Iain Taylor graduated in Celtic and taught Gaelic at primary, secondary and tertiary levels in Uist, Perthshire and Skye. A native of Elgin in Moray, he worked for some years in the Gaelic department of Scottish Television before going on to lecture at Sabhal Mòr Ostaig, the Gaelic College in Skye, from which he retired in 2020.

The
Placenames
of Scotland

IAIN TAYLOR

BIRLINN

First published in 2022 by
Birlinn Ltd
West Newington House
10 Newington Road
Edinburgh
EH9 1QS

www.birlinn.co.uk

ISBN 978 1 78027 771 4

British Library Cataloguing-in-Publication Data
A catalogue record for this book is available
on request from the British Library

Typeset by Hewer Text UK, Edinburgh

Printed and bound by Clays Ltd, Elcograf S.p.A.

Tha an leabhar seo mar chuimhneachan air mo phàrantan,
William John Taylor agus Isobel Stewart à Eilginn.

This book is in memory of my parents,
William John Taylor and Isobel Stewart from Elgin.

Contents

List of Maps

Preface

Placenames are a constant source of debate. Who was *Edwin*, whose name is said to live on in that of Edinburgh? Are the *drum* and *chapel* still to be found in Drumchapel? Which *king* had a *seat* at Kingseat in Perthshire? This book aims to address these and similar questions, but in the field of Scottish placenames, the answers are not always what might be expected at first sight.

In their current form or forms and in their own right, placenames convey meaning whether we seek to analyse their component parts or not. As it stands, *Elgin* (or *Eilginn* in Gaelic), for instance, means the main town in Moray situated on the River Lossie, located between Lossiemouth and Rothes, and between Lhanbryde and Alves. As a word capable of analysis, *Elgin* breaks down into the element *Eilg*, from a root suggesting "noble" and likely a poetic term for Ireland, and a possible diminutive ending -*in*. Thus *Elgin* is shown to be a commemorative name rather than one descriptive of its location or founder. The various Elgins throughout the world do not *per se* mean "little Ireland", but rather suggest that their founders came from Moray and wished to remember Elgin. Likewise, it may be the case that some of Scotland's Norse names commemorate places in Norway rather than describe the new settlements in the new country.

The creation of names in one language superimposed upon preceding ones have helped obscure the origin of many names and cause uncertainty and misunderstanding. Conversely, the settling in Scotland by different groups and cultures over the centuries has given the country's placenames a richness, variety and complexity absent in countries such as Iceland and Denmark, where the bulk of names stem from one language only. It is beyond the scope of this book to delve into the minutiae of Scottish history, but the peoples and influences with an effect on placenames are outlined in the Introduction. Additionally, this book concentrates on names created in Gaelic or possessing a Gaelic form, as hitherto it has not been possible to find the Gaelic names or forms of places in one accessible volume.

In order to save space in the gazetteer sections, this book lists the most common generic elements from the languages in which place-names have been created in this country. In the gazetteer section, each entry takes the following format:

- The current English name of a place is given in bold type followed in brackets by the name of the county or island in which it is located.
- If the place has a current or attested Gaelic name or one approved by Ainmean-Àite na h-Alba, that is then given in plain type.
- This is followed by the derivation of the name in quotation marks, followed by any other relevant comments, with cross-references to other names shown in bold.
- Where a placename in English form, such as *Balmore*, has an obviously Gaelic source, in this case *Baile Mór*, but where that Gaelic original is not in current usage nor found in literary sources, this is shown in the explanatory text rather than in the first line of the entry. Generally, the language from which the placenames are derived is stated in the explanatory text, but where no language is given, it should be assumed that the name was created in Gaelic.
- In some cases, a placename is explained with reference to another name, as in *Strath of Pitcalnie*, where readers should refer back to *Pitcalnie* for the derivation of that name.
- Finally, although since the 1980s Gaelic spelling has used only a grave accent to mark long vowels, this book also uses the old acute accent as an indication of pronunciation, as prior to the 1980s *è* and *é* indicated two distinct sounds, as did *ò* and *ó*. In everyday writing, however, a name written in this book as *Leódhas* should be written as *Leòdhas* to comply with orthographic conventions.

Some points on terminology need to be clarified. A name such as *Drummore* should probably be most correctly termed an "English form" rather an "English name", because although *Drummore* is used in English to identify the most southerly village in Scotland near the tip of the Mull of Galloway, it was created originally in Gaelic, and the village is known as *An Druim Mòr*, "the great ridge", in that language. Likewise, *Siabost* should maybe be termed a "Gaelic form" rather than a "Gaelic name" because although *Siabost* is used in Gaelic to refer to the township on the west side of Lewis between Barvas and Carloway, it is from a Norse name, *Sjábólstaðr*, "sea farm". The English form of that name is *Shawbost*, which came into English via the Gaelic sound system, as did all Nordic names outwith Orkney, Shetland and north-east Caithness. However, *Drummore* is a name in its own right, as are *Siabost* and *Shawbost*, and are recognised as such by the speakers of the languages in question and by this book.

A number of maps are to be found towards the end of the book, showing the distribution of peoples and of important placename elements.

This is not an academic treatise on Scotland's placenames, which lies more within the remit of the School of Scottish Studies and the Scottish Place-Name Society. Rather, this is an attempt to present in accessible format a list of names of settlements, islands, areas, rivers, lochs and mountains. The best sources in print, dealing with place-names at a national and local level, are given in the bibliography. In certain instances it has not been possible to work out what a name means. This is either because the sources themselves are unclear or because it is beyond the linguistic ability of the compiler.

Despite the existence of excellent publications on placenames, there is still a need for study and dissemination of information, and the foundation of a state-funded Placenames Commission along the lines of those in Norway or Ireland would be a welcome development, although Ainmean-Àite na h-Alba based at Sabhal Mòr Ostaig in Skye is involved in very important research and publication. Ainmean-Àite na h-Alba is referred to as 'AÀA' in the text. Readers are also directed to the Scottish Place-Name Society website, which is a great source of information.

Tha mi fada an comain a h-uile duine, nach gabh ainmeachadh an seo, a thug cuideachadh dhomh le bhith a' trusadh ainmean às na sgìrean aca fhèin. Cha phàigh taing sibh.

Introduction

Placenames carry out a number of important functions in any society. As illustrated in the next paragraph, placenames can give an insight into the languages spoken by various peoples at various times, including the present. Perhaps the most basic names are those which describe the landscape of the area in which the place is located, such as *An Gleann Gorm/Glengorm*, "the fresh-green valley", in Mull or *Stoneywood* in Aberdeen. Developing on from this category are names which mention animals, birds or plants growing in the locality, for example *Bathgate* in West Lothian, a Brythonic name meaning "boar wood", or *Fiosgabhaig/Fiskavaig* in Skye, a Norse name signifying "fish bay". Land use forms another category as demonstrated in names such as *Port an Eòrna/Barleyport* in Lochalsh and the Anglian name *Berwick*, indicating a farm where bere or barley was grown. One step on from that are the names which mention specific buildings, agricultural or not, including such names as *Tom an t-Sabhail/Tomintoul* in Banffshire, which mentions a hillock with a barn on it, and *Carnwath* in Lanarkshire, a Brythonic name signifying a new fort. There also exist commemorative names of several types, one important category being those names which tell of a particular type of work carried out in the area. *Sròn a' Chlachair/Stronachlachar* at Loch Katrine tells of the "headland of the stonemason", while *Minigaff* in Kirkcudbrightshire mentions the "hill of the smith", originally a Brythonic name. Individuals and peoples are commemorated in a large set of placenames, such as *Tòrr nam Fiann/Tornaveen*, "the hill of the legendary Fingalian heroes", in Aberdeenshire and *Beàrnasdal/Bernisdale* in Skye, which marks the valley of a Norseman called Bjarn or Bjorn. Particularly numerous throughout Scotland are names coined in commemoration of saints or other ecclesiastical persons, such as *Cill Mhearnaig/Kilmarnock* in Ayrshire, "the church of Ernan/Ernoc", *Mungasdal/Mungasdale* in Wester Ross, a Norse name denoting the valley of a monk and Speyside's *Sgìre Dhrostain*, "the parish of Drostan", the Gaelic name of Aberlour parish (but not village). This last name illustrates a fairly common feature of placenames in Scotland, which is that one place can have unrelated names in different languages. Although *Sgìre Dhrostain* and "Aberlour parish" both describe the same place using a word for "parish", the two names have no other connection. The Gaelic name of the village of Aberlour is *Obar Lobhair*, which was the basis of the current English name. Places with the same name in English may have totally different names in Gaelic depending on their location, for instance there are many places called "Newton" in English, which we might expect to be a translation of *Am Baile Ùr*, "the new farm", and indeed there are some places with that Gaelic name. However, Newton in Argyll is *An Fhadhail Dhubh*, "the black ford", while in North Uist it is *Baile MhicPhàil*, "MacPhail's farm", and in Ross and Tiree *Am Baile Nodha*, "the new farm", using a different word for "new". Apparently simple names can often be less straightforward than they appear at first glance.

As shown above, the placenames of Scotland can be categorised in a number of ways, but for the purposes of this book they will be grouped according to the language or languages in which they were created. This immediately introduces a historical element, in that the various languages of Scotland, although coexisting in different areas at different periods, appeared and disappeared at different times.

With some exceptions, all of Scotland's placenames fall into one of two linguistic groupings, Celtic and Germanic, both of which are branches of the Indo-European language family. The Celtic languages themselves form two groups, Goidelic or Q-Celtic (comprising modern Scottish Gaelic, Irish and Manx) and Brythonic or P-Celtic (comprising modern Welsh, Cornish and Breton, as well as Pictish). The Germanic languages in which placenames in Scotland were created are English (originally Anglian) and Norse.

The oldest names are those of major rivers in particular, as well as those of some islands, which have similarities to names in mainland Europe. These rivers were named by people or peoples who lived in what is now Scotland before the Picts or Britons settled here. The Romans were aware of the names of several of the tribes, and these are to be found on Map 1. W.J. Watson (1993) discusses these tribes, their names and their areas in *History of the Celtic Placenames of Scotland*.

Prior to the arrival of the Scots and Angles, the area north of what is now the Central Belt formed the territories of the Northern and

Southern Picts, speaking P-Celtic with elements such as *aber* in common with the Brythonic language of the Britons to the south. The Pictish territories are shown on Map 2, where the distinguishing feature of the placenames is the element *pett* which means a "share or portion of land", cognate with Welsh *peth* and Gaelic *cuid*. Although *pett* has lasted until the present in anglicised placenames as "Pit-", the gaelicised forms of most such placenames have replaced *pett* with Gaelic *baile*, "settlement, farm, village", although certain names in Gaelic have retained *pett* in the form "Peit". In addition, the specifying element in most "Pit-" names is from Gaelic, as in "Pittyvaich". This suggests that Gaelic used *pett* as a generic term over a long period until it ceased to carry any lexical meaning, at which time it was replaced with *baile*.

Contemporary with the Picts of the north were the Brythonic-speaking Britons south of the Forth–Clyde line in their main territories of Strathclyde, Gododdin and Rheged, also shown on Map 2. Although their territories were, in the main, south of the Forth and Clyde, the capital of Strathclyde was at Dumbarton. Because of the similarity between certain Gaelic and Brythonic elements, such as Gaelic *dùn* and Brythonic *din*, "fort", or Gaelic *eaglais* and Brythonic *eglwys*, "church", a degree of uncertainty exists in stating definitively on linguistic grounds alone in which language certain placenames were created. Brythonic placenames share certain elements in common with Pictish names, but some, such as "Penpont", would be instantly comprehensible to speakers of modern Welsh.

It is reckoned that the Gaelic-speaking Scots were settled in Dal Riada in Argyll by around 450 AD, having come from the territory of Dal Riada in northern Ireland, but this accepted history has been disputed recently, with some scholars unconvinced by the theory of large-scale immigration into Argyll. In any case, the Scots had early contact with the Picts as recorded in Columba's visit to the northern Pictish capital at Inverness in the 6th century AD. The Angles meanwhile had founded their territory of Bernicia centred on Bamburgh in Northumberland around 550 AD, and soon began an expansion which would bring them into conflict and contact with the equally expansionist Scots, who had entered early into Pictish territory and by 840 had united the kingdoms of the two peoples under the king of the Scots. By 945 the Scots had acquired the Brythonic territory of Strathclyde and, within thirty years, Lothian. At the battle of Carham in 1006, the defeat of the Angles put a temporary stop to their expansion, and by around 1050 Gaelic was at its peak and spoken by most people over the territory of what is now mainland Scotland, with the exception of the southern Borders and north-east Caithness, where Gaelic appears to have been spoken only by the landowning aristocracy.

Prior to this, the Angles had been spreading throughout the southern part of what is now Scotland, gaining Rheged in the south-west through marriage by around 635 and capturing the fort of Din Eidyn (now Dùn Éideann or Edinburgh) around five years later. Their expansion northwards was halted by the Picts at the Battle of Nechtansmere in 685, but by the middle of the next century the Angles had control of Kyle in modern Ayrshire. In the north and west the Norse had attacked Iona by around 790 and Dumbarton by 870, and had established their territories in the west and north.

The kingdom of the Scots remained in Gaelic-speaking hands until the marriage of Malcolm Canmore and Margaret in the 11th century, after which time the gradual decline of Gaelic hegemony began. The settling of fertile, low-lying lands and the setting-up of burghs by speakers of English introduced that language to areas previously Gaelic-speaking only.

The more recent linguistic history of Scotland is fairly well known, as is the uneasy coexistence between Gaelic and English, and the entrenchment of Gaelic within the Highlands and Islands to the north and Galloway and Carrick to the south. By the beginning of the 20th century, Gaelic was indigenous only in parts of the counties of Argyll, Bute, Dunbarton, Stirling, Perth, Aberdeen, Banff, Moray, Nairn, Inverness, Ross, Sutherland and Caithness. One hundred years later, with the exception of Gaelic speakers in mainland cities and towns, the language was continuing to be used by and regenerated at community level only in the northern Hebrides.

Because of the long-term coexistence of several languages in different parts of the country, a large proportion of placenames consists of elements from more than one of these languages. The linguistic combinations most frequently found in these hybrids are Gaelic/Norse, Gaelic/Pictish, Gaelic/English, Gaelic/Brythonic, English/Brythonic and English/Norse, as well as three-way combinations such as Gaelic/Norse/English. In the most intensively English part of the country, the Borders, a common type of placename is that of a Gaelic or Norse personal name attached to English *tún*, as in *Maxton*, where Gaelic *Macas* precedes *tún*, showing that despite the fact that *Maxton* is a name created in English, the owner of the farm was a Gaelic-speaker. Similarly, in the north-east, Gaelic personal names can be found attached to Pictish *pett*, as in "Pitmurchie", and in the north, English personal names can be found in combination with Gaelic *baile*, as in "Baledmund".

A fairly unknown set of combinations came about particularly in the south-west, in which Gaelic replaced English, leading to established English names such as *Mellington*, *Swinton* and *Meithbothel* (now *Maybole*) being adopted by the Gaelic-speaking population who added Gaelic affixes to these, resulting in *Dalmellington*, *Dalswinton*, *Meibothelbeg* and *Meibothelmore*. Gradually, English replaced Gaelic, but the names of *Dalmellington* and *Dalswinton* remained, although there is no trace of *Maybolemore* and *Maybolebeg* as distinct entities.

A generic element in a placename is a general term, for example, in a name such as *Newtown*, the generic is *town* because that is the element describing the type of place under discussion, while *New* specifies the type of *town*. One might find that in the vicinity of Newtown there might be an Oldtown, in which *Old* is the specifier, distinguishing this *town* from *Newtown* and all other *towns*.

A commonly encountered pattern of placenames charts the replacement of one language by another, and perhaps by another again, in which the generic element in the first language, having lost lexical meaning to the speakers of the second language becomes simply a "name", and is used as a specifying element with the same generic in the new language, as in *Knockhill* in Fife. When Fife was Gaelic-speaking, the hill in question would have been named simply *Cnoc*, "hill", or *An Cnoc*, "the hill". As Gaelic died out and was replaced by English, this would have changed to *Knock* to fit in with the sound system of English, and would eventually have ceased to connote a hill. However, because the place known by the name of *Knock* was a hill, English speakers came to define it as *Knock Hill*, gradually becoming *Knockhill*.

The change from Norse to Gaelic and then to English can be seen in *Ardtornish Point* in Morvern. This name was originally coined by Norse speakers as *Thorirnes*, "Thorir's headland". As Gaelic replaced Norse, this became *Tòirinis* and ceased to have any lexical meaning.

Gaelic speakers in turn added their word for a headland, *àird*, and the name became *Àird Tòirinis*, which meant nothing to English speakers other than being a name which they pronounced as *Ardtornish*. They in turn recognised the place as a headland and added their generic, *point*, to explain it and give *Ardtornish Point*, a name which now contains three languages' generic terms for a headland. This name neatly shows how one language's generic can become another's specifier. To Norse speakers, the generic was *nes*, "headland", and the specifier *Thorir*. Gaelic-speakers did not recognise *nes* as a generic and used the entire *Thorirnes* as a specifier, adding their own generic *àird*. Then English speakers, failing to perceive *àird* as a generic in *Àird Tòirinis* or *Ardtornish*, added their own generic *point*. If English were to be replaced by another language in the future such as (albeit improbably) Turkish, it might in turn add its own generic to the by-then meaningless *Ardtornishpoint*, leading to *Artornispoynt Burnu*, a name with one original specifying element (*Thorir*) and the same generic in four successive languages (*ness, àird, point, burun*), with each losing its meaning to the subsequent replacement language.

As well as placenames constructed in various languages, there can be problems in interpreting placenames from a single language due to generic or specifying elements or personal names which are no longer in use, and as a result of change and corruption through the passage of time. This latter point is particularly relevant when considering the placenames of marginal areas in which one language is/was being replaced by another, as in Braemar or Upper Banffshire in the 19th century. It is not enough to rely on current pronunciation and interpretation, which may be flawed or influenced by the incoming language, although if the inhabitants of a particular area call a place by a particular name, then that name is as valid as the official or written one.

Watson (1993) is a valuable source of information on the names of Gaelic saints and of rivers in particular, and on the subject of rivers should be read in conjunction with W.F.H. Nicolaisen (1986). Much valuable work has been carried out in recent years in the form of books, academic papers and theses, and articles particularly in the *Scottish Journal of Name Studies*, which raise many questions beyond the scope of this book. As a result, the bibliography at the end of this book is recommended for a wider and deeper examination of the placenames of Scotland.

Gaelic Pronunciation

This brief guide to pronunciation gives approximate equivalents in standard Scottish English (except where otherwise indicated) for the letters and combinations of letters found in Gaelic. The Gaelic alphabet contains 18 letters (a, b, c, d, e, f, g, h, i, l, m, n, o, p, r, s, t, u) but since the language has many more sounds than that, accent marks are used to indicate long vowels, *h* is added after most consonants to change their sound, and when consonants are combined with *i* or *e*, they become palatalised, as indicated below.

Vowels	Approximate sound	English example
a *or* ai	*short* a	cat
à *or* ài	*long* ah	father
ao *or* aoi	*between* ay *and* oo	–
ea *or* ei	*short* e *or* ay	egg *or* take
èi	*long* e	*French* Sèvres
éi *	*long* ay	days
eò *or* eòi	yaw	yawn
eu	*short* ee-u	*Italian* Fiat
i *or* io	*short* i *or* ee	in *or* keep
ì *or* ìo	*long* ee	fiend
ia	*short* ee-u	*Italian* Fiat
iu	*short* yoo	youth
iù	*long* yoo	use
o *or* oi	*short* aw *or* oa	top *or* coat
ò *or* òi	*long* aw	awe
ó *or* ói *	*long* oa	mower
u *or* ui	*short* oo	brood
ù *or* ùi	*long* oo	brewed

Vowels	Approximate sound	English example
b	b	**b**ig
b (+ e/i)	b + y	**B**ute
bh	v	**v**ery
bh (+ e/i)	v + y	**v**iew
c	k	**c**at
c (+ e/i)	k + y	**k**ilt
ch	kh	lo**ch**
ch (+ e/i)	kh + y	*German* i**ch**
cn	kr	**cr**ock
d	d	**d**o [tip of tongue against back of teeth]
d (+ e/i)	j	**j**ig
dh	gh	*voiced equivalent of* kh
dh (+ e/i)	y	**y**es
f	f	**f**ig
f (+ e/i)	f + y	**f**ew
fh	*silent*	–
g	g	**g**o
g (+ e/i)	g	a**g**ue
gh	gh	*voiced equivalent of* kh
gh (+ e/i)	y	**y**es
h	h	hat
l	l	*formed by raising the back of the tongue*
l (+ e/i)	l + y	**l**ure
m	m	**m**ore
m (+ e/i)	m + y	**m**ew
mh	v	**v**at
mh (+ e/i)	v + y	**v**iew
n	n	**n**ot
n (+e/i)	n + y	**n**ew

Vowels	Approximate sound	English example
p	p	**p**at
p (+ e/i)	p + y	**p**ew
ph	f	**f**our
ph (+ e/i)	f + y	**f**ew
r	r	**r**ock
r (+ e/i)	th	**th**is
rt	rsht	har**sh t**one
s	s	**s**ift
s (+ e/i)	sh	**sh**ift
sh	h	**h**at
sh (+ e/i)	h + y	**h**ew
t	t	**t**ug [tip of tongue against back of teeth]
t (+ e/i)	ch	**ch**ew
th	h	**h**at
th (+ e/i)	h + y	**h**ew

* Since the issue of *Gaelic Orthographic Conventions* by the Scottish Examinations Board in 1981, revised subsequently by the Scottish Qualifications Authority, the acute accent mark found in *á, é* and *ó* has been replaced by the grave accent mark as in *à, è* and *ò*. This is merely a spelling convention and does not affect pronunciation, although the abolition of the grave accent has obscured pronunciation rather than clarified it. This book uses the acute accent throughout as an indication of the pronunciation of names, but it should be borne in mind that this is obsolete and words spelled here such as *Leódhas, Géirinis* and *Am Baile Mór* should have the everyday spelling *Leòdhas, Gèirinis* and *Am Baile Mòr*.

Common Generic Elements

This section lists alphabetically the most common generic elements found in Scottish placenames. They are listed according to the form in which they are found in current English and Gaelic placenames and not in their form in the original language. For example, Norse *vík* appears under *-aig*, *-bhaig*, *-vaig* and *-wick* (its realisations in current Gaelic and English forms) rather than under the original Norse *vík*. In addition, it is worth noting that in Gaelic names consisting only of a noun (or a noun with an adjective), the definite article is generally used, as in *Am Baile Mór*, "the big farm", rather than simply *Baile Mór*, "big farm". In English it is unusual to use the definite article in such instances, so that *Newtown* is used rather than *The Newtown*, but the names of rivers usually include the article, as in *the Spey, the Tummel* and *the Tweed*.

It should be remembered that not every name ending in *-a* is from Norse *á* or *øy*, and that the list of generics is a general guide only, which should help with the derivations in the gazetteer sections.

The lists are in the following format:

- firstly, the generic element is given, followed by the word from which it comes in the original language;
- in brackets is an explanation of the term in English;
- finally, there comes an example of a placename including the generic.

The following abbreviations are used: B for Brythonic, E for English or Anglian, G for Gaelic, N for Norse including Danish and P for Pictish.

Element	Origin	Examples
-a	N *á* (river) or	Grìota; Greeta
	N *øy* (island)	Diùra; Jura
aber-	B *aber* (river mouth)	**Aber**deen
ach-	G *achadh* (field)	**Ach**nahannet

Element	Origin	Examples
-aidh	G a locative or dative ending (place of)	Balg**aidh**
-aigh	N *øy* (island)	Barr**aigh**
aird	G *àird* (point)	**Aird** of Sleat
-al	N *fjall* (mountain) or	Lang**al**
	N *vollr* (field)	Man**al**
ald-	G *allt* (stream)	**Ald**ivalloch
-am	N *holmr* (islet)	Grian**am**
ard	G *àird* (point)	**Ard**kinglas
as	N *áss* (ridge)	Bri**as**cleit
auch-	G *achadh* (field)	**Auch**indachy
auchter-	G *uachdar* (upland)	**Auchter**arder
auld-	G *allt* (stream)	**Auld**earn
ault-	G *allt* (stream)	**Ault**more
-ay	N *øy* (island)	Scalp**ay**
bac	N *bakki* (bank)	Am **Bac**
back	N *bakki* (bank)	**Back**ies
bad-	G *bad* (copse; spot)	**Bad**ralloch
bal-	G *baile* (farm; settlement; town)	**Bal**maha
bar-	G *bàrr* (hill, summit)	**Bar**caldine
beck	E *beck* (stream) or	Water**beck**
	N *bekkr* (stream)	**Beck**rivik
bel-	G *baile* (farm; settlement; town)	**Bel**helvie
ben	G *beinn* (mountain)	**Ben** Nevis
-bhagh	N *vágr* (narrow bay)	Steòrna**bhagh**
-bhaig	N *vík* (bay)	Tarsga**bhaig**
-bhal	N *fjall* (mountain)	Snaoisea**bhal**
-bhat	N *vatn* (water)	Loch Langa**bhat**
-bhig	N *vík* (bay)	Bréi**bhig**
-bie	N *byr* (farm)	Hum**bie**
blà-	N *blá* (blue)	**Blà**bheinn
blair	G *blàr* (field; moor; plain)	**Blair**gowrie
bo-	G *both* (hut)	**Bo**henie
bog-	G *bog* (bog; soft)	**Bog**buie
-bol	N *bólstaðr* (farm) or	Circea**bol**
	E *bótl* (dwelling)	May**bole**
bor-	N *borg* (fort; castle)	**Bor**rodale
-bost	N *bólstaðr* (farm)	Sia**bost**
bow	G *bogha* or N *bóða* (submerged rock)	**Bow**more

Element	Origin	Examples
bràc-	G *brekka* (slope)	**Bràc**adal
brae	E *bra* (brae) or	Burn**brae**
	G *bràigh* (upper part)	**Brae**more
breck-	N *brekka* (slope)	Ard **Breck**nish
brig	N *bekkr* (stream) or	Staoini**brig**
	E *brycg* (bridge)	**Brig** O'Turk
bun-	G *bun* (bottom; river mouth)	**Bun**ree
burgh	E *burh* (farm; fort, town)	Edin**burgh**
burn	E *burna* (stream)	Whit**burn**
-bus	N *bólstaðr* (farm)	Cionna**bus**
-by	N *byr* (farm)	New**by**
cairn-	G *càrn* (cairn; hill)	**Cairn**baan
cambus-	G *camas* (inlet; river bend)	**Cambus**lang
camus-	G *camas* (inlet; river bend)	**Camus**cross
car-	B *caer* (fort) or	**Car**michael
	G *cair* (enclosure or fort)	**Car**luke
	G *cathair* (fort)	**Car**mahome
carden	P *carden* (thicket; copse)	**Carden**den
circ-	N *kirkja* (church)	**Circ**ebost
clachan	G *clachan* (churchyard; village with a church)	**Clachan** Sands
-cleit	N *klettr* (rock; hill)	Brias**cleit**
-clete	N *klettr* (rock; hill)	Mala**clete**
clun(e)-	G *cluain* (meadow)	**Clun**y
coul	G *cùl* (back) or	**Coul**in
	G *cùil* (secluded spot)	**Coul**hill
craig	G *creag* (rock)	**Craig**entinny
-cro	N *kró* (small enclosure)	Lini**cro**
-cuidh	N *kví* (cattle pen)	Liana**cuidh**
cul-	G *cùl* (back) or	**Cul**duthel
	G *cùil* (secluded spot)	**Cul**eave
-dal	E *dale* (valley) or	Esk**dale**
	N *dalr* (valley)	Glen Hinnis**dal**
dal-	G *dail* (haugh)	**Dal**marnock
dean	E *denu* (valley)	**Dean**s
del-	G *dail* (haugh)	**Del**nashaugh
-den	E *denu* (valley)	Carden**den**
doch-	G *dabhach* (davoch)	**Doch**four
druim-	G *druim* (ridge)	An **Druim** Mór

Element	Origin	Examples
drum-	G *druim* (ridge)	**Drum**chapel
dum-	G *dùn* (hill; fort; hill fort)	**Dum**barton
dun-	G *dùn* (hill; fort; hill fort)	**Dun**staffnage
eccle(s)-	B *eglwys* or	**Eccle**fechan
	G *eaglais* (church)	**Eccles**machan
edin-	G *aodann* (hill face)	**Edin**bane
fetter-	G *fothair* (shelving or terraced slope)	**Fetter**cairn
fors	N *forss* (waterfall)	**Fors**inard
-four	G *pòr* (pasture)	Trian**four**
free	G *frìth* (deer forest)	**Free**vater
garr-	N *garðr* (enclosure; dyke)	**Garr**abost
-garry	N *gerði* (pasture land)	Osmi**garry**
gart-	G *gart/gort* (enclosed field)	**Gart**more
gask	G *gasg* (projecting tail or strip of land)	Ger**gask**
gate	E *geatu* (road)	**Gate**house
-gearraidh	N *gerði* (pasture land)	Mùi**gearraidh**
geo	N *gjá* (steep sea inlet)	**Geo**crab
-gil(l)	N *gil* (gully; ravine)	Tràili**gil**
glas	G *glas* (stream)	**Glas**nakille
glen	G *gleann* (valley)	**Glen**elg
-go	N *gjá* (steep sea inlet)	Papi**goe**
-gow	B *cau* (hollow)	Glas**gow**
-gro	N *gróf* (river pit)	Sgealas**gro**
ha-	E *haga* (hedge)	**Ha**wick
-hall	N *halh* (haugh)	Fox**hall**
-ham(e)	E *hám* (homestead)	Nor**ham**
holm	N *holmr* (holm; islet) or	**Holm**isdale
	E *hám* (homestead)	Leit**holm**
hope	N *hóp* (bay)	St Margaret's **Hope**
hùs-	N *hús* (house)	**Hùs**abost
-ie	G a locative or dative ending (place of)	Cairn**ie**
inch-	G *innis* (meadow; island)	**Inch**ree
-ingham	E *-ingaham* (homestead of the people of -)	Twyn**ingham**
-ington	E *-ingatun* (farm of the people of -)	Shear**ington**
inver-	G *inbhir* (river mouth)	**Inver**ness
ken-	G *ceann* (end; head)	**Ken**nacraig
kil-	G *cill* (cell; church)	**Kil**marnock

Element	Origin	Examples
killie-	G *coille* (wood)	**Killie**crankie
kin-	G *ceann* (end; head)	**Kin**dallachan
kirk	N *kirkja* (church)	**Kirk**patrick
knock-	G *cnoc* (hill)	**Knock**vologan
kyle	G *caol* (strait) or	**Kyle**akin
	G *coille* (wood)	Balna**kyle**
lag-	G *lag* (hollow)	**Lag**avulin
law	E *hláw* (hill)	Gate**law**bridge
leck-	G *leac* (slab; flagstone)	**Leck**melm
letter-	G *leitir* (gentle slope)	**Letter**fearn
lì	N *hlið* (slope)	**Lì**
lin-	B *llyn* or	**Lin**lithgow
	G *linn* (pool; pond; firth)	**Linn** O'Dee
loch	G *loch* (loch; firth; sea loch)	**Loch** Ness
logie	G *lagaidh* (place with a hollow)	**Logie** Easter
lon	G *lòn* (wet meadow)	**Lon**more
mon-	G *monadh* (hill; moor; upland) or	**Mon**crieff
	G *mòine* (peat; peat moss)	**Mon**organ
mull	G *maol* (rounded headland or hill)	**Mull** of Kintyre
muir	E *mór* (moor)	**Muir** of Ord
-ness	E *naes* (headland)	Black**ness**
	N *nes* (headland)	**Ness**
-nis	N *nes* (headland)	Stoca**inis**
-nish	N *nes* (headland)	Ardtor**nish**
òb	N *hóp* (bay)	An t-**Òb**an
obar-	B *aber* (river mouth)	**Obar** Pheallaidh
-ort	N *fjorðr* (firth; sea loch)	Loch Eise**ort**
os	N *óss* (river mouth)	À**ros**
pen-	B *pen* (end; head)	**Pen**pont
	G *peighinn* (pennyland)	**Pen**ifiler
pit-	P *pett* (share; lands)	**Pit**caple
pol-	G *poll* (pool; mud)	**Pol**bain
-pol	N *bólstaðr* (farm)	Crosa**pol**
quie	N *kví* (cattle pen)	Lini**quie**
rath-	G *ràth* (circular fort)	**Rath**illet
rhu-	G *rubha* (headland)	**Rhu**nahaorine
ros-	G *ros* (headland; wood) or	**Ros**yth
	N *hross* (horse)	**Ros**inish

Element	Origin	Examples
-said	N *saetr* (sheiling)	Liana**said**
-seadar	N *setr* (dwelling) or *saetr* (sheiling)	Grimi**seadar**
sgeir	N *sker* (skerry)	Heill**sgeir**
-sgo	N *skogr* (small wood)	Bircea**sgo**
-shader	N *setr* (dwelling) or *saetr* (sheiling)	Flas**hader**
-shaw	E *sceaga* (wood)	Cobbin**shaw**
-sker	N *sker* (skerry)	Has**ker**
slock-	G *sloc* (hollow; pit)	**Slock**avullin
sròm	N *straumr* (current; stream)	An **Sròm** Dearg
-sta	N *staðir* (dwelling place; farm)	Tol**sta**
stac	N *stakk* (pillar; rock)	**Stac** Pollaidh
-stane	E *stán* (stone) or *-'s tún* (-'s farm)	Brun**stane**
-stead	E *stede* (place)	New**stead**
stein	N *stein* (stone)	**Stein**nis
strath-	G *srath* (wide valley)	**Strath**more
strome	N *straumr* (current; stream)	**Strome**ferry
stron(e)	G *sròn* (nose-shaped headland)	**Strone**ba
tam-	G *tom* (hillock)	**Tam**dhu
tilly-	G *tulach* (green hill; long low ridge)	**Tilly**fourie
tir-	G *tìr* (land)	**Tir**oran
tom-	G *tom* (hillock)	**Tom**doun
-ton	E *tún* (farm)	Rober**ton**
tor-	G *tòrr* (hill)	**Tor**more
tot-	N *toft* (house site)	**Tot**aig
tra-	B *tref* (settlement)	**Tra**quair
tulloch-	G *tulach* (green hill; long low ridge)	**Tulloch**beg
tully-	G *tulach* (green hill; long low ridge)	**Tully**belton
-vaig	N *vík* (bay)	Toka**vaig**
-val	N *fjall* (mountain)	Blashi**val**
-vat	N *vatn* (loch; water)	**Vat**ersay
-wall	N *vollr* (field)	Ding**wall**
-way	N *vágr* (narrow bay)	Carlo**way**
-wick	E *wíc* (village) or	Ber**wick**
	N *vík* (bay)	Ler**wick**
-warth	E *worð* (enclosure)	Pol**warth**

Settlements and Areas

A

A'Chleit (Argyll), A' Chleit
"The cliff or rock", from Norse.

Abban (Inverness), An t-Àban
"The backwater or small stream."

Abbey St Bathans (Berwick)
"The abbey of St Baoithean or
Bathan."The surname
"MacGylboythin", from
MacGilleBhaoithein, "son of the
follower of Baoithean", appeared in
Dumfries in the 13th century, but
has since died out.

Abbotsinch (Renfrew)
"The abbot's meadow", from
English/Gaelic, on lands once
belonging to Paisley Abbey.

Aberarder (Inverness), Obar Àrdair
"The mouth of the Arder."

Aberargie (Perth), Obar Fhargaidh
"The mouth of the angry river",
from *fearg.*

Aberbothrie (Perth)
"The mouth of the deaf stream",
from *bodhar*, "deaf", suggesting a
silent stream.

Abercairney (Perth)
"The mouth of the Cairney", a river
name from *càrnach*, meaning "stony".

Aberchalder (Inverness), Obar
Chaladair
"The mouth of the Calder." Easter
Aberchalder in Stratherrick was
formerly known as *A' Cheann Mhór*,
"the big end".

Aberchirder (Banff), Obar Chiardair
"The mouth of the dark water", from
ciar and *dobhar*. Locally this town is
known as "Foggieloan".

Abercorn (West Lothian)

"Horn-shaped river mouth", cognate
with *còrn*, "horn". It was known to
Bede as "Aebbercurnig", and is of
Brythonic origin.

Abercrombie (Fife), Obar
Chrombaidh
"Bent river mouth", from *crom.*

Aberdalgie (Perth), Obar Dheilgidh
"The mouth of the thorny stream".

Aberdeen (Aberdeen), Obar Dheathain
"The mouth of the Don", a river
named after a deity. Aberdeenshire
is *Siorrachd Obar Dheathain.*

Aberdour (Fife), Obar Dobhair
"The mouth of the water or river."

Aberfeldy (Perth), Obar Pheallaidh
"The mouth of Peallaidh." *Peallaidh*,
which comes from *peallach*, "shaggy",
was an *ùraisg* or water sprite said to
live in this stream. The town is
mentioned in the saying, *Trì iongantasan na h-Alba: drochaid Obar
Pheallaidh, tobraichean Ghlinn Iucha
is cluig Pheairt*, "The three wonders
of Scotland: Aberfeldy bridge, the
wells of Linlithgow and the bells of
Perth". The August fair at Aberfeldy
was known as *Faidhir nan Gròiseag*,
"the gooseberry fair".

Aberfoyle (Perth), Obar Phuill
"The mouth of the sluggish stream."
Poll was borrowed as "pow" into
Scottish English. The market at
Aberfoyle was known as *Féill
Barachan*, from *Féill Bhearchain*, "St
Barchan's fair", a saint associated
with Kilbarchan in Renfrewshire.

Abergairn (Aberdeen), Obar
Gharthain
"The mouth of the Gairn", a noisy

river the name of which comes from *goir*, "call".

Abergeldie (Aberdeen), Obar Gheallaidh
"The mouth of the bright river."

Aberlady (East Lothian)
"Rotten river mouth", from *lobh*, "rot".

Aberlednock (Perth), Obar Liadnaig
"The mouth of the Lednock", an obscure name.

Aberlemno (Angus), Obar Leamhnach
"The mouth of the elm stream."

Aberlour (Banff), Obar Lobhair
"The mouth of the noisy or talkative stream." Aberlour Church and parish respectively are *Cill Drostain* and *Sgìre Dhrostain*, "the church/parish of St Drostan". The town is officially known as Charlestown of Aberlour in memory of the founder of the planned village, Charles Grant of Elchies.

Abernethy (Inverness, Perth), Obar Neithich
"The mouth of the Nethy", a river name suggesting cleanliness and said to be inhabited by water spirits known as *na Neithichean*, "the Nethys".

Aberscross (Sutherland), Abarsgaig
"Muddy strip of land."

Abersky (Inverness), Abairsgigh
"Muddy place."

Abertarff (Inverness), Obar Thairbh
"The mouth of the bull river."

Aberuchill (Perth), Obar Rùchaill
Although local Gaelic speakers understood this to mean "mouth of the red flood", from *Obar Ruadh Thuil*, evidence points to this name containing *coille*, "wood", similar to *Orchill*, meaning that the whole name refers to a river-mouth linked to a wood.

Aberuthven (Perth), Obar Ruadhainn
"The river mouth at the red-brown place."

Abigil (Sutherland), Àbaigil
"River-farm gully", from Norse.

Aboyne (Aberdeen), A-bèidh
These Gaelic and English forms are unclear. The fair held here was known as *Fèill Mhìcheil*, "St Michael's Fair".

Abriachan (Inverness), Obar Itheachan
This name was originally *Obar Bhritheachan*, "mouth of the hill river". *Bodaich Obar Bhritheachan*, "the old men of Abriachan", were apparently notable in the area. The area known as the "Cords of Abriachan" are *Na Cordachan*, referring to a series of narrow fields. The local church is *Cill Fhìonain*, "St Finnan's Church".

Acairseid Mhor (Eriskay, Raasay), An Acarsaid Mhór
"The big anchorage."

Acha (Argyll, Coll), An t-Achadh
"The field."

Achabeg (Skye), An t-Achadh Beag
"The small field."

Achachoish (Argyll), Achadh a' Chòis *or* Achadh a' Chòthais
"The field at the cave or lair."

Achachonleich (Inverness), Achadh a' Chonalaich
This may mean "the stubble field" or "the field at the place of the whirlpool".

Achachork (Skye), Achadh a' Choirce
"Oat field."

Achadaphris (Argyll), Achadh Dà Phris
"The field with two bushes."

Achadesdal (Ross), Acha Deuthasdal
"The field at Desdal", the latter part of which is a Norse valley name with an unclear first element. Gairloch Hotel was originally known as *Taigh-òsta Acha Deuthasdal*, "the Achadesdal hotel".

Achadunan (Argyll), Achadh an Dùnain
"The field at the small hill (fort)."

Achag (Arran), Achag
This appears to be "small field", and is also known as "Upper Corrie" in English.

Achagallon (Argyll, Arran), Achadh Ghallain
"The field with a standing stone." People from Achagallon in Arran were known as *feannagan*, "crows".

Achahoish (Argyll)
See **Achachoish**.

Achallater (Perth), Achadh Chaladair *or* Ach Chaladair
"The field of the Calder."

Achaloist (Mull), An t-Achadh Loisgte
"The burnt field."

Achalone (Caithness)
"The field by the pool", from *Achadh an Lòin*.

Achamore (Coll, Gigha, Nairn), An t-Achadh Mór
"The big field."

Achanalt (Ross), Achadh nan Allt
"The field of the streams." However, a number of names which seem to contain the genitive plural article *nan* may originally have contained *n-*, indicating the genitive plural without the article. As this grammatical feature died out, Gaelic speakers presumably rationalised the presence of the *n* sound as being the genitive plural article. Other such names may include "Cumbernauld", "Lochnell" and "Palnure".

Achanamara (Argyll), Achadh na Mara
"The field by the sea." It is said that this place was originally called *Achadh nam Marbh*, "the field of the dead".

Achandunie (Ross), Achadh an Dùnaidh
"The field at the hill (fort) place."

Achanruie (Perth), Achadh an Ruighe
"The field on the slope."

Achanuaran (Lismore), Achadh an Fhuarain
"The field of the spring."

Achaphubuil (Argyll), Achadh a' Phùbaill
"The field of the tent or pavilion."

Achara (Arran), Acha-Rà
"The field at the circular fort", from an older form, *Achadh an Ràtha*. Local people were nicknamed *meanbh-chuileagan*, "midges".

Acharacle (Argyll), Àth Tharracail
"Torcuil's ford."

Acharanny (Arran), Achadh an Rainich
"The bracken field." A more appropriate Gaelic spelling might be *Achadh an Rainigh*, showing more accurately the form of the genitive singular once the standard form in nouns ending in *-ach* such an *raineach*, but more recently restricted to some southern dialects.

Acharn (Argyll, Perth), Àth a' Chàirn
"The ford by the cairn."

Acharossan (Argyll), Achadh a' Chrosain
"Field of the little cross."

Achateny (Argyll), Achadh an Teine
"The field of the fire."

Achavaich (Sutherland), Achadh a' Bhàthaich
"The field with the byre."

Achavandra (Sutherland), Achadh Anndra
"Andrew's field."

Achavanich (Caithness), Achadh a' Mhanaich
"The monk's field."

Achavarasdal (Caithness)
This Gaelic/Norse name may be "the field at Barr's valley", from *Achadh Bhàrrasdail* and if so this second part may be also found in **Barrisdale**, but an alternative derivation could refer to a field containing an enclosure for horses, also from Norse.

Achavoulaig (Bute), Achadh a' Bhuilg
"The field of the bag" or "the bag-shaped field".

Achavoulin (Arran), Achadh a'
Mhuilinn
"The field of the mill", also known
in English as Millfield.

Achavraie (Argyll), Achadh a'
Bhràighe; (Ross), Achd a' Bhràighe
"The field on the upper land." The
Gaelic form of the Ross name shows
achd in place of *achadh*, which is a
fairly common occurrence in that
area.

Achbreck (Banff)
"Speckled field", from *Achadh Breac*.

Achdalieu (Argyll), Achadh
DoLiubha
"DoLiubha's field", in memory of a
saint. This name shows a relatively
rare diminutive form of the saint's
name where *do*, "your", is placed
before the name itself in order to
express devotion or endearment,
thus giving Achdalieu a more accurate meaning of "the field of beloved
St Liubha". Much more common
than *do* is to use *mo*, "my", as in *Cill
MoLuaig*, "Kilmoluag".

Achduart (Ross), Achadh Dhubhaird
"The field at Duart", which in turn
is "black headland".

Acheilidh (Sutherland), Ach
Choillidh
"Field at the wood place."

Achenbrain (Ayr)
See **Auchenbrain**.

Acheninver (Ross), Achd an Inbhir
"The field at the river mouth."

Achentoul (Perth, Sutherland),
Achadh an t-Sabhail
"The field with the barn."

Acherault (Inverness), Achadh a'
Gharbh Uillt
"Field of the rough burn."

Achfary (Sutherland), Achadh Taigh
Phairidh
"The field at Para's house."

Achgarve (Ross), An t-Achadh Garbh
"The rough field." Local people
were nicknamed *sgairbh*,
"cormorants".

Achgobhal (Perth), Achadh a'
Ghobhail
"The field at the fork."

Achiltibuie (Ross), Achd Ille
Bhuidhe
"The field of the yellow haired boy."
This name sometimes appears as
Àicheallaidh Buidhe, "yellow Achilty",
by analogy with Achilty in Easter
Ross.

Achilty (Ross), Àicheallaidh
This name is not clear, but may be
associated with Celtic *uxellos*, "high",
the origin of "Ochil".

Achimenach (Caithness)
"Middle field", from *Achadh
Meadhanach*.

Achin (Sutherland), Na h-Achaidhean
"The fields."

Achinahuagh (Sutherland), Achadh
na h-Uamha
"The field at the cave."

Achindarroch (Inverness), Achadh
nan Darach
"Field of the oaks."

Achinduin (Lismore), Achadh an
Dùin
"The field by the hill (fort)."

Achingall (East Lothian)
"The field of the non-Gaels", from
Achadh nan Gall.

Achininver (Sutherland), Achadh an
Inbhir
"The field by the river mouth."

Achins (Caithness), Na h-Achaidhean
"The fields."

Achintee (Ross), Achadh an t-Suidhe
"The field of the seat", situated near
the hill called *Meall an t-Suidhe*,
"lump of the seat".

Achintore (Inverness), Achadh an
Todhair
"The bleaching field." The stream
running through Achintore is *Allt
nan Dathadairean*, "stream of the
dyers", or "Ashburn" in English.

Achintraid (Ross), Achadh na
Tràghad
"The field at the beach."

Achintyhalavin (Sutherland), Achadh an Taigh-thalmhainn
"The field of the earth-house."

Achlean (Inverness), An t-Achadh Leathann
"The wide field."

Achlochan (Ross), Achd an Lochain
"The field by the small loch."

Achlunachan (Perth, Ross), Achadh Ghlùineachain or Achadh Lùinneachain
This may be "the field of jointed grass".

Achlusa (Skye), Achadh Lusa
"The field at the bright river", from Gaelic/Norse.

Achmelvich (Sutherland), Achadh Mhealbhaich
"The field of Melvich."

Achmony (Inverness), Achadh a' Mhonaidh
"The field at the uplands."

Achmore (Lewis), An t-Acha Mór; (Perth), An t-Achadh Mór; (Ross), Acha Mór
"The big field." Achmore and Lochganvich are the only inland settlements in Lewis, and a person not up to their job is said to be seòla-dair an Acha Mhóir, "an Achmore sailor". In Lewis, this place was known simply as An t-Ach, "the field".

Achnaba (Argyll), Achadh na Bà
"The field of the cow."

Achnabobane (Inverness), Achadh na Bó Bàine
"The field of the white cow."

Achnabourin (Sutherland), Achadh nam Bùraidhean
"The field of the bellowings."

Achnacairn (Argyll), Achadh nan Càrn
"The field at the cairns."

Achnacarnan (Argyll), Achadh nan Càrnan
"The field by the small cairns."

Achnacarnin (Sutherland), Achadh nan Càrnan
See **Achnacarnan**.

Achnacarry (Inverness), Achadh na Cairidh
"The field by the weir."

Achnaclerach (Ross), Achadh nan Cléireach
"The field of the clerics."

Achnacloich (Argyll, Inverness, Nairn, Skye), Achadh na Cloiche
"The field at the stone." Achnacloich in Skye is often known as "Stonefield". People from Achnacloich in Aird in Inverness-shire were known as crodh laoigh, "calves".

Achnacloigh (Argyll), Achadh na Cloiche
See **Achnacloich**.

Achnacree (Argyll), Achadh na Crithe
"The field at the shaking place." Achnacreebeag is Achadh na Crithe Beag, "small Achnacree".

Achnacroish (Lismore), Achadh na Croise
"The field of the cross".

Achnafauld (Perth), Achadh na Follt or Achadh nam Fàd
The first Gaelic name was used locally but may have been influenced by the anglicised form because the defining element is unclear. AÀA recommend the second Gaelic name, which means the "field of the furrows or peats".

Achnafearn (Inverness), Achadh na Feàrna
"The field of the alder."

Achnagairn (Inverness), Achadh nan Càrn
"The field of the cairns", from an older Achadh na gCàrn.

Achnagarron (Ross), Achadh nan Gearran
"The field of the geldings."

Achnagart (Ross), Ach nan Gart
"The field of the enclosures."

Achnagonalin (Moray), Achadh nan Coitheanalan
"The field of the assemblies or

congregations", from older *Achadh na gCoitheanalan*.

Achnagullan (Sutherland), Achadh nan Cuilean
"The field of the whelps", from an older *Achadh na gCuilean*.

Achnaha (Argyll), Achadh na h-Àtha
"The field by the kiln or stable."

Achnahaird (Ross), Achadh na h-Àirde
"The field by the headland." Brae of Achnahaird is *Bràigh Achadh na h-Àirde*, "Upper Achnahaird".

Achnahannet (several), Achadh na h-Annaid
"The field of the annat church." The old church of Achnahannet near Ardgay is *Cill MoChalmaig*, "Beloved St Colman's Church". In Scotland an *annaid* seems to have been a small church in a remote location of no great significance, and usually not dedicated to any particular saint, unlike in Ireland where an *andóit* was an important church, often containing a saint's relics.

Achnahard (Perth)
See **Achnahaird**.

Achnahinich (Ross), Achadh na h-Ìnich
"The field at the nail place."

Achnahuaigh (Sutherland), Achadh na h-Uagha
"The field of the cave or grave."

Achnairn (Sutherland), Achadh an Fheàrna
"The field of the alder."

Achnaluachrach (Sutherland), Achadh na Luachrach
"The field with the rushes."

Achnanconeran (Inverness), Achadh nan Conbhairean
This may be "the field at the confluences".

Achnasaul (Inverness), Achadh nan Sabhal
"The field with the barns."

Achnasheen (Ross), Achadh na Sìne
"The field of the stormy weather."

Achnashellach (Ross), Achadh nan Seileach
"The field of the willows."

Achnatra (Argyll), Achadh na Tràgha
"The field by the beach."

Achnebron (Ayr), Achadh na Bràthann
"The field of the quern." See **Mauchline**.

Achnegie (Ross), Achadh an Fhiodhaich
"The field at the wooded place."

Achness (Sutherland), Achadh an Easa
"The field at the waterfall or stream."

Acholter (Bute), Achadh a' Choltair
"The field of the coulter", a coulter being part of a plough.

Achosnich (Argyll, Sutherland), Ach Osnaich
This appears to be "the field of sighing", but may originally have contained a different second element which became changed.

Achpopuli (Inverness), Achadh Poible
"The field of the herding hut."

Achranich (Argyll), Achadh an Rainich
"The field with the bracken."

Achray (Perth), Àth Chrathaidh
"Shaking ford."

Achreisgill (Sutherland), Achadh Rìdhisgil
"The field of Reisgill."

Achriabhach (Inverness), An t-Achadh Riabhach
"The brindled field."

Achrimsdale (Sutherland), Achadh Rumasdail
"The field of Rimsdale."

Achscrabster (Caithness)
"The field of Scrabster", from *Achadh Sgrabastail*.

Achtar (Perth), Achadh Teàrra
"Pitch field."

Achtemarack (Inverness), Ach t-Seamraig
"Clover field", from an older *Achadh an t-Seamraig*.

Achterblair (Inverness), Ochdamh a' Bhlàir
"The octave of the moor", an octave being the eighth part of a davoch, which was a land measurement roughly equivalent to 400 Scots acres.

Achtercairn (Ross), Achd a' Chàirn
"The field at the cairn."

Achtoty (Sutherland), Achadh Toitidh
"The field of smoke or fumigation."

Achtriochtan (Argyll), Achadh Triachatain
The second element in this field name is unclear.

Adabrock (Lewis), Adabrog
This Norse fort name contains an unclear first element. Adabrock consists of *Adabrog Àrd* and *Adabrog Ìosal*, "high Adabrock" and "low Adabrock" respectively.

Advie (Moray), Àbhaidh
This name may contain *magh*, "plain".

Affleck (Aberdeen), Achadh Leac
"Slab field."

Ahmore (North Uist), An Àth Mhór
"The big ford."

Aigas (Inverness), Àigeis
This is unclear, but might be "edge ridge", from Norse or "place of the gap", from Gaelic.

Aignish (Lewis), Aiginis
"Edge point", from Norse.

Ailsa Craig (Ayr), Creag Ealasaid *or* Allasan
Although this is said to be "craig of the rocky place", also known simply as *A' Chreag*, "the rock", the "Ailsa" part of the name is from *Alfsigrsøy*, "Alfsigr's island". This rock has been known by a variety of other names, including *Creag Alasdair, Ealasaid a' Chuain*, "Ealasaid of the Ocean", and "Paddy's Milestone". The names *Alasdair* and *Ealasaid* appear to have been used due to their vague similarity in sound to *Alfsigr*. Ailsa Craig

and Sanda in Kintyre are linked in a number of sayings which describe that area of the sea as a bad place to be in stormy weather, *'S truagh gun robh thu eadar Allasan is Àbhainn*, "It's a pity you were between Ailsa Craig and Sanda", and *Cha bu mhath a bhith eadar Allasan is Àbhainn a leithid seo a latha*, "It wouldn't be good to be between Ailsa Craig and Sanda on a day like this."

Airbow (Fife)
"High point of cattle", from *Àird Bó*, which shows the obsolete genitive plural *bó*, which in modern Gaelic would be *bhó*.

Aird (Benbecula, Inverness, Lewis, Ross), An Àird
In Benbecula, Lewis and Ross, this is "the headland", but the Inverness name means "the prominent hill", and has the extended name of *Àird Mhic Shimidh*, "Lord Lovat's Aird". This Aird appears in a number of sayings such as, *Buntàta pronn is uachdar leotha, biadh bodaich na h-Àirde*, "Mashed potatoes and cream, the food of the old men of Aird", and *Is mór stàth na h-Àirde do Mhac Shimidh*, "Lord Lovat benefits greatly from Aird". The nicknames given to the people of various places in this Aird are recounted in another saying, *Fithich dhubha Mhilifiach, piatan Cnoc Bhàin, faoileagan a' Chluain, ruadh-chearcan Baile an Todhair, cabair fhada a' Chonfhadhaich, gearran beaga Baile a' Chonais*, "Black ravens from Milifiach, pet lambs from Knockbain, gulls from Clune, red hens from Balintore, long poles from Convinth, little hares from Balconish." Aird in Wester Ross is also known by the full name of *An Àird Druiseach*, "the brambly headland".

Aird Brenish (Lewis), Àird Bhréinis
"The headland of Brenish."

Aird Dell (Lewis), Àird Dhail
"The headland of Dell."

Aird Dhubh (Ross), An Àird Dhubh
"The black headland." The name of this small settlement in Applecross is spelled "Ard Dhubh" on roadsigns.

Aird Donald (Wigtown)
"Donald's headland", from *Àird Dhòmhnaill.*

Aird of Sleat (Skye), Àird Shléite *or* An Àird
"The headland of Sleat" or "the headland". Local people are nicknamed *faoileagan*, "gulls". See **Sleat**.

Aird Point (Ross), An Àird
"The headland." The English form contains both the Gaelic and English generic terms for a headland.

Airdrie (Lanark); (Nairn), An Àrd Ruigh
"The high slope." AÀA gives the Lanarkshire name as *an t-Àrd-Ruigh*, with the same meaning in English.

Airds (Argyll), Na h-Àirdean
"The headlands." Airds House is *Taigh nan Àird.*

Aird Tong (Lewis), Àird Thunga
"The headland of Tong."

Aird Uig (Lewis), Àird Uig
"The headland of Uig."

Airidhantuim (Lewis), Àirigh an Tuim
"The sheiling by the hillock."

Airlie (Angus), Iarlaidh
This name is unclear but may contain an element meaning "west", however AÀA give *Earlaidh* as the Gaelic name which appears to suggest "east".

Airntully (Perth)
"The point at the green hill", from *Àird an Tulaich.*

Airor (Inverness), Eàrar
This may be "sand spit" or "beach", from Norse.

Airyolland (Wigtown)
This may be "Fillan's sheiling", from *Àirigh Fhaolain.*

Aithmuir (Perth)
"Big ford", from *Àth Mór.*

Aitnoch (Moray), Aitneach
"Juniper place."

Alavig (Harris), Àlabhaig
This may be either "eel bay" or "deep river bay", from Norse.

Alcaig (Ross), Alcaig
"Auk bay", from Norse.

Aldamph (Aberdeen), Allt Damh
"Stream of stags", originally the name of a stream, later attached to a farm.

Aldandulish (Perth), Allt an Dùghlais
"The stream of the black water."

Aldbar (Angus)
This may be "top stream", from *Allt Bhàirr.*

Aldclune (Perth), Allt Cluaine
"Meadow stream."

Aldie (Ross), Alltaidh
"Stream place."

Aldivalloch (Banff), Allt a' Bhealaich
"The stream at the pass."

Aldochlay (Dunbarton), Allt a' Chlaidheimh
"The stream of the sword." This Gaelic form is confirmed by both an older anglicised form and the name of the stream flowing through the settlement which is *Allt a' Chlaidheimh*. Diack (1944) collected a slightly different form locally suggesting *Allt a' Chlaidh*, "the stream at the graveyard", but this could have been a corruption given that both *a' chlaidheimh* and *a' chlaidh* would be pronounced very like each other.

Aldour (Perth), Allt Dobhair
"Water stream."

Aldourie (Inverness), Allt Dobhraig
"Dobhrag stream", *dobhrag* being a diminutive of *dobhar*, "water or river".

Alford (Aberdeen), Àthfort
This name may contain the Gaelic and English words for "ford".

Aline (Lewis), Àth an Linne *or* Àth Linne
"The ford by the pool."

Alisary (Inverness), Amhlasairigh
This Norse name suggests "Olaf's sheiling".

Alladale (Inverness), Aladal
This is Norse for "Ali's valley" or "eel valley".

Allan (Fife); (Ross), Alan Mhór
The name in Fife derives from *Eilean*, representing a meadow, while the Ross name is "big Allan".

Allanbank (Ross), An Réim
The English name refers to this place's riverside location while the Gaelic name is "the course".

Allanfearn (Inverness), An t-Àilean Feàrna
"The alder meadow."

Allangrange (Ross), Alan
The English name is "the barn on the Allan", while the Gaelic name is that of the river.

Allanmore (Aberdeen, Inverness), An t-Àilean Mór
"The large meadow."

Allanquoich (Aberdeen), Àilean Choich
"The meadow in the hollow." An over-correct Gaelic form, *Àilean na Cuaiche*, which has the same meaning, is common.

Allarburn (Inverness), Allt Feàrna
"Alder stream." This is the local name of the village also known as Aultfearn and Kiltarlity. The Gaelic name does not apply to Allarburn in Moray.

Allargue (Aberdeen), Àth Làirig
"Ford of the pass."

Allasdale (Barra), Athalasdal
This may be "Ali's valley", from Norse.

Alligin (Ross), Àiliginn
This is said to mean "jewel", from *àilleag*, but the "l" sound in the name refutes this. Wester Alligin (marked "Alligin Shuas" on maps) is

Bràighe Àiliginn, "upper Alligin", or simply *am Bràighe*, "the upper part". Brybeg or Upper Alligin is *Am Bràighe Beag*, "the small upper part", and Easter or Inver Alligin is *Inbhir Àiliginn*. Local people are *saoidheanan*, "saithes", or *adhaichean*, "livers".

Alloa (Clackmannan), Alamhagh *or* Allamhagh
This may be "wild or rocky plain".

Alloway (Ayr)
See **Alloa**.

Alltbeithe (Inverness), Allt Beithe
"Birch stream."

Alltgobhlach (Arran), Allt Gobhlach
"Forked stream." In several Arran names comprising a noun and qualifying adjective, there is no accompanying definite article, which would be expected and is the norm elsewhere in Scotland as well as Arran in general.

Allt-nan-Subh (Ross), Allt nan Subh
"The stream of the berries."

Alltnaharra (Sutherland), Allt na h-Eirbhe
"The stream by the boundary wall."

Alltnaharrie (Ross), Allt na h-Airbhe
See **Alltnaharra**.

Alness (Ross), Alanais
"Allan place."

Altandhu (Ross), An t-Alltan Dubh
"The black streamlet."

Altanour (Perth), An t-Alltan Odhar
"The dun-coloured streamlet."

Altass (Sutherland), Alltais
"Rock place."

Altavaig (Skye), Alltabhaig
"Swan bay", from Norse.

Altgaltraig (Argyll), Allt Galtraig
"The stream at hogs' bay", from Gaelic/Norse.

Altimarlach (Caithness), Allt nam Mèirleach
"The stream of the robbers."

Altnabreac (Caithness, Ross), Allt nam Breac
"The stream of the trout."

Altnacardich (Inverness), Allt na Ceàrdaich
"The stream at the smithy."

Altnacealgach (Sutherland), Allt nan Cealgach
"The stream of the cheats."

Altnamain (Ross), Taigh a' Mhonaidh
The English name, which also appears as "Aultnamain", is from *Allt na Mèinn*, "the ore stream", while the Gaelic name is "the house on the moor".

Alturlie (Inverness), Allt Rollaidh
The defining element of this stream name is unclear. Alturlie Point is *Gob Allt Rollaidh*.

Altyre (Moray), Alltar
This appears to contain *allt*, "stream", but is unclear in whole.

Alva (Clackmannan)
See **Alloa**.

Alvah (Banff)
See **Alloa**.

Alves (Moray), An Àbhas *or* Àbhais
This may be "water place".

Alvie (Inverness), Albhaidh *or* Allamhaigh
See **Alloa**.

Alyth (Perth), Àilt *or* Allaid
The root of this name may be *ail*, "rock". AÀA recommends *Àilid*.

Amar (Skye), An t-Amar
"The channel."

Amat (Ross, Sutherland), Àmait
"Confluence", from Norse. In Ross, North Amat is *Àmait na h-Eaglais*, "Amat of the church", and South Amat is *Àmait na Tuath*, "Amat of the laity". Amat in Sutherland is *Àmait nan Cuilean*, "Amat of the whelps".

Amhuinnsuidhe (Harris), Abhainn Suidhe
"River Suidhe." The English form is from an older Gaelic spelling.

Amulree (Perth), Àth Maol Ruibhe
"St Maol Rubha's ford." Amulree church is *Cill Maol Ruibhe* or *Cill MoRuibhe*.

An Ard (Ross), An Àird
"The headland." This name refers to a group of settlements in Gairloch.

Anaheilt (Argyll), Àth na h-Eilde
"The ford of the hind."

Anancaun (Ross), Àth nan Ceann
"The ford of the heads."

Angus (Angus), Aonghas *or* Siorrachd Aonghais
This may commemorate Aonghas, the leader of one of the kindred groupings in Dal Riada. Coastal Angus is known as *Machair Aonghais*, "plain of Angus", while the area of the Glens is *Bràigh Aonghais*, "upland of Angus". Angus and the Mearns together were known as *Cìrcheann*, "Circenn", while someone from the coastal area was a *Tròsach*, a name based on a Gaelic form of Montrose.

Anie (Perth), Àth an Fhéidh
"The ford of the deer."

Ankerville (Ross), Cinn Déis Bhig *or* Baile a' Chragain
The English name comes from an 18th-century owner, while the Gaelic name is "little Kindeace". Ankerville was also known locally by the second Gaelic name, which means "farm at the little rock".

Annan (Dumfries), Anainn
This is primarily a river name, dedicated to the goddess Anu. The phrase *eadar Cataibh is Anainn*, "from Sutherland to Annan", is a Gaelic equivalent of *from Land's End to John O' Groats*. Annandale is *Srath Anann*.

Annat (Ross), An Annaid
"The small church." Local people were known as *daoine uaisle*, "gentlefolk". See **Achnahannet**.

Annathill (Lanark)
This may represent a hill at an *annaid*, "small church". See **Achnahannet**.

Annet (Ayr, Perth)
"The small church", from *an Annaid*. See **Achnahannet**.

Annishader (Skye), Anaiseadar *or* Arnaiseadar
"Eagle township", from Norse.

Anstruther (Fife)
The root of this name may be *sruthair*, "stream" or "current", which is common in Ireland, but rarer in Scotland. This town's name is pronounced as "Enster" by local people.

Antfield (Inverness), An t-Achadh Seanganach
"The field of ants."

Appin (Argyll, Perth), An Apainn
"The abbey lands." Appin in Argyll, which probably belonged to the religious community of Lismore, is also known as *Apainn nan Stiùbhartach*, "Appin of the Stewarts", and *Apainn Mhic Iain Stiùbhairt*, "Appin of John Stewart's son", and the inhabitants were nicknamed *cearcan-tomain*, "partridges". The part of Appin between Loch Creran and Loch Linnhe is *An Ceathramh Feàrna*, "the alder quarterland", referring to a quarter of a davoch, which was a land measurement roughly equivalent to 400 Scots acres. Appin in Perthshire is also known as *Apainn nam Mèinnearach*, "Appin of the Menzies", and the Carse of Appin is simply called *an Cars*. Appin in Perthshire was previously known as *Apainn na Gailmnich* or *Apainn nan Cailmnich*, "Appin of the Dows", using an obscure local name by which the Dow family was known.

Applecross (Ross), A' Chomraich
The English name comes from an older Gaelic *Abar Crosain*, "mouth of the cross river", while the present Gaelic name is "the sanctuary", with a longer form *A' Chomraich Abrach*, "the sanctuary of Abar Crosain". It used also to be known as *Comraich Maol Ruibhe*, "St Maol Rubha's sanctuary". To express "in Applecross", Gaelic uses *air a' Chomraich*, "on the sanctuary". A native of the area is an *Abrach*, also nicknamed a *boc*, "buck". Applecross Mains is *Borghdal*, "fort valley", from Norse, and the north coast is *Na Cealan*, possibly "the cells", from Gaelic or a name related to the Norse for "keel".

Aquhorties (Aberdeen)
"Field of the standing stone", from *Achadh Coirthe.*

Arabella (Ross), Am Bog
The English name commemorates the wife of an owner, and the Gaelic name is "the bog".

Araird (Ross), An Araird
"The prominent headland."

Arbirlot (Angus)
"The mouth of the Elliot Burn", containing Brythonic *aber*.

Arboll (Ross), Àrbol
"River farm" or "seal farm", from Norse.

Arbroath (Angus), Obar Bhrothaig
"The mouth of the Brothock."

Arbuthnot (Kincardine), Obar Bhuadhnait
"The mouth of the Buadhnat."

Arcandeith (Ross), Arcan Duibh
"Very black place."

Ardachu (Sutherland), Àrd Achadh
"High field."

Ardachvie (Inverness), Àird Eachaidh *or* Àird Eachbhaidh
"The point on the horse plain."

Ardachy (Argyll), Àrdachaidh
"Place of the high field."

Ardalanish (Mull), Àird Dealanais
This Gaelic/Norse name may be "headland at valley point".

Ardanashaig (Argyll, Scalpay), Àird an Aiseig
"The headland of the ferry."

Ardaneaskan (Ross), Àird an Fheusgain
"Mussel headland." Ardnaneaskan Point is *Rubha Àird an Fheusgain.*

Ard an Runair (North Uist), Àird an Rùnair
This appears to mean "the headland of the secretary", but the element, *rùnair*, may be from Norse for "rowan" or "rough".

Ardargie (Perth)
"Point on the Farg", from *Àird Fhargaidh*. The same river name appears in "Aberargie".

Ardarroch (Ross), Àird Daraich
"Oak headland."

Ardbeg (Argyll, Bute, Islay), An Àird Bheag
"The small headland."

Ardbrecknish (Argyll), Àird Breicinis
"Slope headland", from Norse with Gaelic *àird*, "headland", added.

Ardcharnich (Ross), Àird Cheatharnaich
"Warrior headland."

Ardchattan (Argyll), Àird Chatain
"Catan's headland." The old church here was known as *Baile Bhaodain* (rather than *Cill Bhaodain*), dedicated to St Baetan.

Ardchivaig (Jura), Àird Chiabhaig
This Gaelic/Norse name is "headland of enclosure bay".

Ardchoirk (Mull), Àird a' Choirce
"Headland of the oats."

Ardchrishnish (Mull), Àird Chraoisinis
This has both Gaelic and Norse words for "point", but the Norse specifying element is unclear.

Ardchronie (Ross), Àird Chrònaidh
"The headland at the swarthy place."

Ardchuing (Benbecula), An Àird Chumhang
"The narrow headland." This is also known as "Ard Cumhang".

Ardchyle (Perth), Àrd Choille
"High wood."

Ardclach (Nairn), Àird Chlach
"Stony high point."

Ard Cumhang (Benbecula), An Àird Chumhang
See **Ardchuing**.

Ardeer (Ayr)
This may be "west headland", from *Àird Iar*.

Ardelve (Ross), Àird Eilbh
This may be "the headland at fallow land". The market held here was *Féill na h-Àirde*, "the Ard fair", referring to Ardelve.

Ardencaple (Dunbarton), Àird nan Capall
"Headland of the horses."

Ardendrain (Inverness)
"High point of the (black)thorn", from *Àird an Droighinn*.

Ardentallen (Argyll), Àird an t-Sàilein
"The headland at the small inlet."

Ardentinny (Argyll), Àird an t-Sionnaich
"The headland of the fox."

Ardentrive (Kerrera), Àird an t-Snàimh
"The headland of the swimming."

Ardeonaig (Perth), Àird Eódhanaig *or* Àird Eónaig.
"Adamnan's headland." The local church is *Cill MoCharmaig*, "dear St Cormac's Church". This area used to be known as "Ardewnan", from *Àird Eódhanain* or *Àird Eónain*, but possibly by analogy with nearby places the form of Adamnan's name changed.

Ardersier (Inverness), Àird nan Saor
"The headland of the joiners." This village is also known as *Am Baile Ùr*, "the new village", and was earlier known as *Baile nan Caimbeulach*, "the Campbells' village".

Ardery (Argyll), Àrdaraidh
This appears to be simply "high place".

Ardessie (Ross), Àird Easaidh
"Headland at the waterfall place."

Ardfenaig (Mull), Àird Fìneig
This may be from one of two sources. If it is a wholly Gaelic name, it may be "headland of the Fìneag", a diminutive form of *Fìne*, "Fyne". It could, however, be Gaelic/

Norse, containing Gaelic *àird*, "headland", and Norse *vík*, "bay".

Ardfern (Argyll), Àird Fheàrna
"Alder headland."

Ardfernal (Jura), Àird Fheàrnail
If this is a wholly Gaelic name it may mean "alder headland", but the second part could be Norse for "far hill", giving "headland of the far hill".

Ardfour (Ayr)
"Pasture point", from *Àird Phùir*.

Ardgay (Ross), Àird Ghaoithe
"Windy or marshy point." The Kincardine area market held at Ardgay was called *an Fhéill Éiteachan*, which is unclear in meaning although may be compared with **Carn Etchachan**.

Ardgour (Argyll), Àird Ghobhar
"Goats' headland." Local people were known as *gobhair*, "goats". Ardgour House is *A' Chùil*, "the secluded spot". The name may originally have been *Àird Dhobhar*, "Headland of waters", which is pronounced the same as *Àird Ghobhar*.

Ardgye (Moray)
See **Ardgay**.

Ardhallow (Argyll), Àrd Thalamh
"High land."

Ardhasaig (Harris), Àird Àsaig
This Gaelic/Norse name is "headland at ridge bay".

Ardheisker (North Uist), Àird Heillsgeir
"The headland of the flat or holy rock", from Gaelic/Norse.

Ardheslaig (Ross), Àird Heisleag
"Headland of hazel bay", from Gaelic/Norse. A local person is a *cràiceanach*, denoting a squat or disagreeable person.

Ardincaple (Argyll, Dunbarton), Àird nan Capall
"Horses' headland."

Ardindrean (Ross), Àird an Dreaghainn
"The headland with the thorn bush."

Ardintoul (Ross), Àird an t-Sabhail
"The headland by the barn."

Ardivachair (South Uist), Àird a' Mhachaire
"The headland on the machair", which is flat, fertile land near the sea used for cultivating vegetables.

Ardkenneth (South Uist), Àird Choinnich
"Cainneach's headland."

Ardkinglas (Argyll), Àird Chonghlais
"Point on the Conglass."

Ardlair (Ross), Àird Làir
"Mare headland."

Ardlamont (Argyll), Àird MhicLaomainn
"Lamont's headland."

Ardlui (Dunbarton), Àird Laoigh
"The point on the Lui or Loy."

Ardlussa (Jurra), Àird Lusa
"The point on the Lussa."

Ardmaddy (Argyll), Àird a' Mhadaidh *or* Àird Mhadaidh
"The headland of the wolf or fox."

Ardmair (Ross), Àird Mhèar
This may be "finger headland".

Ardmaleish (Bute), Àird MoLaoise
"St MoLaoise's headland."

Ardmarnock (Argyll), Àird Mhearnaig
"St Ernoc's or M'Ernoc's headland."

Ardmeanach (Mull), An Àird Mheadhanach
"The middle headland."

Ardmenish (Jura), Àird Mhèanais
"The headland of the narrow point", from Gaelic/Norse.

Ardmhor (Barra), An Àird Mhór
"The large headland."

Ardminish (Gigha), Àird Mhèanais
See **Ardmenish**.

Ardmolich (Inverness), An Àird Mholach
"The shaggy headland."

Ardmore (several), An Àird Mhór
Where this name is found on the coast, it is most likely "the large headland", but inland it is "the large height".

Ard More Mangersta (Lewis), Àird Mhór Mhangartaidh
"The large headland of Mangersta."

Ardnacroish (Lismore), Àird na Croise
"The headland of the cross."

Ardnacross (Mull), Àird na Croise
See **Ardnacroish**.

Ardnadam (Argyll), Àird nan Damh
"The point of the stags or oxen."

Ardnagoine (Ross), Àird nan Gaimhne
"The point of the stirks."

Ardnagrask (Ross), Àird nan Crasg
"The point of the crossing places", from older *Àird na g-Crasg*.

Ardnahoe (Bute) Àird na h-Uamha; (Islay), Àird na Hogh
In Bute the name is "the headland with the cave", while in Islay it is "the headland of the burial mound", featuring a final Norse element.

Ardnakille (Scalpay), Àird na Cille
"The headland by the church."

Ardnamonie (South Uist), Àird na Mònadh
"The headland of the peat."

Ardnamurchan (Argyll), Àird nam Murchan
"The headland of the sea hounds." Ardnamurchan Point is *Rubha Àird nam Murchan* or *An Rubha Murchanach*. A local person is a *Murchanach*, nicknamed a *cnòdan*, "gurnet". The rivalry between Ardnamurchan and neighbouring Sunart is recorded in the saying, *Sùrd le Suaineart! Chaidh Àird nam Murchan a dholaidh!*, "Let Sunart rejoice! Ardnamurchan has been ruined!" A byword for a detour is *rathad nam Mealla Ruadh chun na Ranna*, "via Mealla Ruadh to Ranna", indicating a roundabout way to get from one place to another, or more broadly describing a complicated way of doing something. Both the places mentioned are located in Ardnamurchan.

Ardnarff (Ross), Àird an Arbha
"The headland with the corn."

Ardnastang (Argyll), Àird na Staing
"The headland of the ditch."

Ardnastruban (Grimsay), Àird nan Srùban
"The headland of the cockles."

Ardnave Point (Islay), Rubha Àird Néimh
"The point of Ném's headland."

Ardnish (Inverness), Àird Nis
"The headland of Nes or Nis." This place near Arisaig was originally called *nes*, "headland", in Norse, which developed into *nis* in the Gaelic sound system. Gaelic *àird*, "headland", was later added to *nis*, which was a meaningless name to Gaelic speakers.

Ardoch (Moray, Perth)
"High place", from *Àrdach*. The Roman camp at Ardoch in Perthshire was known in Gaelic as *Cathair Mhaothail*, "Muthil fort".

Ardoe (Aberdeen)
This is probably from *Àrdach*, "high place", as Gaelic names ending in *-ach* often became anglicised with a final *-o* in the north-east.

Ardpatrick (Argyll), Àird Phàraig
"Patrick's headland." Ardpatrick Point is *Rubha Àird Phàraig*.

Ardradnaig (Perth), Àird Radanaig
This may be "point on the rat stream".

Ardrishaig (Argyll), Rubha Àird Driseig
The English name is "briar headland", while the Gaelic name is "the point on the briar headland". A local person is a *Rubhach*, known in English as a Pointer. AÀA recommends *Àird Driseig* as the name of the village.

Ardroag (Skye), Àird Ròdhaig
"The headland of Roag", from Gaelic/Norse.

Ardroil (Lewis), Eadra Fhadhail
"Between two sea fords", from *Eadar Dhà Fhadhail*.

Ardroscadale (Bute), Àird Rosgadail
This name, which signifies a headland, appears to contain the Norse *dalr*, "valley", but this may not be the case based on old forms of the name. Nether Ardroscadale is *Am Baile Ìochdrach*, "the lower farm", while Upper Ardroscadale is *Am Baile Uachdrach*, "the upper farm".

Ardross (Fife); (Ross), Àird Rois
The name in Fife is "high point", from *Àrd Ros*, whereas the name in Ross-shire is "the headland or high point of Ross".

Ardrossan (Ayr), Àird Rosain
"The point of the small promontory."

Ardruairidh (South Uist), Àird Ruairidh
"Roderick's headland."

Ardscalpsie (Bute)
This name is the "headland of Scalpsie", from *Àird Scalpasaidh*. See **Scalpsie**.

Ardsheal (Argyll), Àird Sheile
This headland name contains the pre-Gaelic river name *Seile*, quite common in the west.

Ardskenish (Colonsay), Àird Sgithinis
This may be "Skiði's headland", from Norse, with Gaelic *àird* added later.

Ardslave (Harris), Àird Léimhe
This may be "moor headland".

Ardtalla (Islay), Àird Talla
"Rock point", although an earlier form of the name, *Àird Tealbha*, might suggest an alternative derivation.

Ardtalnaig (Perth), Àird Talanaig
The second part of this name is unclear, although the name denotes a headland.

Ardteaghanish (Scalpay), Àird Adhanais
This Gaelic/Norse name may be "the headland of tongue point".

Ardtoe (Argyll), Àird Tobha
"Howe headland", from Gaelic/Norse.

Ardtornish (Argyll), Àird Tòirinis
"The headland of Thorir's promontory", from Gaelic/Norse. Ardtornish Point is *Rubha Àird Tòirinis*.

Ardtun (Mull), Àird Tunna
This may be "enclosure headland", from Gaelic/Norse.

Arduaine (Argyll), An Àird Uaine
"The green headland."

Ardullie (Ross), Àird Ilidh
"The headland of the Ilidh", a name also found further north. See **Helmsdale**.

Arduthie (Kincardine)
"Duthac's point", from *Àird Dhubhthaich*, possibly referring to the saint commemorated in **Tain**.

Ardvannie (Ross), Àird Mhanaigh
This is said to be "monk's headland".

Ardvar (Sutherland), Àird Bhàirr
This may be "top headland".

Ardvasar (Skye), Àird a' Bhàsair
This headland name may contain Norse *voss*, "current", although locally believed to contain a word based on *bàs*, "death". Local people are known as *cearcan*, "hens".

Ardveenish (Barra), Àird Mhèanais
"The headland of the narrow point", from Gaelic/Norse.

Ardverikie (Inverness), Àird Mhairgidh
This may be "the high point of the merkland".

Ardvey (Harris), Àird Mhighe
"The headland at the narrow place", from Gaelic/Norse. There are two places in Harris with this name, each with a more complete Gaelic form, namely *Àird Mhighe Leacan Lì* near Lackalee and *Àird Mhighe Fhionnasbhaigh* near Finsbay.

Ardvorlich (Perth), Àird Mhùrlaig
"The point at the rounded inlet."

Ardvorran (North Uist), Àird a' Bhorrain
It is not clear what the name of this headland means. *Borran* is "buttock"

or "haunch", but it may be related to the word found in *Caolas a' Mhòrain*, the Gaelic name for the Sound of Boreray.

Ardvourlie (Harris), Àird a' Mhulaidh
This name may be "lip headland". A house nearby is named "Mulag House".

Ardvreck (Sutherland), An Àird Bhreac
"The speckled headland."

Ardyne (Argyll), Àird Fhìne
"The point on the Fyne."

Arevegaig (Argyll), Àirigh Bheagaig
This name is unclear, but contains *àirigh*, "sheiling", and Norse *vík*, "bay".

Argyll (Argyll), Earra-Ghàidheal
"The coastland of Gaels", from an older *Oirthir Ghàidheal*. Mid Argyll is *Meadhan Earra-Ghàidheal* or more poetically *Dal Riada*, named after the territory in Ireland where the Scots originated. At its peak, Argyll stretched from Kintyre to Loch Broom. South of Ardnamurchan was known as *an t-Oirthir a Deas*, "the south coast", with the northern area called *an t-Oirthir a Tuath*, "the north coast". A byname for Argyll is *Dùthaich Mhic Chailein*, "the land of the Duke of Argyll". Argyll and Bute together are *Earra-Ghàidheal agus Bòid*.

Arichamish (Argyll), Àirigh a' Chamais
"The sheiling by the bay."

Arichastlich (Argyll), Àirigh Chastulaich
"The sheiling by the steep green hill."

Aridrisaig (Ross), An Àirigh Dhriseach
"The briar sheiling."

Arienas (Argyll), Àirigh Aonghais
"Angus's sheiling."

Arileod (Coll), Àirigh Leòid
"Leòd's sheiling."

Arinacrinachd (Ross), Àirigh nan Cruithneachd

"The sheiling of the Picts", from an earlier form, *Àirigh nan Cruithneach*. Local people were called *druinich*, "druids", possibly a corruption of *Cruithnich*.

Arinafad (Argyll), Àird nam Fàd
"The headland of the divots or furrows."

Arinagour (Coll), Àirigh nan Gobhar
"The goats' sheiling."

Arisaig (Inverness), Àrasaig
"River mouth bay", from Norse. The sheltered nature of the bay was known to fishermen who would recommend *dèan Eige no Àrasaig dheth*, "head for Eigg or Arisaig", in the event of a storm.

Ariundle (Argyll), Àirigh Fhionndail
"The sheiling in the fair valley", from Gaelic/Norse.

Arivirig (Coll), Àirigh Mhaoraich
This appears to mean "shellfish sheiling", but the name may have become corrupted from an original Norse word.

Arivruich (Lewis), Àirigh a' Bhruthaich
"The sheiling on the brae."

Armadale (several), Armadal
"Arm valley", from Norse, referring to a bay. Armadale in West Lothian was named after Armadale in Sutherland.

Arnabol (Sutherland), Àrnabol
"Eagle farm" or "Arne's farm", from Norse.

Arnipol (Inverness), Àrnapol
See **Arnabol**.

Arnabost (Coll), Àrnabost
See **Arnabol**.

Arnbeg (Stirling)
"Small portion", from *Earrann Bheag* or *Earrann Beag*, possibly known locally as *An Earrann Bheag* or *An t-Earrann Beag*, "the small portion", using the definite article. Although *earrann* is normally a feminine noun, it may have been masculine in local Gaelic, as shown in the second forms above.

Arnclay (Perth), Earrann a' Chlaidh
"The portion (of land) at the graveyard."

Arnclerich (Perth)
"The cleric's portion of land", from *Earrann a' Chléirich.*

Arndean (Kinross)
"The dean's portion of land", from *Earrann an Deadhain.*

Arndilly (Moray)
"The point at the green hill", from *Àird an Tulaich*, which is also the Gaelic name of Airntully in Perthshire.

Arnisdale (Inverness), Àrnasdal
"Arne's valley", from Norse.

Arnish (Lewis), Àirinis; (Raasay), Àrnais
"Eagle headland", from Norse.

Arnisort (Skye), Àrnasort
"Arne's firth", from Norse.

Arnmannoch (Kirkcudbright)
"The monks' portion of land", from *Earrann nam Manach.*

Arnmore (Perth, Stirling)
"Big portion", from *Earrann Mhór* or *Earrann Mór*. See **Arnbeg.**

Arnol (Lewis), Àrnol
"Eagle hill", from Norse.

Arnprior (Stirling)
"The prior's portion of land." This was earlier known in English as "Erne-frear", showing more clearly the Gaelic derivation, *Earrann a' Phriair.*

Arnvicar (Perth)
"The vicar's portion of land", from *Earrann a' Bhiocair.*

Aros (Mull), Àros *or* Àras
"River mouth", from Norse.

Arpafeelie (Ross), Arpa-philidh
This name is unclear.

Arran (Arran), Arainn
This is unclear and said to be unrelated to the name "Aran" in Ireland, which is *Árainn* with a long initial "a". However, if the names are linked they mean "kidney-shaped". Arran has the poetic name, *Arainn*

nan Aighean Iomadh, "Arran of the many stags". A native of Arran is an *Arannach* or *Arainneach* also called *coinean mór*, "big rabbit". In Arran the people of various settlements had their own nicknames as in the rhyme, *Meanbhchuileagan Acha-Rà, coilich dhubha an Dubh Ghearraidh, stùcanaich /tùiteallaich Achadh a' Charra, cuileagan-ime Chatagail, feannagan Achadh a' Ghallain,* "Midges from Achara, black cocks from Dougrie, stuck-up/awkward folk from Auchencar, butterflies from Catacol, crows from Achagallon". The coast between North Thundergay and Whitefarland is called *an Luirgeann*, "the shank". The Cock of Arran is also known as *an Coileach Arannach*, "the Arran cock" and *an Coileach Clachaig*, "the stone cock". Arran was traditionally linked with Bute and Islay, as shown in the triad *Bòd is Ìle is Àrainn*. In olden times sailors would have been considered more than fortunate if in one day's sailing they had seen *a' Chearc Leòdhasach, an Coileach Arannach agus an Eireag Mhanannach*, "the Lewis Chicken, the Cock of Arran and the Manx Pullet". The old road from Lamlash to Kilmory was known as *rathad na h-iubhraigh*, "the road of the yew forest".

Arrivain (Perth), Àirigh a' Mheadhain
"The sheiling in the middle."

Arrochar (Dunbarton), An t-Àrar, An t-Àrchar *or* An Tairbeart Iar
The English and first two Gaelic names are obscure but may be related to "Ben Arthur", which is in the Arrochar Alps. The third Gaelic name is "the west isthmus", with the east isthmus being Tarbet Loch Lomond nearby.

Arscaig (Sutherland), Àrsgaig
"Strip of land by a river", from Norse.

Artafallie (Ross), Àirde Fàillidh
This may be "high point of the sods".

Aruadh (Islay), An t-Àth Ruadh
"The red-brown ford."

Ascog (Bute), Àsgaig
"Ash bay", from Norse.

Ashaig (Skye), Aiseag
"Ferry." The full name is *Aiseag Maol Ruibhe*, "St Maol Rubha's ferry", the saint commemorated in Applecross and elsewhere in Skye. The initial vowel can be pronounced long, giving *Àiseag*, which might point to a Norse origin suggesting "ash bay" rather than the Gaelic derivation, which would normally be expected to contain the definite article.

Ashcraig (Arran), Baile Uachdrach
The English name is "ash rock", but the Gaelic one is "upper farm".

Ashentilly (Kincardine)
"Stream at the green hill", from *Eas an Tulaich*.

Ashfield (Argyll), Learg na h-Uinnsinn
The Gaelic name is "the ash slope".

Ashintully (Perth)
"The stream at the green hill", from *Eas an Tulaich*.

Ashmore (Perth), An tEas Mór
"The big waterfall."

Askernish (South Uist), Àisgearnais
This may be "ash field point", from Norse.

Asknish (Argyll), Aisginis
"Ash tree point", from Norse.

Assynt (Ross, Sutherland), Asaint *or* Asainn
"Ridge end", from Norse. Mid Assynt is *Meadhan Asaint*, "the middle of Assynt", and Upper Assynt is *Àrd Asaint*, "high Assynt". An Assynt person is an *Asainteach*. The churchyard in Assynt near Novar in Ross is *Cladh Churadain*, "St Curadan's churchyard".

Astle (Sutherland), Àsdal
"Aspen valley", from Norse.

Atholl (Perth), Athall
"New Ireland", from *Ath Fhótla*, *Fótla* being a poetic term for Ireland. A local person is an *Athallach*. The Forest of Atholl is *Frith Athaill*. A short ditty from the early days of stagecoaching outlines the progress made in a day's travel from Atholl to Badenoch, *Bracaist am Baile Chloichrigh, lunch an Dail na Ceàrdaich, dìnneir an Dail Chuinnidh 's a' bhanais ann an Ràt*, "Breakfast in Pitlochry, lunch in Dalnacardoch, dinner in Dalwhinnie and the wedding in Raitts."

Attadale (Ross), Atadal
This may be "fight valley", from Norse.

Auch (Argyll), Achadh Innis Chalainn
The English name is from "field". The full Gaelic name is "the field at the meadow of Calann".

Auchabrick (Wigtown)
"Speckled field", from *Achadh Breac*.

Auchagallon (Arran), Achadh a' Ghallain
"The field of the standing stone." An alternative derivation is found in *Achadh a' Ghaillinn*, "the field of the storm".

Auchaleffan (Arran), Achadh an Leth-pheighinn
"The field of the half pennyland."

Auchallater (Aberdeen)
See **Achallater**.

Auchareoch (Arran), Achadh Riabhach; (Bute), An t-Achadh Riabhach
"Brindled field." The Arran name lacks the expected definite article.

Aucharrigill (Sutherland), Achadh Uraigil
This Gaelic/Norse name is "the field at the stony ravine".

Auchbreck (Banff)
"Speckled field", from *Achadh Breac*.

Auchenbegg (Lanark)
"Small field", from *Achadh Beag*. This

name shows how, through analogy with other names, "Auchen-" or "Auchin-", which should mean "field of the", came to replace "Auch-", "field", as the generic in many place-names where "Auchen-" and "Auchin-" do not make sense in a Gaelic context.

Auchenblae (Kincardine)
"Field of blossoms", from *Achadh nam Blàth*.

Auchenbowie (Stirling)
"Yellow field", from *Achadh Buidhe*. See **Auchenbegg**.

Auchenbrack (Aberdeen)
"Speckled field", from *Achadh Breac*. See **Auchenbegg**.

Auchenbrain (Ayr), Achadh na Bràthann
"The field of the quern." See **Mauchline**.

Auchencairn (Arran, Kirkcudbright), Achadh a' Chàirn
"The field with the cairn." In Arran, Auchencairn is sub-divided into *Baile Ìochdrach*, "lower farm", and *Baile Uachdrach*, "upper farm".

Auchencar (Arran), Achadh a' Charra
"The field with the standing stone." Locals were known as *stùcanaich*, "stuck-up people", or *tùiteallaich*, "awkward people".

Auchenclech (Aberdeen)
"The field with the stone", from *Achadh na Cloiche*.

Auchencorth (Midlothian)
"The field with the standing stone", from *Achadh na Coirthe*.

Auchencrosh (Ayr)
"The field of the cross", from *Achadh na Croise*.

Auchencrow (Berwick)
This looks like a Gaelic field name, but in the 14th century the name was "Aldenecraw" and, given its location, is more likely of English origin.

Auchencruive (Ayr)
"The field with the tree", from *Achadh na Craoibhe*.

Auchendarg (Aberdeen)
Possibly "red field", from *Achadh Dearg*. See **Auchenbegg**.

Auchendinny (Midlothian)
"Field of the fire", from *Achadh an Teine* or "field of the fox", from *Achadh an t-Sionnaich*.

Auchendryne (Aberdeen), Ach an Droighinn
"The field with the thorn bush."

Auchenfedrick (Dumfries)
"Patrick's field", from *Achadh Phàdraig*. See **Auchenbegg**.

Auchengavin (Dunbarton), Achadh nan Gamhainn
"The field of the stirks."

Auchenhalrig (Moray)
"The field at the deer trap", from *Achadh na h-Eilreig*.

Auchenhard (West Lothian)
"The field at the high point", from *Achadh na h-Àirde*.

Auchenharvie (Ayr)
"The field at the boundary wall", from *Achadh na h-Eirbhe*.

Auchenlay (Perth)
This may be "the doctor's field", from *Achadh an Léigh*, or "the field of the calf", from *Achadh an Laoigh*, but it is uncertain.

Auchenlochan (Argyll), Achadh an Lochain
"The field by the small loch."

Auchenlongford (Ayr)
"The field of the encampment", from *Achadh an Longphuirt*.

Auchenreath (Banff)
"The field on the slope", from *Achadh na Ruighe*.

Auchenrioch (Argyll), Achadh na Riabhach
"Brindled field." The Gaelic name does not make grammatical sense, but shows how *Achadh na*, "field of the", appears to have superseded plain *Achadh*, "field", as a generic in place-names, in a way paralleled in English names starting with "Auchen-" and "Auchin-". See **Auchenbegg**.

Auchenrivock (Dumfries)
"Brindled field", from *Achadh Riabhach*. See **Auchenbegg**.

Auchenroy (Ayr)
"Russet field", from *Achadh Ruadh*. See **Auchenbegg**.

Auchensavil (Argyll), Achadh nan Sabhal
"The field with the barns."

Auchenshuggle (Glasgow)
This may be "the rye field", from *Achadh an t-Seagail*.

Auchentaggart (Dumfries)
"The priest's field", from *Achadh an t-Sagairt*.

Auchentiber (Ayr)
"The field with the well", from *Achadh an Tiobair*.

Auchinairn (Dunbarton)
"The field of the alder", from *Achadh an Fheàrna*.

Auchinbo (Aberdeen)
"Field of the cows", from *Achadh nam Bó*.

Auchindachy (Banff), Ach Choinneachaidh
This may be "the meeting field".

Auchindarroch (Argyll), Achadh nan Darach
"The field of the oaks."

Auchindoir (Aberdeen), Ach an Tòrr
"The field by the hill", but the English form hints at the possibility of *dobhar*, "water", rather than *tòrr* as the second element.

Auchindoun (Banff)
"The field at the hill (fort)", from *Achadh an Dùin*.

Auchindownie (Fife)
Older forms of the name suggest that this was originally *Aodann Dùnaidh*, "hill face of Dùnaidh", rather than deriving from *achadh*.

Auchindrain (Argyll), Achadh an Droighinn
"The field with the thorn bush."

Auchindrum (Aberdeen)
"The field at the ridge", from *Achadh an Droma*.

Auchineden (Stirling)
"The field at the hill face", from *Achadh an Aodainn*.

Auchinhove (Aberdeen)
"The field at the cave or hollow", from *Achadh na h-Uamha*.

Auchinleck (Ayr)
"Field with slabs or flagstones", from *Achadh nan Leac*.

Auchinleith (Aberdeen)
This was formerly written as "Auchincleith" and "Auchincleche", suggesting "the field with the stone", from *Achadh na Cloiche*.

Auchinloch (Dunbarton)
"Field by the loch", from *Achadh an Locha*.

Auchinreoch (Kirkcudbright, Stirling)
See **Auchareoch**.

Auchintarph (Aberdeen)
"The field of the bull or bulls", from *Achadh an Tairbh* or *Achadh nan Tarbh*.

Auchintoul (Aberdeen), Ach an t-Sabhail
"The field at the barn."

Auchleuchries (Aberdeen)
"Reedy field", from *Achadh Luachrach*.

Auchleven (Aberdeen)
"Elm field", from *Achadh Leamhan*.

Auchlyne (Perth), Achadh Loinne
This may mean "stack-yard field", as *loinn* had the meaning of "stack-yard" in Perthshire Gaelic. Normally, however, *loinn* means "good condition or appearance", which may be what is intended. The old chapel at Auchlyne was *Caibeal na Fairg(e)*, "the chapel of the shrine".

Auchmachor (Aberdeen)
"St Machar's field", from *achadh* and *Madhchar*, "St Machar".

Auchmore (Aberdeen, Arran)
See **Achmore**.

Auchmuir (Fife)
Although apparently a name beginning with *achadh*, "field", older forms

of the name suggest that this was *Àth Mór*, "big ford".

Auchnaclach (Aberdeen)
"The field of the stones", from *Achadh nan Clach*.

Auchnaclache (Islay), Uchd nan Clach
"The breast (slope) of the stones."

Auchnacloich (Argyll), Achadh na Cloiche
"The field with the stone."

Auchnafree (Perth), Achadh na Frìthe
"The field at the deer forest."

Auchnagallin (Moray)
This may be "the field of the standing stones", from *Achadh nan Gallan*.

Auchnagatt (Aberdeen)
"The field of the cats", from *Achadh nan Cat*. The older Gaelic spelling, *Achadh na gCat*, shows the voicing of initial voiceless consonants in certain situations.

Auchnahannet (Moray)
See **Achnahannet**.

Auchnarrow (Banff)
"The corn field", from *Achadh an Arbha*.

Auchnastank (Banff), Achadh na Staing
"The field with the ditch."

Auchness (Moray)
"The field at the stream or waterfall", from *Achadh an Easa*.

Auchnoon (Midlothian)
"The field of the lambs", from *Achadh nan Uan*.

Aucholzie (Aberdeen), Ach Choille
"Wood field."

Auchrannie (Arran), Achadh an Rainigh
"The field of bracken", showing the older form of the genitive of *raineach*, still found in the southern Gaelic-speaking areas.

Auchreddy (Aberdeen), Achadh Reite
The first part of the name is "field", but the second is unclear. *Achadh Reite* is also the Gaelic name of New Deer.

Auchroisk (Banff, Moray)
"The field at the crossing place", from *Achadh a' Chroisg*.

Auchtascailt (Ross), Achadh Dà Sgaillt
This may be "field with two bald patches".

Auchterarder (Perth), Uachdar Àrdair
"The upland of the Arder."

Auchteraw (Inverness), Uachdar Abha
"Upland of the Oich." This name shows that the river flowing into Loch Oich was called *Abha* before the name altered to *Obhaich*.

Auchterderran (Fife)
This was not originally a name containing "auchter" or *uachdar*, "upland", but may be related to the element found in "Urchany". The second element is *deòradh*, "dewar, relic-holder".

Auchterflow (Ross), Uachdar Chlò
This may be "windy upland". This place is mentioned in a saying found with local variants in a number of places, *Buntàta proinnt' is uachdar leotha, biadh bodaich Uachdar Chlò*, "Mashed potatoes and cream, the food of the old men of Auchterflow".

Auchtergavan (Perth), Uachdar Ghamhair
"The upland of the winter land."

Auchterless (Aberdeen)
"The upland of the fortified enclosure", from *Uachdar Leasa*.

Auchtermuchty (Fife), Uachdar Mucadaidh
"The upland of the pig place."

Auchterneed (Ross), Uachdar Niad
This may be "the upland of the stream", with a cognate of Brythonic *nant*, "stream".

Auchtertool (Fife)
This may be "Tuathal's upland", from *Uachdar Thuathail*, but a nearby river might instead be the defining element.

Auchtertyre (Moray, Ross), Uachdar Thìre
"The top of the land." In Ross, the name was locally pronounced as *Uachdar Ìridh*.

Auchtogorm (Moray), An t-Ochdamh Gorm
"The green octave or eighth-land." See **Achterblair**.

Auchtow (Perth), Achadh Tubha
The second element of this field name is unclear.

Auchvaich (Inverness), Achadh a' Bhàthaich
"The field of the byre."

Auldcharmaig (Ross), Allt Charmaig
"Cormac's stream."

Auldearn (Nairn), Allt Éire *or* Allt Éireann
"The stream of Ireland." See **Strathearn**.

Aulich (Perth), Abhlaich
"Water place."

Auliston Point (Argyll), Rubha nan Amhlaistean
This appears to mean "the headland of the circumventions".

Aultachruinn (Ross), Allt a' Chruinn
"Stream of the tree."

Aultanrynie (Sutherland), Allt an Reidhinidh
This stream name is unclear although *reidhneach* is applied to a cow yielding no milk. Nearby Loch More is *Loch an Reidhinidh*.

Aultbea (Ross), An t-Allt Beithe *or* Am Fàn
The English and first Gaelic names are "the birch stream" and originally applied to the stream running through the village. The second Gaelic name is "the slope". To express *in Aultbea*, Gaelic uses *air an Allt Bheithe* or *air an Fhàn*, "on Aultbea". An older Gaelic name for Aultbea was *Am Fàn Braonach*, "the slope of the Loch Broom area". Local people are known as *rodain*, "rats" or *Fànaich*, "slope people".

Aultfearn (Inverness)
See **Allarburn**.

Aultgrishan (Ross), Allt Ghrisean
"Brindled stream." *Grìsean* is a contraction of *grìs-fhionn*. Locals are known as *crùbagan*, "crabs", or *Grìseanaich*, "brindled ones".

Aultguish (Ross), An t-Allt Giuthais
"The pine or fir stream."

Aultiphurst (Sutherland), Allt a' Phuirt
"The stream by the port."

Aultivulin (Sutherland), Allt a' Mhuilinn
"The stream of the mill." This village is also known as Millburn.

Aultmore (Banff)
"Big stream", from *Allt Mór*.

Aultnagar (Sutherland), Allt nan Car
"The stream with the turns", from older *Allt na gCar*.

Aultnamain (Ross), Taigh a' Mhonaidh
See **Altnamain**.

Aultnaskiach (Inverness), Allt nan Sgitheach
"The stream of the hawthorns."

Aultonrea (Aberdeen)
"The stream on the slope", from *Allt an Ruighe*.

Aultroy (Ross), An t-Allt Ruadh
"The red-brown stream."

Aultsigh (Inverness), Allt Saidhe
"Bitch stream", streams often being named after animals.

Aundrary (Ross), Anndrairigh
The first part of this Norse field or sheiling name is unclear.

Avernish (Ross), Abhairnis
"Bulky headland", from Norse. Local people were nicknamed *faoile-agan*, "gulls".

Avielochan (Inverness), Aghaidh an Lochain
"The hill face by the small loch." Locally, the name was *Agaidh an Lochain*.

Aviemore (Inverness), An Aghaidh Mhór

"The big hill face." Locally, the name was *An Agaidh Mhór*.

Avoch (Ross), Abhach
"Water place." The local church is *Cill Ainndreis*, "St Andrew's Church".

Avonbridge (Stirling)
"Avon" is a common element in the Celtic languages denoting a river and is found as *abhainn* in Gaelic and Irish and *afon* in Welsh.

Ayr (Ayr), Inbhir Àir
"The mouth of the River Ayr." Ayrshire is *Siorrachd Inbhir Àir*.

B

Back (Lewis), Am Bac
"The bank", from Norse. To express *in Back*, Gaelic uses *air a' Bhac*, "on Back". A native of Back is a *Bacach*, also nicknamed an *adag*, "haddock".

Backhill (Berneray), Cùl na Beinne
"The back of the hill."

Backies (Sutherland), Na Bacannan
"The banks", from Norse.

Back of Keppoch (Inverness), Cùl na Ceapaich
"The back of Keppoch."

Back Settlement (Argyll), Leaca na Sgoir
The English name must refer to the settlement's location at the back of the Ardsheal peninsula in Duror. The Gaelic name is "the slabs at the rock", but some sources refer to the Back Settlement comprising not only *Leaca na Sgoir* but also *Port na Cloiche*, "the port of the stone".

Badachonachar (Ross), Bad Chonachair
Bad is a "spot" or "copse" and *conachair* can mean "uproar", but the second part may be a genitive of the personal name *Conchobhar*, to give "Conchobhar's spot".

Badachro (Ross), An Caolas
The Gaelic name is "the strait", but the English name comes from *Bad a' Chrò*, "the copse or clump by the

sheep-fold", which in Gaelic refers only to Badachro farm.

Badagyle (Ross), Bad a' Ghoill
"The copse of the non-Gael."

Badanloch (Sutherland), Bad an Locha
"The copse by the loch." Badanloch on the north side of the River Helmsdale is *Taobh nan Guinneach*, "the Gunns' side", while the south side of the river is called *Taobh nan Gòrdanach*, "the Gordons' side".

Badanluig (Ross), Bad an Luig
"The copse in the hollow."

Badantional (Ross), Bad an Inneail
"The copse of the tackle or instrument."

Badbea (Ross), Am Bad Beithe
"The birch copse."

Badcall (Ross), Bada Call
"Hazel copse."

Baddoch (Aberdeen), A' Bhadach
"The copse place."

Badenloch (Sutherland), Bad an Locha
"The copse by the loch."

Badenoch (Inverness), Bàideanach
"Drowned place." A short ditty from the early days of coaching outlines the progress made in a day from Atholl to Badenoch: *Bracaist am Baile Chloichrigh, lunch an Dail na Ceàrdaich, dìnneir an Dail Chuinnidh 's a' bhanais ann an Ràt*, "Breakfast in Pitlochry, lunch in Dalnacardoch, dinner in Dalwhinnie and the wedding in Raitts." A person from Badenoch is known as a *Bàideanach*, which is the same word as the name of the area.

Badenscoth (Aberdeen)
"The copse of the flowers", from *Bad nan Sgoth*.

Badentarbat (Ross), Bad an Tairbeirt
"The copse at the isthmus."

Badenyon (Aberdeen), Bad an Eòin
This appears to be "the copse of the bird", but this may be a corruption of an earlier name.

Badfearn (Ross), Am Bad Feàrna
"The alder copse."

Badicaul (Ross), Bada Call
"Hazel copse."

Badinluchie (Ross), Bad an
Fhliuchaidh
"The copse or spot of the wetting."

Badintagairt (Sutherland), Bad an
t-Sagairt
"The priest's copse."

Badivochel (Banff)
"The copse of the herdsman", from
Bad a' Bhuachaille. Previously there
were two separate settlements
known in English as "Badivochel
Beg" and "Badivochel More", showing *Beag* (small) and *Mór* (big).

Badlehavish (Sutherland), Bad Liath
Thamhais
"Thomas's grey copse."

Badluachrach (Ross), Am Bad
Luarach *or* Am Bad Luachrach
"The reedy copse."

Badnafrave (Banff)
"The copse of the roots", from *Bad
nam Freumh.*

Badnegie (Caithness), Bad na
Gaoithe
"The windy or marshy copse."

Badninish (Sutherland), Bad an
Innis
"The copse at the meadow", showing an unusual genitive form of *an
innis.*

Badour (Argyll), Bad Odhair
This appears to be "dun copse", but
may have originally been *Bad
Dobhair*, "water or river copse".

Badralloch (Ross), Am Bad Ràilleach
or Am Bad Tràilleach
The first Gaelic name may be "the
oak copse", but the second appears
to contain *tràill*, "slave".

Badscally (Ross), Bad Sgàlaidh
"Eerie spot or copse."

Badvo (Perth), Bad a' Bhoth
"The copse at the hut."

Badvoon (Ross), Gràdal
The English name may come from

Bad a' Mhuin, "the copse at the hilly
clump", while the Gaelic name is
"grey valley", from Norse.

Bailanfhraoich (Sutherland), Baile an
Fhraoich
"The farm of the heather."

Baile Boidheach (Argyll), Am Baile
Bòidheach
"The beautiful farm or settlement."

Baile Mor (Iona), Am Baile Mór
"The big farm."

Bailliemore (Kerrera), Am Baile Mór
"The big farm."

Balachroan (Inverness), Baile a'
Chròthain
"The farm with the small sheep fold."

Balallan (Lewis), Baile Ailein
"Alan's township."

Balameanoch (Perth)
See **Balemeanach**.

Balanloan (Perth)
"The farm by the pond", from *Baile
an Lòin.*

Balanreich (Perth)
"The heather farm", from *Baile an
Fhraoich.*

Balantyre (Perth), Baile an t-Saoir
"The joiner's farm."

Balarumindhu (Colonsay), Baile
Raomainn Dubh
"Raomann's black farm."

Balaruminmore (Colonsay), Baile
Raomainn Mór
"Raomann's big farm."

Balavetchy (Colonsay), Baile a'
Mhaide
"The farm of the stick."

Balavil (Inverness, Ross), Baile a'
Bhile
"The farm at the sacred tree or rock
edge."

Balbaird (Fife)
This appears to be "the poet's farm",
from *Baile a' Bhàird*, but *bàrd* can
also mean a meadow, so the name
might be "the farm of the meadow".

Balbairdie (Fife)
This may be "the poet's farm" or "the
farm with the meadow", from *Baile*

a' Bhàird, but if the Gaelic was *Baile Bàrdaidh* it may be "the farm at the poet's place" or possibly "the farm of the meadow place".

Balbardie (West Lothian)
See **Balbairdie**.

Balbeg (Inverness), Am Baile Beag
"The small farm."

Balbeggie (Fife, Perth)
This may be "place of the small farm", from *Baile Beagaidh*.

Balblair (Inverness, Nairn, Ross), Baile a' Bhlàir
"The farm on the moor."

Balbrydie (Angus), Baile Bhrìghde
"Bridget's farm." An additional version of the name was collected by Diack (1944) and may be spelled *Baile Bhrùide*.

Balcaskie (Fife)
This may be "the farm at the projecting ridge", from *Baile Gasgaidh*, earlier *Baile Gasgain*.

Balchalum (Perth), Baile Chaluim
"Calum's farm."

Balcherry (Ross), Baile a' Cheathraimh
"The farm on the quarter-land."

Balchladich (Sutherland), Baile a' Chladaich
"The farm by the shore."

Balchraggan (Inverness), Baile a' Chreagain
"The farm at the little rock."

Balchrick (Sutherland), Baile a' Chnuic
"The farm at the hill."

Balchristie (Fife)
"Christopher's farm", from *Baile Chrìsdein*.

Balcladaich (Inverness), Baile a' Chladaich
"Farm by the shore."

Balcladich (Caithness)
See **Balcladaich**.

Balcomie (Fife)
"Colman's farm", from *Baile Cholmain*.

Balconie (Ross), Bailcnidh
"Strong place."

Balconish (Inverness), Baile a' Chonais
"The farm of the dispute." Local people were nicknamed *gearran beaga*, "little hares".

Balcormo (Fife)
"Cormac's farm", from *Baile Charmaig*, as seen in an older English form, "Balcormak".

Balcruvie (Fife)
"Wooded farm", from *Baile Craobhaigh*. This was also "Pitcruvie", showing how Pictish *pett*, "lands", changed to Gaelic *baile* with the same meaning.

Baldernock (Dunbarton)
"Ernoc's or D'Ernoc's farm", from *Baile Dearnaig*. See **Achdalieu**.

Baldinnie (Fife)
This may be "the farm of the sons of Donnagan or Donnachan", from *Baile Mac Dhonnagain/Dhonnachain*.

Baldoon (Ross), Baile an Dùin
"The farm by the hill (fort)."

Baldornoch (Perth)
"Pebbly farm", from *Baile Dòrnach*.

Baldovan (Angus)
"Deep spot or place", from *Ball Domhain*.

Baldutho (Fife)
"Duthac/Dubhthach's farm", from *Baile Dhubhthaich*.

Balechurn (Raasay), Baile a' Chùirn
"The farm at the cairn."

Baledmund (Perth), Baile Admainn
"Admann's farm."

Balegra (Arran), Baile Ìochdrach
"Lower farm." There is a corresponding Baluagra or *Baile Uachdrach*, "upper farm".

Baleloch (North Uist), Baile an Locha
"The farm by the loch."

Balemartin (Tiree), Baile Mhàrtainn
"Martin's farm."

Balemeanach (Skye), Am Baile Meadhanach
"The middle farm."

Balephuil (Tiree), Baile a' Phuill
"The farm by the bog or pool."

Balerno (Midlothian), Am Baile
Àirneach
"The sloe farm."

Baleshare (North Uist), Am Baile
Sear
"The east farm." The church here
was *Teampall Chrìosd*, "Christ's
Chapel".

Balevulin (Tiree), Baile a' Mhuilinn
"The farm at the mill."

Balfour (several)
"Pasture farm", from *Baile Phùir*.

Balfron (Stirling)
This may be from *Baile Freòin* and
connected with the river name in
Glen Fruin, which seems to stem
from *freòine*, "fury", but older anglicised forms of the name go against
this derivation.

Balgarva (South Uist), Baile
Gharbhaidh
"Garbhach's farm."

Balgate (Inverness), Baile a' Gheata
"The farm at the road."

Balgaveny (Banff)
"The farm with the stirk", from *Baile
a' Ghamhna*.

Balgaverie (Fife)
"Winter farm", from *Baile
Geamhraidh*.

Balgay (Angus)
"Windy or marshy farm", from *Baile
Gaoithe*.

Balgeddie (Fife)
See **Bargeddie**.

Balgone (East Lothian)
This may be "the farm of the dogs",
from *Baile nan Con*, earlier spelled
Baile na gCon.

Balgonie (Fife)
See **Balgown**.

Balgorney (West Lothian)
"Miry farm", from *Baile
Gronnaigh*.

Balgour (Perth)
"The farm with the goats", from
Baile nan Gobhar.

Balgove (Fife)
"The smith's farm", from *Baile a'
Ghobha*.

Balgown (Skye), Baile a' Ghobhainn
"The smith's farm."

Balgownie (Aberdeen)
See **Balgown**.

Balgrummo (Fife)
"Gormag's farm", from *Baile
Ghormaig*.

Balgy (Ross), Balgaidh
"Bag-shaped place." Local people
are known as *balgairean*, "foxes/
scoundrels", which is a play on
words given that *Balgaidh* and
balgairean both begin with the same
syllable.

Balhagarty (Kincardine)
This may be "farm at the priest's
place", from *Baile Shagartaidh*.

Balhalloch (Aberdeen)
This is said to be "old women's
farm", from *Baile Chailleach*,
although the name may refer to
nuns, as in **Nunton**.

Balharvie (Fife)
"The farm with the boundary wall",
from *Baile na h-Airbhe*.

Baligarve (Lismore), Am Baile
Garbh
"The rough farm."

Baligrundle (Lismore), Baile
Grunndail
This may be "the farm at Grunndal",
this being Norse for "green valley".

Balindore (Argyll), Baile an Dobhair
"The farm by the water or river."

Balinoe (Tiree), Am Baile Nodha
"The new farm."

Balinrait (Nairn)
"The farm at the circular fort", from
Baile an Rait.

Balintore (Angus, Inverness, Ross),
Baile an Todhair
"The farm of seaweed or bleaching."
Balintore in Angus is some distance
from the sea, and the name here
probably refers to bleaching. The old
name of Balintore in Ross is *Port an*

Ab, "the abbot's port", which led to local people being known as *abaich*, "abbot people", as well as *sgalltairean*, "jellyfish". Residents of the area of Balintore known as *am Bàrd*, "the Park", were known as *bàrdanaich*, "park people".

Balintraid (Ross), Baile na Tràghad
"The farm by the beach."

Balivanich (Benbecula), Baile a' Mhanaich
"The monk's farm." Nearby is Nunton, or *Baile nan Cailleach.*

Balkaithley (Fife)
"Cathalan's farm", from *Baile Chathalain.*

Balkeith (Sutherland), Baile na Coille
"The farm by the wood." The English name suggests that this may have been formed with Brythonic *coed* rather than *coille*, "wood".

Balknock (Skye), Baile nan Cnoc
"The farm in the hills."

Balla (Eriskay), Am Baile
"The village."

Ballabeg (Perth)
"The small farm", from *Am Baile Beag.*

Ballachraggan (Perth)
"The farm at the small rock", from *Baile a' Chreagain.* Older forms suggest that the original may have been *Baile nan Creagan*, "the farm at the little rocks".

Ballachrask (Inverness)
"The farm at the crossing place", from *Baile a' Chraisg.*

Ballachrosk (Aberdeen)
"The farm at the crossing place", from *Baile a' Chroisg.*

Ballachulish (Argyll, Inverness), Baile a' Chaolais
"The village at the narrows." The old name was *Caolas Mhic Phàdraig*, "the narrows of Patrick's son", and the people of South Ballachulish were nicknamed *muinntir an sglèat*, "the slate people". North Ballachulish is *Seann Bhaile a' Chaolais*, "old

Ballachulish". Two hotels in Ballachulish were known by different names in Gaelic and English, Loch Leven Hotel being *Taigh an Rubha*, "the house on the headland", and Ballachulish Hotel known as *Taigh a' Chnaip*, "the house by the hillock".

Ballachurn (Banff)
"The farm at the cairn", from *Baile a' Chùirn.*

Ballagan (Stirling)
"The farm in the hollow", from *Baile an Lagain.*

Ballaglas (Grimsay), Am Baile Glas
"The grey-green township."

Ballanlish (Banff)
"The farm with the garden or fortified enclosure", from *Baile an Leis.*

Ballantrae (Ayr), Baile na Tràgha
"The farm by the beach." The old name was *Cill Chuithbeirt*, "St Cuthbert's Church", which is also the Gaelic name of Kirkcudbright.

Ballantruan (Banff)
"The farm by the little stream", from *Baile an t-Sruthain.*

Ballantrushal (Lewis), Baile an Truiseil
"The farm at the Truiseal stone", a standing stone the name of which comes from Norse *thrus*, "goblin".

Ballater (Aberdeen), Bealadair *or* Bealdair
This name is unclear except for the fact that it is not a *baile* name. Easter Ballater is *Bealadair Shìos* and the Pass of Ballater is *Creagach Bhealadair*, "the rocky place of Ballater". An Aberdeenshire Gaelic saying mentions the latter place, *Faodaidh gun tachair sinn a-rithist mun tachair Creagach Bhealdair*, "Perhaps we'll meet again before the rocks of Ballater do."

Ballaterach (Aberdeen), Baile Leitreach
"The slope farm."

Ballchladdich (Sutherland), Baile a' Chladaich
"The farm by the shore."

Ballchraggan (Ross), Lòn nam Ban
The English name is from *Baile a' Chreagain*, "the farm at the small rock", while the Gaelic name is "the women's meadow". Nearby is a clootie well known as *Fuaran Bean Mhuiristean*, possibly "the spring of Morrison's wife". Clootie wells are found in various parts of the country and are places where people tie rags or "cloots" to trees near a well in an attempt to have an ailment cured. The most famous clootie well is probably *Tobar Churadain*, "St Boniface/Curadan's well", between Tore and Munlochy in the Black Isle.

Ballechin (Perth), Baile Eachainn
"Eachann's farm."

Balleigh (Ross), Baile an Lighe *or* Baile an Lighiche
"The doctor's farm."

Ballencrieff (East Lothian, West Lothian), Baile na Craoibhe
"The farm by the tree."

Ballentoul (Perth), Baile an t-Sabhail
"The farm with the barn."

Ballianlay (Bute), Baile Fhionnlaigh
"Finlay's farm."

Ballicock (Perth), Baile Ceòg
This farm name is unclear.

Balliefurth (Moray)
"The farm at the port", from *Baile a' Phuirt*.

Balliekine (Argyll), Bàinleacainn; (Arran) A' Bhàinleacainn
"White broad slope." People from the Arran place of this name were nicknamed *calmain*, "pigeons", while the place itself was subdivided into *Baile Ìochdrach*, "lower farm", and *Baile Uachdrach*, "upper farm".

Balliemeanoch (Argyll), Am Baile Meadhanach
"The middle farm."

Balliemore (Argyll), Am Baile Mór; (Inverness) A' Bhealaidh Mhór
In Argyll this is "the big farm", but the Inverness name is "the big broom", referring to the type of bush.

Ballieward (Inverness), Baile a' Bhàird
"The farm with the meadow."

Ballifeary (Inverness), Baile na Faire
"The farm of the watch or guard."

Balligill (Sutherland), Bàiligil
This may be "grassy ravine", from Norse.

Ballinaby (Islay), Baile an Aba
"The abbot's farm."

Ballinakill (Argyll), Baile na Cille
"The farm at the church."

Ballindalloch (Banff), Baile na Dalach
"The farm at the haugh", which is a low-lying riverside meadow.

Ballindean (Fife, Perth)
This may be "the dean's farm", from *Baile an Deadhain*.

Ballindeor (Argyll), Baile an Deòir
"The farm of the relic keeper."

Ballindewar (Perth)
See **Ballindeoir**.

Ballindollo (Angus)
See **Ballindalloch**.

Ballindoun (Inverness)
"The farm at the hill (fort)", from *Baile an Dùin*.

Ballingall (Fife)
"The farm of the non-Gaels", from *Baile nan Gall*.

Ballingrew (Perth), Baile nan Craobh
"The farm by the trees", from older *Baile na gCraobh*.

Ballinlagg (Moray)
This appears to be "the farm in the hollows", from *Baile nan Lag*.

Ballinloan (Perth)
"The farm by the pond", from *Baile an Lòin*.

Ballinluig (Perth), Baile an Luig
"The farm in the hollow."

Ballinroich (Ross), Baile an Rothaich
"Munro's farm."

Ballintomb (Moray)
"The farm at the hillock." There are
two places with this name, the one
near Knockando being the site of
the planned village of Archiestown,
named after Sir Archibald Grant.

Ballintore (Inverness), Baile an Todhair
See **Balintore**.

Ballintuim (Perth), Baile an Tuim
"The farm at the hillock."

Ballivicar (Islay), Baile a' Bhiocair
"The vicar's farm."

Ballo (Fife)
"Pass", from *Bealach*.

Balloan (Inverness, Nairn), Baile an
Lòin
"The farm by the pond."

Balloch (Dunbarton), Bealach;
(Inverness), Baile an Locha
In Dunbarton, the name means
"pass". In Inverness it is "the farm by
the loch".

Ballochbuie (Aberdeen), Am Bealach
Buidhe
"Yellow pass." Ballochbuie Forest is
Frìth Bhealaich Bhuidhe.

Ballochgoy (Ayr, Bute)
In Bute this is possibly "windy pass",
from *Bealach Gaoithe*, given that
"Windyhall" is on the other side of
Rothesay. However, AÀA recommend *Bealach Gaidh*, the second
element of which is unclear.

Ballochmartin (Cumbrae)
"Martin's pass", from *Bealach
Mhàrtainn*.

Ballochmyle (Ayr)
"Blunt pass", from *Bealach Maol*.

Ballochyle (Argyll), Baile a' Chaoil
"The farm at the strait."

Ballogie (Aberdeen)
"The farm in the place of the
hollow" or rather "the farm of
Logie", from *Baile Lagaidh*.

Ballone (Inverness), Baile an Lòin
"The farm by the pond."

Ballycaul (Bute)
"MacCall's farm", from *Baile
MhicCathail*.

Ballycurrie (Bute)
This is "Currie's farm", from *Baile
MhicMhuirich*.

Ballygown (Arran, Mull), Baile a'
Ghobhainn
"The smith's farm."

Ballygrant (Islay), Baile a' Ghràna
This may be "the grain farm".

Ballygrogan (Argyll), Baile Ghrogain
"Grogan's farm."

Ballygrundle (Lismore), Baile
Grunndail
See **Baligrundle**.

Ballyhaugh (Coll), Baile Hogh
"The farm at Hogh", this being
Norse for "mound".

Ballyhennan (Dunbarton)
"Seanan's farm", from *Baile Sheanain*.

Ballymeanoch (Arran), Baile
Meadhanach
"Middle farm." It is worth noting
that the definite article is missing
from this name where it would be
expected, given its simple noun and
adjective format. This is a common
feature of Arran place-names,
although examples do exist of the
more usual structure.

Ballymichael (Arran), Baile Mhìcheil
"Michael's farm."

Ballymony (Islay), Baile a' Mhonaidh
"The farm at the hill or upland."

Balmacaan (Inverness), Baile Mac
Cathain
"The farm of the son of Cathan."

Balmacara (Ross), Baile Mac Ara *or*
Baile Mac Carra
"The farm of the son of Ara or Carra."

Balmachree (Inverness)
This may be "MoChridhe's farm",
from *Baile MoChridhe*, in memory of
a now-forgotten Gaelic saint, but
Baile mo chridhe could be "my beloved
farm", although this is unlikely.

Balmaclellan (Kirkcudbright)
"Maclellan's farm", from *Baile
MhicIllfhaolain* or "the farm of
Gillfhaolain's son", from *Baile Mac
Illfhaolain*.

Balmacnaughton (Perth), Baile Mac Neachdain
"The farm of Neachdan's son."

Balmacqueen (Skye), Baile MhicCuithein
"MacQuien's farm."

Balmaghie (Kirkcudbright)
"MacGhie's farm", from *Baile MhicAoidh*, or "the farm of Aodh's son", from *Baile Mac Aoidh*.

Balmaglaister (Inverness), Baile Mac Glasdair.
This appears to mean "the farm of the son of Glasdar", but the name was originally *Bad a' Ghlaistir*, "the grassy copse".

Balmaha (Stirling), Baile MoThatha
"St MoThatha's farm." The generic element here may originally have been *bealach*, "pass".

Balmain (Fife, Perth)
"Middle farm", from *Baile Meadhain*.

Balmainish (Skye), Baile Mhànais
"Magnus's farm."

Balmakeith (Nairn), Baile MacCàidh *or* Baile MacDhàidh
"Davidson's farm."

Balmakewan (Kincardine)
"MacEwan's farm", from *Baile MhicEóghainn*, or "Ewan's son's farm", from *Baile Mac Eóghainn*.

Balmalcolm (Fife)
"Malcolm's farm." The forename here is probably *Maol Chaluim* rather than just *Calum*.

Balmanno (Perth)
"The monks' farm", from *Baile Manach* in earlier Gaelic which would now be *Baile Mhanach*.

Balmartin (North Uist), Baile Mhàrtainn
"Martin's farm."

Balmeanach (Skye), Am Baile Meadhanach
"The middle farm."

Balmedie (Aberdeen)
This may be "middle farm", from *Baile Meadhain*, which would give

the same meaning as Pitmedden in the same area.

Balmenach (Banff)
See **Balmeanach**.

Balmerino (Fife)
The first element is *baile* and the second is said to refer to a St Merinach.

Balmoral (Aberdeen), Baile Mhoireil *or* Both Mhoireil
This is said to mean "majestic farm", but the phonetics do not support this. Locally the name was *Both Mhoireil*, which suggests that the place might have been named after a saint, because there are many examples of saints' names following *both* in placenames.

Balmore (Dunbarton); (Inverness), Am Baile Mór and A' Bhuaile Mhór
The Dunbarton name is the same as the first Inverness name on the north side of Loch Ness, which is "the big farm", while the second Inverness name on the south side of Loch Ness is "the big fold".

Balmuchy (Ross), Baile Mhuchaidh
It has been suggested that the name contains a Brythonic personal name, but there is an old Gaelic word *much*, "mist", which might be the origin here, suggesting a misty farm.

Balmuckety (Angus)
"The farm at the pig place", from *Baile Mucadaidh*.

Balmule (Fife)
"The farm of Maol's son", from *Baile Mac Mhaoil*.

Balmullo (Fife)
"The farm at the summit or summits", from *Baile a' Mhullaich* or *Baile Mullach*, the latter being the plural form, which would be *Baile Mhullach* in modern Gaelic.

Balmungie (Ross), Baile Mhungaidh
"The farm at the place of mugwort", from *mong*.

Balmungo (Fife)
See **Balmungie**.

Balmyle (Perth)
This was earlier Balmain, which may represent *Baile Meadhain*, "middle farm".

Balnaba (Wigtown)
"The abbot's farm", from *Baile an Aba*.

Balnabeen (Ross), Baile na Binn
"The farm of judgement." This was located near a gallows hill.

Balnaboath (Ross), Baile nam Both
"The farm with the huts."

Balnabodach (Perth), Baile nam Bodach
"The farm of the old men."

Balnabreich (Banff)
This is possibly "the farm on the bank", from *Baile na Bruaiche*.

Balnabroich (Perth)
See **Balnabreich**.

Balnabruich (Caithness)
See **Balnabreich**.

Balnacarn (Inverness), Baile nan Càrn
"The farm at the cairns."

Balnaclash (Moray)
"The farm at the ditch", from *Baile na Claise*.

Balnacoil (Sutherland), Baile na Coille
"The farm at the wood."

Balnacoole (Arran), Baile na Cùil
"The farm in the secluded spot."

Balnacoul (Banff, Moray)
See **Balnacoole**.

Balnacra (Ross), Beul-àtha na Crà
"The ford of the salmon trap."

Balnacraig (Inverness, Perth), Baile na Creige
"The farm at the rock."

Balnacroft (Aberdeen), Baile na Creit
"Settlement of the croft." The spelling indicates the Aberdeenshire pronunciation of *croit* as *creit*.

Balnadelson (Sutherland), Baile an Dìollaid
"The farm of the saddle."

Balnafettack (Inverness), Baile nam Feadag
"The farm of the plovers."

Balnagall (Ross), Baile nan Gall
"The farm of the non-Gaels."

Balnageith (Moray)
"Windy or marshy farm", from *Baile na Gaoithe*. *Gaoth* means "wind", but in older placenames can also stand for "marsh".

Balnaglach (Inverness), Baile nan Clach
"The farm of the stones", from older *Baile na gClach*.

Balnagore (Arran), Baile nan Gobhar; (Ross), Baile nan Corr
In Arran this is "the farm of the goats", while in Ross the name is "the farm of the cranes", from an older *Baile na gCorr*.

Balnagowan (Lismore), Baile nan Gobhann
"The smiths' settlement."

Balnagown (Nairn, Ross), Baile nan Gobhainn
See **Balnagowan**.

Balnagrantach (Inverness), Baile nan Granndach
"The Grants' farm."

Balnaguard (Perth), Baile nan Ceàrd
"The tinkers' farm", from older *Baile na gCeàrd*.

Balnaguisich (Ross), Baile na Giuthsaich
"The farm at the pine wood."

Balnaha (Perth, Ross)
"The farm with the barn or kiln", from *Baile na h-Àtha*.

Balnahard (Mull), Baile na h-Àirde
"The farm on the headland."

Balnahaun (Inverness)
"The farm at the river", from *Baile na h-Abhann*.

Balnain (Inverness), Baile an Fhàin, Beul an Àthain
The first Gaelic name is located near Loch Ness and is "the farm on the slope". The second is near the Spey and is "the mouth of the small ford".

Balnakailly (Bute), Baile na Coille
"The farm at the wood."

Balnakeil (Sutherland), Baile na Cill
"The farm at the church."

Balnakeilly (Perth), Baile na Cille
See **Balnakeil**.

Balnakilly (Perth), Baile na Cille
See **Balnakeil**.

Balnaknock (Skye), Baile nan Cnoc
"The farm at the hills."

Balnakyle (Ross), Baile na Coille
"The farm at the wood."

Balnald (Perth), Baile nan Allt
"The farm at the streams."

Balnamoan (Perth)
This is probably "the peat farm",
from *Baile na Mòna*.

Balnamoon (Angus)
See **Balnamoan**.

Balnapaling (Ross), Baile nam
Péiling
"The township of the palings",
where plots of land were separated
by wooden palings.

Balnasuim (Perth), Baile nan Sum
"The farm of the soumings", the
method used to calculate the ratio of
cattle to sheep on a given piece of
land.

Balnault (Ross), Baile an Uillt
"The farm at the stream." The
English pronunciation suggests that
it came from an earlier Gaelic form,
Baile nan Allt, "the township at the
streams", or includes the genitive *n*
sound referred to in **Achanalt**.

Balnespick (Inverness), Baile an
Easbaig
"The bishop's farm."

Balniel (Fife)
"Neil's farm", from *Baile Néill*.

Balno (Moray), Am Baile Nodha
"The new farm."

Balnoe (Aberdeen)
See **Balno**.

Balnuig (Ross), Baile an Aoig
This is said to mean "the township
of death".

Balnuilt (Aberdeen, Nairn), Baile an
Uillt
"The farm at the stream."

Balole (Islay), Baile Olla
"Olaf's farm."

Balornock (Glasgow)
This is said to be "Louernoc's hut",
from Brythonic, and not a Gaelic
baile name.

Balphetrish (Tiree), Baile Pheadrais
"Petrus's farm."

Balquhidder (Perth), Both Chuidir *or*
Both Phuidir
The meaning of this name is unclear
except that *both* is a "hut". A native
of the area is a *Puidreach*, which may
be the origin of the Perthshire
surname, Buttar. Balquhidder Fair
was known as *Féill Aonghais*, "St
Angus's Fair". The Braes of
Balquhidder is *Srath Bhoth Phuidir*,
"the strath of Balquhidder".

Balranald (North Uist), Baile
Raghnaill
"Ranald's farm."

Balrobert (Inverness), Baile Reabairt
"Robert's farm", the Gaelic name
showing an unusual form of "Robert".

Balrymonth (Fife)
"The farm on the royal moor", from
Baile Rìmhinn. See **St Andrews**.

Baltersan (Wigtown)
This may be "cross farm", from *Baile
Tarsainn*, "township across".

Baluagra (Arran), Baile Uachdrach
"Upper farm", also known in
English as Meadowside. There is a
corresponding Balegra or *Baile
Ìochdrach*, "lower farm".

Baluain (Perth), Am Baile Uaine
"The green farm."

Balulive (Islay), Baile Uilbh
"Ulive's farm", named after the
founder of the settlement.

Balure (Argyll), Baile Ùr a' Bharra
Challtainn *or* Am Baile Ùr
"The new farm (of Barcaldine)."

Balvaird (Ross), Baile a' Bhàird
"The poet's farm" or "the farm at the
meadow", as *bàrd*, which usually
means "poet", is also found with the
meaning of "meadow".

Balvalachlan (Perth), Baile
MhicLachlainn
"MacLachlann's farm."

Balvaron (Inverness), Baile a' Bharain
"The baron's farm."

Balvarran (Perth), Baile a' Bharain
"The baron's farm", possibly referring
to the Baron of Straloch.

Balvatten (Inverness), Baile a'
Bhadain
"The farm at the little copse."

Balvenie (Banff), Baile Bhainidh *or*
Both Bhainidh
"St Beathan's farm", in memory of
the 11th-century Bishop of
Mortlach. Braemar Gaelic pronunciation suggests spellings such as
Bail' Bhìnidh and *Both Bhìnidh*, but
these forms may have been influenced by the anglicised "Balvenie".

Balveolan (Argyll), Baile Bheòlain *or*
Baile a' Bheòlain
"Beòlan's farm." This personal name
is found in the Irish *Ó Beoláin*,
"Boland".

Balvicar (Seil), Baile a' Bhiocaire
"The vicar's farm."

Balvonie (Inverness), Baile a'
Mhonaidh
"The farm at the uplands or hills."

Balvraid (Inverness), Baile Bhràid
"Upland farm", containing a genitive
form of *bràigh*, "upper part".

Bamff (Perth), Banbh
Banbh, with *Eilg, Éire* and *Fótla*,
were poetic names for Ireland and
commemoratively applied to several
places in Scotland, as here.

Banavie (Inverness), Bainbhidh *or*
Banbhaidh
"Pig place", although this may be a
reference to Ireland. See **Bamff**.

Banbeath (Fife)
"The farm at the birch", from *Baile
na Beithe.*

Banchor (Nairn), Beannchar
"Horn-shaped place." This is a name
common to Scotland, Ireland and
Wales. In English in the other

countries it is known as *Bangor*, but
in Irish it is *Beannchar*, as here.

Banchory (Kincardine), Beannchar
This is also known in English as
Banchory Ternan, named after
Torranan, as opposed to Banchory
Devenick near Aberdeen, where St
Devenick, an associate of St Machar,
is commemorated. See **Banchor**.

Bandon (Fife)
"The farm at the hill (fort)", from
Baile an Dùin.

Bandrum (Fife)
"Farm at the ridge", from *Baile an
Droma.*

Bandry (Dunbarton), Am Bàn Doire
"The fair oak grove." This name was
understood locally to derive from
Am Bàn Àirigh, "the fair sheiling",
but this appears not to have been
the original form.

Banff (Banff), Banbh
See **Bamff**. Upper Banffshire is
Bràigh Bhanbh, "the upland of
Banff" and the county of Banffshire
is *Siorrachd Bhanbh.*

Bangour (West Lothian)
This may represent *Beinn Ghobhar*,
"hill of goats".

Bankhead (Perth), Dul Corrachaidh
"The head of the bank" in English,
but the Gaelic name is "the haugh
of the odd field". This place used to
be known as Dalcorachy.

Banknock (Stirling)
"The farm at the hills", from *Baile
nan Cnoc,* as confirmed in
Ballinknok, an older form of the
anglicised name.

Bannachra (Dunbarton), Beannchar
See **Banchory**.

Bannockburn (Stirling), Allt a'
Bhonnaich
"The bannock stream." The Gaelic
name has taken the "bannock" of the
English form to mean "scone",
although the origin may be different.
The Battle of Bannockburn is *Blàr
Allt a' Bhonnaich* in Gaelic.

Bantaskin (Stirling)
"The farm or place of the gospel."
Earlier evidence shows that this
name included the Pictish element
pett together with *soisgeul* "gospel".

Barassie (Ayr)
Folk etymology has it that this
name came from the "braw sea", but
the origin of the name is more likely
to be *Bàrr Fhasaidh*, "the top of the
stance or place".

Baravullin (Argyll), Bàrr a' Mhuilinn
"The summit by the mill."

Barbaraville (Ross), An Cladach
The English name commemorates
the wife of a former proprietor. The
Gaelic name is "the shore".

Barbauchlaw (East Lothian)
This is said to be "the farm of the
crozier", from *Baile Bachlach*, as seen
more clearly in the older English
form, Balbaghloch.

Barcaldine (Argyll), Am Barra
Calltainn
"The hazel summit." Barcaldine
House was known as *Taigh Inbhir
Dheargain*, "the house at the mouth
of the red stream" and Barcaldine
Castle was *An Caisteal Dubh*, "the
black castle". Balure at Barcaldine is
Baile Ùr a' Bharra Challtainn, "the
new village of Barcaldine".

Bardrochat (Ayr)
This name probably means "the farm
at the bridge", from *Baile na
Drochaid*. In placenames of the
south-west, *baile*, which is generally
anglicised as "Bal-", sometimes
appears as "Bar-", causing confusion
with names deriving from *bàrr*,
"summit or hill".

Barevan (Nairn), Bréibhinn
"Éibhinn's summit", from an earlier
Bàrr Éibhinn, commemorating a saint.

Bargeddie (Lanark)
An older form of the name shows
this to contain *baile* rather than *bàrr*
and to be "the farm at the strip of
arable land", from *Baile Geadaidh*.

Barglass (Aberdeen), Am Blàr Glas
"The grey-green field."

Bargrennan (Kirkcudbright)
This may mean "the township at the
sunny spot" or "the hill at the sunny
spot", from *baile* or *bàrr* and *grianan*.
See **Bardrochat**.

Barjarg (Dumfries)
"Red hill" or "red township", from
bàrr or *baile* and *dearg* (red).

Barlanark (Glasgow)
This apparently hybrid Gaelic/
Brythonic name suggests "the hill at
the clearing", from *bàrr* and
Brythonic *lanerc*, "clearing", which
would give a Gaelic form of *Bàrr
Lannraig*.

Barleyport (Ross), Port an Eòrna
The Gaelic and English names mean
the same and refer to a port where
barley was traded.

Barlia (Bute), Am Bàrr Liath
"The grey hill(top)."

Barlinnie (Glasgow)
Like nearby Barlanark, this may be a
hybrid Gaelic/Brythonic name or a
wholly Gaelic name meaning "the
hill by the pool", from *bàrr* and either
Brythonic *llyn* or Gaelic *linn*, "pool".

Barmollach (Argyll), Bàrr Molach
"Shaggy summit."

Barmuckity (Moray)
"The summit at the pig place", from
Bàrr Mucadaidh.

Barmore (Bute), Am Bàrr Mór
"The big hill(top)."

Barmulloch (Glasgow)
This appears to be "the hill of the
summit or summits", from *bàrr* and
mullach, but earlier forms of the
name suggest a Brythonic origin
with a different meaning.

Barnacarry (Argyll), Bàrr na Cairidh
"The hill by the weir" or "the top of
the weir".

Barnagad (Argyll), Bàrr nan Gad
"The hill of the twigs or withes."

Barnakill (Argyll), Bàrr na Coille
"The top of the forest."

Barnhill (Angus); (Jura), Cnoc an t-Sabhail
"Hill of the barn." Barnhill in Angus was earlier known as Ecclesmonichto, from *eaglais* (church) dedicated probably to St Nechtan, using a diminutive form, *MoNeachdan*. The Gaelic name above only applies to Barnhill in Jura.

Barnluasgan (Argyll), Bàrr an Luasgain
"The hill of the shaking."

Barnultoch (Wigtown)
"The hill or farm of the Ulstermen", from *Bàrr nan Ultach* or *Baile nan Ultach*. See **Bardrochat**. However, this name may be *Bàrr n-Ultach* or *Baile n-Ultach* without the definite article.

Barnyards (Inverness), An t-Sràid
The Gaelic name means "the street".

Barra, Barraigh
"Finbar's island", from Norse. A native of Barra is a *Barrach*. The island's isolation is mentioned in the saying, *Ged's fhada a-muigh Barraigh, ruigear e*, "Although Barra is far out, it can be reached". Barra Head on the southerly island of Berneray is *Ceann Bharraigh*.

Barrapoll (Tiree), Goirtean Dòmhnaill
The English name is "the farm at the rocky mound", from Norse. The Gaelic name is "Donald's enclosed field", named after an official of the Duke of Argyll.

Barrhill (Ayr)
In the south-west, *bàrr* appears to be used for "hill" although in the north it is restricted to "top" or "summit". Thus "Barrhill" is an example of the Gaelic element *bàrr* being later defined by the addition of English "hill".

Barrisdale (Inverness), Bàrrasdal
"Barr's valley", from Norse.

Barrlockhart (Wigtown)
This may be "the hill of the encampment", from *bàrr* and *long-phort/longart*, "encampment". There is a place in Argyll also known as *Bàrr an Longairt*. See **Bardrochat**.

Barsolus (Dumfries)
This is thought to be "light or bright hill", from *bàrr* and *solas*, but see **Bardrochat**.

Barthol Chapel (Aberdeen)
The older name of this place was Fithkil, from *Fiodh Chill*, "wooden church".

Barvas (Lewis), Barbhas *or* Barabhas
"The fort by the river mouth", from Norse. The second spelling shows the epenthetic vowel between *r* and *bh* not normally shown in Gaelic orthography. A local saying, *iasgach muinntir Bharbhais*, "the fishing of the Barvas folk", refers to the alleged habit of the people here of waiting to see how other areas got on with the fishing before starting themselves.

Bassaguard (Fife)
"The priest's farm", from *Baile an t-Sagairt*.

Batabeg (Moray)
"Little boat", from *Bàta Beag*, referring to the small ferry which used to operate across the mouth of the Findhorn.

Baugh (Tiree), Am Bàgh
"The bay."

Bayble (Lewis), Pabail
"Priest village", from Norse. Lower Bayble is *Pabail Iarach* and Upper Bayble is *Pabail Uarach*.

Bayfield (Ross: Black Isle), Croit Seocaidh; (Ross: Nigg), Cinn Déis Bhig *or* Cinn Déis Robson Shuas; (Skye), An Sligneach
While the English name is simply "field by the bay" in all cases, the Gaelic names vary from place to place. Bayfield in the Black Isle is "Jockie's croft", while in Nigg it is "big Kindeace" or "Robertson's upper Kindeace", referring to a

Robertson who lived here in the 17th century. See **Kindeace**. In Skye, Bayfield is "the shell place".

Bayhead (Lewis, North Uist), Ceann a' Bhàigh
"The head of the bay."

Bayherivagh (Barra), Bàgh Shiarabhagh
This is a Gaelic/Norse name, containing both languages' words for "bay" and an unclear first Norse element, although possibly containing *sjá*, "sea".

Baymore (Grimsay), Am Bàgh Mór
"The big bay."

Bays (Harris), Na Bàigh
"The bays." The hilly area inland from Bays is *Bràigh nam Bàgh*, "the upper part of Bays".

Beach (Mull), Am Beitheach
"The birch wood."

Beachan (Aberdeen, Moray), Am Beitheachan
"Little birch wood."

Beacravik (Harris), Beicribhig
"Stream bay", from Norse.

Beasdale (Inverness), Biasdail
The first element of this Norse valley name is unclear.

Beaufort Castle (Inverness), Caisteal Dhùnaidh
The seat of the Lovats was renamed from *Dùnaidh*, "fort place", to Beaufort. Beaufort Home Farm is *Dùnaidh Ùr*, "new Dounie", while Dounie itself is *Seann Dùnaidh*, "old Dounie".

Beauly (Inverness), A' Mhanachainn
The English name is said to be "beautiful place", from French *beau lieu*, and was probably imported from England. The Gaelic name is "the monastery", an abbreviated form of *Manachainn Mhic Shimidh*, "Lovat's monastery". A more poetic name was *Manachainn nan Lios*, "the monastery with the enclosed gardens". The fair held here was known as *Féill na Manachainn*.

Bedersaig (Harris), Beudarsaig
This may be "pasture land bay", from Norse.

Bedrule (Roxburgh)
"Bethóc's rule", referring to lands owned by Bethóc or Beathag, the wife of a nobleman from Nithsdale. The order of elements in the place-name changed from Celtic "Rulebethock" through "Bethrowll" to its present form, marking the change in language from Celtic to Germanic.

Beglan (Inverness), Beag Ghleann
"Small glen."

Beldorney (Aberdeen), Baile Dòrnaigh
"The farm at the pebbly place", one-time home of Sìleas na Ceapaich, a major poet at the turn of the 17th and 18th centuries and daughter of MacDonald of Keppoch, who moved to Beldorney after her marriage to Alexander Gordon of Camdell.

Belgaverie (Wigtown)
This is believed to represent *Baile Geamhraidh*, "winter township".

Belhelvie (Aberdeen)
"Sealbhach's farm", from *Baile Shealbhaigh*, showing the old form of the genitive case in nouns ending in -*ach*. AÀA recommends *Baile Shealbhaich*.

Belivat (Nairn), Buaile Fhiodhaid
"The cattle fold at the wooded place."

Bellabeg (Aberdeen), Am Baile Beag
"The small farm."

Belladrum (Inverness), Bealadruim
This very old name is "ford mouth ridge".

Bellanoch (Argyll), Beul-àtha nan Eich
"The ford mouth of the horses." This name with an unusual geni-tive plural form was recorded from a native speaker from Mid Argyll.

Bellie (Moray)
"Broom place", from *Bealaidh*.

Belliheglish (Banff)
"Farm at the church", from *Baile na h-Eaglais*. Nearby is the old church of St Peter's.

Bellochantuy (Argyll), Bealach an t-Suidhe
"The pass at the seat."

Bell Rock (Fife), Innis Ceap
This is also known in English as Inchcape, from Gaelic, meaning "island of the stumps".

Bellsgrove (Argyll), Doire nan Clag
"The grove of the bluebells."

Bellyclone (Perth)
"The farm of Gilleòin's son", from *Baile Mac Ghilleòin*.

Belmaduthy (Ross), Baile Mac Duibh
"The farm of Dubh's son."

Belnacraig (Aberdeen), Baile na Creige
"The farm by the rock."

Belnahua (Luing), Beul na h-Uamha
"The mouth of the cave."

Benadrove (Lewis), Beinn na Dròbh
"Hill of the cattle sale."

Ben Armine (Sutherland), Beinn Àrmainn
This Gaelic/Norse name is "mountain of the steward or commander".

Benbecula, Beinn nam Fadhla *or* Beinn a' Bhaoghla.
"Mountain of the sea fords." As Benbecula is mainly low-lying, the name may have originated in *Peighinn nam Fadhla*, "the pennyland of the fords". Poetically, the island is known as *an t-Eilean Dorcha*, "the dark island". A local is a *Badhlach* or *Baoghlach*.

Benbuie (Dumfries)
"Yellow mountain", from *Beinn Bhuidhe*.

Benderloch (Argyll), Meudarloch
"Mountain between two lochs", a contraction of *Beinn eadar dà loch*. Local people were nicknamed *eireagan dathte*, "coloured pullets".

Bendochy (Perth)
This may be "horn place", referring to the horn-like bends on the River Isla, from *Beannachaidh*. However, Bennochy in Fife is "blessing place", possibly an area of Church lands, and the Perth name might be from the same source.

Benlister (Arran), Peighinn an Fhléisteir
"The pennyland of the archer."

Benmore (Argyll), A' Bheinn Mhór
"The big mountain."

Bennan (Arran), Am Beannan
"The cliff." Bennan Head is *Ceann a' Bheannain*.

Bennecarrigan (Arran), Beinn na Cànraigeann
The meaning of the second part of this name is unclear, although the first is "mountain".

Bennetfield (Ross), Baile Bheineit
Although "Benedict's field" in English, the Gaelic name is "Benedict's farm".

Bennochy (Fife)
See **Bendochy**.

Benside (Lewis), Beinn na Saighde
"The mountain of the arrow."

Benvie (Angus)
See **Banavie**.

Berie (Lewis), A' Bheirgh
"The rock or stone", from Norse.

Berisay (Lewis), Beirgheasaigh
"Rock island" or "stone island", from Norse.

Bernera (Bernera, Inverness), Beàrnaraigh
"Bjørn's island", from Norse. The island of Bernera or Great Bernera is also known as *Beàrnaraigh Ùig*, "Bernera of Uig", and *Beàrnaraigh Leòdhais*, "Bernera of Lewis". A local is a *Beàrnarach*.

Berneray (Barra, Berneray), Beàrnaraigh
"Bjørn's island", from Norse. The full names of Berneray near Barra are *Beàrnaraigh Cheann Bharraigh*,

"Berneray of Barra Head", and *Beàrnaraigh an Easbaig*, "Berneray of the bishop". Berneray between Uist and Harris is known as both *Beàrnaraigh Na Hearadh*, "Berneray of Harris", and *Beàrnaraigh Uibhist*, "Berneray of Uist". A native of this island is known as a *Beàrnarach* or *Bagan*.

Bernisdale (Skye), Beàrnasdal
"Bjørn's valley", from Norse. Aird Bernsidale is *Àird Bheàrnasdail*, "the headland of Bernisdale", while Park Bernisdale is *Pàirc Bheàrnasdail*, "the park of Bernisdale".

Berriedale (Caithness), Bearghdal
This may be Norse "valley at the rocky hill".

Berwickshire (Berwick), Siorrachd Bhearaig
Berwick itself is "barley farm", from English. For some time the town of Berwick was known as South Berwick to distinguish it from North Berwick in East Lothian. Berwick town is known in Gaelic as *Bearaig* and *Abaraig*.

Bethelnie (Aberdeen)
"St Nathalan's hut or farm", from *Both Nathalain* or *Baile Nathalain*. This is the old name of Meldrum parish.

Bettyhill (Sutherland), Am Blàran Odhar
The English name is that of Elizabeth, Countess of Sutherland, while the Gaelic name is "the dun-coloured field or moor".

Bighouse (Sutherland), Bìogas
"Barley house", from Norse. Lower Bighouse is *An Tòrr*, "the hill", and Upper Bighouse is *Bìogas Àrd*, "high Bighouse".

Big Sand (Ross), Sannda Mhór
"Big sand river", from Norse/Gaelic.

Bindal (Ross), Bindeil
"Sheaf valley", from Norse.

Birchburn (Arran), An t-Allt Beithe
"The birch stream."

Birchfield (Inverness), Cùl a' Mhuilinn; (Ross), Achadh na h-Uamhach
The English name is self-explanatory, but the two places have different Gaelic names. In Inverness this is "the back of the mill", while in Ross it is "the field at the cave".

Birichen (Sutherland), Bioraichean
This may mean "sharp points".

Birkhall (Aberdeen), Tòrr Beatha *or* Tòrr Beithe
The English name is "birch haugh", while the Gaelic names are "birch hill".

Birkisco (Skye), Birceasgo
"Birch wood", from Norse.

Birnam (Perth), Biorman, Biornam *or* Braonan
This may be "homestead by the stream", from English, as suggested by the first two Gaelic forms, but *Braonan* is a Gaelic name related to the element found in *Loch Bhraoin* or Loch Broom, and meaning "little damp place". This dampness may also be what is referred to in a local saying: *Tha ceò air Branac*, "there's mist on Birnam Hill".

Birness (Aberdeen)
This may be "damp place", from *Braonais*.

Birnie (Moray), Braonaigh
"Damp place." Birnie was earlier known as Brenach, from *braonach*, "damp".

Birse (Aberdeen), Braois *or* Breis
This may be from *preas*, "bush" or "thicket". The parish is *Sgìre Bhraois* or *Sgìre Bhreis*.

Bishopbriggs (Dunbarton), Drochaid an Easbaig
This was originally "the bishop's riggs" although it now appears to be "the bishop's bridges".

Black Crofts (Argyll), Na Croitean Dubha
The names in both languages mean the same.

Blackfold (Inverness), Am Buaile Dubh
"The black fold", referring to a fold for cattle or other animals. *Buaile* is usually feminine in gender, but appears to have been masculine in this area.

Blackford (Perth), Srath Gaoithe
"Black ford" in the English name is not reflected in the Gaelic name of "marshy or windy strath", which is the source of the older English name, Strageath.

Black Isle (Ross), An t-Eilean Dubh
"The black island", although this is a peninsula. It was known as *Eilean Dubhthaich*, "Duthac's island", from which the current name is a contraction. The area used also to be known as *An Àird Mheadhanach*, "the middle headland" and *Eadar Dhà Dhàil*, "between two haughs".

Blacklunans (Perth), Bealach Glùinneig *or* Bealach Lùnaig
This name may be "the pass of jointed-grass".

Blackmill (Luing), Am Muileann Dubh
"The black mill."

Blackrock (Islay), A' Charraig Dhubh
"The black rock." Local people were known as *ròcaidich*, "ravens".

Blackwaterfoot (Arran), An Dubh Abhainn, Bun na Dubh Abhann *or* Bun na h-Abhann
"The mouth of the black river", a translation of the second Gaelic name. The first Gaelic name translates as "the black river", while the third is "the river mouth".

Blaich (Argyll), Blàthaich
This may be "blossom place".

Blair (Fife, Inverness)
"Field, plain", from *Blàr*. In Inverness, the place was divided into Ardblair, from *Àird Bhlàir*, "upper Blair", and Fanblair, from *Fàn Bhlàir*, "lower Blair".

Blair Atholl (Perth), Blàr Athaill *or* Blàr Athall
"The plain of Atholl." Old Blair is *Seann Bhlàr* and Upper Blair is *Blàr Uachdar*.

Blairbeg (Arran), Am Blàr Beag
"The small plain."

Blairboych (Arran), Blàir Bòidheach
"Beautiful plain", showing an unexpected form of *blàr* and no definite article.

Blaircessnock (Perth)
This may be *Blàr Seisgeannach*, "marshy plain or moor".

Blairdaff (Ayr)
"Field of oxen", from *Blàr Damh*, which would be *Blàr Dhamh* in modern Gaelic.

Blairfettie (Perth), Blàr Pheitigh
"The moor of the place of pits", referring to the Pictish term *pett*.

Blairfindie (Banff), Blàr Fionndaidh
This may be "the field at the white place".

Blairfoid (Ross), Blàr Choighde
This may be a Gaelic/Brythonic name, "the plain at the wood".

Blairgowrie (Perth), Blàr Ghobharaidh
"The plain of Gowrie." This was also known locally as *Blàr na Gobharaidh*, with the same meaning.

Blairhullichan (Stirling), Blàr Thulachain
"The field at the small green hill."

Blairingone (Kinross)
"The plain of the hounds", from *Blàr nan Con*, earlier *Blàr na gCon*.

Blairinroar (Perth)
This may be "the plain of the skirmish", from *Blàr an Ruathair*.

Blairish (Perth), Blàrais
"Plain place."

Blairlogie (Stirling)
"Field or plain of Logie", from *Blàr Lagaidh*.

Blairmore (Argyll, Arran, Nairn, Sutherland), Am Blàr Mór; (Inverness), Blàr Mór

"The big field or plain." In Inverness this is "big Blair" or "big plain". See **Blair.**

Blairnamarrow (Banff), Blàr nam Marrow
"The field of the dead."

Blairnavaid (Stirling)
"The field of the peats or furrows", from *Blàr nam Fàd,* formerly *Blàr na bhFàd.*

Blairninich (Ross), Blàr an Aonaich
"The moor of the market."

Blair Uachdar (Perth), Blàr Uachdar
"Upper Blair."

Blairy (Inverness), Blàiridh *or* Blàraidh
"Field or plain place."

Blarmachfoldach (Inverness), Blàr Mac Faoilteach
This is not clear and, although the Gaelic name seems to mean "field of the son of Faoilteach", may have altered through the centuries.

Blarmore (Inverness), Am Blàr Mór
"The big field or plain."

Blarnaleavoch (Ross), Blàr na Leitheach *or* Blàr na Leamhach
The first Gaelic name is "field of the half place" while the second is "the elm field".

Blarour (Inverness), Blàr Dhobhair
"The water or river field."

Blashaval (North Uist), Blathaiseabhal
"Blue sea mountain", from Norse.

Bleaton Hallet (Perth), Am Pladan
This was originally a hill name to which a previous proprietor added his surname. The hill in question is *Monadh Phladain,* locally pronounced *Mon Phladain.*

Blebo (Fife)
This is said to be from *Blàth Bholg,* "bag-shaped blossom land".

Blelack (Aberdeen)
See **Blebo**. Diack (1944) recorded local Gaelic pronunciation of this name as "bllalak".

Blochairn (Glasgow)
This appears to be "the farm by the cairn", from *Baile a' Chàirn.*

Blughasary (Ross), Blaoghasairigh
The first element of this Norse name is unclear, although a field or sheiling is referred to.

Boath (Angus, Ross)
The Angus name appears to be from *Both Mhearnaig,* "St Ernoc's or M'Ernoc's hut", while the Ross name is *Na Bothachan,* "the huts".

Boat of Garten (Inverness), Coit a' Ghartain *or* A' Choit
"The boat at Garten" or "the boat", where a ferry operated prior to the construction of the bridge.

Bochastle (Perth), Both Chaisteil
"The hut at the castle."

Bochonie (Perth), Both Chòmhnaidh
This may be "St Comhghan's hut".

Bogach (Barra), A' Bhogach
"The boggy place."

Bogallan (Ross), Bog Alain
"The bog of Allan."

Bogany (Bute)
"Boggy place", from *Boganach* or *Boganaidh.*

Bogary (Arran), Na Bogaire
This may be "the bog place", although the Gaelic name is a plural.

Bogbain (Inverness), Am Bog Bàn; (Ross), Am Bac Bàn
In Inverness this is "the fair bog", but in Ross, "the fair bank", from Norse *bakki.*

Bogbuie (Ross), Am Bog Buidhe
"The yellow bog."

Bogendreep (Kincardine), Bog an Dreich
"The bog at the hill face."

Bogindollo (Angus)
"The bog in the haugh", from *Bog na Dalach.*

Bognie (Aberdeen)
See **Bogany**.

Bog of Gight (Aberdeen)
"The windy or marshy bog", from *Bog na Gaoithe.*

Bogrow (Ross), Am Bogaradh
"The bog place."

Bohally (Perth), Both Àlaidh
This hut name probably has the corrupted name of a saint as its second element.

Boharm (Banff), Both Sheirm
See **Bohally**.

Bohenie (Inverness), Both Shìnidh
See **Bohally**. A saying about local placenames goes, *Tha còig bothan an Loch Abar, còig gasgan ann am Bàideanach 's còig còigean ann an Srath* Éireann, "There are five boths in Lochaber, five gasgs in Badenoch and five còigs in Strathdearn". The five boths in Lochaber are Bohenie, Bohuntine, Bolyne, Both Chàsgaidh and Both Lugha.

Bohespick (Perth), Both Theasbaigh
"Bishop's hut."

Bohuntine (Inverness), Both Fhionndain
"Fintan's hut", possibly referring to the saint of that name. See **Bohenie**.

Boisdale (South Uist), Baghasdal
"Baegi's valley", from Norse. North Boisdale is *Baghasdal* or *Baghasdal a Tuath*, while South Boisdale is *An Leth Mheadhanaich*, "the middle half". The old church in South Boisdale was *Caibeal Dhiarmaid*, "St Diarmid's Chapel". The moorland to the east of Boisdale and north of Garynamonie is *a' Mhòrainn*, locally understood to mean "the large division".

Boleskine (Inverness), Both Fhleisginn
This refers to a hut, but the second element is unclear though may contain *fleasg*, "withe".

Bolfracks (Perth), Both Bhrac *or* Both Frac
This name is unclear, although the Gaelic form contains "hut". Locally the name is pronounced *Both Frac* and this may be related to *Leitir*

Fraic, "Letterfrack" in County Galway, which contains a personal name.

Bolnabodach (Barra), Buaile nam Bodach
"The old men's fold or pen."

Bolnapiart (Banff), Buaile nam Peart
This name may be "the fold of the copses", including the Brythonic word *pert* which gave the name *Peairt* or **Perth**.

Boltachan (Perth), Bualtachan
"Sheep or cattle pens."

Bolyne (Inverness), Both Fhloinn
"Flann's hut." See **Bohenie**.

Bomakellock (Banff), Both MoCheallaig
"Beloved St Ceallag's hut."

Bona (Inverness), Am Bànath
"The fair ford." The graveyard here was *Cladh Churadain*, "St Curitan's churchyard", commemorating the saint associated with Fortrose and Clootie Well near there.

Bonahaven (Islay), Bun na h-Abhainn
"The mouth of the river." The English form of the name appears to have gone out of use.

Bonar Bridge (Sutherland), Drochaid a' Bhanna
"The bridge at Bonar", meaning "bottom ford", from *am Bannath*. The site of the present-day village was formerly known as *Baile na Croit*, "farm of the hump". In North Sutherland Gaelic, the name was pronounced *Drochaid a' Bhonn-àth*, which more accurately represents its meaning.

Bonaveh (Colonsay), Bun a' Bheithe
"The foot of the birch." This may refer to the root of a birch tree, but might actually mean "mouth of the birch stream".

Bonawe (Argyll), Bun Abha
"The mouth of the Awe."

Bonhard (Fife, West Lothian)
"Farm at the high point", from *Baile na h-Àirde*.

Bonhill (Dunbarton), Bun Olla
This appears to be a gaelicisation of an English name the early forms of which included "Binnuill" and "Bonuil".

Bonjedward (Roxburgh)
The second part of this name contains the older English form of the name "Jedburgh", and the first element appears to be *bun*, "river mouth".

Bonnavoulin (Argyll), Bun a' Mhuilinn
"The river mouth of the mill." This is also spelled "Bunavullin" in English.

Bonskeid (Perth), Both na Sgaod
The second part of this hut name is unclear.

Boor (Ross), Bùra
"Bower river", from Norse.

Boreland (Dumfries); (Perth), Am Borlainn *or* A' Bhorlainn
This appears to be "the sloping land", but may have originated in English, referring to land used to feed the landlord's household, as in the name in Dumfries. In Boreland near Loch Tay in Perthshire, the old church was known as *Caibeal Chiarain*, "St Ciaran's Chapel".

Borenich (Perth), Both Reithnich
This name sounds as though it is "bracken hut", but the second element might be the name of a saint, which also appears to form the defining element in the church name "Kilrenny".

Boreraig (Skye), Boraraig
"Fort bay", from Norse. The old church in the cleared village of Boreraig in south Skye was *Teampall Chaon*, dedicated to St Congan.

Boreray, (North Uist), Boighreigh; (St Kilda), Boraraigh
"Fort island", from Norse. A native of Boreray off North Uist is a *Boighreach* or *sgarbh*, "cormorant". The saying *Na toir bó á Paibeil's na toir bean á Boighreigh* is "Don't take a

cow from Paible or a wife from Boreray".

Borgie (Sutherland), Borghaidh
"Fort river", from Norse.

Borline (Inverness, Skye), Borlainn
See **Boreland**.

Borlum (Inverness), Bòrlum
"Strip of arable land."

Borneskitaig (Skye), Borgh na Sgiotaig
"Fort at the division bay", from Gaelic/Norse.

Bornish (South Uist), Bòirnis
"Fort headland", from Norse.

Borrisdale (Harris), Borghasdal
"Fort valley", from Norse.

Borriston (Lewis), Borghasdan
This Norse name contains "fort".

Borrobol (Sutherland), Borghbol
"Fort farm", from Norse.

Borrodale (Argyll, Skye, South Uist), Borghdal
"Fort valley", from Norse.

Borsham (Harris), Boirseam
This Norse name may be "fort holm".

Borve (Harris), Na Buirgh; (Skye), Borbh; (elsewhere), Borgh
The Harris name is "the forts". Elsewhere it is "fort", from Norse.

Bosta (Bernera), Bostadh
"Small farm", from Norse. Local pronunciation suggests a preferable spelling of *Bòstadh*.

Bothkennar (Stirling)
"St Cainnear's hut", from *Both Cainneir*, referring to a saint also commemorated in Glen Cannel.

Bot na h-Acaire (Perth), Both Uachdair
"Upper hut." The English form came from a misreading of earlier anglicisation, "Bothvechtar".

Botriphnie (Banff)
Local Gaelic pronunication was transcribed by Diack (1944) as "vatreini", suggesting spellings such as *Bhad Reidhnigh* or *Bhoth Draighnigh*, both open to interpretation. The first element could be *bad*,

"copse" or *both*, "hut", while the second is unclear, but may include *reidhneach*, "cow yielding no milk", or *droigheann*, "thorn".

Bottacks (Perth), Na Botagan
"The peat banks."

Bottle Island (Ross), Eilean a' Bhotail
"The island of the bottle", so called because of its shape. An alternative name was *Eilean Druim Briste*, "broken ridge island".

Bousd (Coll), Babhsta
"Small farm", from Norse.

Bovain (Perth), Both Mheadhain
"The middle hut."

Bower (Caithness), Bàgair
This Norse name may be "bowers".

Bowglass (Harris), Am Bogha Glas
"The grey reef."

Bowmore (Islay), Bogha Mór *or* Am Bogha Mór
"Big reef."

Boyndie (Banff), Bòinndidh
This name was originally that of a river and may be "eternal goddess", from old Gaelic *buandea*. The current Gaelic name, used in Easter Ross, may be a gaelicisation of the English form. Boyndie beach is *Tràigh Bhòinndidh* in Gaelic.

Boysack (Angus)
This is said to be from *Baile Ìosaig*, "Isaac's township".

Braal (Caithness), Breitheal
"Broad field", from Norse.

Bracadale (Skye), Bràcadal
"Slope valley", from Norse.

Bracara (Inverness), Bracara *or* Brachdara
This name is unclear.

Bracla (Inverness)
See **Brackloch**.

Brackla (Nairn)
See **Brackloch**.

Brackletter (Inverness), Breac Leitir
"Speckled slope."

Brackley (Argyll), Am Bracal
"Slope field" or "slope valley", from Norse.

Brackloch (Sutherland), A' Bhraclaich
"The badger's sett."

Bracora (Inverness)
See **Bracara**.

Bracorina (Inverness), Brac na Daraich
The second element in the name is "oak", but the first is unclear. This English form which appears on maps has been influenced by the name of Bracara, which is nearby.

Brae (Ross), A' Bhruthach *or* A' Bhruthaich
"The brae."

Braebost (Skye), Bréabost
"Broad farm", from Norse.

Braedownie (Angus)
This seems to be from *Bràigh Dhùnaidh*, "the upper part of Downie".

Braegarrie (Aberdeen), Bràigh a' Ghàraidh
"The upper part of the Garrie."

Braegrudie (Sutherland), Bràigh Ghrùididh
"The upper part of Grudie."

Braehorrisdale (Ross), Bràigh Thòrasdail
"The upper part of Torrisdale."

Braeintra (Ross), Bràigh an t-Sratha
"The upper part of the strath."

Braelangwell (Ross), Bràigh Langail
"The upper part of Langwell."

Brae Leny (Perth), Bràigh Lànaigh
"The upper part of Leny." The place was earlier known as *Luirgeann*, "shank or ridge".

Brae Lochaber (Inverness), Bràigh Loch Abar
"Upper Lochaber." A native of the area is a *Bràigheach*.

Braelude (Perth), Bràigh Leòid
"The upper part of Lude."

Braemar (Aberdeen), Bràigh Mhàrr (district), Baile a' Chaisteil (village)
The district is "the upper part of Mar" and the village is "village at the castle". The village comprises *Achadh an Droighinn* or Auchendryne, "field

of the thorn bush", west of the river and *Baile a' Chaisteil* or Castleton to the east. The village was earlier known as *Cinn Drochaid*, "bridge end". There were four fairs or markets held in Braemar: in April, *An Fhéill Fhuar*, "the cold fair"; in June, *Féill an t-Samhraidh*, "the summer fair"; in September, *Féill an Fhoghair*, "the autumn fair"; and in December, *An Fhéill Anndrais*, "St Andrew's fair".

Brae Moray (Moray), Bràigh Mhoireibh
"The upper part of Moray."

Braemore (Caithness, Ross), Am Bràigh Mór
"The large upland."

Brae of Achnahaird (Ross), Bràigh Achadh na h-Àirde
"The upper part of Achnahaird."

Brae Rannoch (Argyll, Perth), Bràigh Raineach
"The upper part of Rannoch."

Brae Roy (Inverness), Bràigh Ruaidh
"The upper part of the River Roy."

Braes (Skye), Am Bràighe
"The upper part." The full name is *Bràighe Thròndairnis*, "upper Trotternish", or *Bràighe Phort Rìgh*, "the upper part of Portree".

Braes of Abernethy (Inverness), Bràigh Obar Neithich
"The upper part of Abernethy."

Braes of Balquhidder (Perth), Srath Bhoth Phuidir
The Gaelic name is "the strath of Balquhidder".

Braes of Callander (Perth), Bràigh Chalasraid
"The upper part of Callander."

Braes of Cromar (Aberdeen), Bràigh Crò Mhàrr *or* Bruthaichean Crò Mhàrr
"The upper part of Cromar" or "the braes of Cromar". The second Gaelic form may be a re-translation into Gaelic from a mistranslation into English assuming *bràigh* to mean "brae".

Braes of Doune (Perth), Bràigh Dhùin
"The upper part of Doune."

Braes of Foss (Perth), Bràigh Fasaidh
"The upper part of Foss."

Braes of Glen Orchy (Argyll), Bràigh Ghlinn Urchaidh
"The upper part of Glen Orchy."

Braes of Mause (Perth), Bruthaichean Mheallaibh
"The braes of Mause."

Braes of Ullapool (Ross), Bruthaichean Ulapuil
"The braes of Ullapool."

Brae Tongue (Sutherland), Bràigh Thunga
"The upper part of Tongue."

Braeval (Banff, Perth), Bràigh a' Bhaile
"The upper part of the farm."

Bragar (Lewis), Bràgar *or* Bràgair
This Norse name may be "pretty field". Local pronunciation reflects the second Gaelic form.

Braglen (Argyll), Bràigh a' Ghlinne
"The upper part of the glen."

Brahan (Ross), Brathann
This may be "quern place".

Braichlie (Aberdeen), Brachlach
This may be the same name as in **Brackloch**.

Branahuie (Lewis), Bràigh na h-Aoidhe
"The upper part of the Eye isthmus." See **Point**.

Branault (Argyll), Bràigh nan Allt
"The upper land at the streams"

Brawl (Sutherland), Breitheal
"Broad field or hill", from Norse.

Breacachadh (Coll), Breac Achadh
"Speckled field."

Breaclete (Bernera), Breacleit
"Broad cliff", from Norse. Local pronunciation collected by Oftedal (1954) suggests a preferable spelling of *Britheacleit*.

Breadalbane (Perth), Bràid Albainn *or* Bràghaid Albainn
"The upper part of Alba or

Scotland." A native of the area is a *Bràighdeach*.

Breakish (Skye), Breacais
This may be "speckled place". Lower Breakish is *Breacais Ìosal* and Upper Breakish is *Breacais Àrd*.

Breakough (Cumbrae)
"Speckled place", from *Breacach*.

Breasclete (Lewis), Briascleit *or* Brèascleit
"Cliff with the broad ridge", from Norse. Local pronunciation collected by Oftedal (1954) suggests a preferable spelling of *Britheascleit*.

Brechin (Angus), Breichin *or* Brichin
This name is said to represent a dedication to the Brythonic St Brychan. An earlier Gaelic form appears as *Breichne*, probably with the same derivation.

Breckrey (Skye), Am Breacaradh
The Gaelic name suggests that this may be "the speckled place" (see **Bogrow**), but given its location, this may be of Norse origin and contain the element *brekkr*, "slope".

Breich (West Lothian)
"Bank", from *Bruaich*.

Brenachie (Ross), Breanagaich
The meaning of this name is unclear.

Brenachoil (Perth), Breun Choille
"Putrid wood."

Brenchoille (Argyll), Breun Choille
See **Brenachoil**.

Brenish (Lewis), Bréinis
"Broad headland", from Norse.

Brevig (Barra, Lewis), Bréibhig
"Broad bay", from Norse. Brevig in Lewis is situated on Broad Bay, which is also known as *an Loch a Tuath*, "the north loch".

Bridgend (Arran), Ceann an Drochaid; (Inverness), Ceann na Drochaid; (Islay) Beul an Àtha
The Arran and Inverness names are "the end of the bridge", while the Islay name is "the ford" or "the mouth of the ford". It is interesting that the Arran name shows *drochaid*,

"bridge", to be masculine as it is in Irish, although generally this is a feminine noun in Scottish Gaelic.

Bridge of Awe (Argyll), Drochaid Abha
"The bridge over the Awe."

Bridge of Balgy (Perth), Drochaid Bhalgaidh
"The bridge at Balgy." The old churchyard here is *Cladh Bhranno*, "Brandubh's churchyard".

Bridge of Brown (Banff), Drochaid Bhruthainn
"The bridge over the Brown", a river name unconnected with English "brown".

Bridge of Cally (Perth), Drochaid Challaidh
"The bridge at Cally", meaning "hazel place".

Bridge of Dee (Aberdeen, Kincardine, Kirkcudbright)
"The bridge over the Dee", possibly from *Drochaid Dhé*.

Bridge of Don (Aberdeen), Drochaid Dheathain
"The bridge over the Don."

Bridge of Earn (Perth), Drochaid Éireann
"The bridge over the Earn."

Bridge of Fiddich (Banff)
"The bridge over the Fiddich", possibly from *Drochaid Fhiodhaich*.

Bridge of Gaur (Perth), Drochaid Ghamhair
"The bridge over the Gaur."

Bridge of Marnoch (Aberdeen), Drochaid na Màrnaich
This is said to mean "St Ernoc's or St M'Ernoc's bridge", but might be "the bridge of the Mar men" using an irregular genitive form.

Bridge of Oich (Inverness), Drochaid Obhaich *or* Drochaid an Iar Àth
The Gaelic names are "bridge of Oich" and "bridge of the west ford" respectively.

Bridge of Orchy (Argyll), Drochaid Urchaidh *or* Drochaid Urcha

"The bridge over the Orchy." The latter name is the one used locally.

Bridge of Tarf (Perth), Drochaid Tairbh
"The bridge over the Tarf."

Brig O'Turk (Perth), Ceann Drochaid
The English name mentions the "Turk" or "boar river" but the Gaelic name is "bridge end". An earlier name attached to this place was "Duncraggan", from *Dùn Chreagain*, "hill of the little rock", but from an earlier *Druim Chreagain*, "ridge of the little rock".

Brin (Inverness), Braoin
This name may refer to damp ground. Brin Mains is *Cnoc nan Cnaimhseag*, "the hill of the whortleberries".

Brinacory (Inverness), Braonacairidh
This name is unclear.

Broadford (Skye), An t-Àth Leathann
"The broad ford."

Brochel (Raasay), Brochaill
This name is unclear, but may be from Norse "fort hill" or "fort field".

Brochroy (Argyll), Am Bruthach Ruadh
"The red-brown brae."

Brock (Tiree), Am Brog
"The fort", from Norse.

Brockies Corner (Inverness), Taigh Bhròcaidh
The Gaelic name is "Brockie's house".

Brodick (Arran), Tràigh a' Chaisteil
The English name is "broad bay", from Norse. This has been gaelicised as *Breadhaig* but this name is used only to refer to the part of the village known as "Douglas Row" in English. The Gaelic name of Brodick as a whole is "the beach by the castle".

Brogaig (Skye), Brògaig
"Fort bay", from Norse.

Broker (Lewis), Brocair
This may be "forts", from Norse.

Brolass (Mull), Bròlas
This name is unclear.

Brolum (Lewis), Brothluim
This name appears to contain Norse for "holm".

Broomhill (Inverness), An Tom Bealaidh; (Ross: Kindeace), Àird nan Cathag; (Ross: Urray), Cnoc a' Bhealaidh or An Cnoc Bealaidh
Broomhill, the current terminus of the Speyside railway near Nethy Bridge in Inverness-shire, is "the broom hillock". In Ross, the Kindeace Gaelic name is "the high point of the jackdaws", while the Urray names both mean "the broom hill".

Broomton (Ross), Baile a' Bhealaidh
"The farm of the broom", referring to the plant.

Brora (Sutherland), Brùra
"Bridge river", from Norse, a name originally applied to the river and then to the village, which earlier was *Inbhir Bhrùra*, "mouth of the Brora". Brora is also called locally, *Brùra nam maraichean*, "Brora of the mariners".

Broughdarg (Aberdeen), A' Bhruthach Dhearg
"The red brae."

Broxburn (West Lothian)
"Badger stream." The village was earlier known as Easter Strathbroc, the latter part of which is from Gaelic *Srath Broc*, "badger strath". See **Uphall**.

Bruachaig (Ross), Bruachaig
"Small bank."

Bruachbane (Perth), Am Bruthach Bàn
"The white brae."

Bruachrobie (Sutherland), Bruthach Robaidh
"Robbie's brae."

Bruar (Perth), Bruthar
It is unclear what is meant in this name, although it may contain an old Gaelic element for "heat",

possibly referring to the whirlpools at the Falls of Bruar.

Brucefield (Ross), Cnoc an Tighearna
The Gaelic name is "the hill of the lord", while the English name commemorates the proprietor, Robert Bruce MacLeod. North Brucefield is *Loch Sirr*.

Brue (Lewis), Brù
"Bridge", from Norse.

Bruernish (Barra), Bruthairnis
This may be "bridge headland", from Norse.

Bruichladdich (Islay), Bruach a' Chladaich
"The bank of the shore." Locally the name is pronounced as *Bruach a' Chladaigh*. There is evidence to suggest that the name was originally *Bruthach a' Chladaich*, "the brae at the shore". See **Acharanny**.

Bruichnain (Ross), Bruach an Éidhinn
"The ivy bank."

Bruist (Berneray), Brùsta
"Bridge village", from Norse.

Brunigil (Skye), Brùnaigil
"Brown ravine", from Norse.

Brybeg (Ross), Am Bràighe Beag
"The small upper part." See **Alligin**.

Buailedhubh (South Uist), A' Bhuaile Dhubh
"The black pen."

Buaile-uachdrach (South Uist), A' Bhuaile Uachdrach
"The upper pen."

Buailnaluib (Ross), Buaile na Lùib
"Pen at the bend."

Bualintur (Skye), Buaile an Todhair
"The bleaching pen" or "seaweed fertiliser pen". Given this place's location by the sea, the latter interpretation is more likely.

Buchan (Aberdeen), Buchan *or* Bùchainn
This name may stem from Brythonic *bwch*, "cow". The name was recorded as *Búkan* in Norse,

although not of Norse origin, and Diack (1944) collected the pronunciations transcribed as "būching" or "būchinn", both indicating a long first vowel.

Buchanan (Stirling), Bochanan
"The hut of the canon", from an older *Both a' Chanain*. A local person is known as a *Cananach*, "Buchanan person".

Buchanty (Perth), Buchantaidh
This name is unclear, although it may be a locative form of the name, "Buchan".

Buckie (Banff), Bucaidh
This may be "buck place", from *boc*, "buck". A native of this area and the north-east coast generally is a *Bucach*. In North Sutherland Gaelic, the Buckie area was known as *An Taobh Bucach*, "the Buckie side/area".

Bught (Inverness), Cill Bheathain *or* Am Bucht
The English name is "pen", while the Gaelic name is "Bean's church". However, Gaelic speakers now call the area *am Bucht* from the English name. Bught Park is known as *Pàirc nam Bochd*, "the park of the poor", but this is an attempt to interpret Bught as a Gaelic word.

Buinach (Moray), Buidheanach
"Yellow place."

Bullion (West Lothian)
This name refers to boggy land, from English. The older name was Croftangry, maybe from *Croit an Rìgh*, "the king's croft".

Bunacaimb (Inverness), Bun na Caime
"The mouth of the crooked stream."

Bunachton (Inverness), Both Neachdain
"Nechtan's hut."

Bunanuisg (Islay), Bun an Uisge
"The mouth of the water."

Bunarkaig (Inverness), Bun Airceig
"The mouth of the Arkaig."

Bunavoneddar (Harris), Bun
Abhainn Eadarra
"The mouth of the Eadarra river."

Bunavullin (Argyll, Eriskay), Bun a'
Mhuilinn
"The river mouth of the mill." The
place in Argyll is also spelled
"Bonnavoulin" in English.

Bunchrew (Inverness), Bun Chraoibh
"The foot of the tree."

Bundalloch (Ross), Bun Dà Loch
"The mouth of two lochs."

Bunessan (Mull), Bun Easain
"The base of the little waterfall."
Local people here were nicknamed
othaisgean, "sheep".

Bunloit (Inverness), Bun Leothaid
"Slope foot."

Bunnabhain (Islay), Bun na
h-Abhainn
"The mouth of the river." This was
formerly written in English as
"Bonahaven".

Bunoich (Inverness), Bun Obhaich
"The mouth of the Oich."

Bunrannoch (Perth), Bun Raineach
"The mouth of the Rannoch."

Bunree (Inverness), Bun an Ruighe
"The foot of the slope."

Bunzion (Fife)
"Peak", from *Binnean*.

Burghead (Moray), Am Broch
The English name is "head of the
fort", with Norse *borg*. The Gaelic
name is from the local English
name, The Broch, a name also
applied to Fraserburgh.

Burgie (Moray)
This appears to be Norse *borg*, "fort",
with a Gaelic locative.

Burnhervie (Aberdeen)
"The stream at the boundary wall",
with *eirbhe* preceded by Scottish
English "burn". The whole name
may be a part-translation from a
Gaelic name. See **Alltnaharra**.

Burnside (Ross), Taigh an Daimh
The English name refers to "the side
of the stream" but the Gaelic name

is "the house of the stag or ox". This
Gaelic name only applies to
Burnside in Ross.

Burrelton (Perth), Both Bhùirnich *or*
Both Bhùirm
The English name commemorates
the founder of the planned village,
George Burrel. The Gaelic names
are unclear although they contains
both, "hut", and possibly reference to
a saint.

Bush, The (Bute), Taigh an Tuim
The Gaelic name is "the house on
the hillock".

Bute (Bute), Bód *or* Bòid
This name may have its source in old
Gaelic *bót*, "fire". A native of Bute is
a *Bódach* or *Bòideach*, which gives the
anglicised surname "Boyd". A saying
claims, *Chan ann am Bòid uile a tha
an tolc; tha cuid dheth sa Chumaradh
bheag làimh ris*, "Not all evil is in
Bute; there is some in little
Cumbrae nearby". Bute was traditionally linked with Arran and Islay,
as shown in the saying *Bód is Ìle is
Arainn*. The Forest of Bute is *Coille
Bhòid/Bhòid*.

Butt (Arran), Am Buta
"The short rig (in a field)", from
Norse.

Butterstone (Perth)
"Buttar's farm", from English. Buttar
is a surname which may be related
to *Puidreach*, an adjective connected
to Balquhidder.

Buttock Point (Bute), A' Phutaig
This may be "the small ridge of
land".

Butt of Lewis (Lewis), Rubha
Robhanais
The English name refers to this
headland's location at the tip of
Lewis, while the Gaelic name is "the
point of the hole headland", the
latter element being from Norse,
and referring to the hole known as
the Eye of the Butt through which
the sea pushes.

C

Cabaan (Ross), An Cadha Bàn
"The white pass."

Cabrach (Banff, Jura), A' Chabrach
"The antler place."

Cabrich (Inverness)
See **Cabrach**.

Cadboll (Ross), Cadabal
"Cat village", from Norse. An alternative spelling and pronunciation is given as *Cathabul*. This is possibly a tribal reference to the people usually associated with Caithness and Sutherland.

Caensa (Tiree), Ceòsaibh
"Hollows", from the Norse term also found in **Keose**.

Caillach Head (Argyll), Sròn na Caillich
"The old woman's or witch's promontory."

Cailness (Stirling), Cùl an Eas
"The back of the waterfall or stream." The name was formerly spelled "Culness" in English.

Caiplich (Inverness), A' Chaiplich
"The horse place", from *capall*.

Cairnaqueen (Aberdeen), Càrn na Cuinge
"The cairn at the narrow pass." This is often rendered as *Càrn na Cuimhne*, "the memorial cairn", which sounds similar.

Cairnbaan (Argyll), An Càrn Bàn
"The white cairn."

Cairnbanno (Aberdeen)
This may be "peaked cairn", from *Càrn Beannach*.

Cairnbrogie (Aberdeen)
"Brogan's cairn", from *Càrn Bhrògain*.

Cairnbulg (Aberdeen), Càrn Builg
"Bag-shaped cairn." See **Cairnwell**.

Cairndow (Argyll), An Càrn Dubh
"The black cairn."

Cairney (Perth)
"Copse place", from Pictish *carden* with a Gaelic ending.

Cairngall (Aberdeen)
"The cairn of the non-Gaels", from *Càrn nan Gall.*

Cairngate (Fife)
"The cairn of the cats", from *Càrn na gCat*, an old form of present *Càrn nan Cat.*

Cairnie (Aberdeen)
There are two places with this name in Aberdeen. The first, near Skene, derives from Pictish *carden*, and is "copse place", while the second, in Strathbogie, comes from *càrn* and is "cairn place".

Cairn na Burgh Beg (Mull), Cearnaborg Beag
"Small Cearnaborg", a Norse name possibly meaning "fort on good land".

Cairnoch (Stirling)
"Cairn place", from *Càrnach.*

Cairnryan (Wigtown), Càrn Rìoghaine
This fairly recent English name refers to a cairn on Loch Ryan, but previously the village was called Macheraskeoch from *Machair an Sgìthich*, "the hawthorn machair or plain". The Gaelic form of "Cairnryan" is recommended by AÀA.

Cairns (Fife)
"Corner place", from *Ceàrnais.*

Cairntradlin (Aberdeen)
"Triduana's cairn", from *Càrn Traillein.*

Cairnwell (Aberdeen), Càrn a' Bhalg or An Càrn Bhailg
"The bag-shaped cairn." Both Gaelic names show non-standard features in the genitive forms. The bad weather associated with this area is summed up in the rhyme, *Cur is cathadh am Bealach Dearg, sneachd is reòthadh an Càrn a' Bhalg, cùl ri gaoith air Làirig Bhealaich, grian gheal am Maoilinn*, "Drifts and storms at Bealach Dearg, snow and frost at the Cairnwell, back to the

wind at Làirig Bhealaich, bright sun at Moulin".

Caithness (Caithness), Gallaibh
The English name is "cat headland", originally from Norse and referring to the tribal name of the people of Caithness and Sutherland. The Gaelic name is "territory of the foreigners or non-Gaels", namely the Norse who settled in large numbers in this area. The extreme north-east of Caithness is *Roinn Ghallaibh*, "the point of Caithness", from *rinn*, "point", rather than *roinn*, "division". A person from Caithness is a *Gallach*.

Calbha Beag (Sutherland), Calbha Beag
"Small calf island", from Norse/Gaelic.

Calbost (Lewis), Calbost
"Kali's farm", from Norse.

Caldour (Roxburgh)
This name may be "hard water", related to *Caladar*, a common river name.

Calgary (Mull), Calgarraidh
This may be "Kali's sheiling or pasture land", from Norse.

Caliach Point (Mull), Rubha na Caillich
"The old woman's or witch's headland."

Callander (Moray), Caladar; (Perth), Calasraid
The name in Moray is "hard water", a common river name, while in Perth it is "harbour street", possibly referring to the town's riverside location, and pronounced *Caltraid* in local Gaelic. The fair held at Callander in Perthshire was *Féill MoCheasaig*, "St Kessock's Fair" and *Féill Chalasraid*, "Callander Fair". The Braes of Callander are known as *Bràigh Chalasraid*, "the upper part of Callander", while Milton of Callander is *Baile a' Mhuilinn*, "the farm with the mill".

Callanish (Lewis), Calanais
This may be "Kali's headland", from Norse. The Standing Stones of Callanish are *Tursachan Chalanais*, possibly from Norse *thrus*, "goblin", as also found in **Ballantrushal**.

Callert (Inverness), Callaird
"Hazel headland."

Calligarry (Skye), Cailigearraidh
This may be "Kali's sheiling or pasture land", from Norse, as in Calgary in Mull. People from Calligarry in Skye are known as *cearcan breaca*, "speckled hens".

Callyons (Fife)
"Small wood", from *Coillean*.

Calnakill (Ross), Cal na Cille *or* Cal 'a Cille
"The meadow at the church." Local people are known as *slatan-mara*, "tangle stems". A Wester Ross saying lists the nicknames of people from a number of Applecross settlements as follows, *Slatan-mara Cal na Cille, Bodaich bhiorach an Lòin Bhàin, Rùcanaich Chùthaig agus tùchanaich na Feàrn*, "Tangle-stems from Calnakill, sharp old men from Lonbain, rumblers from Cuaig and the hoarse folk of Fearns".

Calrossie (Ross), Calrosaidh
This may be "meadow wood place".

Calvay (South Uist), Calbhaigh
"Calf island", from Norse.

Calvine (Perth), Cail Mhinn *or* Cail Mhìn
"Kids' meadow" or "smooth meadow".

Calziemuck (Perth)
This appears to be "the wood of pigs", from *Coille Muc*. In modern Gaelic, the name would be *Coille Mhuc*.

Camaghael (Inverness), Cam Dhail
"Crooked haugh or meadow."

Camasine (Argyll), Camas Éidhinn
"Ivy bay."

Camaslongart (Ross), Camas Longairt
"Encampment bay."

Camasnacroise (Argyll), Camas na Croise
"Cross bay."

Camasnaharry (Ross), Camas na h-Eirbhe
"The bay at the boundary wall."

Camault (Inverness)
"Crooked stream", from *Camallt*.

Cambus (Stirling)
"River bend", from *Camas*. *Camas* in inland locations denotes a bend or loop on a river, while on the coast it is a generally semi-circular bay.

Cambusbarron (Stirling)
This may be "the baron's river bend", from *Camas a' Bharain*.

Cambusbeg (Perth)
This is "little Cambus", from *Camas Beag* and is in contrast to Cambusmore.

Cambuscurrie (Ross), Camas Curaidh
This appears to be "coracle bay".

Cambusdrenny (Perth)
This appears to be "river bend at the thorny thicket", from *Camas Draighnigh*.

Cambuskenneth (Stirling)
This appears to be "Kenneth's river bend", but the personal name was not *Coinneach* but *Cionnadh*, which is no longer current as a first name in modern Gaelic, but does appear in surnames such as "MacKenna".

Cambuslang (Lanark), Camas Long
"River bend of ships." This was the furthest point up the Clyde navigable by large vessels.

Cambusmore (Perth), Camas Mór; (Sutherland), An Camas Mór
In Perth this is "large Cambus", in contrast to Cambusbeg. In Sutherland the name is "the large bay".

Cambusnethan (Lanark)
"The bend on the Nethan."

Cambus O'May (Aberdeen), Camas a' Mhuigh
"The river bend on the plain."

Camdell (Aberdeen), Camdhail
"Crooked meadow."

Camelon (Stirling), Camlan
This name is unclear, but said to be where King Arthur met his death. In English the first syllable is pronounced locally as in "came".

Camghouran (Perth), Camgharan
"Crooked river", from older *Cam Dhobhran*.

Camisky (Inverness), Camuisgidh
"Crooked water."

Cammachmore (Kincardine)
"Big bent place", from *Camach Mór*.

Cammo (Midlothian)
"Bent place", from *Camach*.

Camore (Sutherland), An Cadha Mór
"The big pass."

Campbeltown (Argyll), Ceann Loch Chille Chiarain *or* Ceann Loch
The planned settlement was named after Archibald Campbell, but was earlier known as Lochhead, a translation of *Ceann Loch*. The full Gaelic name is "the head of the loch at St Ciaran's Church".

Campsie (Perth), Camais *or* Camaisidh
"River bend."

Camserney (Perth), Camas Fheàrnain
"The river bend at Fearnan." See **Fearnan**.

Camuscross (Skye), Camas Cros
"Cross bay."

Camusinas (Argyll), Camas Aonghais
"Angus's bay."

Camusluinie (Ross), Camas Luinge
"Ship bay."

Camuslusta (Skye), Camas Lusta
"The bay of Lusta."

Camusmore (Skye), An Camas Mór
"The large bay."

Camusnagaul (Argyll, Ross), Camas nan Gall
"The bay of the non-Gaels."

Camusrory (Inverness), Camas Ruairidh
"Roderick's bay."

Camusteel (Ross), Camas Teile
"Linden bay."

Camusterrach (Ross), Camas Tearach
"Eastern bay."

Camustianavaig (Skye), Camas Dìonabhaig
This Gaelic/Norse name contains both languages' words for "bay", while the first Norse element may be *dyn*, "noisy".

Candacraig (Aberdeen), Cionn na Creige
"The end of the rock." This is basically the same name as "Kennacraig" and "Kincraig".

Canna (Canna), Canaigh
This may be "can island". A native of Canna is a *Canach*, and the Laird of Canna is *Fear Chanaigh*. The island was also known by the byname, *an t-Eilean Tarsainn*, "the (a)cross island", may be because of its location between the mainland and Uist. See **Small Isles**.

Cannich (Inverness), Canaich
"Bog cotton place."

Cantray (Inverness), Canntra
This Brythonic name may be "white settlement".

Cantraydoune (Inverness), Canntra an Dùin
"Cantray by the hill (fort)."

Caol (Inverness), An Caol
"The narrows". The full name is *Caol Loch Abar*, "narrows of Lochaber".

Caolasnacon (Argyll), Caolas nan Con
"The narrows of the dogs", referring to the small waves caused by the tide against the wind.

Caoles (Coll, Tiree), An Caolas
"The narrows." The full name of Caoles in Coll is *An Caolas Colach*, "the Coll narrows", while in Tiree it is *An Caolas Tiristeach*, "the Tiree narrows".

Caol Ila (Islay), Ruadhphort
"Red-brown harbour." The English name comes from *Caol Ìle*, the name of the strait separating Islay and Jura which was applied to the distillery

founded here. The village was divided into *Ruadhphort Beag* and *Ruadhphort Mór*, "small and large Ruadhphort", respectively.

Caolis (Vatersay), An Caolas
See **Caoles**.

Cape Wrath (Sutherland), Am Parbh *or* An Carbh
The Gaelic and English names come from a Norse word for "turning", where ships would turn south after passing along the north coast. The second Gaelic name is used in Lewis while the first is more widespread. The Cape Wrath peninsula as a whole is known locally as *Taobh a' Phairbh*, "the Cape Wrath side or area".

Capisdale (Skye), Capasdal
This may be "champion's valley", from Norse.

Cappenoch (Dumfries)
"Tillage place", from *Ceapanach*.

Caputh (Perth), Càpaig *or* a' Cheapaich
The first Gaelic name may be from a Brythonic word for "birch wood", while the second is "the tillage land", and may have been coined to give the name an understandable meaning in Gaelic. The old ferry at Caputh was known locally as *bàt' Chàpaig*, "the Caputh boat".

Cara (Gigha), Cara
This Norse name may be "Kari's island".

Carabus (Islay), Càrabus
"Copse farm", from Norse.

Caradal (Skye), Càradal
"Copse valley" or "Kari's valley", from Norse.

Caragrich (Harris), Caragraich
The meaning of this name is unclear.

Carberry (East Lothian)
Given this place's location, the name is most likely of Brythonic origin, denoting a fort. AÀA recommend *Craobhbarraidh*.

Carbeth (Stirling)
This may be "birch cairn", from *Càrn Beithe*, as the name was "Carnbeth" in the 16th century.

Carbisdale (Sutherland), Càrbasdal
"Copse farm valley", from Norse, which is also the old name of nearby Culrain. The Battle of Carbisdale is known in Gaelic as *Blàr Chreag a' Chóinneachain*, referring to a nearby hill.

Carbost (Skye), Càrbost *or* Carabost
"Copse farm", from Norse.

Cardhu (Moray)
This may be "black mossy land", from *Càthar Dubh*. The name is also spelled "Cardow" in English.

Cardnach (Moray)
"Copse place", from Pictish with a Gaelic suffix.

Cardno (Aberdeen)
See **Cardnach**.

Cardonald (Glasgow), Cair Dhòmhnaill
This may be "Donald's fort", from *Cathair Dhòmhnaill*, but the Gaelic name given above is that recommended by AÀA and suggests "Donald's enclosure".

Cardow (Moray)
See **Cardhu**.

Cardross (Dunbarton)
"Copse headland", from Gaelic *Càrdainn Ros*, containing Pictish *carden*. AÀA recommends that the name be spelled *Càrdanros*.

Carfin (Lanark), An Càrn Fionn
An old form of the name is "Carnefyn", which appears to suggest a Brythonic derivation such as "Nefyn's fort or cairn". However, the stress in the English name is on the second syllable, which suggests "white cairn", as above.

Cargill (Perth), Car Ghàidheal
This may be "seat of the Gaels".

Carie (Perth), Càraidh
Cairidh is "weir", and this may be a corruption of that.

Carinish (North Uist), Càirinis
"Kari's headland", from Norse.

Carlo (Arran), Rubha na Beithe
The English name dates from the late 19th century and replaced the earlier Birchpoint, which was a translation of the Gaelic name.

Carloway (Lewis), Càrlabhagh
"Karl's bay", from Norse. Upper Carloway is *Mullach Chàrlabhaigh*, "the top of Carloway".

Carluke (Lanark), Cair MoLuaig
The Gaelic word *cair*, "enclosure", is different from *cathair*, "seat", but the two have fallen together as a result of their closeness in pronunciation, and AÀA recommend the name given above, which is "MoLuag's enclosure". Around the 13th century Carluke was known as *Eaglais MoLuaig*, "St MoLuag's Church".

Carmahome (Arran)
This is said to be from *Cathair MoChoilm*, "the seat of St Columba".

Carmichael (Lanark)
"Michael's fort", from Brythonic. In the 12th and 13th centuries this place was known as "Kermichel" and "Karemigal", cognate with Gaelic *Cathair Mhicheil*.

Carminish (Harris), Cairiminis
This Norse headland name is unclear.

Carmunnock (Lanark)
This may be "monks' seat", from Brythonic, as suggested by an old form of the name, "Cormannoc", cognate with older Gaelic *Cathair Manach*, now *Cathair Mhanach*.

Carmyle (Lanark)
"Blunt fort", from Brythonic, cognate with Gaelic *Cathair Mhaol*. However, AÀA recommend *Cair Maol*, which is "blunt enclosure".

Carmyllie (Angus), Càrn Mhìlidh
This may be "warriors' cairn", a name known to Gaelic speakers in Glenshee and Braemar.

Carna (Argyll), Càrna
This may be "Kari's island", from Norse.

Carnach (Argyll, Ross), Càrnach; (Perth), Caorannach
In Argyll and Ross this is "cairn place", but the place near Callander in Perthshire is "rowan-tree place".

Carnan (South Uist), An Càrnan
"Small cairn." The full name is *Càrnan an Ìochdair*, "small cairn of Iochdar".

Carnasserie (Argyll), Càrn Asaraidh
"Cairn at the path."

Carnbee (Fife)
This may be "mountain cairn", from *Càrn Beinne*.

Carndearg (Muck), An Càrn Dearg
"The red cairn."

Carnish (Lewis), Càrnais
This may be "Kari's headland", from Norse.

Carnoch (Argyll), A' Chàrnach; (Inverness), Càrnach; (Ross), A' Chàrnaich
"The stony place."

Carntyne (Glasgow)
This may be "fire cairn", from Gaelic *Càrn Teine* or a Brythonic cognate, however AÀA recommend *Càrn-Tìn* with an unclear second element.

Carnwath (Lanark)
An old form of the name, Carnewyth, suggests "new fort", from *Caer Newydd*, a Brythonic cognate of Gaelic *Cathair Nuadh*.

Caroy (Skye), An Cadha Ruadh
"The red-brown pass."

Carrabus (Islay), Càrabus
This may be of the same origin as **Carbost**. People from Carrabus were nicknamed *coilich gheala*, "white cocks".

Carradale (Argyll), Càradal *or* Càradail
"Copse valley" or "Kari's valley", from Norse. Carradale House is *Taigh Mór Chàradail*.

Carr Brae (Ross), Bruthach Charra
"The slope at the rock shelf."

Carrbridge (Inverness), Drochaid Chàrr *or* Drochaid Charra
Both names are found, the former being preferred locally and said to mean "the bridge at the marsh". An alternative derivation for the latter form is "the bridge at the rock shelf".

Carrick (Argyll, Ayr), Carraig
"Rock."

Carriden (Midlothian)
While this was believed to be Brythonic "fort of Eidyn", containing the personal name found in "Edinburgh" and *Dùn Éideann*, there is an argument that it may stem from Pictish *carden*, "thicket", although this is unlikely given its location.

Carrishader (Lewis), Càiriseadar
"Kari's dwelling" or "Kárinn's dwelling", from Norse. Local pronunciation suggests a preferable spelling of *Càiriseadair*.

Carron (Moray, Stirling), Carrann
The Stirling name is from "rough water" and the Moray name may be from the same source.

Carron Valley (Stirling), Srath Carrann
"The strath or valley of the River Carron." This was the site of a battle referred to in Gaelic documents. The Gaelic name is the same as that of Strathcarron in Wester Ross.

Carsaig (Argyll), Càrsaig
This may be "Kari's bay", from Norse.

Carse of Bayhead (Ross), Moroich Chinn Déis
The Gaelic name is "the carse of Kindeace".

Carse of Gowrie (Perth), Cars Ghobharaidh
The English name is self-explanatory, and this Gaelic name is a translation of it.

Carse of Stirling (Stirling), Carsach
The Gaelic name, meaning "carse
place", was used in the 12th century
and is a gaelicised form of English
"carse".

Carsie (Perth)
This is either an English diminutive
of "carse" or a name based on English
"carse" with a Gaelic locative.

Carskiey (Argyll), Carraig Sgéithe
"Wing rock", first applied to a rock
in the bay.

Carsphairn (Kirkcudbright)
This name is unclear, but presumably Gaelic. The first element is *cars*,
"carse", from English, and the
second may be *feàrna*, "alder", but
this name is under debate.

Carstairs (Lanark), Caisteal Tarrais
"Castle of Tarras." The name was
"Casteltarras" in the 12th century
but had altered to "Carstaris" by the
16th.

Cartomy (Ross), Càthar Tomaidh
This may be "mossy ground at the
hillock place".

Carwhin (Perth), Coire Chunna
"Cunna's corrie." Cunna is also
commemorated at the graveyard of
Cladh Chunna in Glen Lyon.

Cashel (Dunbarton), Caiseil; (Stirling)
"Stone fort", from *Caiseal*.

Cashel Dhu (Sutherland), An Caiseal
Dubh
"The black stone fort."

Cashlie (Perth), Caislidh
"Place of the stone fort." This was
known poetically as *Caislidh nan
clach móra*, "Cashlie of the great
stones".

Cassilis (Ayr)
This is from *caiseal*, "stone fort", with
an English plural attached.

Cassindonald (Fife)
"Donald's projecting ridge", from
Gasg Dhòmhnaill.

Castlebay (Barra), Bàgh a' Chaisteil
"The bay of the castle", referring to
Kisimul Castle.

Castle Campbell (Clackmannan),
Caisteal a' Ghlòim
While the English name mentions
the owners of the castle, the
Gaelic name is "castle in the
chasm".

Castle Coeffin (Lismore), Caisteal
Chaifeann
This name allegedly commemorates
a Norse noble called *Caifeann* in
Gaelic.

Castle Corbet (Ross), An Caisteal
Dearg
The English name mentions the
owners of the castle, but the Gaelic
name is "the red castle".

Castlecraig (Ross: Black Isle), Taigh
na Creige; (Ross: Nigg) Caisteal
Chrag
The English name is "castle rock",
similar to the Gaelic name of the
place in Nigg. The Black Isle name
is "the house by the rock".

Castle Douglas (Kirkcudbright),
Caisteal nan Dùghlasach
"Castle of the Douglases", referring
to nearby Threave Castle.

Castle Heather (Inverness), Caisteal
Leathoir
"Castle on the slope." The English
name, which used to be "Castle
Leather", is a corruption of the
Gaelic.

Castle Leod (Ross), Cùl Dà Leothaid
or Cùltaigh Leòid
The English name does not refer to
a castle held by Leòd, but is a
corruption of the Gaelic names
which both mean "at the back of
two slopes".

Castle Menzies (Perth), Caisteal
Uaimh
The English name refers to the
Menzies family, who became prominent in the district after the depar-
ture of the Dow family. The Gaelic
name translates as "Weem Castle"
and refers to the local area. See **Dull**
and **Weem**.

Castle Stalker (Argyll), Caisteal
Eilean an Stalcaire
The Gaelic name is "the castle on
the island of the stalker or
falconer".

Castle Sween (Argyll), Caisteal
Tuinn
"Svein's castle", based on a Norse
personal name. The Gaelic name
seems to contain an unusual form of
the personal name.

Castle Tioram (Argyll), An Caisteal
Tioram
"The dry castle", so called because it
is located on *Eilean Tioram*, "dry
island", which denotes an island
accessible at low tide, a name which
means the same as "Orinsay" or
Orasaigh, which has its origins in
Norse.

Castleton (Arran), Baile a' Chaisteil
"The village by the castle."

Castletown (Caithness), Baile a'
Chaisteil
"The village by the castle."

Castle Urquhart (Inverness), Caisteal
na Sròine
The Gaelic name is "Strone castle",
the castle also being known as *An
Caisteal Dubh*, "the black castle" and
Caisteal Dubh na Sròine, "the black
castle of Strone".

Catacol (Arran), Catagal
This Norse name refers to a ravine,
but the first part of the name is
unclear. People from here were
known as *cuileagan-ime*, "butterflies".
The coast between Catacol and
Lochranza is *an Luirgeann*, "the
shank".

Cathkin (Lanark)
"Common land", from *Coitcheann*.

Catlodge (Inverness), Caitleag
"Sheep cote."

Cattadale (Islay, Sutherland), Catadal
"Cat valley", from Norse. The
Sutherland name may refer to the
tribal name of the people of
Caithness and Sutherland.

Causamul (North Uist), Cabhsamul
This may be "cow island", from Norse.

Causer (Moray), Cabhsair
"Causeway or pathway."

Caversta (Lewis), Cabhartaigh
"Kofri's farm", from Norse.

Caw (Scalpay), An Cadha
"The pass."

Cawdor (Nairn), Caladar
"Hard water", a name usually
applied to rivers. This was the seat of
a sept of the Campbells known as
Caimbeulaich bhoga Chaladair, "the
soft Campbells of Cawdor". The
Cawdor parish or area was known as
Sgìre Chaladair.

Ceannacroc (Inverness), Ceann nan
Cnoc *or* Ceanna-Chnoc
"The end of the hills."

Cellar Head (Lewis), An Seilear
This name may refer to shells, from
Norse.

Ceres (Fife)
"West or back place", from *Siarais*.

Challoch (Wigtown)
"Anvil", from *teallach*, as in the hill
name *An Teallach*.

Challochmunn (Ayr)
This may be "Munna's anvil", from
Teallach Mhunna. *Munna* is a
byname of the saint also known as
Fionntan or "Fintan".

Changue (Ayr)
This may be "tongue", from *teanga*,
referring to a strip of land.

Chanonry Point (Ross), Gob na
Cananaich *or* Rubha na Cananaich
"The point of the chanonry" which
is at Fortrose or *A' Chananaich*, "the
chanonry", referring to the abbey of
Curadan, who was also known as St
Boniface.

Chapelhill (Ross), Cnoc an t-Seipeil
"The hill at the chapel."

Chapelpark (Inverness), Croit
MoLuaig *or* Pàirc an t-Seipeil
Gaelic has two names for this place
near Dulnain Bridge, "St MoLuag's
croft" and "the field at the chapel".

Chapelton (Bute), Baile a' Chaibeil; (Inverness), Baile an t-Seipeil
"The farm at the chapel."

Charleston (Inverness, Ross), Baile Theàrlaich
"Charles's farm." Charleston in Inverness used to be known as *Achadh nam Bodach*, "field of the old men".

Charlestown (Ross), Am Baile Dearg
The English name commemorates a former owner while the Gaelic name is "the red farm". Formerly this was known as *an Clachan*, "the churchyard". Charlestown House is *An Taigh Dearg*, "the red house".

Charlestown of Aberlour (Banff), Obar Lobhair
See **Aberlour**.

Charlottefield (Perth), An Dailean Mór
The Gaelic name is "the large haugh".

Cheesebay (North Uist), Bàgh a' Chàise
"Spume bay." *Càise*, "spume", is an uncommon word of Norse origin which sounds identical to the word for "cheese", hence the English mistranslation.

Chesthill (Perth), Seasdal
"Terraced meadow", of which the English name is an approximation in sound.

Chicken Head (Lewis), A' Chearc
The Gaelic name of this headland is simply "the hen", so called because of its shape.

Chipperton (South Uist), Tiobartan
"Well place", containing *tiobar* rather than the usual *tobar* for "well". The well itself was *Tobar Thiobartain* and said to be *air fìor iomall an domhain*, "at the very edge of the world".

Chirmorie (Ayr)
This appears to be "St Mary's land", from *Tìr Mhoire*.

Churchtown (Raasay), An Clachan
"The churchyard" or "the village with a church". *Clachan* is often anglicised as "Kirkton".

Cilmalieu (Argyll), Cill MoLiubha
"St MoLiubha's Church."

Clabhach (Coll), A' Chlabaich
This name is unclear but may mean something like "the open-mouthed place", referring to a topographical feature.

Clachaig (Argyll), Clachaig
"Stone place."

Clachamish (Skye), Clach Amais
This appears to mean "target stone", but an older form of the name shows that it was *Cladh a' Chamais*, "graveyard by the bay".

Clachan (Argyll, Lismore, North Uist, Seil), An Clachan
"The churchyard" or "the village with a church". In North Uist the full Gaelic name is *Clachan na Lùib* or *Clachan a' Ghlùib*, "the churchyard at the glebe". In Seil the full name is *Clachan Saoil*, "the kirkton of Seil".

Clachanmore (Wigtown)
"The big village", from *An Clachan Mór*.

Clachan of Campsie (Stirling), Clachan Chamais
"The kirkton of Campsie."

Clachan of Glendaruel (Argyll), Clachan Ghlinn Dà Ruadhail
"The kirkton of Glendaruel."

Clachan Sands (North Uist), Clachan Shannda
"The churchyard of Sanda", which is "sand river", from Norse. The graveyard here is called *Cladh a' Chlachain*, "the graveyard of Clachan".

Clachieran (Bute), Cladh Chiarain
"The graveyard of St Ciaran."

Clachnacuddin (Inverness), Clach na Cùdainn
"The stone of the tub", where local women did their washing.

Clachnaharry (Inverness), Clach na
h-Aithrigh
"Repentance stone."

Clachtoll (Sutherland), A' Chlach
Thuill
"The stone with a hole."

Clachuil (Ross), Clach Thuill
"Stone with a hole."

Clackmannan (Clackmannan), Clach
Mhanainn *or* Clach Mhanann
"The stone of Manau", a district of
the Brythonic people of the Forth
area. Clackmannanshire is *Siorrachd
Chlach Mhanainn* or *Siorrachd
Chlach Mhanann*.

Clackriach (Aberdeen)
"Brindled stone", from *Clach
Riabhach*.

Cladach (Arran), An Cladach
"The shore."

Claddach (Bute), An Cladach
"The shore."

Claddach Baleshare (North Uist),
Cladach a' Bhaile Shear
"The shore opposite Baleshare."

Claddach Carinish (North Uist),
Cladach Chàirinis
"The shore opposite Carinish."

Claddach Illeray (North Uist),
Cladach Iolaraigh
"The shore opposite Illeray."

Claddach Kirkebost (North Uist),
Cladach Chirceboist
"The shore opposite Kirkebost."

Claddach Knockline (North Uist),
Cladach Chnoc an Lìn
"The shore opposite Knockline."

Claddach Kyles (North Uist),
Cladach a' Chaolais
"The shore at the narrows."

Cladich (Argyll), An Cladach
"The shore."

Cladoch (Arran), An Cladach
"The shore."

Claggan (Argyll, Inverness), An
Claigeann
"The skull", a word used to denote
the most productive field on a
farm.

Claigen (Skye), An Claigeann
See **Claggan**.

Claonaig (Argyll), Claonaig
This Norse name denoting a bay has
an unclear initial element.

Clare (Ross), An Clàr
"The small plain."

Claremont (Fife)
"Flat hill" or "rough pasture", from
Clàr Mhon(adh).

Clashindarroch (Aberdeen)
"Ditch by the oak", from *Clais an
Daraich*.

Clashmahew (Wigtown)
"St MoChua's ditch", from *Clais
MoChua*.

Clashmore (Sutherland), A' Chlais
Mhór
"The big ditch."

Clashnabuiac (Ross), Clais nam
Buidheag
"The ditch of the yellow flowers."

Clashnamuiach (Ross), Clais nam
Maigheach
"The ditch of the hares."

Clashnessie (Sutherland), Clais an
Easaidh
"The ditch by the small waterfall."

Clauchaneasy (Wigtown)
"Jesus's churchyard", from *Clachan
Iosa*.

Clauchlands (Arran)
This may be from *clachlann*, "stone
enclosure".

Clauchog (Arran), Clachaig
"Stony place."

Clava (Inverness), Clabhalag
The meaning of this name is unclear.

Claybokie (Aberdeen), Cladh
Bhòcaidh
"The graveyard of the ghost."

Clay of Allan (Ross), Criadhach
Alain Mhóir
"Claylands by the big Allan."

Claypark (Lewis), A' Bhuaile
Chrèadha
The Gaelic name is "the clay pen".

Cleadale (Eigg), Clèadail
This Norse name refers to a valley,

and the first element may refer to a ridged slope.

Cleascro (Lewis), Cliasgro
This Norse name may be "river pit at ridged slope".

Cleland (Lanark)
This is probably "clay land", from English.

Clerkhill (Sutherland), Cnoc a' Chléirich
"The clerk's or cleric's hill."

Cliad (Barra), Cliaid; (Coll), Cliad
This Norse name may be a form of *klettr*, "rock or cliff".

Cliasmol (Harris), Cliasmol
This Norse name contains *holm*, "small island", but the first part is unclear, although it may contain a personal name.

Cliff (Lewis), Clibh; (Ross), A' Chliubh
These Norse names mean "cliff". Cliff House in Ross is *Taigh na Cliubhann*.

Clifton (Perth), Achadh nan Tuirighnean; (Ross), Baile na Creige
The English name is "cliff village", which is also the meaning of the Gaelic name in Ross, while in Perth the Gaelic name is "the field of the kings".

Clochan (Banff)
"Churchyard" or "kirkton", from *Clachan*.

Clochfoldich (Perth), Cloich Phollaich
"Indented stone."

Cloch Point (Renfrew)
"Point of the stone", possibly a part-translation of *Rubha na Cloiche*, of which there are several around the country.

Cloddach (Moray)
"River meadow", from *Cladach*. This word normally means "shore", but is also the usual term in Manx Gaelic for a river meadow.

Closeburn (Dumfries)
"St Osbran's or Osbern's Church",

from *Cill Osbrain*, as reflected in the 12th-century form of the name, "Kyleosbren". It is unclear whether St Osbran of Ireland or St Osbern of England is the saint in question.

Clova (Angus), Clàbha
The meaning of this name is unclear.

Clovulin (Argyll), Cladh a' Mhuilinn
This appears to mean "the cemetery at the mill".

Cluanie (Arran, Ross), Cluainidh
"Meadow place."

Cluer (Harris), Cluthair
This Norse name appears to be in plural form, but its meaning is unclear.

Clunas (Nairn), Cluanais
"Meadow place."

Clune (Inverness), An Cluain *or* A' Chluain
"The meadow."

Clunes (Inverness), Na Cluainean (Lochaber); A' Chluain (Aird)
"The meadows" and "the meadow" respectively. The old name of Clunes in Aird was *Fionn Ghaisg*, "white Gask", referring to a strip of land projecting from a plateau. Local people were known as *faoileagan (na Cluain)*, "seagulls (of Clunes)".

Clunie (Perth), Cluainidh
"Meadow place."

Cluniemore (Perth), Cluainidh Mhór
"Big Cluny."

Cluniter (Argyll), Claon Oitir
"Sloping promontory."

Cluny (Aberdeen, Fife)
See **Clunie**.

Clydebank (Dunbarton), Bruach Chluaidh
"The bank of the Clyde."

Clydesdale (Lanark), Dail Chluaidh
"The valley of the Clyde."

Clynder (Dunbarton), An Claon Dearg
"The red slope."

Clyne (Sutherland), Clìn
"Slope", from an original *cluain*. Clyne parish is *Sgìre Chlìn*.

Cnocantubha (Arran), Cnocan an Tugha
"The hillock of the thatch."

Cnocbreac (Jura), An Cnoc Breac
"The speckled hill."

Coalsnaughton (Clackmannan)
This may be "Nechtan's land", from *Cas Neachdain*, where *cas* is used for "land" rather than "foot", as also happens in Irish placenames.

Coast (Ross), An t-Eirtheaire
"The coast." First Coast is *an t-Eirtheaire Shìos*, "the lower coast", and Second Coast is *an t-Eirtheaire Shuas*, "the upper coast". Gaelic uses *air an Eirtheaire* to express "in Coast". Second Coast had the alternative names *an t-Eirtheaire Donn*, "the brown coast", and *an t-Eirtheaire Bhos*, "the coast here".

Cochno (Dunbarton)
This may mean "place of little hollows", from Gaelic *Cuachanach*, but may also be from a Brythonic source based on *coch*, "red".

Cockbridge (Aberdeen), Drochaid a' Choilich
This appears to be "the bridge of the cockerel", but *coileach* also means "eddy", which may be the intended meaning here.

Cockenzie (East Lothian), Cùil Choinnich
"Kenneth's secluded spot."

Coigach (Ross), Cóigeach *or* A' Chóigeach
"Place of fifths", referring to land division, the fifths comprising Achnahaird, Achlochan, Acheninver, Achavraie and Achduart and known together as *na còig achaidhean*, "the five fields". The area is also known as *Sgìre na Cóigich*, "the district of Coigach".

Coignafearn (Inverness), Cóig na Feàrna
"The fifth of the alder", referring to land divisions. This is located in Strathdearn, which contains five

cóigs or divisions, namely Coignafearn, Coignascallan, Cóig na Sìthe, Cóig a' Mhuilinn and Cóig nam Fionndaraich. See **Strathdearn**.

Coignascallan (Inverness), Cóig nan Sgàlan
"The fifth of the shelters or huts." See **Coignafearn**.

Coilacreich (Aberdeen), Coille a' Chrithich
"The aspen wood."

Coilantogle (Perth)
This may be "nook of the rye", from *Cùil an t-Seagail*.

Coilleag (Eriskay), A' Choilleag
"The cockle beach."

Coillemore (Arran), Coille Mór
"Large wood." This name is unusual in that the definite article would be expected, as would *mhór*, the feminine form of the adjective, rather than the masculine *mór*.

Coillore (Skye), Coille Òra
This was originally the name of a wood, but the spelling in Gaelic and English obscure the meaning of the second element.

Colaboll (Sutherland), Colabol
"Coal farm", from Norse.

Colbost (Skye), Cealabost *or* Caileabost
This may be "keel farm" or "farm with a drying shed", from Norse.

Coldbackie (Sutherland), Callbacaidh
"Cold bank" or "charcoal bank", from Norse.

Coldwells (Ross), Am Bealaidh
The "cold wells" referred to in the English name are absent from the Gaelic, which means "the broom", referring to the shrub.

Col Glen (Argyll), An Caol Ghleann
"The narrow glen", which is the same name as that of the Sma' Glen in Perthshire.

Colintraive (Argyll), Caol an t-Snàimh
"The narrows of the swimming", where cattle were swum across between Cowal and Bute.

Coll (Coll), Cola; (Lewis), Col
The island of Coll has a pre-Celtic name and is known by the epithet, *Cola Chreagach Chiar*, "dark rocky Coll". A native of the island is a *Colach*. The character of the people is referred to disparagingly in a couple of rhymes such as *Chan fhaic am Muileach nach sanntaich am Muileach; na shanntaicheas am Muileach, goididh an Colach; 's na ghoideas an Colach, cuiridh an Tiristeach am folach*, "What the Mull man sees, he wants; what the Mull man wants, the Coll man steals; what the Coll man steals, the Tiree man hides". Another is *Chan eil an cùil no an cuilidh nach fhaic sùil a' Mhuilich, 's chan eil an àird no 'n ìosal nach laimhsich làmh an Ìlich. Na dh'fhàgadh am Muileach, ghrad-sgrìobadh an Colach bhuaithe e, ach 's mairg a dh'earbadh a chuid no anam ris a' chealgaire Bharrach*, which has similar sentiments, but manages to disparage the people of Islay and Barra too. *Cola* is frequently spelled as *Colla* although this latter form does not reflect the pronunciation. Coll in Lewis is "summit", from Norse. Upper Coll is *Col Uarach*, Inner Coll is *Ceann a-Staigh Chuil*, and Outend Coll is *Ceann a-Muigh Chuil*. The nearby beach is *Tràigh Chuil*.

Collam (Harris), Colam
This may mean "summit holm", from Norse.

Collychippen (Dunbarton), Cùil a' Chipein
"The secluded spot at the place of (tree) stumps."

Colmonell (Ayr), Cill Cholmain Eala
"The church of St Colman Eala", which is the same name as that of Kilcalmonell in Argyll. It is interesting that the English form has lost the reference to a church contained in *Cill*, anglicised as "Kil-".

Colnabaichin (Aberdeen), Cùil nam Bàthaichean
"The secluded spot at the byres."

Colonsay (Colonsay), Colbhasa
"Kolbein's island", from Norse. A native of Colonsay is a *Colbhasach*, also nicknamed a *coinean mór*, "big rabbit".

Colzium (Midlothian)
"Narrow leap", from *cuingleum*.

Comar (Inverness), Comar
"Confluence."

Comar Kirkton (Inverness), Clachan Comair
"Churchyard of Comar."

Comer (Stirling)
This may be "confluence", from *comar*.

Comrie (Perth), Cuimrigh; (Ross), Comraigh
"Sanctuary." The fair in Comrie in Perthshire was known as *Féill MoCheasaig*, "dear St Kessock's Fair".

Conaglen (Argyll), Conghleann
"Hound valley."

Conchra (Argyll, Ross), Conchra
"Place of cruives", a type of pen or fold.

Conicavel (Moray)
This may be "narrow place at the fish trap", from *Cong a' Chabhail*.

Conisby (Islay), Coinneasbaidh
This is a Norse farm name and may contain the same first element as in **Cuniside**, indicating that the farm was owned by a woman. A folk-etymology derives the name from *Còmhnaidh an Easbaig*, "the residence of the bishop". Local people were known as *ceàrdan*, "tinkers".

Connage (Inverness), A' Choinnis
This may mean "the joint meadow".

Connel (Argyll), A' Chonghail *or* A' Choingheal
"The whirlpool", the full name being *A' Chonghail/A' Choingheal Latharnach*, "the Lorn Connel". The Falls of Connel are *Sruth na Conghail*, "the current of Connel".

Connista (Skye), Conasta
The first part of this Norse farm name is unclear.

Conon (Skye), Connain
This commemoration of the saint Connan was originally applied to the nearby river and then to the township.

Cononbrae (Ross), Bog Domhain
The English name refers to the River Conon, while the Gaelic name means "deep bog".

Conon Bridge (Ross), Drochaid Sguideil
The English name refers to the River Conon and while the Gaelic also mentions a bridge, its second part is a Norse valley name, although its defining element is unclear. Local people were nicknamed *geòcairean*, "gluttons".

Conon House (Ross), Taigh Chonainn
"House of the Conon", a river name possibly meaning "hound stream".

Conordon (Skye), An Còmhnardan
"The small plain."

Conrick (Dumfries); (Inverness), A' Chòmhrag
The Inverness name means "the confluence" and the Dumfries name may be from the same source.

Contin (Ross), Cunndainn
This may be "confluence". The local fair was *Fèill Ma Ruibhe*, "St Maol Rubha's fair", later relocated to Dingwall.

Contullich (Ross), Conntulaich
"Place of joint hills."

Conveth (Kincardine), Coinmheadh
"Free quartering." This refers to the obligation placed on the area to provide sustenance free of charge to passing troops. Conveth is the old name of the parish of Laurencekirk.

Convinth (Inverness), An Confhadhach
"The place of storms."

Coomb Island (Sutherland)
See **Neave Island**.

Coppay (Harris), Copaigh
"Cup island", from Norse, a reference to the island's shape.

Corarder (Inverness), Coire Àrdair
"Corrie of the Arder."

Corgarff (Aberdeen), Corr Garaidh
This appears to mean "end of the den".

Corkamull (Mull), Corcamul
"Oat ridge", from Norse.

Corkisary (Ross), Corcasairigh
This may be "oat sheiling", from Norse, or it might be a Norse sheiling or field name with a personal name as the first element.

Cornabus (Islay), Còrnabus
"Corn farm", from Norse.

Cornaig (Tiree), Còrnaig
"Corn bay", from Norse. Cornaigbeg is *Còrnaig Bheag*, "little Cornaig", and Cornaigmore is *Còrnaig Mhòr*, "big Cornaig".

Corncattrach (Aberdeen)
"The corrie with the stone fort", from *Coire na Cathrach*.

Corndavon (Aberdeen), Coire an Dà Bheinn
"The corrie in the two mountains."

Cornhill (Sutherland), Cnoc an Airbh
The English form is a translation from Gaelic.

Cornton (Ross), Baile an Loch
While the English name is "corn farm", the Gaelic name is "the farm by the loch".

Coroghan (Canna), An Corra Dhùn
"The uneven hill (fort)."

Corpach (Inverness), A' Chorpaich
"The place of bodies", possibly meaning that the dead were ferried from here for burial.

Corran (Inverness, Skye), An Corran
"The narrow spit." The full name of Corran by Ardgour is *Corran Àird Ghobhar*, "the narrow spit of Ardgour".

Corrie (Arran), An Coire
"The corrie." The full name used to
be *Coire Cnoc Dubh*, "the corrie of
the black hill", from which the genitive case is absent. Upper Corrie is
Achag, possibly "little field" and also
known as "Achag" in English. High
Corrie is *An Coire Àrd*, while North
High Corrie is *Guala Bàn*, "white
shoulder".

Corriecravie (Arran), Coire
Chraobhaidh
"Corrie at the tree place."
Corriecravie Moor was known
locally as *An Cnoc Reamhar*, "the fat
hill", after a prominent nearby
feature.

Corriehiam (Arran), Coire Chaim
This appears to be "crooked corrie".

Corriemoillie (Ross), Coire
Mhuillidh
"Milling corrie."

Corriemulzie (Ross), Coire
Mhuillidh
"Milling corrie."

Corrievorrie (Inverness), Coire
Mhóruigh
"The corrie on the big slope"

Corrimony (Inverness), Coire
Mhonaidh
"The corrie on the uplands." The
local graveyard was *Cladh
Churadain*, "St Curitan's churchyard", the same name as the graveyard in Bona.

Corrour (Inverness), Coire Odhar
"Dun corrie", but the original name
may have been *Coire Dhobhair*,
"corrie by the water".

Corry (Ross), An Coire
"The corrie."

Corrychoillie (Inverness), Coire
Choingligh
"The corrie at the narrow place."

Corrygills (Arran), Coire Ghoill
Although this appears to be "corrie
of the non-Gael", it may be from
Norse *korfagil* (raven gully) or
karigil (Kari's gully).

Corrynahera (Jura), Coire na
h-Earadh
"The corrie at the division."

Corry of Ardnagrask (Ross), Coire
Àird nan Crasg
"The corrie of Ardnagrask."

Corskie (Moray)
This may be "crossing place", from
Crasgaidh.

Coruanan (Inverness), Coire Uanain
This appears to be "lamb's corrie".

Corunna (North Uist), Corùna
This was named after the battle in
Spain during the Napoleonic wars.

Corvost (Ross), Coire-bheist
This name is locally interpreted as
"corrie of the beast", but since the
stress is on the first syllable the
name's origin must lie somewhere
else.

Coshieville (Perth), Cois a' Bhile
"By the rock edge or sacred tree."
Coshieville near Glen Lyon had a
market known as *Féill MoChoid*
commemorating St Coedi. Easter
Coshieville is *Dùn MhicMhatha*,
"Matheson's fort".

Cottartown (Inverness), Baile nan
Coitearan
"The cotters' farm."

Cotterton (Ross), Achadh nan Coitear
The English name is "cotters' farm",
but the Gaelic name is "the cotters'
field".

Coul (Ross), A' Chùil
"The secluded spot."

Coulags (Ross), Na Cùileagan
"The little secluded spots."

Coulhill (Ross), Cnoc na Cùil
"The hill at the secluded spot." The
old name was *Baile na Cùil*, "farm at
the secluded spot".

Coulin (Ross), Cùmhlainn
"Place of enclosures." The old name
was *Teamradal*, "timber dale", from
Norse.

Coull (Aberdeen), A' Chùil *or* Cùil
"The secluded spot." Coull parish is
Sgìre Chùil.

Coulport (Dunbarton), An Cùl Phort
"The back port", possibly referring
to its location at the back of
Rosneath peninsula.

Coulregrein (Lewis), Cùl ri Gréin
"Back to the sun."

Coupar Angus (Perth), Cùbar
Aonghais
"The *cùbar* of Angus", *cùbar* being
from a Brythonic word possibly
meaning "confluence" and cognate
with Gaelic *comar*.

Cour (Argyll), An Cùr
This is unclear, but if from Norse,
may refer to cattle folds.

Courthill (Ross), Cnoc a' Mhòid
"The hill of the meeting place or
court."

Couttie (Perth)
"The *cùbar* of Ultan's son", from
Cùbar Mac Ultain. See **Coupar
Angus** and **Cupar**.

Cove (Ross), An Uamhghaidh
The Gaelic name is "the place of
caves". Local people are known as
buic, "bucks".

Cowal (Argyll), Comhal *or*
Comhghall
"Comhghall's land", the leader of
one of the four sections of Dal
Riada. A local is a *Comhalach*. The
Kerry or Kyles district is *An
Ceathramh Comhalach*, "the Cowal
quarterland", and a native of that
area is a *Ceathrach*, "Kerry
person".

Cowden (Perth), A' Challtainn
"The hazel wood."

Cowie (Kincardine, Stirling)
This may be "hazel place", from
Collaidh.

Coylet (Argyll), Cuingleathad
"Narrow slope."

Coylton (Ayr)
"Coel's farm." See **Kyle**.

Coylumbridge (Inverness), Drochaid
na Cuingleum
"The bridge of Coylum", which itself
means "narrow leap".

Crackaig (Jura), Cracaig;
(Sutherland), Crachdaig
"Crow bay", from Norse.

Cradlehall (Inverness), Am Baile
Dearg
The Gaelic name is "the red farm".

Craggan (Perth)
"Small rock", from *Creagan*.

Cragganmore (Banff), An Creagan
Mór
"The big rock."

Cragganvallie (Inverness), Creagan a'
Bhealaidh
"Little rock of the broom."

Craggie (Sutherland), Cragaidh
"Rock place."

Craig (Ross), Creag Ruigh
Mhorghain *or* A' Chreag
"The rock at Morgan's slope" or "the
rock". An alternative interpretation
is based on *morghan*, "gravel" or
"shingle". Another form of the name
is *Creag Ni Mhorghain*, "Morgan's
daughter's rock". The Craig River is
Abhainn na Creige or *Abhainn Bràigh
Thathaisgeail*.

Craigellachie (Banff), Creag
Eileachaidh
"The rock at the stony place."

Craigellie (Aberdeen)
This may be "the rock at the stony
place", from *Creag Eiligh*.

Craigendoran (Dunbarton), Creag an
Dobhrain
"The rock of the otter."

Craigengall (West Lothian), Creag
nan Gall
"Rock of the non-Gaels."

Craigentinny (Midlothian), Creag an
t-Sionnaich
"The rock of the fox."

Craigesk (Midlothian)
"The rock at the Esk", from *Creag
Easg*.

Craighouse (Jura), Taigh na Creige
"The house by the rock."

Craigie (Angus, Ayr, Perth, West
Lothian)
"Rock place", from *Creagaidh*.

Craigievar (Aberdeen), Creag Mhàrr
"The rock of Mar."

Craigleith (East Lothian)
"The rock of Leith", from *Creag Lìte*.

Craiglumphart (Fife)
This is "the rock at the encampment", from *creag* and *longphort*.

Craigmaddie (Dunbarton), Creag a'
Mhadaidh
"The rock of the fox or wolf."

Craigmailing (West Lothian)
This may be "rock at the smooth
rounded hill", from *Creag Mhaoilinn*.

Craigmarry (West Lothian)
This may be "the rock of killing",
from *Creag a' Mharbhaidh*.

Craigmawhannel (Ayr)
This appears to be "dear St Conall's
rock", from *Creag MoChonaill*.

Craigmore (Bute), A' Chreag Mhór
"The big rock."

Craigmyle (Aberdeen)
"Rounded rock", from *Creag Mhaol*.

Craignavie (Perth), Creag
Neamhaidh
"The rock at the sacred place."

Craignish (Argyll), Creiginis
"Rocky headland", from Norse.
Local people were nicknamed *òigich*,
"youngsters", and *fithich dhubha*,
"black ravens". Craignish Point is
Rubha Chreiginis.

Craignure (Mull), Creag an Iubhair
"The rock of the yew."

Craigo (Angus)
"Rock place", from *Creagach*.

Craig Phadrig (Inverness), Creag
Phàdraig *or* Làrach an Taigh Mhóir
The English and first Gaelic names
are "Patrick's rock", while the second
Gaelic name, used by local Gaelic
speakers, is "the site of the big
house".

Craigs (Ross), Taigh na Creige
The English name is "rocks", while
the Gaelic name is "the house by the
rock".

Craigston (Barra), Baile na Creige
"The village by the rock."

Craigstrome (Benbecula),
Creagastrom
"Rocky current", from Norse.

Craigton (Ross, Sutherland), Baile na
Creige
"The village by the rock." There is a
Craigton in Glasgow and one in
Angus which may contain the
surname "Craig" rather than refer-
ring to a rock.

Crail (Fife), Cair Ail
"Fort at the rock", showing a Pictish
borrowing into Gaelic of *cair* in the
sense of "fort". An older form of the
anglicised name, "Caraile", shows
the derivation more clearly.

Cramond (Midlothian)
"Fort on the Almond", from
Brythonic. The derivation is clear in
an old form of the name,
"Caramonth".

Cranachan (Inverness), Crannachan
"Tree place."

Crandart (Angus), Crannaird
"Tree point." Diack (1944) spelled
the Gaelic form of this name as "'n
grunngart", suggesting perhaps *An
Crannghart*, which may represent
"the tree field".

Cranloch (Moray)
"Tree place", from *crannlach*.

Crannach (Aberdeen), Crannach
"Tree place."

Crarae (Argyll), Carr Eighe
The elements in the Gaelic name
can be interpreted as "rock ledge"
and "file", giving an overall meaning
of "file-shaped rock ledge" but, if the
English form is an accurate reflec-
tion of an older name, an alternative
interpretation might include *crò* or
crà, "enclosure" and *réidh*, "level".

Crask (Sutherland), An Crasg
"The crossing." The Crask Inn is
known as *Taigh a' Chraisg*, "Crask
house".

Crathes (Kincardine), Crathais
This appears to mean "shaking
place".

Crathie (Aberdeen), Craichidh
This may mean the same as **Crathes** and **Cray**.

Craw (Arran), An Crà, An Cràdha *or* A' Chré
All the variations in the name stem from *crò*, "sheep pen", originally a Norse word.

Cray (Perth), Crathaidh
"Shaking place."

Creagan (Argyll), An Creagan
"The small rock." There is a Creagan in Perthshire which appears to be from the same origin.

Creagorry (Benbecula), Creag Ghoraidh
"Godred's rock."

Creich (Mull), Crèich; (Sutherland), Craoich
This may mean "tree place".

Cremannan (Stirling)
This is thought to stem from either *Crò Mhanainn* or *Crò Mhanann*, "the enclosure of Manau" a Brythonic district around the Forth, or from *Crò Mheannan*, "kids' enclosure".

Crepkill (Skye), Creipigil
This was originally Norse *Cresgil*, "cross ravine".

Cretshengan (Argyll), Croit Sheangain
"Seangan's croft."

Crianlarich (Perth), A' Chrìon Làraich
This appears to be "the wasted site", but the first element may originally have been *critheann*, "aspen", rather than *crìon*, "wasted or feeble".

Crieff (Perth), Craoibh
"Tree place." The December market held here was known as *Féill Tómais*, "St Thomas's Fair".

Crimond (Aberdeen)
This may be "shaking moor" or "boundary moor", from *crith* or *crìoch* and *monadh*.

Crinan (Argyll), An Crìonan
This seems to be "the wasted or debilitated place". Crinan Moss is *A' Mhòine Mhór*, "the big peat moss".

Croachy (Inverness), Cruachaidh
"Hard field."

Crobeg (Lewis), Crò Beag
"Small enclosure", from Norse/Gaelic.

Crochandoon (Arran), An Cnocan Donn
"The brown hillock."

Croe Bridge (Ross), Drochaid a' Chrò
"The bridge at the enclosure."

Croft (Ross), Croit Thollaidh
The Gaelic name is "croft at Tollie".

Croftamie (Stirling), Croit Sheumaidh
This appears to be "Jamie's croft".

Croftdavid (Perth), Croit Dhàidh
"David's croft."

Croftjames (Ross), Croit Sheumais
"James's croft."

Croftmore (Perth), A' Chroit Mhór
"The big croft."

Croftnahaven (Inverness), Croit na h-Abhann
"The croft by the river."

Croggan (Mull), An Crògan
This name seems to refer to a paw-shaped piece of land, from *cròg*, "paw". Local people were nicknamed *eich dhonna*, "brown horses".

Croick (Ross), A' Chròic
"The antlers", possibly referring to a branch in the glen or river.

Croir (Bernera), Crothair
"Enclosures", from Norse.

Cromar (Aberdeen), Crò Mhàrr
"The enclosure of Mar." Braes of Cromar is *Bràigh Crò Mhàrr* and *Bruthaichean Crò Mhàrr*.

Cromarty (Ross), Cromba
"Crooked bay." The Cromarty Firth is *Caolas Chrombaigh*. The saying, *Ged a rachadh Cromba leis a' mhuir*, "Even though Cromarty were to slip into the sea", was used to denote an unlikely occurrence.

Cromasaig (Ross), An Cromasadh *or* Cromasaig
"The crooked stance."

Crombie (Fife)
"Crooked river." The older name was Abercrombie from *Obar Chrombaidh*, "mouth of the crooked river".

Cromdale (Moray), Crombail
"Crooked haugh." The original form of the name, *Cromdhail*, shows the component parts more clearly. The parish was known as *Sgìr' MoLuaig*, "St MoLuag's parish", and the Cromdale Hills are *Beinn Chrombail* or *Beinn Chromdhail*.

Cromlix (Perth)
This may refer to standing stones and come from Gaelic *crom leac* (cognate with the better-known Brythonic *cromlech*) with an English plural attached.

Cromore (Lewis), Crò Mór
"Large enclosure", from Norse/Gaelic.

Cromra (Inverness), Cromrath
"Crooked circular fort."

Cross (Lewis), Cros
"Crossing place", from Norse.

Crossaig (Argyll), Crosaig
"Cross bay", from Norse.

Crossal (Skye), Crosal
"Cross hill", from Norse.

Crossapoll (Tiree), Crosabol
"Cross farm", from Norse.

Crossbost (Lewis), Crosabost
"Farm of the crosses", from Norse.

Crosscraig (Perth), Troisearraig
Both Gaelic and English names contain a reference to some kind of crossing, but the Gaelic name says nothing about a rock or craig.

Crossmyloof (Glasgow), Crois MoLiubha
This seems to be "dear St Liubha's cross". Locally the name is believed to stem from the saying "cross my loof with silver" where "loof" is alleged to mean "hand".

Crossroads (Sutherland), Blàr nan Cnàmhnan
"Field of the bones." This is part of the wider area of Melness.

Cross Skigersta Road (Lewis), An Rathad Ùr
The road between Cross and Skigersta is known as "the new road" in Gaelic.

Crowlin Islands (Ross), Na h-Eileanan Cròlaigeach *or* Na h-Eileanan Cròlainneach
The "Crowlin" part of the name may mean "hard land".

Crowlista (Lewis), Crabhlasta
This may be "farm of the meadow with a pen", from Norse.

Croy (Ayr, Dunbarton, Nairn), Crothaigh
This is said to stem from *cruaidh*, "hard".

Crubenmore (Inverness), Crùbainn Mhór
"Large crouching place", possibly a reference to the nearby hills.

Crulivaig (Lewis), Crùlabhaig
This Norse name may be "bay at the meadow with a pen".

Cuach (Inverness), A' Chuach
"The hollow."

Cuagach (Eigg), A' Chuagach
This is said to be "twisted place", but may originate from Norse for "bay at the enclosure".

Cuaig (Ross), Cùthaig
"Cow bay", from Norse. The bay itself is called *Òb Chùthaig*. Local people are known as *rùcanaich*, "rumblers", or *tùthagan*, "patches".

Cuderish (Perth), Cudrais
This may mean "common land".

Cuidrach (Skye), A' Chuidreach
This may be "common land". South Cuidrach is *Peighinn an Dùine*, "pennyland of the hill fort".

Cuier (Barra), Cuithir
"Cattle folds", from Norse.

Cuigeas (Tiree), Cu-dhéis
This may contain Norse *kví*, "enclosure". An alternative English name is "Quaish".

Cuil (Argyll, Ross), A' Chùil
"The secluded spot."

Cuilghailtro (Argyll), Cùil Ghailltreo
"Secluded spot of the non-Gaels'
settlement." This name appears to
contain Brythonic *tref*, "settlement",
although the location is outwith the
area of the main groupings of
Brythonic names.

Cuillich (Ross), Cuinglich
"Narrow place."

Cuithe (Arran), An Cuithe
"The cattle fold", from Norse *kví*.

Culaneilan (Ross), Cùl an Eilein
"The back of the island."

Culbin Sands (Moray), Bar Inbhir
Éireann
The sands here are called "the sand
bar at the mouth of the Findhorn" in
Gaelic.

Culbo (Ross, Sutherland), Cùrabol
"Knob-shaped farm", from Norse.

Culbokie (Ross), Cùil Bhòcaidh *or*
An Cùil Bhàicidh
"The secluded spot of the ghost or
goblin."

Culburnie (Inverness), Blàr na
Feadaig *or* Cùl Bhraonaigh; (Ross),
Cùil Braonaigh
The Inverness names are "the plover
field" and "the back of the damp
place" respectively, while the Ross
name is "the secluded spot at the
damp place". People from Culburnie
in Inverness-shire were known as
pigheidean, "magpies".

Culcabock (Inverness), Cùil na
Càbaig
This name appears to mean "the
quiet spot of the kebbuck of cheese",
but the original name was possibly
Cùl na Ceapaich, "the back of the
tillage land". Additionally, the name
Càpaig is found in **Caputh**, and this
may be another origin of the name.
An even older name of this place
was *Clachan Donnchaidh*, "Duncan's
village".

Culcharry (Nairn), Cùl a' Charra
This appears to be "the back of the
marsh".

Culchonich (Ross), A' Chùil
Chóintich
"The mossy secluded spot."

Culduie (Ross), Cùil Duibh
"Black secluded spot."

Culduthel (Inverness), Cùl Daothail
or Cùil Daothail
This name's meaning is unclear,
although it includes *cùl*, "back", or
cùil, "quiet spot". *Daothail* is said to
come from *tuathail*, "north side",
however there is a personal name,
Tuathal, which may be the origin of
this name.

Culeave (Ross), Cùil Liabh
"The back of the moors", from an
older *Cùil Shliabh*.

Culisse (Ross), Cùl an Lios
"The back of the fortified enclosure."

Culkein (Sutherland), An Cùl-cinn
"The common grazings."

Culkein Drumbeg (Sutherland),
Cùl-cinn an Droma Bhig
"The common grazings of
Drumbeg."

Cullen (Banff)
The old English name was
"Invercullen", which was said to
mean "the mouth of the holly
stream", from *Inbhir Cuilinn*. Gaelic
speakers in Banffshire and Braemar
pronounced the name approximately
as *Cuileann* and *Cùileann*, but as
Diack (1944) points out, the
pronunciation of Gaelic placenames
in marginal areas can be unreliable.
However, although AÀA recommend *Cuileann* as the name of the
town, the change from "Invercullen"
to "Cullen" matches a similar change
in the names of Ayr, Brora, Girvan
and Nairn, where the English forms
lost "Inver" but the Gaelic ones
retained *Inbhir*, suggesting that
Inbhir Cuilinn is a more appropriate
form of the name.

Cullerne (Moray)
"The back of the Findhorn", from
Cùl Éireann.

Cullicudden (Ross), Cùl a' Chùdainn
"The back of the tub", referring to a topographical feature. Cullicudden parish is *Sgìre Mhàrtainn*, "St Martin's parish", now the name of **Resolis** parish into which Cullicudden was subsumed.

Cullipool (Luing), Culapul
This Norse name may be "coal farm".

Culloden (Inverness), Cùil Lodair
This may be "the secluded spot at the shelving slope".

Culmaily (Sutherland), Cùil Mhàilidh
Cùil is a "secluded spot", but the second element is unclear. However, see **Dalmally** and **Kilmallie**.

Culnacraig (Ross), Cùl na Creige
"The back of the rock."

Culnaknock (Skye), Cùl nan Cnoc
"The back of the hills."

Culnamean (Skye), Cùl nam Beann
"The back of the mountains."

Culrain (Sutherland), Cùl Ràthain
"The back of the small circular fort." The older name was *Càrbasdal*, "copse farm valley", from Norse, now applied to Carbisdale.

Culross (Fife), Cuileann Ros
"Holly point."

Culsh (Aberdeen), A' Chùilt
"The secluded spot."

Culter (Aberdeen, Kincardine), Cùldair
This may be "back water". Peterculter is on the north side of the Dee with Maryculter on the south bank in Kincardineshire.

Cults (Aberdeen, Fife), A' Chùilt
"The secluded spot."

Culzie (Ross), Caolaisidh
"Place of the narrow meadow."

Cumbernauld (Dunbarton), Comar nan Allt
"The confluence of the streams."

Cumbrae (Cumbrae), Cumaradh
"Place of the Cymric people" referring to the Brythonic people of Strathclyde. A derogatory saying about Bute also takes a sideswipe at Cumbrae, *Chan ann am Bòid uile a tha an t-olc; tha cuid dheth sa Chumaradh bheag làimh ris*, "Not all evil is in Bute; some is in little Cumbrae nearby". Cumbrae is also known as "Great Cumbrae" or *Cumaradh Mór*, while Little Cumbrae is *Cumaradh Beag*. The fair held in Great Cumbrae was known as *Féill MoCheasaig*, "dear St Kessock's Fair".

Cummingston (Moray)
"The town of the Cummings." This is locally known as "the Collach", perhaps from *an coileach* meaning "the eddy".

Cumnock (Ayrshire), Cumnag
The Gaelic form is a transliteration of the English. New Cumnock is *Cumnag Nuadh*.

Cuniside (Sutherland), Caonasaid
"Lady's farm", from Norse.

Cunninghame (Ayr), Coineagan
The meaning of this name is unclear, but predates the arrival of English and is thus not a *ham* or "homestead" name.

Cupar (Fife), Cùbar *or* Cùbar Fìobha
Cùbar is a Brythonic word, maybe meaning "confluence". In Gaelic, Cupar was known as *Cùbar Fìobha*, "Cupar of Fife", to distinguish it from *Cùbar Aonghais*, "Coupar of Angus". The town cross is known as *Crois Chùbair*.

Curin (Ross), Caorthainn
"Rowan place."

Curragh (Ayr)
"Wet plain", from *Currach*.

Currie (Midlothian), Curraich *or* Curraigh
"Wet plain", from an oblique form of *currach*.

Cushnie (Aberdeen)
This may mean "cold place". Diack (1944) collected the pronunciation "cushĕnĭ", which suggests the

spelling *Cuiseanaidh*, although AÀA recommend *Cuisnidh*. See **Troup Head**.

Cyderhall (Sutherland), Siara
"Sigurd's howe", from Norse. The English form of the name was "Sydera" before the ornate creation of "Cyderhall". This is the burial place of Sigurd Eysteinson, who subjugated Caithness and Sutherland for the Norse.

D

Daan (Ross), Dathan
"Small davoch."

Dailly (Ayr), The English form is an abbreviation of Gaelic, "haugh of the devotee of St Ciaran".

Dailuaine (Banff), An Dail Uaine
"The green haugh."

Dairsie (Fife)
"Oak stance", from *dair* and *fasadh*, giving *Darfhasaidh*. This is also known as Osnaburgh in English.

Dalachale (Banff)
"The kail haugh", from *Dail a' Chàil*.

Dalarossie (Inverness), Dail Fhearghais
"Fergus's haugh." The English version comes from an older Gaelic form with the same meaning, *Dail Fhearghasa*.

Dalavich (Argyll), Dail Abhaich
"Haugh at the water place."

Dalavil (Skye), Dail a' Bhil
This may be "haugh at the rock edge", from Gaelic, or "valley at the rock edge", from Norse/Gaelic.

Dalbagie (Aberdeen), Dail Bàididh
The second element of this haugh name may contain a reference to flooding.

Dalbeattie (Kirkcudbright)
This contains *dail*, "haugh", but the second element is unclear. It is said to be from *beithe*, "birch", but the phonetics do not suggest this. It may represent *biataiche*, "provider of food".

Dalbeg (Lewis), Dail Beag *or* An Daile Beag
"Small valley", from Norse/Gaelic. Dalbeg and Dalmore are together known as *Na Dailean*, "the valleys".

Dalbeth (Glasgow)
This may be "birch haugh", from *Dail Bheithe*.

Dalblair (Ayr)
"The haugh on the plain", from *Dail a' Bhlàir*.

Dalcapon (Perth), Am Baile Ìochdrach
The English form comes from *Dail Ceapan*, which is possibly "the haugh of stumps" and is now the Gaelic name of the place known as Milton of Dalcapon in English. Dalcapon itself is called "the lower farm" in Gaelic.

Dalcataig (Inverness), Dail Cataig
The second element of this haugh or meadow name is unclear.

Dalcharn (Sutherland), Dail Chàirn
"Cairn haugh."

Dalchlachaig (Perth), Dail Chlachaig
"Haugh at the stone place."

Dalchork (Sutherland), Dail Choirce
"Oat haugh."

Dalchosnie (Perth), Dail Chosnaidh
This may be "haugh of the defender or defending".

Dalchreichart (Inverness), Dul Chreachaird *or* Dail Chreachaird
This appears to be "the haugh at the raiding point".

Dalcrombie (Inverness), Dail Chrombaidh
"The haugh at the crooked river."

Dalcross (Inverness), Dealgan Ros
"Thorn point." Influenced by English, a new Gaelic name has arisen for this place, *Dail Chrois*, which appears to mean "cross haugh".

Daldhu (Perth), An Dail Dubh
"The black haugh."

Daldorn (Perth)
This may be "otter haugh", from *Dail Dobhrain* or *Dail Dobhran*, the

former being singular and the latter an old plural form of *dobhran*, "otter".

Dalfad (Aberdeen), An Dail Fhada
"The long haugh." Locally the name was pronounced *An Dail Fhad'*.

Dalgety Bay (Fife), Bàgh Dhealgadaidh
"Bay of Delgaty", which in turn comes from *Dealgadaidh*, "thorny place".

Dalginch (Fife)
"Thorn meadow", from *Dealg Innis*.

Dalginross (Perth), Dealganros
See **Dalcross**.

Dalguise (Perth)
This may be "pine haugh", from *Dail Ghiuthais*.

Dalhalvaig (Sutherland), Dail Healabhaig
"The haugh of Healabhaig", a Norse name possibly meaning 'flat bay'.

Dalharrold (Sutherland), Dail Harraild
"Harald's haugh", in memory of an Earl of Orkney defeated in battle here.

Daliburgh (South Uist), Dalabrog
"Valley fort", from Norse. Until recently this was known as "Dalibrog" in English.

Dalilea (Argyll), Dail an Léigh
"The doctor's haugh." Another Gaelic name is *Dail Eildhe*, the second part of which is unclear and which would be stressed on the first syllable of the second word, thus differing from current Gaelic and English pronunciation.

Dalintart (Argyll), Dail an Tairt
This appears to be "the haugh of the thirst or dryness".

Dalintober (Argyll), Dul an Tobair
"The haugh of the well."

Dalivaddy (Argyll), Dail a' Mhadaidh
"The haugh of the wolf."

Dalkeith (Midlothian), Dail Chéith
"Valley with the wood", from Brythonic.

Dall (Perth), An Dail
"The haugh."

Dallachy (Moray)
"Haugh field or place", from *Dalachaidh* or *Daileachaidh*.

Dallas (Moray), Dalais
"Haugh place." The present village replaced the older Dolais Mychel or *Dalais Mhìcheil*, "Dallas of St Michael", which was located at Torechastle.

Dalleagles (Ayr)
"Church haugh", from *dail* and *eaglais*.

Dallyfour (Aberdeen), Dail a' Phùir
"Haugh at the pasture land."

Dalmagarry (Inverness), Dail Mac Gearraidh
"Gearraidh's son's haugh."

Dalmahoy (Midlothian)
"St MoThua's haugh", from *Dail MoThua*.

Dalmaik (Aberdeen)
"St Mayota's haugh", from *Dul M'Aodhaig*.

Dalmally (Argyll), Dail Mhàilidh
The name is originally from *Dul Mhàilidh*, a haugh name with an unclear second element which is said to be the name of a saint. See **Culmaily** and **Kilmallie**. Glen Orchy Church, which is located here, was *Clachan an Dìseirt* – "the churchyard of the hermitage" – and refers back to an older name, *Dìseart Chonnain*, "St Connan's hermitage". The parish of Glen Orchy was known as *An Dìseart*, "the hermitage".

Dalmarnock (Glasgow, Perth)
"St Ernoc's or M'Ernoc's haugh", from *Dail Mhearnaig*. AÀA recommend *Dail Meàrnaig*.

Dalmellington (Ayr)
"Meling's farm", from English, to which Gaelic *dail*, "haugh", was later prefixed, suggesting that Gaelic replaced English in the area, giving rise to a conjectural Gaelic form

such as *Dail Mheileangtain*, "the haugh at Melingtun".

Dalmeny (West Lothian), Dùn Mheinidh
Although the English name appears to be a haugh name possibly containing the name of the saint commemorated in **Kilmeny**, earlier forms of the name such as "Dunmanyn" and "Dunmany" suggest a hill (fort). The second element may be that found in "Slamannan" and "Clackmannan", giving a conjectural *Dùn Mhanainn* or *Dùn Mhanann* as the original basis of the name. The Gaelic name given above is recommended by AÀA.

Dalmigavie (Inverness), Dail Mhigeachaidh
"Haugh at the marshy hill face."

Dalmore (Lewis), Dail Mór *or* An Daile Mór; (Ross), An Dail Mór; (Sutherland), Dail Mhór
In Lewis, the name means "the big valley", from Norse/Gaelic. See **Dalbeg**. In Ross and Sutherland it is Gaelic, "big haugh".

Dalmuir (Dunbarton), An Dail Mhór
"The big haugh."

Dalmunzie (Perth), Dail Mhungaidh
"Mungo's haugh."

Dalnabreck (Argyll, Perth), Dail nam Breac
"The haugh of the trout." The place in Strathardle in Perthshire was known locally as *Dail na Bric*, which means the same but does not use the genitive case.

Dalnacardoch (Perth), Dail na Ceàrdaich
"The haugh of the smithy." See **Atholl**.

Dalnacloich (Ross), Dail na Cloiche
"The haugh of the stone."

Dalnacroich (Ross), Dail na Croiche
"The haugh of the gallows."

Dalnafree (Sutherland), Dail na Frìthe
"The haugh at the deer forest."

Dalnagairn (Perth), Dail nan Càrn
"The haugh of the cairns", from older *Dail na gCàrn*.

Dalnaglar (Perth), Dail nan Clàr
"The haugh of the slabs", from older *Dail na gClàr*.

Dalnamein (Perth), Dail na Mèinn
"The haugh with the mine or ore."

Dalnaspidal (Perth), Dail na Spideil
"The haugh at the hospice." The old name was simply *An Spideal*, "the hospice or spittal".

Dalnatrat (Argyll), Dail na Tràghad
"The haugh by the beach."

Dalnavert (Inverness), Dail nam Feart
"The haugh of the graves", from older *Dail na bhFeart*.

Dalnavie (Ross), Dail Neimhidh
"The haugh of the sacred place."

Dalnawillan (Caithness)
"The haugh of the mill", from *Dail a' Mhuilinn*.

Dalneigh (Inverness), Dail an Eich
"The horse haugh."

Dalness (Argyll), Dail an Easa
"The haugh at the waterfall."

Dalnessie (Sutherland), Dail an Easaidh
"The haugh at the waterfall place" or "the haugh at the little waterfall".

Dalpatrick (Lanark, Perth), Dail Phàdraig
"Patrick's haugh."

Dalraddy (Aberdeen, Inverness), Dail Radaidh
This may mean "dark or ruddy haugh", from a dialect word, *rodaigh*. A saying concerning the place in Inverness-shire is, *Bha cailleach ann an Dail Radaidh, dh'ith i adag 's i marbh*, "There was an old woman in Dalraddy who ate a haddock while dead". Gaelic sentence structure and gender make it unclear whether it was the woman or the haddock that was dead; a good example of how difficult it is to translate wordplay from one language to another.

Dalreavoch (Sutherland), An Dail Riabhach
"The brindled haugh."

Dalreoch (Ayr, Dunbarton), An Dail Riabhach
"The brindled haugh."

Dalrigh (Perth), Dail Rìgh
"King's haugh." This name may originally have contained *ruigh* (slope), but is now understood to refer to King Robert Bruce after a battle fought here. See **Clifton**.

Dalry (Midlothian); (Ayr), An Dail Fhraoich; (Kirkcudbright), Clachan Eòin
In Ayrshire, this appears to be "the heather haugh", but an alternative derivation may be "the haugh at the slope", from *dail* and *ruigh*, with either derivation being applicable to the place in Midlothian. The village in Kirkcudbright is also known as St John's Town of Dalry and the Gaelic name is simply "St John's village".

Dalserf (Lanark)
"St Serf's haugh", possibly from *Dail Sheirbh.*

Dalswinton (Dumfries)
"Swine farm", from English, to which Gaelic *dail*, "haugh", was prefixed later when Gaelic replaced English in the area, giving rise to a conjectural form *Dail Suantain*, "the haugh at the swine farm".

Dalvey (Moray, Perth)
"Birch haugh", from *Dail Bheithe.*

Dalvorar (Aberdeen), Dail a' Mhorair
"The lord's haugh."

Dalvoulin (Inverness), Dail a' Mhuilinn
"The haugh at the mill."

Dalvraid (Sutherland), Dail a' Bhràghaid
"The haugh at the upland."

Dalwhinnie (Inverness), Dail Chuinnidh
"Warrior's haugh." See **Atholl**.

Dalziel (Inverness, Ross), Dail Ghil; (Perth), Dail Gheollaidh

The name in Inverness and Ross is "white haugh", while in Perth it is "haugh at the white or bright place".

Dandaleith (Moray)
This may be "the hill (fort) of two halves", from *Dùn Dà Leth.*

Danna Island (Argyll), Danna
This Norse island name is unclear.

Dares (Inverness), Daras
"Door." A local measure is *mìle o Dhubhras gu Daras*, "a mile from Dores to Dares".

Dargill, (Perth), Deargail
"Red place" or "red rock".

Darnaway (Moray), Taranaich
"Thunder plain."

Dasher (Stirling)
"South-facing land", from *Deisear.*

Dava (Moray), An Damhath
"The ox or stag ford"

Davaar Island (Argyll), Eilean Dà Bhàrr
"Barr's island."

Davidston (Ross), Baile Dhàidh
"David's farm."

Daviot (Aberdeen); (Inverness), Deimhidh
The Inverness name is cognate with that of the Demetae tribe, similar to *Dyfed* of Wales and is of Brythonic origin. It is unclear whether the Aberdeen name is from the same source.

Davoch (Banff)
A *dabhach* or "davoch" was a measurement of land approximately 400 Scots acres in size.

Deanich (Ross), An Dianaich
"The steep place."

Dechmont (West Lothian), Deagh Mhonadh
This seems to be "good hill", from *deagh mhon(adh)*, but may have had a Brythonic origin.

Deecastle (Aberdeen), Ceann na Coille
The English name is unrelated to the Gaelic one, which means "wood end".

Deeside (Aberdeen, Kincardine), Oir Dhé
"The side or edge of the Dee." Upper Deeside is *Bràigh Dhé*, "the upper part of the Dee", while Lower Deeside is *Inbhir Dhé*, "the mouth of the Dee". The Dee itself is *Uisge Dhé*, "the water of Dee", a name with connotations of divinity, and occurs in the saying, *Spé, Dé is Tatha, na trì uisge as motha fon adhar*, "Spey, Dee and Tay, the three greatest rivers under the sun".

Degnish (Argyll), Daiginis
The first part of this Norse headland name is unclear.

Delavorar (Banff), Dail a' Mhorair
"The lord's haugh."

Delfour (Inverness, Moray), Dail Phùir
See **Dallyfour**.

Delgaty (Aberdeen)
"Thorn place", from *Dealgadaidh*.

Dell (Inverness), An Dail; (Lewis), Dail
In Inverness the name is "the haugh", also known by the full name *Dail MhicEachainn*, "MacEachen's haugh". The Lewis name is "valley", from Norse. In Lewis, North Dell is *Dail bho Thuath*, South Dell is *Dail bho Dheas* and Aird Dell is *Àird Dhail*, "headland of Dell".

Delliefour (Inverness), Dail a' Phùir
See **Dallyfour**.

Dell of Morile (Inverness), Baile nam Bodach
The English name refers to a dale near Morile, while the Gaelic name is "the old men's farm".

Delmore (Inverness)
"The big haugh or valley", from *An Dail Mór*.

Delnabo (Banff), Dail nam Bó
"The haugh of the cows."

Delnadamph (Aberdeen), Dail nan Damh
"The haugh of the oxen or stags."

Delnashaugh (Banff)
"The haugh of the willows", from *Dail nan Seileach*.

Delny (Inverness), Deilgnidh
"Prickly place."

Dennyhogles (Fife)
"Hill (fort) of the church", from *Dùn na hEaglais*.

Derculich (Perth), Dearglaich
"Red place." Upper Derculich is *Dearglaich Uthard*, while the Laigh of Derculich is *Ìochdar Dhearglaich*, "the lower part of Derculich".

Dereneneach (Arran), Doire nan Each
"The oak grove of the horses."

Derraid (Moray), An Doire Roid
"The bog myrtle grove."

Derry (Aberdeen), An Doire
"The oak grove."

Dervaig (Mull), Dearbhaig
This Norse name may be "deer bay". Local people were nicknamed *mathain*, "bears".

Desher (Inverness), Deisear
"North-facing land."

Deskford (Banff), Deasgart
This is pronounced "Deskart" locally and does not refer to a ford. It may be "south field", from Gaelic *deas* and *gart*, but this is uncertain.

Dhoon (Kirkcudbright)
"Hill fort", from *dùn*.

Diabaig (Ross), Dìobaig
"Deep bay", from Norse. Upper Diabaig is *Dìobaig an Àird*, but Gaelic has no specific name for Lower Diabaig. A saying stresses its isolation in earlier times: *'S fhada bhon lagh Dìobaig, 's fhaide na sin sìos Mealbhaig*, "Diabaig is far from the law and Melvaig even further". Locals are known as *cnòdain* or *cnùdanan*, "gurnards". The weather locally is referred to in *Fras agus ialach, earrach muinntir Dhìobaig*, "Showers and sunny spells, the Diabaig people's springtime".

Dibidale (Lewis, Rum), Dìobadal
"Deep valley", from Norse.

Diebidale Forest (Ross), Frìth
Dhìobadail
"Deer forest of Diebidale", which
itself is "deep valley", from Norse.

Dieraclete (Harris), Dìricleit
"Deer cliff", from Norse.

Digg (Skye), An Dìg
"The ditch or furrow." Local people
were nicknamed *bogais*, "bugs" or
"timber moths".

Dingwall (Ross), Inbhir Pheofharain
The English name is "court field",
from Norse. The Gaelic name is
"mouth of the Peffer". The town has
the byname of *Baile a' Chàil*, "the
kail village", anglicised as
"Balechaul". The fair here, formerly
held at Contin, was *Fèill MaRuibhe*,
"St Maol Rubha's fair", while the
fair held in July was *Fèill Choluim*,
referring possibly to Columba.

Dinnet (Aberdeen), Dùnaidh
"Fort place." The English version
seems to derive from an older Gaelic
or possibly Brythonic form. The
Moor of Dinnet is *Sliabh Muileann
Dùnaidh*, "the moor on the mill of
Dinnet".

Dippen (Argyll), Duipinn; (Arran),
An Dipinn
This may be "black pennyland", from
dubh and *peighinn*, or "two pennyland", from *dà* and *peighinn*,
although in both cases one would
expect *f* rather than *p* in the names.

Diriebught (Inverness), Tìr nam
Bochd
"Land of the poor", apparently
because this was owned by the
Church, which donated the profit as
alms to the poor. Originally,
however, this may have been *Doire
nam Bochd*, "oak grove of the poor",
or even *Doire nam Boc*, "oak grove of
the bucks".

Dirnanean (Perth), Doire nan Eun
"Oak grove of the birds."

Divach (Inverness), Dìobhach
The meaning of this name is unclear.

Dochanassie (Argyll), Dabhach an
Fhasaidh
"The davoch at the stance."

Dochcarty (Ross), Dabhach Gartaidh
This may be "the davoch at the place
of the enclosed field".

Dochfour (Inverness), Dabhach
Phùir
"The davoch of pasture land."

Dochgarroch (Inverness), Dabhach
Gairbheach
"The davoch at the rough place."

Dochmaluag (Ross), Dabhach
MoLuaig
"St MoLuag's davoch."

Dochnaclear (Ross), Dabhach nan
Cliar
"The davoch of the clerics."

Dochnalurg (Inverness), Dabhach na
Lurgainn
"The davoch of the shank."

Dola (Sutherland), Dóla
The meaning of this name is unclear,
but may feature a river.

Doll (Sutherland), An Dail
"The haugh."

Dollar (Clackmannan)
This may be "haugh place", from
Dolar.

Dollerie (Perth), Doillearaidh
"Dark place." This name is the oppo-
site of **Soilzarie** or *Soillearaidh* near
Glenshee.

Donavourd (Perth), Dùn a' Bhùird
"The table hill (fort)."

Donibristle (Fife)
This may be "Breasal's or Uí
Bhreasail's fortress", from *Dùnadh
Bhreasail* or *Dùn Uí Bhreasail*.

Doodilmore (Islay), Dudal Mór
The first part of this Norse valley
name is unclear. *Mór*, "big", has been
added possibly to distinguish here
from a *Dudal Beag* which may have
existed at one time.

Dores (Inverness), Dubhras
"Black wood" or "black headland". A

local saying measures *mìle o Dhubhras gu Daras*, "a mile from Dores to Dares".

Dorlin (Argyll), An Dòirlinn
"The tidal isthmus or promontory."

Dornie (Ross), An Dòrnaidh
"The pebble place." Dornie ferry was known as *Aiseag na h-Àirde*, referring to its landing place at Ardelve. Gaelic uses *air an Dòrnaidh* to express "in Dornie".

Dornoch (Sutherland), Dòrnach
"Pebble place." This was known as *Dòrnach na goirt*, "Dornoch of starvation" and the fair held here was *Féill Bharr*, "St Barr's fair".

Dornock (Dumfries)
See **Dornoch**.

Dorusduan (Ross), Doras Dubhain
"Door of the black stream", referring to the mouth of the stream.

Dosmuckeran (Ross), Dos Mucaran *or* Dos Mhucarain
This suggests "thicket of the pig place". Dosmuckeran House is *Taigh Dhos Mhucarain*.

Douglas (Lanark), Dùghlas
"Black stream", from an older *Dubhghlas*.

Dougrie (Arran), An Dubh Gharadh *or* An Dubh Ghearraidh
"The black dyke" or "the black fertile land", though probably the former. Local people were nicknamed *coilich dhubha*, "black cocks".

Doularg (Ayr)
"Black slope", from *Dubh Learg*.

Doune (Perth, Ross), An Dùn
"The hill (fort)." Doune in Perth is known as *Baile an Dùine*, "the town of Doune", and the Braes of Doune are *Bràigh Dhùin*. The fair held here was *Faidhir Dhùin* or *Faidhir Dhùnaidh*.

Doune Carloway (Lewis), Dùn Chàrlabhaigh
"The fort of Carloway", referring to the broch. This township is usually referred to as *An Dùn*, "the hill

(fort)". Local people are referred to in the saying *Muinntir an Dùin, bidh iad fada gun èirigh*, "the people of Doune Carloway never get up early".

Dounie (Perth), An Dùnaidh; (Ross), Dùnaidh
"Hill (fort) place." Easter Dounie in Perthshire is *Dùnaidh Shìos*.

Dounreay (Caithness), Dùnrath
"Fortified mound."

Dowally (Perth)
This may be "place at the black rock", from *Dubhailigh*.

Downies (Perth), Dùnais
"Hill (fort) place."

Draikies (Inverness), Dreigidh
The meaning of this name is unclear.

Drainie (Moray)
"Thorn place", from *Droighnidh*, as in Drynie.

Drem (East Lothian)
"Ridge", from *Druim*.

Drimindarroch (Inverness)
"The ridge of the oak or oaks", from *Druim an Daraich* or *Druim nan Darach*.

Drimnin (Argyll), Na Druimnean *or* Na Drumainean
"The ridges."

Drimsdale (South Uist), Dreumasdal
The first part of this Norse valley name is unclear, although it may be a personal name.

Drishaig (Argyll), Driseig
This appears to be from Gaelic *dris*, "briar" or "bramble", but given its location may be a Norse bay name.

Droman (Sutherland), An Droman
"The small ridge."

Dron (Perth), Drongaidh *or* An Dronn
"Ridge place" or "the ridge". The saying, *Rathad mór leathann réidh, rathad muileann Drongaidh*, "A smooth broad main road, the road to Dron mill", referred to something which did not exist.

Drudaig (Ross), Drùdaig
The first part of this Norse bay name is unclear.

Druimachoish (Argyll), Druim a' Chòthais
"The ridge at the cave or lair."

Druimarbin (Inverness), Druim Earbainn
"Roe-deer ridge."

Druimavuic (Argyll), Druim a' Bhuic
"The ridg of the buck."

Druimdrishaig (Inverness), Druim Driseig
"Briar or bramble ridge."

Drum (Aberdeen, Kinross, Stirling)
"Ridge", from *Druim*. Locally these places would have been known in Gaelic as *An Druim*, "the ridge".

Drumachine (Arran), Druim a' Chaoin; (Perth), Druim a' Chaoine
This may be "smooth ridge".

Drumachloy (Bute)
"The ridge of the burial ground or ditch", from *Druim a' Chlaidh*. An alternative interpretation is *Druim a' Chlaidheimh*, "the ridge of the sword".

Drumadoon (Arran), Druim an Dùin
"The ridge by the hill (fort)." Drumadoon Point is *Rubha a' Bharra*, "the point at the extremity" or *Rubha an Dùin*, "the point at the hill (fort)".

Drumain (Fife)
"Middle ridge", from *Druim Meadhain*.

Drumaird (Fife)
"The high ridge", from *Druim Àrd*.

Drumbane (Perth)
"The fair or fallow ridge", from *An Druim Bàn*.

Drumbeg (Sutherland), An Druim Beag; (West Lothian)
"The small ridge" is the meaning of the name in Sutherland, and the West Lothian name is most likely the same.

Drumblade (Aberdeen)
The first part of this name is Gaelic *druim*, "ridge", while the second may be from Brythonic for "flower" or "blossom".

Drumbowie (West Lothian)
See **Drumbuie**.

Drumbroider (Stirling)
"Bruadar's ridge", from *Druim Bhruadair*.

Drumbuie (Inverness, Ross), An Druim Buidhe
"The yellow ridge", Drumbuie in Ross is known jocularly as *Druim Buidhe nan deargannan*, "Drumbuie of the fleas".

Drumcarro (Fife)
"Rocky or uneven ridge", from *Druim Carrach*.

Drumchapel (Glasgow), Druim a' Chaibeil
AÀA recommend the above form, which is "ridge of the chapel", however, an alternative is "horse ridge", from *druim chapall*.

Drumchardine (Inverness), Druim Chàrdainn
"Copse ridge", from Gaelic/Brythonic.

Drumchork (Ross, Sutherland), Druim a' Choirc
"The oat ridge."

Drumclog (Lanark), Druim Clog
"Rock ridge" composed of Gaelic *druim*, "ridge", and Brythonic *colg*, "rock".

Drumcross (Renfrew), Druim na Croise; (West Lothian), Druim Crois
In Renfrewshire this is "ridge of the cross" but in West Lothian may be "cross ridge".

Drumcroy (Ross), Druim Chruaidh
"Hard ridge."

Drumcudden (Ross), Druim a' Chùdainn
"The ridge of the tub."

Drumdelgie (Aberdeen)
"Prickly ridge", from *druim* and *dealg*, giving a conjectural form of *Druim Dealgaidh*.

Drumderfit (Ross), Druim a Diar
This is said to be "ridge of tears", the
local story being that the old name
was *Druim Dubh*, "black ridge", until
a battle was fought which gave rise
to the saying, *Bu Druim Dubh an-dé
thu, ach's Druim a Deur an-diugh*,
"You were Black Ridge yesterday,
but today you are the Ridge of
Tears". It is more likely, given the
English form, that the second part
originated in Pictish, meaning
something quite different, and
adapted by Gaelic speakers to make
sense to themselves.

Drumdevan (Inverness), An Druim
Dìomhain
"The idle ridge." This is a ridge on
which nothing will grow. *An Druim
Dìomhain* was the original name of
the Drummond area of Inverness
and is the Gaelic name of
Drumduan near Nairn.

Drumdow (Ayr)
"Black ridge", from *Druim Dubh*.

Drumduan (Nairn)
See **Drumdevan**.

Drumduff (West Lothian)
"Black ridge", from *Druim Dubh*.

Drumdurno (Aberdeen)
This may be "pebbly ridge", from
Druim Dòrnach.

Drumfearn (Skye), An Druim
Fheàrna
"The alder ridge." Local people are
known as *coin*, "dogs".

Drumfin (Fife)
"White ridge", from *Druim Fionn*.

Drumforber (Kincardine)
This appears to be "Cairbre's ridge",
from *Druim Chairbre*.

Drumguish (Moray), An Druim
Giuthais
"The pine ridge."

Drumlamford (Ayr)
"Encampment ridge", from *druim*
and *longphort*.

Drumlanrig (Dumfries)
"Ridge at the clearing", from *druim*

and *lannraig*, the latter from
Brythonic *lanerc*.

Drumlean (Perth), An Druim
Leathann
"The broad ridge."

Drumlemble (Argyll), Druim Lèamal
The second element of this ridge
name may be a Norse field name but
is unclear.

Drumloist (Perth), An Druim
Loisgte
Although this is literally "burnt
ridge", this term was used to indicate an ancient cooking site.

Drummin (Inverness), Drumainn
"Ridge place."

Drummond (Inverness), An
Druimein; (Perth, Ross), Drumainn
The Perth and Ross names mean
"ridge place", while the Inverness
name is simply "the small ridge". See
Drumdevan.

Drummonernoch (Perth)
"The Drummond of Earn or
Ireland", from *Drumainn
Éireannach*.

Drummore (Perth, Wigtown), An
Druim Mór
"The big ridge."

Drumnadrochit (Inverness), Druim
na Drochaid
"The ridge at the bridge."

Drumoak (Aberdeen), Druim
M'Aodhaig
"St Mayota's ridge."

Drumochter (Inverness, Perth),
Druim Uachdair
"Top ridge." This is also known as
Druim Uachdair nam Bó,
"Drumochter of the cattle".

Drumore (Argyll, Nairn), An Druim
Mór
"The big ridge."

Drumossie (Inverness), Druim
Athaisidh
"Ridge of the great haugh." Nearby
Loch Ashie is *Loch Athaisidh*.

Drumpellier (Lanark)
This appears to be "ridge of the

spear shafts", but earlier forms of the name point to Brythonic *din*, "fort", as the first element.

Drumrunie (Ross), Druim Raonaidh
"Ridge at the field place."

Drumry (Dunbarton)
"Slope ridge", from *druim* and *ruigh*. Nearby is Kingsridge, the name of which developed through confusion between *ruigh*, "slope", and *rìgh*, "king", which both sound alike. The same confusion occurred in the names of Kingseat and Portree. AÀA recommend *Druim Rìgh*.

Drums (Aberdeen), Druim Airgididh
The English name is "ridges", while the Gaelic name is "ridge at the silver place" or "silver ridge".

Drumsallie (Inverness), Druim na Saille
"The willow ridge."

Drumsleet (Kirkcudbright)
This may be "the ridge of hills", from *druim* and *sléibhte*.

Drumsmittal (Ross), Druim Smiotail
The second part of this ridge name is unclear.

Drumtuthil (Fife)
"Tuathal's ridge", from *Druim Tuathail*, a personal name.

Drumuie (Skye, Sutherland), Druim Muighe
"The ridge on the plain." Drumuie in Sutherland was known as *Druim Muighe a' bhàrr*, "Drumuie of the cream."

Drumullie (Inverness), Druim Mùillidh
"Milling ridge." An alternative derivation given by Watson is *Druim Ulaidh*, "treasure ridge", relating to a tale of treasure known locally.

Drumvaich (Perth)
This appears to be *Druim a' Bhàthaich*, "the ridge of the byre".

Drumwhirn (Kirkcudbright)
This may be "rowan ridge", from *druim* and *caorthann*.

Drunkie (Perth)
This may be "ridge place", from *Drongaidh*, which is a name also found in **Dron**, and was also the earlier name of the place now called Invertrossachs.

Dry Harbour (Raasay), An Acarsaid Thioram
"The dry anchorage."

Drymen (Stirling), Druiminn
"Ridge place."

Drynachan (Nairn), Droighneachan
"Thorn place."

Drynan (Skye), Droighnean
"Thorns."

Drynie (Ross), Droighnidh
"Thorn place."

Drynoch (Skye), An Droighneach
"The thorn place."

Dualin (Perth), Dubh Àilean
"Black meadow."

Duart (Mull, Perth), Dubhaird
"Black headland."

Duartbeg (Sutherland), Dubhaird Bheag
"Small Duart."

Duartmore (Sutherland), Dubhaird Mhór
"Large Duart."

Dufftown (Banff), Baile nan Dubhach
"The town of the Duffs", named after the Duff family of Banffshire. The Gaelic name is recommended by AÀA. Previously the settlement had been known as **Balvenie**.

Duffus (Moray), Dubhais
"Black place."

Duible (Sutherland), Daigheabal
This may be "bog farm", from Norse.

Duiletter (Argyll), An Dubh Leitir
"The black slope."

Duirinish (Ross, Skye), Diùranais *or* Diùirinis
"Deer headland", from Norse. Duirinish in Skye is known as *dùthaich nam mogan*, "land of the mogan shoes", and the locals are called *moganaich*. *Mogan* was a type

of thick stocking incorporating a sole similar to footwear worn by the Saami people. In Ross, the village is known as *Diùranais an eòrna*, "Duirinish of the barley", and is close to *Port an Eòrna* or Barleyport.

Duisdale (Skye), Dùisdeil
The first part of this Norse valley name is unclear, but may be the same personal name as found in **Dusary**. Duisdalebeg is *Dùisdeil Bheag*, "little Duisdale", and Duisdalemore is *Dùisdeil Mhór*, "big Duisdale". The area north of Duisdalemore towards the shore is *Leitir Chaillich*, which suggests "the slope of the nun(s)".

Duisky (Argyll), Dùisgidh *or* Dubhaisgidh
"Black water."

Dull (Perth), Dul
"Haugh" or "meadow". Appin of Dull is *Apainn nam Mèinnearach*, "The Menzies' Appin".

Dullater (Dunbarton, Perth)
See **Duiletter**.

Dulnain Bridge (Inverness, Moray), Drochaid Thulnain
"The bridge over the Dulnain."

Duloch (Fife)
"Black loch", from *Dubh Loch*.

Dulsie Bridge (Nairn), Drochaid Dhulfhasaidh
"The bridge at the haugh place."

Dumbarton (Dunbarton), Dùn Breatann
"Fort of the Britons", as mentioned in the saying, *Trì gearastain na h-Albann – Dùn Breatann, Dùn Chailleann is Madaigein na Mòin*, "Three fortresses of Scotland – Dumbarton, Dunkeld and Rannoch Moor". Dumbarton Rock is *Ail Chluaidh*, "the rock of the Clyde", sometimes *Creag Chluaidh* with the same meaning, and was the capital of the Brythonic territory of Strathclyde. A Perthshire saying claims a very deaf person is *cho bodhar ri Creag Chluaidh*, "as deaf as Dumbarton Rock". Dunbartonshire is *Siorrachd Dhùn Breatann*.

Dumbreck (Glasgow), An Dùn Breac
"The speckled hill (fort)."

Dumcrieff (Dumfries)
"Hill (fort) of the tree(s)", from *dùn* and *craobh*.

Dumfin (Dunbarton), Dùn Fhinn
"Fionn or Fingal's fort."

Dumfries (Dumfries), Dùn Phris
"Hill (fort) at the thicket." However, old forms of the name suggest *druim* or *dronn*, "ridge", rather than *dùn*, "hill (fort)". Dumfriesshire is *Siorrachd Dhùn Phris* and Dumfries and Galloway is *Dùn Phris agus Gall-ghàidheil.*

Dunaad (Argyll), Dùn Athad
"Fort on the Add."

Dunach (Argyll), Dùnach
"Hill (fort) place."

Dunachton (Inverness), Dùn Neachdain
"Nechtan's fort."

Dunain (Inverness), Dùn Eun
This appears to be "birds' hill", but could be "John's hill (fort)", from *Dùn Eathain*. Local Gaelic speakers pronounced the name as *Dùn Ian*. Dunain Mains is *Baile Mór Dùn Eun*, "the big farm of Dunain". Craig Dunain is *Creag Dhùn Eun.*

Dunalister (Perth), Dùn Alasdair
"Alasdair's fort." The old name was *Mùrbhlagan*. See **Murlaggan**.

Dunalunt (Bute)
This is unclear but contains Gaelic *dùn.* The second part may be Norse *há-land*, "high land" or *há-lundr*, "high wood", giving an estimated Gaelic form *Dùn Álannd.*

Dunan (Arran, Skye), An Dùnan
"The hillock."

Dunans (Skye), Na Dùnanan
"The hillocks."

Dunaverty (Argyll), Dùn Àbhartaich
"Àbhartach's fort."

Dunbar (East Lothian), Dùn Barra
This appears to be a Gaelic name meaning "Barr's fort", but given the town's location, this is probably a name of Brythonic origin.

Dunbartonshire (Dunbarton), Siorrachd Dhùn Breatann *or* Siorrachd Dhùn Breatainn
This name, with "Dun-" rather than "Dum-", was created to distinguish the county from the town of Dumbarton. The part of the county between Loch Lomond, Loch Long and the Clyde was known to local Gaelic speakers as *An t-Eilean Leamhnach*, "the Leven Island".

Dunbeath (Caithness), Dùn Beithe *or* Dùn Bheatha(dh)
"Birch hill (fort)" or "Beatha's fort".

Dunbeg (Argyll), An Dùn Beag
"The small hill (fort)."

Dunblane (Perth), Dùn Bhlàthain
"Blane's hill (fort)." Old forms of the name suggest that *dul* (meadow) rather than *dùn* (fort) was the original generic in the name.

Dunbog (Fife)
This looks like a Gaelic name meaning "soft or damp hill", but an older form suggests that it is from *dùn* and *bolg* and means "bag hill", possibly referring to its shape.

Duncansby (Caithness), Dùn Gasbaith
The English version suggests "Duncan's farm". The Gaelic name used by the poet Rob Donn MacAoidh, which contains the term for a hill (fort) and an obscure second element, is simply a gaelicisation of the Norse name and is also applied to Duncansby Head. In North Sutherland Gaelic, Duncansby Head was more recently called *Ceann Dhungain* or *Ceann Dhonnchaidh*, "Duncan's head".

Duncanstown (Ross), Bog a' Mhiodair
The Gaelic name is "the bog at the pasture land", but since *miodar*, "pasture land", is similar to the word for a mitre, a local story arose about a bishop losing his mitre in the bog here.

Duncow (Dumfries)
"Hazel hill", from *Dùn Coll* which in modern Gaelic would be *Dùn Choll*. An old form of the anglicised name, "Duncoll", shows this derivation very clearly.

Duncraig (Ross), Dùn na Creige
"Hill of the rock." This name is fairly recent and supplanted the earlier *Am Fasadh Àlainn*, "the beautiful spot".

Dundarave (Argyll), Dùn Dà Ràmh
This appears to mean "fort of two oars", but may have become corrupted over the centuries.

Dundas (Stirling, West Lothian), Dùn Deas
"South hill (fort)."

Dundee (Angus), Dùn Deagh *or* Dùn Dé
It was believed that this contained a personal name based on "fire", but it is now believed that the second part of the name is a byform of "Tay" or *Tatha*, giving an overall meaning of "fort on the Tay". Dundee was known to Gaelic speakers in Aberdeenshire as *Baile Ailleag*, whose meaning is unclear.

Dundonald (Ayr, Fife)
"Donald's hill (fort)", from *Dùn Dòmhnaill*.

Dundonnell (Ross), An Srath Beag, An Locha Beag *or* Achadh Dà Dhòmhnaill
The English name is "Donald's fort", from an older Gaelic form, *Dùn Dòmhnaill*. The first Gaelic name is "the little strath", and the second is "the little loch", also the name of Little Loch Broom. The third Gaelic name is "the field of two Donalds". Dundonnell Lodge is *An t-Eilean Daraich*, "the oak island", while Dundonnell Hotel is *Taigh-òsta an t-Sratha Bhig*, "the hotel of the small strath".

Dun Dornadilla (Sutherland), Dùn Dornaigil
This mixed Gaelic/Norse name is "hill (fort) at the thorny ravine".

Dundreggan (Inverness), Dul Dreagain
"Dragon haugh", a term used to denote a warrior or hero.

Dundrennan (Kirkcudbright)
"Thorn hill", from *dùn* and *droighnean.*

Dunduff (Ayr, Fife)
"Black hill (fort)", from *Dùn Dubh.*

Dundurcus (Moray)
"The hill (fort) at the place of boars", from *Dùn Turcais.*

Dundurn (Perth), Dùn Dùirn
"Fort of the fist", a former Pictish stronghold.

Dunearn (Fife); (Nairn), Dùn Éireann
In Nairn this is "hill (fort) on the Findhorn", but in Fife may be a commemorative name and be "the hill (fort) of Ireland".

Dunfermline (Fife), Dùn Phàrlain
This is generally understood to be "Pàrlan's fort", a personal name usually anglicised as "Bartholomew". However, the name is older and possibly tribal or belonging to a kin-group.

Dungainachy (Benbecula), Dùn Gainmheacha
"Sandy hill."

Dungavel (Ayr)
"Forked hill", from *dùn* and *gobhal.*

Dunglass (Berwick, East Lothian)
"Grey-green hill", from either Gaelic or more probably Brythonic.

Dunhallin (Skye), Dùn Hàlainn
"Hill (fort) of Hallin."

Dunidea (Perth), Dùnaidh Dé
This name may mean the same as "Dundee", although it appears to mean "fortress of god" or "fortress on the Dee". See **Dundee**.

Dunino (Fife)
This may be "the fort on the prominent hill", from *Dùn an Aonaich.*

Dunira (Perth), Dùn Iarath
"Hill (fort) at the west ford."

Dunkeld (Perth), Dùn Chailleann
"Hill (fort) of the Caledonians", a tribal name also occurring in "Rohallion" and "Schiehallion". The name occurs in the saying, *Trì gearastain na h-Albann – Dùn Breatann, Dùn Chailleann is Madaigein na Mòin*, "Three fortresses of Scotland – Dumbarton, Dunkeld and Rannoch Moor".

Dunlichity (Inverness), Dùn Fhlicheadaidh
"Hill (fort) of Flichity."

Dunlop (Ayr), Dùn Lob
"Puddle hill" as recommended by AÀA, however an alternative may be found in "hill at the bend", from *Dùn Lùib.*

Dunlossit (Islay), Dùn Losaid
"Hill by the Lossit."

Dunlugas (Aberdeen)
This may be "slug hill", from *Dùn Lùgais.*

Dunmaglass (Inverness), Dùn Mac Glais *or* Dùn Mach Glais
This appears to be "the fort of Glas's son".

Dunmore (Fife, Perth, Stirling); (Argyll), An Dùn Mór
"The big hill (fort)."

Dunneaves (Perth), Taigh Neimhidh
"The house at the sacred place."

Dunnet (Caithness), Dùnaid
Although the Gaelic name suggests "hill (fort) place", the origin of this name may be Norse, given its location in north-east Caithness.

Dunnichen (Angus), Dùn Eachainn
The Gaelic form suggests "Eachann's hill (fort)", but the original was *Dùn Neachdain*, "Nechtan's hill (fort)", as this is near the site of the 7th-century battle at Nechtansmere or *Linn Garan.*

Dunnivaig (Islay), Dùn Naomhaig
"Naomhag's or Naomhan's fort."

Dunollie (Argyll), Dùn Olla *or* Dùn Ollaigh
"Onlach's or Ollach's fort."

Dunoon (Argyll), Dùn Omhain
"Hill (fort) on the river." Locally the name was pronounced *Dùn Omhaigh.*

Dunork (Fife)
"Hill (fort) of the swine", from *Dùn Orc.*

Dunottar (Kincardine)
This may be "fort on the shelving slope", from *dùn* and *fothair.* The name was previously "Dunfoeder", which may indicate a Pictish cognate of *fothair.*

Dunphail (Moray), Dùn Fàil
"Palisade fort."

Dunragit (Wigtown), Dùn Reicheit
"The fort of Rheged", a Brythonic territory before the arrival of the Scots.

Dunringell (Skye), Dùn Ruingeil
This Gaelic/Norse name may be "fort at the rough ravine".

Dunrobin (Sutherland), Dùn Robain
"Robin's fort" was known as *Dùn Robain a' chàil,* "Dunrobin of the kail".

Duns (Berwick)
Although the name refers to a hill, it is not clear whether it was coined in Anglian, Brythonic or Gaelic, and any one is possible.

Dunscore (Dumfries)
If this is a Gaelic name, it may mean "hill (fort) at the pinnacle".

Dunsgaith (Skye), Dùn Sgàthaich
"The fort of Sgàthach", a witch who trained Cù Chulainn in the martial arts, according to legend in both Scotland and Ireland.

Dunsinane (Perth), Dùn Seunain
This name may refer to the fort of someone called Seunan or Seanan.

Dunskeath Ness (Ross), Rubha Dhùn Sgàth
"Promontory at the fort of Sgàth", which may be a personal name also found in **Dunsgaith** in Skye.

Dunskellar (North Uist), Dùn Sgealair
This Gaelic/Norse name is "fort by the sheilings".

Dunstaffnage (Argyll), Dùn Stafhainis
"Fort by the staff headland", from Gaelic/Norse.

Duntarvie (West Lothian)
"Hill (fort) at the bull place", from *Dùn Tarbhaidh.*

Duntelchaig (Inverness), Dùn Deilcheig
"Snail hill."

Duntocher (Dunbarton), Dùn Tòchair
"Fort at the causeway", however, an earlier form of the name was "ridge at the causeway", from *Druim Tòchair.*

Duntroon (Argyll), Dùn Treò *or* Dùn Treòin
This fort may have been named after someone called *Treun,* "mighty".

Duntulm (Skye), Dùn Tuilm *or* Dùn Thuilm
"Fort at the island", from Gaelic *dùn* and Norse *holmr,* "island".

Dunure (Ayr), Dùn Iubhair
"Yew hill."

Dunvegan (Aberdeen), Dùn Bheathagain *or* Dùn Mheagain; (Skye), Dùn Bheagain
In Skye this is "Beagan's fort", and Dunvegan Head is *Ceann Dùn Bheagain.* The Aberdeenshire names, although spelled differently, may be from the same source.

Dunvornie (Ross), Dùn Bhoirinidh
"Hill (fort) in the stony place." In County Clare in Ireland is a geologically and botanically well-known area called *an Bhoireann,* "the stony place", called the Burren in English. This appears to be the same word as in the Ross name.

Dupplin (Perth), Dubh Linn
The Gaelic name suggests "black pool", which is also the origin of "Dublin".

Durie (Fife)
"Water place", from *Dobharaidh*,
earlier *Dobharan*.

Durine (Sutherland), Dubhrinn
"Black headland." See **Durness**.

Durnamuck (Ross), Doire nam Muc
"The oak grove of the pigs."

Durness (Sutherland), Diùirnis *or*
Diùranais
"Deer headland", from Norse. An
alternative name was *Dubhrinn*,
"black headland", which still exists
as the Gaelic origin of "Durine". The
area as a whole is known as *Am
Machair* or *A' Mhachair*, and a resi-
dent of the area is known as a
Machaireach, "low-land person".

Durno (Aberdeen)
This may be "pebbly place", from
Dòrnach.

Duror (Argyll), Dùror *or* Dùrar
"Hard water." The complete name is
Dùror na h-Apann, "Duror of
Appin", where the old church was
called *Cill Chaluim Chille* and dedicated to St Columba. The unusually
named Pineapple House was originally known as *Taigh an Tuim*, "the
house at the hillock".

Durris (Kincardine), Duras *or* Dòrs
This may be "black wood".

Dusary (North Uist), Duthasaraidh
This Norse field name may contain
the same personal name as in
"Duisdale".

Dutchman's Cap (Mull), Am Bac
Mór
The island's shape gave rise to its
English name, but the Gaelic means
"the big bank", from Norse *bakki*,
"bank".

Duthil (Inverness), Daothal
This may be a byform from *tuathail*,
"north side", but see **Culduthel**.

Dyke (Moray), Dìg
"Ditch" or "furrow". The parish was
known as *Sgìre Dhig*.

Dysart (Fife), An Dìseart
"The hermitage."

E

Eaglescairnie (East Lothian)
This may be "church at the cairn
place", and although it can be inter-
preted from Gaelic sources as
Eaglais Chàrnaidh, it is possibly
Brythonic given its location.

Eaglesfield (Dumfries)
"Church field", from Gaelic or
Brythonic with English "field".

Eaglesham (Renfrew)
"Church homestead", from Gaelic or
Brythonic with English "ham".

Eagleton (Lewis), Baile na h-Iolaire
or Cnoc na h-Iolaire
The Gaelic names are "eagle farm"
and "eagle hill", although the Gaelic
names are probably translations
from an original English.

Earlish (Skye), Eàrlais
This Norse name may be "earl's river
mouth" or "earl's ridge".

Earshader (Lewis), Iorseadar *or*
Iarsadar
"Beach farm" or "Ævarr's farm", from
Norse. Local pronunciation
collected by Oftedal (1954) suggests
Iarsadar as the preferable spelling.

Easdale (Easdale), Éisdeal
"Horse dale", from Norse.

East Calder (West Lothian), Caladar
an Ear
Calder is "hard water", from
Caladar, a common river name
throughout Scotland. East Calder is
part of a larger area, along with
Midcalder and West Calder.

Easter Ross (Ross), Ros an Ear
This eastern part of Ross is also
known in Gaelic as *Taobh Sear Rois*,
"the east side of Ross", although this
is not used locally.

Easterton (Perth), Easgardan
"East farm", from English, of which
the Gaelic is an adaptation.

Eastertyre (Perth), Ìochdar Thìre
"Bottom of the land." The English
is an adaptation of the Gaelic
name.

Easter Tulloch (Inverness), Baile nan Cròigean *or* Baile nan Groigean
The present Gaelic name is said locally to mean "farm of the puddocks". It is in the east part of Tulloch and was earlier known as *Tulach Ìochdarach*, "lower Tulloch".

East Kilbride (Lanark), Cille Bhrìghde an Ear; (South Uist), Taobh a' Chaolais
The English name is "St Bridget's Church" with "east" added to distinguish these places from West Kilbride. In Lanarkshire the Gaelic name is the same and differentiates this place from West Kilbride in Cunninghame. In South Uist the Gaelic name is "the side of the strait", referring to the place's location on the shore of the Sound of Barra. The English name distinguishes it from the next township, known in English as West Kilbride but in Gaelic as simply *Cille Bhrìghde*, "St Bridget's Church" or "Kilbride".

Eathie (Ross), Àthaigh
"Ford place" Upper Eathie is *Bràigh Àthaigh*, "upper part of Eathie".

Ebost (Skye), Eubost
"Isthmus farm", from Norse.

Ecclefechan (Dumfries)
This is most likely Brythonic for "small church".

Eccles (Berwick)
"Church", originally from Brythonic rather than Gaelic *eaglais*.

Ecclesmachan (West Lothian)
"St Machan's Church", from Gaelic *Eaglais Mhachain* or Brythonic sources. Locally the place was also known as "Inchmachan", from *Innis Mhachain*, "St Machan's haugh or meadow".

Echline (West Lothian)
"Paddock", from *eachlann*.

Edderton (Ross), Eadardan
"Between-fort", from *eadardùn*. Edderton Farm is *Baile nam Foitheachan*, "farm with the lawns or greens". The area between Tain and Edderton is *A' Mhorbhaich* or *A' Mhormhoich*, "the carse".

Eddleston (Peebles)
"Edulf's farm", from English. This place has had several names, reflecting the linguistic groups who settled here. The oldest was Brythonic *Penteiacob*, "the head of Jacob's house", followed by "Gilmertoun", "Gillemhoire's farm", from English but containing a Gaelic personal name. Finally came the English name, which developed into the present form.

Eddrachillis (Sutherland), Eadarra-Chaolas *or* Eadar Dhà Chaolas
"Between two straits."

Ederline (Argyll), Eadarlinn
"Between two pools", from *Eadar dhà Linn*.

Edinample (Perth), Aodann Ambail
"Hill face by the vat or cauldron."

Edinbane (Skye), An t-Aodann Bàn
"The white hill face." Upper Edinbane is *An Uaig*, possibly "the cave".

Edinburgh (Midlothian), Dùn Éideann
"Eidyn's fort", from Brythonic *Din Eidyn*, of which the Gaelic name is a cognate form which was part-translated into English to form "Edinburgh". It is commonly believed that the English name is "Edwin's burgh", but the name existed before English language and names were introduced into the area.

Edinchip (Perth), Aodann a' Chip
"The hill face with a block or stump."

Edingight (Banff)
"The windy hill face", from *Aodann na Gaoithe*.

Edinkillie (Moray)
"The hill face at the wood", from *Aodann na Coille*.

Edinvillie (Banff)
"The hill face at the rock edge", from *Aodann a' Bhile.*

Edra (Perth), Eadarra-leacach *or* Eadar Dhà Leacach
This is "between two slab-places", and the English form used to reflect more accurately its Gaelic origins, being recorded as "Edraleachdach" into the 20th century.

Edrachalda (Sutherland), Eadarra-chalda *or* Eadar Dhà Chalda
"Between two Caldas", referring to the land between rivers Calda Beag and Calda Mór. The river name is Norse for "cold river".

Edradour (Perth), Eadarra-dhobhar *or* Eadar Dhà Dhobhar
"Between two rivers."

Edradynate (Perth), Eadarra-dhoimhnid *or* Eadar Dhà Dhoimhnid
"Between two deep places."

Edragoul (Perth), Eadarra-ghobhal *or* Eadar Dhà Ghobhal
"Between two forks."

Edramucky (Perth), Eadarra-mhucaidh *or* Eadar Dhà Mhucaidh
"Between two pig places."

Edzell (Angus), Éigill
The meaning of this name is unclear.

Eigg (Eigg), Eige
This may be "notch", referring to the shape of Sgùrr Eige or to the depression running across the island. Eigg was known as *Eilean nam Ban Móra*, "the island of the great women", and a native of the island is an *Eigeach*, also nicknamed a *fachach*, "puffin".

Eilanreach (Inverness), An t-Eilean Riabhach
"The speckled island."

Eilean Aigas (Inverness), Eilean Àigeis
"The island or meadow of Aigas."

Eilean Anabuich (Harris), An t-Eilean Anabaich
"The unripe island", referring to poor soil.

Eilean Clourig (Sutherland), Eilean Clobhraig
This may be Norse "clover bay" or "cleft bay", with Gaelic for "island" attached. This is often seen on maps as *Eilean Cluimhrig.*

Eilean Fladday (Raasay), Eilean Fhladaigh
"Flat island", from Norse, with Gaelic "island" attached.

Eilean Imersay (Islay), Eilean Iomarsaigh
This Norse island name may contain a personal name with Gaelic "island" attached.

Eilean Loain (Argyll), An t-Eilean Lòmhain
The meaning of this island name is unclear.

Eilean Tigh (Raasay), Eilean Taighe
"House island."

Eishken (Lewis), Éisgean
This Norse name may contain "ash tree".

Elachnave Islands (Argyll), Na h-Eileacha Naomha
"Holy rocks."

Elchies (Moray), Eileachaidh
"Rocky place." The English name is a plural.

Elcho (Perth)
This is said to be "stony or rocky place", from *ailcheach.*

Eldrable (Sutherland), Eilldreabal
"Beacon farm" or "altar farm", from Norse.

Elgin (Moray), Eilginn
"Ireland." *Eilg*, like *Banbh, Éire* and *Fótla*, was a byname for Ireland, attached by the Scots to many places during their settlement. An area of Elgin was known as "Little Ireland" until recently. A native of Elgin was known as an *Eilgneach*, the same term applied to Glenelg people. The full Gaelic name is *Eilginn Mhoireibh*, "Elgin of Moray", and it is called *Eilginidh* in Wester Ross.

Elgol (Skye), Ealaghol
This may be a Norse name for a field, and might include the word for wild angelica.

Elie (Fife)
If this is a Gaelic name it means "landing place", from *Ealaidh*. From neighbouring Earlsferry there was a sea link to Lothian. In Mull there is also a coastal place known as *An Ealaidh*, "the landing place".

Elishader (Skye), Eiliseadar
"Dwelling by the cave", from Norse.

Ellenbeich (Seil), Eilean na Beithich
"Island of the birchwood", but the name was understood locally to have been *Eilean nam Beathach*, "island of the cattle/farm animals".

Ellister (Islay), Aolastradh
"Dwelling by the cave", from Norse.

Ellon (Aberdeen), Eilean
"Meadow." *Eilean* is normally "island" but the meaning was extended to cover "meadow" as was also the case with *innis*.

Elphin (Sutherland), An Ailbhinn
"Rock peak."

Elrick (Aberdeen)
"Deer trap", from *Eilreig*.

Elrig (Wigtown)
"Deer trap", from *Eilreig*.

Embo (Sutherland), Éireabol
This seems to be "beach farm", from Norse, but an older form, "Ethenboll", suggests "Eyvind's farm" originally, also from Norse. Embo was *Éireabol nan coileagan*, "Embo of the cockles".

Enaclete (Lewis), Einicleit
"Brow cliff", from Norse.

Englishtown (Inverness), A' Ghall Bhaile
The Gaelic name is "the non-Gaels' farm".

Enoch (Dumfries, Renfrew), An Eanach
"The bog" which is the derivation recommended by AÀA in preference to *aonach* which can be "hill", "market place" or "moor".

Enochdhu (Perth), An t-Aonach Dubh
"The black moor or hill."

Ensay (Harris), Easaigh
"Ewe island", from Norse.

Enzie (Banff), An Éinne *or* An Éinnidh
"The angular piece of land."

Eochar (South Uist), An t-Ìochdar
See **Iochdar**.

Eoligarry (Barra), Eòlaigearraidh
This Norse name might be "pasture land of wild angelica".

Eorodale (Lewis), Eòradal
"Jórunn's valley", from Norse.

Eoropie (Lewis), Eòrapaidh
"Jórunn's farm", from Norse.

Eorsa (Mull), Eòrsa
"Beach island", from Norse.

Erbusaig (Ross), Earbarsaig
"Erp's bay", from Norse, although apparently containing a non-Norse personal name. The place was known as *Earbarsaig nan con clomhach*, "Erbusaig of the scabby dogs".

Erchite (Inverness), Earchoighd
"Wood side", probably from Pictish.

Erchless (Inverness), Earghlais
"River side."

Eriboll (Sutherland), Éireabol
"Beach farm", from Norse.

Eriska (Argyll), Aoraisge
"Erik's island", from Norse.

Eriskay, Éirisgeigh
"Erik's island", from Norse. Eriskay is known as *Eilean na h-Òige*, "island of youth", and a native of the island is an *Éirisgeach*.

Erista (Lewis), Eireasta
This Norse name appears to mean "farm at Harris", and lies close to the boundary between Uig and Harris.

Erracht (Inverness), An t-Eireachd
"The meeting place."

Erradale (Ross), Earradal
"Beach valley." North Erradale is *Earradal a Tuath* or *Earradal Shìos*, the latter being "lower Erradale",

and South Erradale is *Earradal a Deas* or *Earradal Shuas*, the latter being "upper Erradale". Inver in Erradale is *Inbhir Earradail*. The coast from North Erradale to Aultgrishan is *A' Chipeanach*, "the stump place".

Erraid (Mull), Eilean Earraid
"Foreshore island." This is similar to the pre-Norse name of Shona.

Errogie (Inverness), Earaghaidh *or* Earagaidh
It is unclear whether this name contains *aghaidh*, "hill face".

Ersary (Barra), Earsaraidh
This may be "beach field", from Norse.

Erskine (Renfrew), Arasgain
This apparently Brythonic name is unclear but may contain an element meaning "side".

Eskadale (Inverness), Éisgeadal
"Ash valley", from Norse. Eskadale Square is *Càrn a' Ghobhainn*, "the smith's cairn".

Eskechraggan (Bute), Easg a' Chreagain
"The fen at the small rocky or rocky place."

Esknish (Islay), Easganais
This is most likely "ash point", from Norse.

Essengael (Perth), Easan Geal
"White or bright streamlet."

Essendy (Perth)
"Place at the streamlet", from *easan* with a locative or diminutive ending such as *Easandaidh*, a formation regularly found here.

Essich (Inverness), Easaich
"Stream or waterfall place."

Esslemont (Aberdeen)
"Low hill", from Brythonic *iselfynydd* or Gaelic *Ìosal Mhonadh*.

Essmitchell (Perth)
"Michael's or Mitchell's waterfall or stream", from *Eas Mhìcheil*, earlier *Eas Mìcheil*.

Ethie (Angus)
"Ford place", from *Àthaigh*.

Ettrick (Bute), Atrag *or* Atraig
This name is unclear but seems to be of Norse origin, containing either *vík*, "bay", or *hryggr*, "ridge". Lower Ettrick is *Atrag/Atraig Ìochdarach* and Upper Ettrick is *Atrag/Atraig Uachdarach*.

Ettridge (Inverness), Eadrais
"Between two streams or waterfalls", from an older *eadar dà eas*.

Evanton (Ross), Am Baile Nodha *or* Am Baile Ùr
The English name is "Ewan's village" while the Gaelic names are both "the new village", to distinguish it from the older settlement across the river.

Evelix (Sutherland), Éibhleag
"Ember", referring to a sparkling stream. The English form has a plural ending.

Ewe Island (Ross), Eilean Iubh
"The island of Ewe", meaning "yew".

Ewich (Perth), Iubhaich
"Yew wood." *Deòradh a' Choigrich*, "the keeper of St Fillan's staff", lived here.

Exmagirdle (Perth)
"St MoGhrill's Church", from *Eaglais MoGhrill*, commemorating one of Columba's disciples.

Eye Peninsula (Lewis), An Aoidh
"The isthmus", from Norse. This area is also known as *An Rubha*, "Point". People from here are *Rubhaich*, also *sùlairean*, "gannets".

Eynort (Skye), Aoineart
"Sea loch at the isthmus", from Norse.

Eyre (Raasay), Eighre
"Beach" or "sand spit", from Norse.

F

Faddoch (Ross), An Fhàdaich
"The place of peat sods."

Faichem (Inverness), Faicheam
This may contain *faiche*, "lawn" or

"green". Lower Faichem is *Faicheam Ìosal* and Upper Faichem is *Faicheam Àrd*.

Faillie (Inverness), Fàille
This name may refer to "sods", as in **Artafallie**. Faillie was known as *Fàille grianach Srath Narann*, "sunny Faillie of Strathnairn".

Fain (Ross), Na Féithean
"The bog channels."

Faindouran (Banff)
This may be "the bog channel of the otter" or "the channel of the little river", from *Féith an Dobhrain*.

Fairybridge (Skye), Beul-àtha nan Trì Allt
The English name is a reminder of the Fairy Flag in Dunvegan Castle, while the Gaelic name is "the ford of the three streams".

Falkirk (Stirling), An Eaglais Bhreac
"The speckled church." The name of this place was first recorded as "Ecclesbrith", from Brythonic, meaning "speckled church". As Gaelic replaced Brythonic, the cognate Gaelic form, *An Eaglais Bhreac*, superseded it. This was later translated into Scots "Fawkirk" with the same meaning, later amended to the present English form. The Latin, *Varia Capella*, has the same meaning. A Wester Ross form of saying "clear off" is *Thoir an Eaglais Bhreac ort*, "get yourself to Falkirk".

Falkland (Fife), Fàclann
Although generally believed to represent "falcon land", from English, this name is now believed to derive from *Falclann*, with connotations of washing or scrubbing.

Falside (Sutherland), Feallasaid
"Mountain sheiling or dwelling", from Norse.

Fanagmore (Sutherland), An Fheannag Mhór
This appears to be "the large lazybed", a lazybed being a narrow strip of cultivable soil built up in rocky ground.

Fanmore (Sutherland), Am Fàn Mór
"The large slope."

Fannyfield (Ross), Am Bog Riabhach
The English name commemorates the daughter of a former prorietor, while the Gaelic name is "the brindled bog".

Faolin (Ross), An Fhaoilinn; (Skye), Fadhlainn *or* Faolainn
"Field or stony place by the shore."

Farlary (Sutherland), Fàrrlaraidh
The meaning of this name is unclear.

Farness (Ross), Feàrnais
"Alder place."

Farout Head (Sutherland), An Fharaird
"The projecting headland." The English name is a corruption and has "head" added.

Farquhar's Point (Argyll), Rubha Fhearchair
The English form is a translation from Gaelic.

Farr (Inverness, Sutherland), Fàrr
The meaning of this name is unclear. The Farr Stone at Bettyhill in Sutherland is *Clach Fhearchair*, "Farquhar's stone".

Fasach (Skye), Fàsach *or* Am Fàsach
"(The) wilderness." Upper Fasach is *Bràigh an Fhàsaich*, "the upper part of Fasach".

Fasag (Ross), Am Fasag
"The place or stance."

Fasagrianach (Ross), An Fhasadh Chrìonaich
"The place of the rotten tree." Local people were *muinntir na Fasadh Chrìonaich*, showing an unusual genitive form.

Fascadale (Argyll), Faisgeadal
The first element of this originally Norse valley name is unclear.

Faskally (Perth), Fas-Choille
This appears to mean "wood place" with the stress on the initial syllable.

Fasnacloich (Argyll), Fas na Cloiche
"The place of the stone."

Fasnakyle (Inverness), Fas na Coille
"The place by the wood."

Fasque (Kincardine), Fàsg
It is unclear what this name means.

Fassfern (Inverness), Am Fasadh Feàrna
"The alder place."

Fassock (Perth), Am Fasadh
"The place or stance."

Fealar (Perth), Féith Làir
This may be "ground channel".

Fearder (Aberdeen), Féith Àrdair
"Bog channel of the Arder."

Fearn (Ross), Manachainn Rois
The English name is "alder", from
Gaelic *feàrn*. The Gaelic name is
"the monastery of Ross", distin-
guishing it from *Manachainn Mhic
Shimidh*, "Lovat's monastery", at
Beauly. Fearn is recorded as *Nova
Farina* in Latin. Easter Fearn is
Feàrn Àrd, "high Fearn", Wester
Fearn is *Feàrn Ìochdarach*, "lower
Fearn", and Mid Fearn is *Feàrn
Meadhanach*. Hill of Fearn is *Baile
an Droma*, "township on the ridge",
while the parish of Fearn is *Sgìre na
Manachainn*, "the parish of the
monastery". The market here was
Féill na Manachainn, "the market of
the monastery" or "Fearn market".

Fearnach (Argyll), Feàrnach
"Alder place."

Fearnan (Perth), Feàrnan
"Alders." The old name was *Sròn
Feàrnain*, "promontory of Fearnan",
and the churchyard was *Cladh na
Sròine*, "the graveyard at the
promontory".

Fearnbeg (Ross), Na Feàrna Beaga
"The small alders." Local people are
known as *eireagan*, "pullets".

Fearnmore (Ross), Na Feàrna Móra
"The large alders." Local people are
known as *coin*, "dogs".

Fearnoch (Argyll), An Fheàrnach
"The alder place", which is located
in Cowal.

Fearns (Raasay), Na Feàrnaibh;
(Ross), Na Feàrna *or* Na Feàrnan
"The alders." In Raasay, North
Fearns is *Na Feàrnaibh a Tuath* and
South Fearns is *Na Feàrnaibh a
Deas*. In Ross, Fearns comprises
Fearnbeg and Fearnmore, and local
people are known as *tùchanaich*,
"hoarse folk".

Feaull (Coll, Skye), Feall
"Mountain", from Norse. In Coll a
byword for a detour was *Rathad
Feall do dh'Ameireaga*, "to America
via Feaull".

Febait (Ross), An Fhéith Bhàite
"The drowned bog channel."

Fender Bridge (Perth), Drochaid
Aindridh
The English name refers to the
River Fender, while the Gaelic name
is "Andrew's bridge".

Fendom (Ross), Na Fànaibh
"The gentle slopes."

Fenechrich (Inverness), Féith na
Crìche
"The bog channel at the boundary."

Feochaig (Argyll), Feòchaig
This Norse name refers to a bay, but
the first element is unclear.

Feolin (Jura), Fadhlainn *or* Faolainn
"Field or stony place by the shore."
An older name was *Aoireann a'
Chaoil*, "the raised beach at the
narrows".

Feorlig (Skye), Feòirlig
"Farthing land." This place was
known as *Feòirlig na crèadha*,
"Feorlig of the clay or clay-rich soil".

Feorlin (Argyll), Feòirling
"Farthing land."

Feorline (Argyll), Feòirling; (Arran),
An Fheòrlainn
"The farthing land."

Ferindonald (Ross, Skye), Fearann
Dòmhnaill
"Donald's land."

Feriniquarrie (Skye), Fearann
MhicGuaire
"MacQuarrie's land."

Ferintosh (Ross), Sgìre na Tòiseachd
The Gaelic name is "the chief's district", while the English name is from an earlier Gaelic form, *Fearann na Tòiseachd* , "the chief's land".

Fernaig (Ross), Feàrnaig
"Alder place."

Ferness (Nairn)
"Alder place," from *Feàrnais.*

Fernilea (Skye), Fearann an Leagha *or* Fearann an Lighiche
"The doctor's land."

Fernoch (Argyll), Feàrnach
"Alder place."

Ferntower (Perth), Cùilt Rainich
The Gaelic name may be "secluded place of bracken".

Fersit (Inverness), Fearsaid Mhór *or* An Fhearsaid
"Large sand spit" or "the sand spit".

Ferter (Ayr)
"Fortress", from *fartair.*

Feshiebridge (Inverness), Drochaid Fhéisidh
"Bridge over the Feshie."

Fetterangus (Aberdeen)
"Angus's shelving or terraced slope", from *Fothair Aonghais.*

Fettercairn (Kincardine), Fothair Chàrdainn
"Shelving or terraced slope at the copse", containing Pictish *carden.*

Fetteresso (Kincardine)
This may be "waterfall slope", from *fothair* and *easach*, as suggested by an earlier anglicised form of the name, "Fodresach".

Fetterletter (Aberdeen)
"Terraced or shelving slope", from *fothair* and *leitir.*

Fetternear (Aberdeen)
This may be "west shelving slope", from *fothair an iar.*

Fiaray (Barra), Fiaraigh
"Ebb-tide island", from Norse.

Fidden (Mull), Na Fìdean
"The sea meadows", from Norse with a Gaelic plural.

Fiddes (Kincardine)
This may be "wood place", from *Fiodhais.*

Fidigarry (Lewis), Fidigearraidh
"Fertile sea meadow", from Norse.

Fife (Fife), Fìobh *or* Fìobha
This appears to be an old tribal or personal name, and first appears as *Fib*, one of the divisions of Pictland. Fife Ness is *Rubha Fìobha*, "the headland of Fife". A Fife person is a *Fìobhach.*

Finaltan (Ross), Na Fionnalltan
"The fair streams."

Finary (Islay), Fìneairigh
The first element of this Norse name is unclear, while the second denotes a field or sheiling.

Finavon (Angus)
"Wooden sanctuary or sacred lands", from *Fiodh Neimheadh.*

Fincastle (Perth), Fonn a' Chaisteil
"The land of the castle."

Findhorn (Moray), Inbhir Éireann
"The mouth of the Findhorn." The Culbin Sands are *Bar Inbhir Éireann*, "the sand bar of the mouth of the Findhorn".

Findochty (Banff), Fonn Dhoichtidh
Fonn can mean "lands" and the second element may be the genitive form of a name. Locally the name is pronounced approximately as "Finnichty" with the stress on the second syllable. Gaelic speakers in Braemar and Upper Banffshire recorded by Diack (1944) pronounced the name as "fanna-güchti", with the stress on the third syllable.

Findo Gask (Perth)
A *gasg* is a projecting tail or strip of land. The first element may refer to Findoca, a saint commemorated locally.

Findon (Ross), Fionndun *or* Fionndan
"White hill (fort)."

Findrassie (Moray), Fiondrosaigh
"Place of the great wood."

Finegand (Perth), Féith nan Ceann
"The stream of the heads", from
earlier *Féith na gCeann*.

Finlaggan (Islay), Port an Eilein
The English name comes from
Gaelic *Fionn Lagan*, "white hollow",
which was attached in corrupted
form to the nearby loch as *Loch
Bhìollagain*. The Gaelic name is "the
island port", referring to *Eilean na
Comhairle*, "the island of the coun-
cil", in the loch where *Comhairle nan
Eilean*, "the Council of the Isles"
met during the Lordship of the
Isles.

Finlarig (Angus)
"White pass", from *Fionn Làirig*.

Finmont (Fife)
"White or fair upland", from *Fionn
Mhonadh*. This name is also found in
Kininmonth.

Finnart (Argyll, Perth), Fionnaird
"White point." Finnart Lodge in
Perthshire is *Dail MhicRath*,
"MacRae's haugh", and Finnart
Church is *Eaglais a' Bhràighe*, "Brae
Church", referring to Brae
Rannoch.

Finsbay (Harris), Fionnasbhagh
"Finn's bay", from Norse.

Fintray (Aberdeen)
"White settlement", from Gaelic
fionn, "white", and *treabh*, a gaelicisation of Brythonic *gwyn* and *tref*.

Fintry (Angus, Stirling)
See **Fintray**.

Finzean (Aberdeen), Fìnnean
It is unclear what this name means.

Fionnphort (Mull), Fionnphort
"White harbour."

Firmor (Ross), An Fhaighear Mhóir
"The great raised beach."

First Coast (Ross), An t-Eirtheaire
Shìos
"The lower coast."

Fiscary (Sutherland), Fiosgairidh
"Fish sheiling", from Norse.

Fisherfield (Ross), Innis an Iasgaich
The Gaelic name is slightly different
as "the fishing meadow".

Fishnish (Mull), Finnsinis
"Fish point", from Norse.

Fiskavaig (Skye), Fiosgabhaig
"Fish bay", from Norse.

Fiunary (Argyll), Fionnairigh
"White sheiling."

Fivepenny (Lewis), Na Cóig
Peighinnean
"The five-penny land." The full name
of Fivepenny near Borve is *Cóig
Peighinnean Bhuirgh* while in Ness it
is *Cóig Peighinnean Nis*.

Fivig (Lewis), Fìbhig
"Sheep bay", from Norse.

Fladabay (Harris), Fleòideabhagh
"Float bay", from Norse.

Fladda (Mull), Flada
"Flat island", from Norse.

Fladda-chuain (Skye), Flada a'
Chuain
"Flat island of the Minch", from
Norse/Gaelic.

Flanders Moss (Stirling), A'
Mhòinteach Fhlànrasach
"The Flanders peat moss", a
reminder that many Flemish people
settled in the east of the country.
Flanders itself is *Flànras, Flannras*
and *Flairisg* in Gaelic.

Flannan Isles (Lewis), Na h-Eileanan
Flannach
This may be "the red islands".

Flashader (Skye), Flaiseadar
"Flat farm", from Norse.

Fleenas (Nairn), Flìonais
The meaning of this name is unclear.

Fleenasnagael (Nairn), Flìonais nan
Gàidheal
"Fleenas of the Gaels."

Flesherin (Lewis), Na Fleisirean
"The flat skerries", from Norse.

Flichity (Inverness), Flicheadaidh
"Wet place." A saying warns, *Fhad's
a bhios an t-allt aig Flicheadaidh a'
ruith dhan taobh tuath, bidh mallachd
air Flicheadaidh*, "As long as the

Flichity stream runs northwards, Flichity will be cursed". The hotel here was known as *Taigh an Àilein*, "the house on the meadow". Nearby is *Dùn Fhlicheadaidh* or Dunlichity, "hill (fort) of Flichity".

Flisk (Fife)
This may be from *fleasg*, "withe", found as a river name in Ireland. Nearby is Fliskmore, "big Flisk", probably from *Fleasg Mòr*.

Flodda (Benbecula), Flodaigh
"Float island", from Norse.

Flodday (Barra, Benbecula), Flodaigh
"Float island", from Norse.

Floddaybeg (North Uist), Flodaigh Beag
"Little Flodday", from Norse/Gaelic.

Floddaymore (North Uist), Flodaigh Mór
"Big Flodday", from Norse/Gaelic.

Flodigarry (Skye), Flòdaigearraidh
"Wet meadow or pasture land", from Norse.

Flowerdale (Ross), Am Baile Mór
The English name is "flower dale", and the Gaelic name, "the big farm". Flowerdale House is *An Taigh Dìge* or *An Taigh Gìge*, "the moat house", the full name being *Taigh Dìge nan Gorm Leac*, "moat house with the blue slates".

Fluchlady (Ross), Fliuch Leathadaidh
"Wet slope place."

Fochabers (Moray), Fachabair *or* Fothabair
The meaning of this name is unclear, although it contains an element suggesting marshy or muddy land.

Fodderletter (Banff, Moray), Foirleitir; (Nairn), Farrleitir
"Terraced or shelving slope", from *fothair* and *leitir*. In Banffshire, Easter Fodderletter is *Foirleitir Shìos*, while Wester Fodderletter is *Foirleitir Shuas*.

Fodderty (Ross), Fodhraitidh
"Lower fort place."

Foindle (Sutherland), An Fhionndail
"The fair valley or haugh."

Fonab (Perth), Fonn an Aba
"The abbot's land."

Ford (Argyll), Àth na Crà *or* An t-Àth
"The ford with the salmon trap" or "the ford". Local people were nicknamed *coin-odhar*, "otters".

Fordell (Fife)
"Over-haugh", from *Fordail*.

Fordie (Perth), An Fhardail
"The over-haugh."

Fordoun (Kincardine), Fordun
"Over-fort." This is a Gaelic equivalent of the Brythonic/Pictish-based "Gourdon" situated further south.

Forest Lodge (Argyll), Taigh na Frìthe
The type of forest referred to here is a treeless deer forest, *frìth* in Gaelic from French *forêt*.

Forfar (Angus), Baile Fharfair *or* Farfar
This may be "shelving slope". The Gaelic name has *baile*, "town", attached.

Forgandenny (Perth)
"Eithne's place above the bog", from *Forgrann Eithne*.

Forgie (Banff)
This may be "shelving slope at the marsh" or "windy shelving slope", from *Fothair Gaoithe*.

Formartine (Aberdeen), Fearann Mhàrtainn
"Martin's land."

Formont (Fife)
"Great or projecting hill", from *Formhon(adh)*.

Forneth (Perth), Fòraist
The English name seems to come from an older Gaelic name while the current Gaelic name is a gaelicisation of "forest".

Fornighty (Nairn), Achadh Ghoididh
The Gaelic name is "the field of theft", but the English name which was recorded earlier as "Fathenachten" is unclear but may contain the personal name *Neachdan*.

Forres (Moray), Farrais
"Small copse."

Forsinain (Sutherland), Forsain Fhàn
"Lower Forsain", containing Norse
fors, "waterfall".

Forsinard (Sutherland), Forsain Àrd
"Upper Forsain", containing Norse
fors, "waterfall".

Forss (Caithness)
"Waterfall", from Norse *fors*.

Fort Augustus (Inverness), Cille
Chuimein
The English name commemorates
William Augustus, the Duke of
Cumberland, whose troops won the
Battle of Culloden. The Gaelic name
is "St Cuimein's Church", a saint
also commemorated in the original
form of **Kirkcolm**.

Forter (Angus), Fortair
"Fortress."

Forteviot (Perth), Fothair Tabhaicht
"Tabhacht's shelving slope." This
was the capital of the southern Picts.

Fort George (Inverness), An
Gearasdan *or* Dùn Deòrsa
The English and second Gaelic
name refer to King George of
Britain, on the throne when this fort
was built in 1748. The first Gaelic
name is a gaelicisation of English
"garrison" and is also the Gaelic
name of Fort William.

Forth Valley (Stirling), Srath For
"Valley of the Forth." *For*, the river's
name in Perthshire Gaelic, was
applied to the lower stretches of the
river only, the upper part being
known as *An Abhainn Dubh*, "the
black river".

Fortingall (Perth), Fartairchill
"Fort church." The markets held
here were *Féill Ceit nan Gobhar*, the
goat market in December, *Féill Ceit
an Fhrois*, the seed market in April
and *Féill MoChoid*, the lamb market
in August. The first two markets are
said to commemorate St Catherine,
but the August fair is dedicated to

St Coedi. In fact, all three may originally have been dedicated to this
saint, who is also commemorated in
nearby Coshieville.

Fortrie (Aberdeen, Banff)
"Big settlement", from Gaelic/
Brythonic *for* and *treabh*, giving
Foirtreabh.

Fortry (Aberdeen, Banff)
See **Fortrie**.

Fortrose (Ross), A' Chananaich
The English name may be "over-
headland" or "great headland",
from Gaelic, while the Gaelic
name is "the chanonry", after the
religious settlement here which led
to Fortrose being poetically termed
Cananaich nan clag, "Fortrose of
the bells". Chanonry Point is
Rubha na Cananaich or *Gob na
Cananaich*.

Fort William (Inverness), An
Gearasdan
The current English name refers to
the fort at Achintore named after
William of Orange. The town then
became known as Maryburgh after
William of Orange's wife until it
came into the hands of the Duke of
Gordon and was renamed
Gordonsburgh. Later, it was named
Duncansburgh after Sir Duncan
Cameron of Fassfearn, and lastly
reverted to its current English name
in memory of the Duke of
Cumberland. The Gaelic name is a
gaelicisation of "garrison" and, as this
is also one of the names of Fort
George, has a more complete
version in *Gearasdan Loch Abar*, "the
garrison of Lochaber".

Foss (Perth), Fasadh
"Place" or "stance".

Fossoway (Kinross), Fasadh Mhaigh
This may be "stance plain".

Foula (Shetland)
"Bird island", from Norse.

Foulford (Perth), Am Féith Salach
"The dirty bog channel."

Fourpenny (Sutherland), Na Ceithir Peighinnean
"The four pennylands", referring to a land measurement.

Foveran (Aberdeen), Fobharan
"Place of wells."

Fowlis (Aberdeen, Angus, Perth, Ross), Foghlais *or* Fólais
"Small stream" or "sub-stream".

Foxhole (Inverness), A' Bhogsolamh *or* A' Bhog-Solla
The Gaelic name is not clear, but may refer to damp ground and willow trees, and the English name is an adaptation from Gaelic.

Fox Point (Ross), Rubha a' Mhadaidh Ruaidh
The English form is a translation from Gaelic.

Foy (Ross), An Fhothaidh
"Lawn", from *faiche*. Foy Lodge, also known as Inverbroom Lodge, is *Taigh na Fothaidh*.

Foyers (Inverness), Foithear
"Shelving slope." The Falls of Foyers are *Eas na Smùide*, "the smoky waterfall". The Laird of Foyers was *Fear Foithreach*.

Foynesfield (Nairn), Seipeil Fhìonain
The Gaelic name is "Finnan's Chapel" rather than "field".

Fraserburgh (Aberdeen), A' Bhruaich
The English name commemorates Sir Alexander Fraser of Philorth in the 16th century. Earlier the place had been known as Faithlie in English as well as the local name, The Broch. The Gaelic name means "the bank", and is an attempt by Gaelic speakers to substitute a Gaelic word for an unclear English one, in this case, "broch".

Freeburn (Inverness), Allt na Frìthe
"The stream by the deer forest." The English name is a part-translation from Gaelic.

Frendraught (Aberdeen)
This appears to be "the land at the bridge", from *Fearann na Drochaide*.

Fresgill (Caithness), Freisgil
"Noisy gully", from Norse.

Freuchie (Fife), Fraochaidh
"Heather place", also the old name of Grantown on Spey in Moray.

Friesland (Coll), Freaslan
This name commemorates Friesland in the Netherlands.

Friockheim (Angus)
This was earlier "Friock", from *fraoch*, "heather", until German *heim* was added in the 19th century by the landowner.

Frobost (South Uist), Fròbost
This Norse farm name contains an unclear initial element.

Fuday (South Uist), Fùideigh
The first part of this Norse island name is unclear.

Fuiay (Barra), Fùidheigh
"House island", from Norse.

Furnace (Argyll, Ross), An Fhùirneis
"The furnace" was an early industrial site. Furnace in Argyll was earlier known as *Inbhir Leacainn* or Inverleacain, "river mouth at the broad hill face".

Fyal (Perth), Féith Mheall
"Boggy channel among the lumpy hills."

Fyrish (Ross), Faoighris
This may be from Norse, containing the word for "pine tree".

Fyvie (Aberdeen)
This name has been the cause of much speculation and it is possible that a diminutive form of *fiodh*, "wood", is its origin, but not in the sense of a forest, which is *coille* in Gaelic. A 13th-century spelling, "Fyuin", in which *u* stands for *v*, is of little help.

G

Gaick (Inverness), Gàdhaig
"Cleft." Gaick is known as *Gàdhaig nam feadan fiar*, "Gaick of the crooked streams", and features in the saying, *'S mór a b' fheàrr leam a bhith*

an Druim Uachdair na bhith an Gàdhaig nan creagan gruamach, "I would rather be in Drumochter than in Gaick of the gloomy crags". A local curse was *Dìol Bhaltair an Gàdhaig ort*, "Walter's fate in Gaick to you", referring to Walter Comyn, who was pecked to death here by eagles. An incident known as *Call Ghàdhaig* occurred in 1799 when a party of people perished here in a storm.

Gairloch (Ross), Geàrrloch
"Short loch." Gairloch Hotel was known as *Taigh-òsta Acha Deuthasdal* and the Old Inn was *Taigh-òsta Cheann an t-Sàil*. The Strath of Gairloch is *Srath Gheàrrloch*. Local people are known as *truisg*, "cod".

Gairlochy (Inverness), Geàrr Lòchaidh
"The short Lochy."

Gairnshiel (Aberdeen), Àirigh Gharthain
"Sheiling at the Gairn."

Gallanach (Argyll), A' Ghallanach; (Coll), A' Ghallanaich
"The coltsfoot place" or "the place of the standing stone".

Gallan Head (Lewis), Gob a' Ghallain *or* An Gallan Ùigeach
Gallan is a standing stone, prominent rock or headland and *gob* is a beak. The second Gaelic name is "the Uig headland".

Gallin (Perth), Gealainn
"White or bright place."

Gallovie (Inverness), Gealaghaidh
"White or bright hill face."

Galloway (Kirkcudbright, Wigtown), Gall-ghàidheil
"Foreign Gaels", referring to Gaels of mixed Gaelic-Scandinavian origin. The Mull of Galloway is *Maol Ghall-ghàidheil*, "rounded headland of Galloway", or *Maol nan Gall*, "rounded headland of the non-Gaels"; the Machars are *Machair Ghall-ghàidheil*, "plain of

Galloway"; and the Rhinns are *Ranna Ghall-ghàidheil*, "divisions of Galloway", or *Na Rannaibh*, "divisions".

Galltair (Inverness), Galltair
This name is unclear but may contain *Gall*, "non-Gael". Previously the definite article was used, so that the name was *An Galltair*. See also **Rhigolter**.

Galmisdale (Eigg), Galmasdal
This Norse valley name appears to contain a personal name as its first element.

Galson (Lewis), Gabhsunn
"Pig sound", from Norse. North Galson is *Gabhsunn bho Thuath* and South Galson is *Gabhsunn bho Dheas*.

Galtrigill (Skye), Galtraigil
This may be "hog ravine", from Norse.

Ganavan (Argyll), A' Ghaineamh Bhàn
"The white sand."

Garbat (Ross), An Garbh Bad
"The rough copse." Garbat Forest is *Frìth a' Gharbh Bhaid*.

Garbole (Inverness), An Garbhbaill
"The rough boll", from *garbh* and *boll* referring to the amount of seed required to sow the land.

Garelochhead (Dunbarton), Ceann a' Gheàrrloch
"The head of the short loch."

Garenin (Lewis), Na Gearrannan
"The fertile lands by the sea."

Gargadale (Arran), Gargadail
"Warriors' valley", from Norse.

Garguston (Ross), Baile Ghargaidh
"Gargach's township."

Garioch (Aberdeen), Gairbheach
"Place of roughness." The Battle of Harlaw is known in Gaelic as *Cath Gairbheach*, "Battle of Garioch", showing that *Gairbheach* does not decline in the genitive case.

Garlogie (Aberdeen)
"Short Logie", from *Geàrr Lagaidh*.

Garmond (Aberdeen)
This may be "rough hill", from *Garbh Mhon(adh)*.

Garmoran (Argyll, Inverness), A' Gharbh Mhorbhairne
"The rough sea gap" or "rough Morvern".

Garmouth (Moray), A' Ghairmich
It is unclear whether this name originated in Gaelic or in English. The village is near the mouth of the Spey, and this may be reflected in the English form of the name. However, if the Gaelic name is original, the English may be a corruption or rationalisation of a name based on "calling", possibly with reference to the sound of the Spey or the sea.

Garnock Valley (Ayr)
See **Glen Garnock**.

Garrabost (Lewis), Garrabost
"Enclosed farm", from Norse.

Garrafad (Skye), An Garradh Fada
This may be "the long field", from Norse *garðr* and Gaelic *fada*.

Garrick Bridge (Ross), Drochaid Gharaig
"Bridge over the Garag."

Garrisdale (Canna), Gàrrasdal
"Field valley", from Norse.

Garros (Skye), Gàrros *or* Gearas
"River mouth at the enclosed field", from Norse.

Garrydhu (North Uist), An Gearraidh Dubh
"The black fertile land."

Garrygall (Barra), An Gearraidh Gadhal
This name refers to fertile land but the defining element is unclear.

Garrygannichy (South Uist), Gearraidh Gainmheacha
"Sandy fertile land."

Garryhallie (South Uist), Gearraidh Sheilidh
"Fertile land with willows."

Garscadden (Glasgow), Gart Sgadain
This appears to be "herring field",

but the *sgadan* element may have become corrupted.

Garscube (Glasgow), Gart Sguaib
"Sheaf field."

Gartally (Inverness), Car Dàlaidh
This name may refer to a "rock ledge" and a "haugh".

Garthbeg (Inverness), Gart Bheag
"Small Garth." *Gart* is an enclosed field.

Gartchonzie (Perth)
This appears to be "Kenneth's field", from *Gart Choinnich*.

Gartcosh (Lanark)
This field name from *gart*, with a second element maybe from *còs*, "cave" or "hollow", gives "field at a cave or hollow".

Gartenbeg (Inverness), An Gairtean Beag
"The small enclosed field."

Gartenmore (Inverness), An Gairtean Mór
"The large enclosed field."

Garth (Perth), Gart
"Enclosed field." The castle here is *Caisteal Ghairt*, "Garth Castle", but was also known as *Caisteal a' Chuilein Chursta*, "castle of the cursed whelp", referring to the son of the Wolf of Badenoch.

Garthonzie (Stirling)
This may be "Kenneth's field", from *Gart Choinnich*.

Gartincaber (Perth)
This may be "the field of the stakes or horns", from *Gart nan Cabar*.

Gartloch (Lanark)
"Enclosed field by the loch", from *Gart Locha*.

Gartloist (Islay), An Gart Loisgte
"The burnt enclosed field."

Gartly (Aberdeen), Gartaidh
Based on the Gaelic form of the name, this appears to be "field place" or "small field", from *gart*. However, older forms of the name suggest that *Gar an Tulaich*, "the den at the green hill", is the derivation of the name which is the same as that of Grandtully in Perthshire.

Gartmore (Perth), An Gart Mór
"The large enclosed field."

Gartnatra (Islay), Gart na Tràgha
"Enclosed field by the beach."

Gartnavel (Glasgow), Gart nan Abhall
"Enclosed field of the apple trees."

Gartness (Stirling), Gart an Easa
"Enclosed field by the stream."

Gartocharn (Dunbarton), Gart a' Chàirn
"Enclosed field with a cairn."

Gartsherrie (Lanark)
This may be "colt field", from *Gart Searraigh*, an older form of modern *Gart Searraich*, but *Searrach* here may be a personal name.

Gartymore (Sutherland), Gartaidh Mór
"Big field place."

Garvaig (Ross), Garbhaig
"Small rough place" or "small rough stream".

Garvald (East Lothian)
This seems to be "rough stream", from *Garbh Allt*, although AÀA recommend *An Garbh-Allt*.

Garvamore (Inverness), An Garbhath Mór
"The large rough ford."

Garvan (Argyll), An Garbhan
"The small rough one", referring to a stream or piece of land.

Garve (Ross), Gairbh
"Rough place." The Strath of Garve is *Srath Ghairbh* and the loch is *Loch Mhaol Fhinn*, "loch of Fionn's devotee". Local people were called *buic*, "bucks".

Garvellachs (Argyll), Na Garbh Eileacha
"The rough rocks."

Garvock (Fife)
"Rough place", from *Garbhag*.

Garynahine (Lewis), Gearraidh na h-Aibhne
"The fertile land by the river."

Garynamonie (South Uist), Gearraidh na Mònadh

"The fertile land by the peat." The slope leading southwards up to Garynamonie is called *Bruthach Donnchaig*, called "Duncan's brae" in English.

Garyvard (Lewis), Gearraidh a' Bhàird
"The poet's fertile land."

Gask (Aberdeen, Fife, Perth), Gasg
"Projecting tail or strip of land."

Gaskan (Inverness), An Gasgan
"The tail-shaped piece of land."

Gatehouse (Islay), Taigh na Geata
"The house at the gate."

Gaza (Ross), Gàsa
This is a biblical reference prompted by the sandy hills here.

Geanies (Ross), Gàthan
"Sea ravine", from Norse, with Gaelic then English plurals attached.

Geary (Skye), Geàrraidh
"Fertile land."

Gearymore (Skye), An Gearraidh Mór
"The large piece of fertile land."

Geddes (Nairn), Geadais *or* Geadas
"Place of the plot of land."

Gedintailor (Skye), Gead an t-Sailleir
"Plot of the salter."

Gedloch (Moray)
This may be "plot place", from *Geadlach*. It is not a loch name.

Geisgeil (Sutherland), Gìsgil
"Gushing ravine", from Norse.

Gella (Angus)
"White ford", from *Gealath*.

Gellovie (Inverness), Gallabaidh
This name is unclear and appears not to be the same as **Gallovie**.

Gelston (Kirkcudbright)
"Gillìosa's farm", from English with a Gaelic personal name meaning "devotee of Jesus".

Genachil (Aberdeen), An t-Seann Choille
"The old wood." The local pronunciation is reflected in the spelling *An t-Seana Choill*.

Geocrab (Harris), Geocrab
"Crab ravine", from Norse.

Georgetown (Perth), Na Barrags
The English name commemorates a
King George, while the Gaelic is a
transliteration of "barracks".

Gergask (Inverness), Garbh Ghaisg
"Rough tail of land projecting from
a plateau." A ditty about names of
various neighbouring districts goes,
*Tha cóig bothan an Loch Abar, cóig
gasgan ann am Bàideanach 's cóig
cóigean ann an Srath Éireann*, "There
are five boths in Lochaber, five gasgs
in Badenoch and five cóigs in
Strathdearn". The gasgs, which are
tails of land projecting from a
plateau, are Gergask, Gasga Mhór,
Gasga Bheag, Drumgask and Gasg
an Lóin.

Gerinish (South Uist), Géirinis
This Norse name may mean "pasture
headland". East Gerinish is *Caolas
Liubharsaigh*, "strait of Liursay",
while West Gerinish is simply
Géirinis.

Geshader (Lewis), Géiseadar
"Goat township", from Norse. Local
pronunciation as collected by
Oftedal (1954) suggests a preferable
spelling of *Géiseadair*.

Gesto (Skye), Geusdo *or* Geusto
"Goat farm" or "goat harbour", from
Norse.

Gigalum (Gigha), Gioghalum *or*
Gigealam
"Holm of Gigha."

Gigha (Gigha), Giogha
"God's island", from Norse. A Gigha
person is a *Gioghach*, also nicknamed
a *gamhainn*, "stirk".

Gighay (Barra), Gioghaigh
"God's island", from Norse.

Gilberts Bridge (Perth), Drochaid
Ghilbeart
Both names mean the same thing.

Gillen (Skye), Na Gilean
"The ravines", from Norse with a
Gaelic plural.

Gilmerton (Midlothian, Perth)
"Gillemoire's farm", from English
but with a Gaelic personal name
meaning "devotee of Mary".

Gilston (Midlothian, Moray)
"Gille's farm", from English, but
with a Gaelic personal name meaning "devotee".

Girvan (Ayr), Inbhir Gharbhain
This was previously Invergarvane,
from the Gaelic name meaning
"mouth of the rough river". The
current English name is simply that
of the river.

Gisla (Lewis), Giosladh
"Hostage river" or "Gisl's river",
from Norse.

Gizzen Briggs (Ross), Drochaid an
Obh
The English name of this sandbar is
"leaky bridge", from Norse, while
the Gaelic name also refers to a
bridge allegedly once linking Ross
and Sutherland.

Glackour (Ross), A' Ghlaic Odhar
"The dun-coloured hollow."

Gladsmuir (East Lothian), Sliabh a'
Chlamhain
"The kestrel moor", from Scottish-
English gled, "kestrel". The Battle of
Prestonpans in Gaelic is *Blàr Sliabh
a' Chlamhain*, "battle of Gladsmuir".

Glaick (Ross), A' Ghlac
"The hollow."

Glame (Raasay), Glàm
This may be a form of *glòm*, "chasm".

Glamis (Angus), Glàmais
This may be "chasm place".

Glascarnoch (Ross), A' Ghlas Càrnach
This may be "the rocky hollow" or
"hollow of cairns".

Glasgo (Aberdeen)
See **Glasgow**. The village of
Blackburn was formerly known as
Broadford of Glasgo, and the local
area contains names such as
Glasgoforest and Glasgoego, the
latter apparently containing the
surname Eggo (*Ciogach* in Gaelic).

Glasgow (Lanark), Glaschu
"Green hollow", from Brythonic. In
Perthshire Gaelic the name was
pronounced as *Glasgu*.

Glasnakille (Skye), Glas na Cille
"The stream at the church."

Glasphein (Skye), A' Ghlaispheinn
"Grey-green pennyland", from an original *A' Ghlas Pheighinn*. This place is
commemorated in a song, *Suirighe na
Glaispheinn*, "the wooing of Glasphein".

Glass (Aberdeen)
"Stream" or "meadow", from *glas*.

Glassans (Islay), Na Glasfhasadhnan
"The grey-green stances."

Glassard (Colonsay), Glasaird
"Grey-green headland."

Glassaugh (Banff)
"Grey-green place" or "grassy land",
from *Glasach*.

Glassel (Kincardine)
This may be "grey-green place", from
Glasail.

Glassert (Perth)
See **Glassard**.

Glassingall (Perth)
This may be "the stream of the non-
Gaels", from *Glas nan Gall*.

Glecknabae (Bute)
This appears to be "the hollow of the
birch", from *Glac na Beithe*.

Gledfield (Ross), Leth Chlamhaig *or*
Lòn na Speireig
The English name is "kestrel field",
from Scottish-English gled,
"kestrel". The first Gaelic name is
"the half strath of the kestrel", and
the second is "wet meadow of the
sparrowhawk".

Glen (Barra), An Gleann
"The glen."

Glenachulish (Argyll, Inverness),
Gleann a' Chaolais
"The glen at the narrows."

Glen Affray (Perth), Gleann Aifrinn
"The glen of the offering."

Glen Affric (Inverness), Gleann Afraic
"The glen of the Affric." This glen
contains *Coille Ruigh na Cuileig*,

"wood at the midge slope", the largest remaining portion of the
Caledonian Forest.

Glen Allachie (Banff), Gleann
Aileachaidh
"The glen at the rocky place."

Glen Alladale (Argyll), Gleann
Athaladail
This may mean "eel valley", from
Norse with *gleann* added.

Glen Almond (Perth), Gleann Amain
"The glen of the Almond."

Glen Ample (Perth), Gleann Ambail
"The glen at the cauldron or vat."

Glenapp (Ayr)
"Alpin's glen", from *Gleann Ailpein*.

Glen Aray (Argyll), Gleann Aora
"The glen of the Aray."

Glen Arklet (Stirling), Gleann
Aircleid
"The glen of the difficult slope."

Glen Aros (Mull), Gleann Àrois
"Glen at the river mouth", from
Gaelic/Norse.

Glen Artney (Perth), Gleann
Artanaig
This may be "Artanag's glen", based
on old Gaelic *art*, "bear".

Glen Ashdale (Arran), Gleann
Éisdeal
"Ash valley", from Norse with
gleann, "glen" attached. The Gaelic
name looks coincidentally like that
of the island of Easdale, but comes
from a different source.

Glen Aven (Banff), Gleann Athainn
"The glen of the very bright river."
In earlier literature, the Gaelic name
was given as *Gleann Athfhinn*.

Glen Baloch (Inverness), Gleann a'
Bhealaich
"The glen at the pass."

Glen Banchor (Inverness), Gleann
Bheannchair
"The glen at the horned place."

Glenbarr (Argyll), Am Bàrr
The Gaelic name is "the summit" or
"the hill", while the English may be
from an older Gaelic form meaning,

Gleann a' Bhàrr, "the glen at the summit/hill".

Glen Barton (Dumfries)
This may be "the glen of the Britons", from *Gleann Breatann*.

Glen Batrick (Jura), Gleann Badraig
"The glen at pasture bay", from Gaelic/Norse.

Glenbeg (Moray), An Gleann Beag
"The small glen."

Glen Bernisdale (Skye), Gleann Bheàrnasdail
"The glen of Bernisdale."

Glenbervie (Kincardine)
"The glen of the boiling water", from *Gleann Biorbhaigh*.

Glen Birnie (Midlothian)
"The glen at the damp place", from *Gleann Braonaigh*.

Glen Borrodale (Argyll), Gleann Bhorghdail
"Fort valley", from Norse with *gleann* added.

Glen Breakerie (Argyll), Gleann Breacairidh
If this name is wholly Gaelic, it is "the glen at the speckled place", but if Gaelic/Norse, it means "the glen at the slope field or sheiling".

Glenbreck (Peebles)
"Speckled glen", from *An Gleann Breac*.

Glen Brerachan (Perth), Gleann Bhriathrachain *or* Gleann Briathrachain
"The glen of the little talkative stream."

Glen Brittle (Skye), Gleann Breadail
This may be "broad valley", from Norse, with *gleann* added.

Glen Buchat (Aberdeen), Gleann Buichead
"Buichead's glen."

Glen Buckie (Perth), Gleann Bucaidh
"The glen of the buck stream."

Glen Callater (Aberdeen), Gleann Chaladair
"The glen of Callater." See **Aberchalder**.

Glen Calvie (Ross), Gleann Chailbhidh
This may contain *calbh*, "plant stalk", and mean "glen at the plant stalk place". A Glen Calvie person is a *Cailbheach*, "Calvie person".

Glen Cannel (Mull), Gleann Cainneir
"St Cainnear's glen."

Glencaple (Dumfries)
"Horse glen", from *Gleann Capall*, which in present-day Gaelic would be *Gleann Chapall*.

Glen Carragrich (Harris), Gleann Tharmasaig
The defining elements in the English and Gaelic names are unclear, but the Gaelic name ends in Norse "bay".

Glen Cassley (Sutherland), Gleann Charsla
"The glen at the castle place."

Glenchromag, (Bute), Gleann Chromaig
"The glen of Cromag", which in turn means "bent or crooked place".

Glen Clova (Angus), Gleann Chlàbhaidh
The meaning of this glen name is unclear.

Glen Cloy (Arran)
This appears to be *Gleann Cloiche*, "stony glen", but an alternative interpretation is that the name is *Gleann Clothaidh*, a contraction of *Gleann MhicLothaidh*, "Fullarton's glen", referring to the Fullartons of Kilmichael.

Glencoe (Argyll), Gleann Comhann *or* Gleanna Comhann
"The glen of the Coe." This is often said to be "glen of weeping" as a result of the Massacre of Glencoe but the name existed long before that event as the river name appears to be pre-Gaelic. Glencoe Village is *A' Chàrnach*, "the stony place", the English name being a fairly recent invention.

Glen Conon (Skye), Gleann
Chonnain
This appears to be "valley of St
Connan".

Glen Convinth (Inverness), Gleann a'
Chonfhadhaich
"The glen in the stormy place."

Glencorse (Midlothian), Gleann
Crosg
"Glen of the crossings."

Glen Creran (Argyll), Gleann
Creurain
The second part of this glen name is
unclear.

Glen Cribesdale (Argyll), Gleann
Creabasdail
This may be "cliff valley", from
Norse, with *gleann* added.

Glen Crossaig (Argyll), Gleann
Chrosaig
"Valley of cross bay", from Gaelic/
Norse.

Glendale (Skye, South Uist), Gleann
Dail
A Gaelic/Norse name with both
elements meaning "valley". In South
Uist, North Glendale is *Ceann a
Tuath Ghlinn Dail* and South
Glendale is *Ceann a Deas Ghlinn
Dail*. A native of Glendale in Skye is
a *Daileach*, while the old church
there is *Cill Chomhghain*, "St
Comhghan's Church".

Glendaruel (Argyll), Gleann Dà
Ruadhail
This was was thought to mean "glen
of the two red places", but recent
research suggests that the site of the
church here may be pre-Christian
and commemorate Dà Ruadha, a
deity possibly connected with Dà
Dearga. This would give a meaning
of "glen of Dà Ruadha". Loch
Riddon is *Loch Ruadhail* with the
same element.

Glen Dee (Aberdeen), Gleann Dé *or*
Gleann Dhé
"Glen of the Dee", a river name with
connotations of divinity.

Glen Derby (Perth), Gleann Geunaid
The Gaelic name is "glen of the
goose stream", which led to the
anglicised form of Glen Gennet,
later abandoned when a Victorian
landowner wished to immortalise
his home town of Derby.

Glen Derry (Aberdeen), Gleann
Doire
"Glen of Derry", which in turn
means "oak grove".

Glen Dessary (Inverness), Gleann
Deasairidh
"Glen in the south-facing place."

Glendevon (Perth)
"The glen of the black river", from
Gleann Duibhe.

Glendhu (Dumfries)
"Black glen", from *Gleann Dubh*.

Glen Dibidale (Ross), Gleann
Dìobadail
"Deep valley", from Norse with
gleann added.

Glen Dochart (Perth), Gleann
Dochard
The river name in this glen may be that
found in the name "Cart", but with
negative connotations of scouring.

Glen Docharty (Ross), Gleann
Dochartaich
This may be "glen of great scouring".

Glen Doe (Inverness), Gleann Dotha
This is said to commemorate a water
sprite named *Dotha* or *Dogha*, but
the name may simply be "bad
water". Glendoebeg is *Gleann Dotha
Beag*, "little Glen Doe".

Glendoick (Perth), Gleann Doig
"Cadoc's glen."

Glen Doll (Angus), Gleann Dòl
This name, the Gaelic form of which
was recorded by Diack (1944), refers
to the river which is unclear in
meaning.

Glen Douglas (Dunbarton), Gleann
Dùghlais
"The glen of the black river."

Glen Dye (Kincardine), Gleann Dàidh
This appears in Gaelic to be "David's

glen", but the origins are obscure. Cairn Dye is now *Càrn an Tàilleir*, but it is unlikely that "Glen Dye" is from that source.

Gleneagles (Perth), Gleann Eagas *or* Gleann Eagais

The second element of the Gaelic name connotes a "notch", while the second element of the English one suggests a church and a form such as *Gleann na h-Eaglais*. Local Gaelic pronunciation always went in favour of the first form, although mention of a "church" is long-standing in non-local sources.

Glenegedale (Islay), Gleann Eigeadail

"Edge valley", from Norse with *gleann* attached.

Glen Elchaig (Ross), Gleann Eilcheig

The meaning of this name is unclear.

Glenelg (Inverness), Gleann Eilg

"Glen of Ireland", a commemorative name. A person from Glenelg is an *Eilgneach*, and locals were nicknamed *othaisgean*, "yearlings" or "hogs".

Glen Elgin (Moray), Gleann Eilginn

"The glen of Elgin."

Glen Ericht (Perth), Gleann Eireachd

"Assembly glen."

Glen Errochty (Perth), Gleann Eireachdaidh

"Assembly glen."

Glen Esk (Angus), Gleann Easg

"The glen of the Esk."

Glen Etive (Argyll), Gleann Éite

"The glen of the Etive", a name with connotations of foulness. *Éiteag*, a water goddess, is said to have lived in the river. A person from this area is an *Éiteach*.

Glen Ey (Aberdeen), Gleann Eidh

The defining element in this name is unclear.

Glen Eynort (Skye), Gleann Aoineart

"The glen of Eynort."

Glen Falloch (Perth), Gleann Falach

"Ringed glen."

Glen Farclas (Banff), Gleann Farghlais

"The glen of the over-stream."

Glen Farquhar (Kincardine)

"Farquhar's glen", from *Gleann Fhearchair*.

Glen Fender (Perth), Gleann Fhionndair

"The glen of the Fender."

Glen Feochan (Argyll), Gleann Faochain

The defining element here is unclear.

Glen Fernate (Perth), Gleann Feàrnaid

"The glen of the alder stream."

Glen Feshie (Inverness), Gleann Féisidh

"The glen of the boggy haugh river."

Glen Fiddich (Banff), Gleann Fhiodhaich

"The glen at the wood place." It is often assumed that this name is based on *fiadh*, "deer", but in fact the root is *fiodh*, "wood".

Glen Finglas (Perth), Gleann Fhionnghlais

"The glen of the fair stream." The church here was *Cladh nan Ceasanach*, "graveyard of Kessock's people", referring to the saint.

Glen Finlas (Argyll), Gleann Fhionnghlais

See **Glen Finglas**.

Glenfinnan (Inverness), Gleann Fhionnainn, Gleann Fhionghain *or* Gleann Fhìonain

The first Gaelic name represents local pronunciation but is unclear. The second and third Gaelic names are "Fingon's glen" and "Finnan's glen" respectively. There is a certain amount of confusion regarding the personal name here, because the area is also associated with Finnan, who is commemorated in *Eilean Fhìonain*, "Island Finnan", in Loch Sheil. The building housing

Glenfinnan House Hotel used to be known as *Taigh na Slataich*, "the house at the rod place".

Glen Forsa (Mull), Gleann Forsa
"Valley of the waterfall river", from Gaelic/Norse.

Glen Fruin (Dunbarton), Gleann Freòin
This name may include that of a river, the name of which is based on *freòine*, "rage". The road from Loch Long to Glen Fruin was known as *Rathad Mór nan Gàidheal*, "high road of the Gaels". The name of this glen might be related to that of Balfron.

Glen Fyne (Argyll), Gleann Fìne
The river name here appears to be based on *fìon*, "wine". A person from the area is a *Fìneach*, also nicknamed a *muc bhiorach*, "porpoise".

Glen Gairn (Aberdeen), Gleann Gharthain
"The glen of the calling river." Lower Glen Gairn is *Iochdar Ghlinn Gharthain*. Glen Gairn Church is *Cill Mo Thatha*, "St Mo Thatha's Church", a saint apparently also commemorated in Balmaha, and the fair in Glen Gairn was *Fèill Mo Thatha*, locally *Fèill Macha*, called in English "St Mungo's Fair".

Glen Garnock (Ayr)
"The glen of the crying river." See **Glen Girnock**.

Glen Garrisdale (Jura), Gleann Gharrasdail
"Field valley", from Norse with Gaelic *gleann*.

Glen Garry (Inverness), Gleann Gharadh *or* Gleanna Gharadh; (Perth: Atholl), Gleann Gar; (Perth: South), Gleann Gamhair
In Inverness-shire and Atholl, this name is "copse glen". In South Perthshire it may mean "winter glen". A person from Glen Garry in Inverness-shire is a *Garranach*.

Glen Garvie (Aberdeen)
"The glen of the rough river", from *Gleann Gharbhaidh*.

Glen Gelder (Aberdeen), Gleann Ghealdair
"The glen of the white or bright water."

Glen Gennet (Ayr)
"The glen of the goose stream", from *Gleann Geunaid*. A glen in Perthshire with the same original name was renamed by a 19th-century landowner as **Glen Derby**.

Glen Girnock (Aberdeen), Gleann Goirneig
"The glen of the crying river."

Glen Glass (Ross), Gleann Ghlais
"The glen of the stream."

Glen Glaster (Inverness), Gleann Ghlasdair
"The glen of the grey-green water."

Glen Gloy (Inverness), Gleann Glaoidh
"The glen of the gluey or viscous river."

Glen Golly (Sutherland), Gleanna Gollaidh
"The glen of the blind river", maybe referring to an overgrown river. This is known as *Gleanna Gollaidh nan craobh*, "Glen Golly of the trees".

Glen Gorm (Mull), An Gleann Gorm
"The green glen." *Gorm* usually means "blue" but also covers the colour of fresh vegetation.

Glen Goulandie (Perth), Gleann Gobhlandaidh
This may be "the glen at the forked place".

Gleann Gour (Argyll), Gleann Ghobhar
"Goats' glen."

Glen Gravir (Lewis), Gleann Ghrabhair
"The glen of Gravir."

Glen Grivie (Sutherland), Gleann Ghrìobhaidh
"The glen at the claw place."

Glen Grudie (Ross), Gleann Ghrùididh
"The glen of the Grudie", referring to gravel.

Glen Gynack (Inverness), Gleann Gòineig
The river name here is obscure.

Glen Haultin (Skye), Gleann Shealtainn
This appears to be "glen of Shetland", and may refer to settlement by Norse people who had come from there.

Glenhinnsdal (Skye), Gleann Hinneasdail
"Hengist's valley", from Norse with *gleann* attached.

Glen House (Mull), Tìr Chonaill
The Gaelic name is "Conall's land", and is also the Gaelic name of County Donegal in Ireland.

Glen Isla (Angus), Gleann Ìl *or* Gleann Ìle
"The glen of the Isla." A local is an *Ìleach*.

Glenjorrie (Ayr)
"The pilgrim's or dewar's glen", from *Gleann an Deòraidh*.

Glen Ketland (Argyll), Gleann Ceitilein
This name is unclear but may contain an element cognate with Brythonic *coed*, "wood".

Glenkill (Arran)
Although commonly derived from *Gleann na Cille*, "valley of the church", the alternative *Gleann na Coille*, "valley of the wood", is likely given the absence of a church in the area.

Glenkindie (Aberdeen), Gleann Cinnidh
The name of the river here may be "champion" or "warrior".

Glen Kinglas (Argyll), Gleann Chonghlais
"The glen of the dog river."

Glen Kyles (Harris), Gleann a' Chaolais
"The glen at the narrows."

Glen Latterach (Moray)
"Sloping glen", from *Gleann Leitreach*.

Glen Lednock (Perth), Gleann Liadnaig
The meaning of this name is unclear.

Glen Leraig (Sutherland), Gleann Leireag
"Larch glen."

Glen Levishie (Inverness), Gleann Lìbhisidh
"The glen of Levishie."

Glenlia (Inverness), An Gleann Liath
"The blue-grey glen."

Glen Liever (Argyll), Gleann Lìbhir
"The glen of Liever."

Glenlivet (Banff), Gleann Lìobhait
"The glen of the Livet."

Glen Lochay (Perth), Gleann Lòchaidh
"The glen of the Lochy."

Glen Lochsie (Perth), Gleann Lòchsaidh
This may be "the glen at the dark place", from *lòch* and *fasadh*.

Glen Lossie (Moray), Gleann Losaidh
"The glen of the plant river."

Glen Loyne (Inverness), Gleann Loinn
"Loyne" may originate in *loinn*, "beauty".

Glenluce (Wigtown), Gleann Lus
Lus is "plant" or "herb", here perhaps implying an overgrown river.
Glenluce Village is *Clachan Ghlinn Lus*.

Glen Lui (Aberdeen), Gleann Laoigh
"The glen of the calf river."

Glen Luss (Dunbarton), Gleann Luis
See **Glenluce**.

Glen Lyon (Perth), Gleann Lìomhann
"The glen of the Lyon", a name conveying smoothness. This was also known as *an Crom Ghleann*, "the crooked glen". MacGregor's patrimony in Glen Lyon is *an Tòiseachd*, "the lord's land", while the

churchyard is *Cladh Chunna*, "St Cunna's Churchyard". Glen Lyon House is *Tulaich a' Mhuilinn*, "the hill of the mill".

Glenmallie (Argyll), Gleann Màilidh
See **Dalmally** and **Kilmallie**.

Glen Markie (Inverness), Gleann Mharcaidh
"The glen of the horse river."

Glen Marxie (Ross), Gleann Mharcfhasaidh
"The glen at the horse stance."

Glen Massan (Argyll), Gleann Masain
"Masan's glen." This was the place beloved of Deirdre in legend.

Glen Mazeran (Inverness), Gleann Masarain
This name is unclear.

Glenmeanie (Ross), Gleann Mèinnidh
This name may be related to "Main" in Ross.

Glenmoidart (Argyll), Gleann Mhùideart
"The glen of Moidart."

Glenmore (several), An Gleann Mór
"The great glen."

Glen Moriston (Inverness), Gleann Moireasdan
This is said to be "the glen of the great water", referring to the river, but the phonetics do not support this. The church lands were *Clachan Mheircheird*, in memory of *M'Eircheard*, "St Erchard".

Glenmoy (Angus)
"Glen at the plain", from *Gleann na Mòighe*.

Glen Muick (Aberdeen), Gleann Muice
"Glen of the pig river." The fair here was *Féill Mhoir* or *An Fhéill Muire*, "St Mary's fair". A native of Glen Muick is a *Mucarnach*.

Glen Nevis (Inverness), Gleann Nibheis
This is commonly believed to be "the glen of terror", from *uabhas*, but the

basis of the name has an Indo-European root with connotations of wetness. Glen Nevis had a negative reputation and in one poem is called *amar sgùrainn an domhain mhóir*, "slop-pail of the wide world".

Glen of Lintrathen (Angus), Gleann Tréithean
The second part of this name is unclear, and it is notable that *linn* or Brythonic *llyn*, "pool", is absent from the Gaelic name. "Lintrathen" itself was recorded by Diack (1944) from speakers of Perthshire Gaelic as *lan-tréin* and *lyann-tré-an*.

Glen of Rothes (Moray), Gleann Ràthais
"The glen of Rothes."

Glen Ogil (Angus)
See **Glen Ogle**.

Glen Ogle (Perth), Gleann Ogail
The meaning of this name is unclear, but is unrelated to *òg*, "young".

Glen Orchy (Argyll), Gleann Urchaidh *or* Gleann Urcha
"The glen of the Orchy." The glen was called *Gleann Urcha nam badan*, "Glen Orchy of the copses", showing local pronunciation. The parish of Glen Orchy was known as *An Dìseart*, "the hermitage", which is referred to in the Gaelic name of nearby **Dalmally**. The fair held in Glen Orchy was *Féill Chonnain*, "St Connan's Fair", referring to the saint commemorated in Dalmally. The Braes of Glen Orchy are *Bràigh Ghlinn Urchaidh* or *Bràigh Ghlinn Urcha*, "the upper part of Glen Orchy". A local saying about the weather went *Fhad 's a bhios ceò air Cruachan, cha bhi pathadh air Urchaidh*, "As long as there's mist on Cruachan, Orchy won't go thirsty".

Glen Ormisdale (Arran), Gleann Ormasdail
"Orm's valley", from Norse, with *gleann* attached.

Glen Orrin (Ross), Gleann Oirrinn
or Gleann Orthainn
"The glen of the offering", referring
to church lands of Urray at the
confluence of the Conon and Orrin.

Glen Pean (Inverness), Gleann Peathain
This name is unclear and may be
from Pictish.

Glen Prosen (Angus), Gleann Pràsaig
or Gleann Pràsain
This name is unclear but may
contain a personal name.

Glen Quiech (Angus)
See **Glen Quoich**.

Glen Quoich (Inverness), Gleann
Chuaich
"The glen of the hollow." This glen
was allegedly haunted by a sprite
named *Cuachag*. The hills and
mountains around Glen Quoich are
known as *Monadh Chuaich*, "the
Quoich range".

Glenramskill (Argyll), Gleann
Ramasgail
"Valley at raven gully", from Gaelic/
Norse.

Glenrath (Peebles)
"Glen with a circular fort", from
Gleann an Ràtha.

Glen Rinnes (Banff), Gleann
Ruaidhneis
"The glen at the red-brown haugh."

Glen Rosa (Arran), Gleann Ruasaidh
"Glen of the horse river", from
Gaelic/Norse.

Glenrothes (Fife), Gleann Ràthais
See **Glen of Rothes**.

Glen Roy (Inverness), Gleann Ruaidh
"The glen of the River Roy." See
Parallel Roads.

Glen Sanda (Argyll), Gleann Shannda
"The glen of the sand river", from
Gaelic/Norse. Glensanda Castle is
Caisteal na Gruagaich, "the maiden's
castle".

Glen Scorrodale (Arran), Gleann
Sgoradail
"Skorri's valley", from Norse, with
gleann added.

Glensgaich (Ross), Gleann
Sgathaich
This name may refer to the pruning
of branches from trees in the area.

Glen Shant (Arran), Gleann Sianta
"Holy glen." Older forms of the
name suggest that this was originally *Crann Sianta*, "holy tree".

Glenshee (Perth), Gleann Sìth
"Fairy glen." The fabled Gaelic
hero Diarmaid is said to have been
killed by a wild boar at Ben
Gulabin near the Spittal of
Glenshee, although several places
in Scotland and Ireland lay claim
to this distinction.

Glensheil (Ross), Gleann Seile
"The glen of the Sheil", a pre-Gaelic
river name. Glensheil Church is
Eaglais Riabhachain, "church at the
brindled place", while the old church
was *Cill Chaointeort*, "St Kentigern's
Church". A Glensheil person is a
Seileach.

Glenshian (Inverness), Gleann an
t-Sìthein
"The glen with the small fairy hill."

Glen Shira (Argyll), Gleann Siara
"The glen of the eternal river."

Glen Sloy (Dunbarton), Gleann
Sluagh *or* Gleann Sluaigh
"The glen of the host."

Glenstrae (Argyll), Gleann Sreith
This may be "the glen of the row".

Glen Strathfarrar (Ross), Gleann
Srath Farair
"The glen of the strath of the
Farrar."

Glen Tanar (Aberdeen), Gleann
Tanair
"The glen of the thundering river."

Glen Tarff (Inverness), Srath Obar
Thairbh
The River Tarff is mentioned in both
names, but the Gaelic name translates as "the strath of Abertarff".

Glen Tilt (Perth), Gleann Teilt
The river mentioned in this name is
pre-Gaelic.

Glen Tolsta (Lewis), Gleann Tholastaidh
"The glen of Tolsta."

Glen Tromie (Inverness), Gleann Tromaidh
"The glen of the elder tree river." A song about this place says, *Gleann Tromaidh nan siantan, leam bu mhiann bhith nad fhasgadh*, "Stormy Glen Tromie, I wish I were in your shelter".

Glen Trool (Ayr)
"The glen of the stream", from *Gleann an t-Sruthail.*

Glen Truim (Inverness), Gleann Truim
"The glen of the elder tree river."

Glen Turret (Perth), Gleann Turraid
"The glen of the dry river", one which shrinks in volume in summer.

Glenuachdrach (Skye), An Gleann Uachdrach
"The upper glen."

Glenuig (Inverness), Gleann Ùige
"Glen at the bay", from Gaelic/Norse.

Glen Urquhart (Inverness), Gleann Urchadain
"The glen of Urquhart." The churchyard here is *Cladh Churadain*, "St Curadan's Churchyard" and the holy well was *Tobar Churadain*, "St Curadan's well".

Glenvicaskill (Skye), Gleann MhicAsgaill
"MacAskill's glen."

Glenwhilk (Perth)
"Reed glen", from *Gleann Chuilc.*

Glenwhinnie (Ayr)
This may be "warrior glen", from *Gleann Chuinnidh.*

Glespin (Lanark)
This may be "grey-green pennyland", from *Glas Pheighinn.*

Glutton (Ross), Glotan
"Gorge."

Goathill (Lewis), Cnoc nan Gobhar
"The hill of the goats."

Goat Island (Lewis), Eilean a' Ghobhail
"The forked island." The English translation came about through confusion between *gobhal*, "fork", and *gobhar*, "goat".

Gobagrennan (Argyll), Gob a' Ghrianain
"The promontory at the sunny spot."

Gobernuisgach (Sutherland), Gob an Uisgich
"The point at the water place."

Golspie (Sutherland), Goillspidh
"Gully village", from Norse. Golspie is *Goillspidh nan sligean dubh*, "Golspie of the mussels".

Golval (Sutherland), Golbhal
"Galli's field" or "field with a loud stream", from Norse.

Gometra (Mull), Gómastra
"Godmund's island."

Gordon (Berwick)
See **Gourdon**.

Gordonbush (Sutherland), Gar-eisgeig
The more recent English name replaced the Gaelic name based on Gaelic/Norse meaning "copse at the waste strip of land". Gordonbush was divided into two parts, *a' Bhealaidh*, "the broom", above the road and *Cill Chaluim Cille*, "St Columba's Church", below.

Gordon Castle (Moray), Bogan Gaoithe
The site of Gordon Castle occupies land known as "windy or marshy bog" in Gaelic.

Gordon Hall (Inverness), Lag an Nòtair
The Gordons were landowners here at the site known as "the notary's hollow" in Gaelic.

Gorstan (Ross), An Goirtean
"The small enclosed field", also known as *Goirtean Ghairbh*, "the small enclosed field at Garve",

Gorstanvorran (Inverness), Goirtean a' Mhoirein

This may be "Murray's enclosed field".

Gortan (Ross), An Goirtean
"The small enclosed field." The full name of Gortan in Lochcarron is *An Goirtean Fraoich*, "small enclosed heathery field".

Gortaneorn (Argyll), An Goirtean Eòrna
"Small enclosed barley field."

Gortantaoid (Islay), Goirtean an Taoid
"The small enclosed field of the halter." An alternative derivation is *Goirtean an t-Saoid*, "the small enclosed field of the cattle drive".

Gorthleck (Inverness), Goirtlig *or* Gortlaig
This name is unclear, although the English form suggests that it may have come from *gart/gort* and *leac* to give "slab field". Lyne of Gorthleck is *Loinn Ghoirtlig*, where *loinn* means "enclosed field". Nearby is *Loch Gart* or Loch Garth.

Gorton (Coll), An Goirtean
"The small enclosed field."

Gortonallister (Arran), Goirtean Alasdair
"Alasdair's small enclosed field."

Gott (Tiree), Got
This Norse name is unclear. A local saying meaning that someone stopped halfway through something is, *Ma stad iad mu Ghot, stad iad mu Ghot.*

Gourdon (Kincardine)
"Great fort", from Brythonic. This was previously "Gordoun" and is closely related to "Fordoun", which shows initial Gaelic *f* rather than Brythonic *g*.

Gourock (Renfrew), Guireag
"Pimple", referring to the hill above the town.

Govan (Glasgow), Baile a' Ghobhainn
The Gaelic name is "the smith's farm", and while the original name may have contained a reference to a

smith, it is likely that it stems from Brythonic with the Gaelic name being a later attempt by Gaelic speakers to give the name a form comprehensible to them.

Govig (Harris), Góbhaig
"Ravine bay", from Norse.

Gowrie (Perth), Gobharaidh
"Gabhran's land." Gabhran was king of Dal Riada during the 6th century. The divisions of Gowrie are *Blàr Ghobharaidh*, "Blair of Gowrie", and *Cars Ghobharaidh*, "Carse of Gowrie".

Gramsdale (Benbecula), Gramasdal
"Gram's valley", from Norse.

Grandtully (Perth), Gar an Tulaich
"The den at the green hill." The Vale of Grandtully is *An Dail*, "the haugh".

Granish (Inverness), Grèanais
This name is unclear but contains a suffix meaning "place".

Grantown on Spey (Moray), Baile Ùr nan Granndach *or* A' Bhaile Ùr
The planned town here is "the new town of the Grants" or just "the new town" in Gaelic, also referred to locally at one time as "Valoor". Prior to this the settlement was known as Freuchie, from *Fraochaidh*, "heather place".

Grasspoint (Mull), Achadh na Creige
The Gaelic name is "the field at the rock" and is unrelated to the English one.

Gravir (Lewis), Grabhair
"Ravines", from Norse.

Grealin (Skye), Grèalainn *or* Greallainn
The meaning of this Norse name is unclear.

Grean (Barra), Grinn
"Green", from Norse.

Great Bernera (Bernera), Beàrnaraigh
"Bjørn's island", from Norse. "Great" in the English form distinguishes this island, also known as

Bernera, from Little Bernera. In Gaelic this is known as *Beàrnaraigh Leòdhais*, "Bernera of Lewis", and *Beàrnaraigh Ùig*, "Bernera of Uig", the district of Lewis to which Bernera is attached. A Bernera person is a *Beàrnarach*.

Great Cumbrae (Cumbrae), Cumaradh Mór
"Large island of the Cymric people", meaning the Britons of Strathclyde.

Great Glen (Inverness), An Gleann Mór
"The great glen", also known as *Glenmore.*

Green, The (Tiree), Biosta *or* Port Bhiosta
The English name may be from Norse "green" or "den". The Gaelic name may be "(port of) the farm dwelling", from Norse.

Greenan (Bute)
"Sunny place", from *Grianan.*

Greenhill (Tiree), Grianal
"Green field", from Norse. The English version of the name came via Gaelic and was rationalised to its present form to give meaning in English.

Greenock (Renfrew), Grianaig
This may be "sunny place", from Gaelic. Given the town's location, a Norse derivation is unlikely. An old Gaelic name of the place was *Gónait*, which is unclear.

Greenstone Point (Ross), Rubha na Cloiche Uaine *or* Rubha na Lice Uaine.
"The point of the green stone or slab."

Greep (Skye), A' Ghrìpe
"The cliff", originally from Norse.

Greinem (Harris), Grianam
"Green islet", from Norse.

Grenicle (Skye), Gréinigil
This Norse name may be "green ravine".

Greshornish (Skye), Grìsinis
"Swine headland", from Norse.

Gress (Lewis), Griais
"Grassy place."

Greystone (Aberdeen), Dail Iarainn
The English name may be either "grey stone" or "Gray's farm", from English. The Gaelic name is "iron haugh". Diack (1944) recorded the name as "chlach glas", representing *A' Chlach Glas* (sic), "the grey stone", which may be a more modern name of which the English is a translation.

Gribun (Mull), Grìobainn *or* Bun na Sgrìob
The meaning of the main name is unclear, but the second Gaelic name, used locally, is "the foot of the scree". Local people are *eich*, "horses".

Grigadale (Argyll), Griogadal *or* Girigeadal
The first part of this Norse valley name is unclear.

Grimersta (Lewis), Grìomarsta
"Grima's dwelling", from Norse.

Griminish (Benbecula, North Uist), Grìminis
"Grima's headland", from Norse.

Grimsay (Grimsay), Griomasaigh
"Grim's island", from Norse.

Grimshader (Lewis), Grimiseadar
"Grim's township", from Norse.

Grishapool (Coll), Griseabol
"Pig farm", from Norse.

Groay (Harris), Gròaigh *or* Grothaigh
"Stream island", from Norse.

Grogarry (South Uist), Gròigearraidh
"Stream meadow", from Norse.

Grosebay (Harris), Greòsabhagh
"Grass bay", from Norse.

Grotaig (Inverness), Grodaig
It is unclear what this name means. It has the appearance of a gaelicised Norse name, and there is evidence of other Norse names in the wider area.

Grudie (Ross), Grùididh
"Gravel place."

Gruids (Sutherland), Na Grùidean
"The gravelly places."

Gruinard (Ross), Gruinneard *or*
Gruinneart
"Shallow firth", from Norse. Wester
Gruinard is *Gruinneard Shuas*,
"upper Gruinard". Big Gruinard is
Gruinneard Mhór and Little
Gruinard is *Gruinneard Bheag*.
Gruinard Island, nicknamed
"Anthrax Island" following British
government experiments in germ
warfare there, is *Eilean Ghruinneart*.
Gruinart (Islay), Gruinneart
See **Gruinard**.
Grula (Skye), Grùla
This may be "stony river", from Norse.
Grulin (Eigg), Grùlainn
"Stony land."
Gruline (Mull), Grùilinn
"Stony land."
Grumbeg (Sutherland), Gnùb Beag
or Grùb Beag
"Small knob-shaped hill."
Gualachulain (Argyll), Guala
Chuilinn
"Holly ridge." See **Gualin**.
Gualin (Sutherland), A' Ghualainn
"Ridge." This generally means
"shoulder" but is used to mean a
long ridge.
Guay (Perth)
This may mean "marsh", from *gaoth*,
but the Gaelic name was recorded as
Gallainn, which may refer to a
standing stone.
Guershader (Lewis), Giùrseadar
"Farm near a chasm", from Norse.
See **Stornoway**.
Gullane (East Lothian), A' Ghualainn
"The shoulder or ridge."
Gunna (Coll, Tiree), Gunna *or*
Gunnaigh
"Gunnar's island", from Norse.
Gunna is mentioned in the lines of a
song, *Thoir mo shoraidh thar
Ghunnaigh gu Muile nam mór
bheann*, "Farewell beyond Gunna to
Mull of the great mountains".
Guridil (Rum), Giùradal
"Chasm valley", from Norse.

Gylen (Kerrera), Na Goibhlean
"Forks" or "forked places". This
name has appeared in a number of
spellings, such as *Gaoidhlean,
Gaoilean* and *Goibhlean*. It has been
used in literature with the definite
article. The castle here was known
locally as *Dùn Donnchaidh*,
"Duncan's fort".

H
Habost (Lewis), Tàbost
"High farm", from Norse.
Hacklete, Haclait (Benbecula), Tàcleit
(Bernera)
"High rock or cliff", from Norse.
Haddo (Aberdeen)
"Half davoch", from English. This is
an anglicised or half-anglicised
equivalent of the more common
"Lettoch".
Half Davoch (Moray)
See **Haddo**.
Halistra (Skye), Halastra
This Norse name is unclear but may
contain an element referring to a
farm.
Halkirk (Caithness), Hàcraig
"Haugh Church", from English.
Halladale (Sutherland), Healadal
This may be "hallowed valley", from
Norse.
Hallaig (Raasay), Halaig
This Norse name may be "high slope
bay".
Hallin (Skye, South Uist), Hàlainn
"Sloping land", from Norse.
Halmadary (Sutherland),
Halmadairigh
This may be Norse "Hjalmund's
sheiling".
Hamera (Skye), Hamara
"Hill" or "rock", from Norse.
Hameraverin (Skye), Hamara
Bhoirein
"Hollow at the hill or rock", from
Norse.
Hamersay (Harris), Hamarsaigh
"Rock island", from Norse.

Hamilton (Lanark), Hamaltan
"Hamill's town", from English.

Handa (Sutherland), Eilean Shannda
"Island at the sandy river", from
Gaelic/Norse.

Harlaw (Aberdeen), Arla
"Hard hill", from English. The
Battle of Harlaw is *Cath Gairbheach*,
"the battle of Garioch".

Harlosh (Skye), Heàrrlois
This Norse name appears to refer to
a river mouth, but the first element
is unclear.

Harrapool (Skye), Harrapol
"Hari's farm", from Norse.

Harris, (Harris, Islay, Rum), Na
Hearadh
"Division" or "portion". In south
Harris, the west side is *a' Mhachair*,
"machair land", as opposed to the
east side, which is *na Bàigh*, "bays".
The hilly area above the east coast is
Bràigh nam Bàgh, "upland of the
bays". A Harris person is a *Hearach*
or *Tearach*. Harris in Islay is called
by the full name of *Na Hearadh
Ìleach* while Harris in Rum is *Na
Hearadh Rumach*.

Hartfield (Ross), Coille Mhùiridh
While the English name refers to a
field of deer, the Gaelic name is "the
wood at the rampart place".
However, another version of the
Gaelic name is *Coille a' Bhùiridh*,
"the wood of bellowing", which
might refer to stags, but may be an
attempt to give the name "meaning".
Hartfield is referred to as *Coille
Mhùiridh dà thaobh na h-aibhne*,
"Hartfield on both sides of the
river".

Hasker (North Uist), Haisgeir
"Ocean rock", from Norse.

Haugh (Inverness), An Talchan
The Gaelic form is a gaelicisation of
English "haugh" with a diminutive
ending.

Haun (Eriskay), Na Hann
"Harbour", from Norse.

Haunn (Mull), Na Hann
See **Haun**.

Hayfield (Perth), Gallanach
"Place of the standing stone" or
"place of coltsfoot".

Heanish (Tiree), Hianais
"Outlying headland", from Norse.

Heaste (Skye), Heasta
"Horse farm", from Norse. Local
people are nicknamed *mèirlich*,
"thieves".

Heatherfield (Skye), An Torran Uaine
The Gaelic name is "the small green
hillock".

Heathfield (Ross), Cail Fhraochaidh
The Gaelic name is "meadow at the
heathery place".

Hebrides, Innse Gall
The English name is unclear but
stems from a misreading of
"Hebudes", itself from "Ebudae".
The Gaelic name is "islands of the
non-Gaels", referring to the islands'
once Norse population. The Outer
Hebrides are *na h-Eileanan a-Muigh*
and the Inner Hebrides *na h-Eileanan a-Staigh*. A Gaelic equivalent
of "carry coals to Newcastle" is *eich a
thoirt a dh'Innse Gall*, "take horses to
the Hebrides".

Heights of Brae (Ross), Am Bràigh
The Gaelic name is "the upper part",
which often appears as "brae" in
English, despite meaning something
different.

Heights of Dochcarty (Ross), Bràigh
Dabhach Gartaidh
The Gaelic name is "the upper part
of Dochcarty".

Heights of Inchvannie (Ross),
Bràigh Innis Mheannaidh
The Gaelic name is "the upper part
of Inchvannie".

Heights of Kinlochewe (Ross),
Bràigh Cheann Loch Iùbh
The Gaelic name is "the upper part
of Kinlochewe".

Heisker (North Uist), Heillsgeir
"Flat rock", from Norse.

Helensburgh (Dunbarton), Baile
Eilidh
Before the construction of planned
town, named after the founder's
wife, this was known as Malig,
Milrigs and Mulig. The planned
town itself was first known simply as
"New Town".

Hell's Glen (Argyll), Gleann Iarainn
or An Gleann Beag
The first Gaelic name is "iron glen",
which led to the English form,
because *iarann*, "iron", sounds like
ifrinn, "hell". The second Gaelic
name is "the small glen".

Helmsdale (Sutherland), Bun Ilidh
The English name is "Helm's valley",
from Norse. The Gaelic name is "the
mouth of the Ilidh", the Gaelic name
of the Helmsdale River. The Strath of
Kildonan is *Srath Ilidh* in Gaelic,
named again after the river. A person
from Helmsdale and district is an
Ileach as opposed to an *Ìleach*, who is
someone from Islay, Glen Isla or
Strath Isla. West Helmsdale is
Achadh Adlaidh, which is a field name
with an unclear second element.

Herbusta (Skye), Hearbusta *or*
Tearbusta
"Lord's farm", from Norse.

Heribost (Skye), Heireabost
See **Herbusta**.

Herishader (Skye), Heiriseadar
"Lord's place", from Norse.

Hermetray (Harris), Hearmatraigh
"Hermund's island", from Norse.

Heylipol (Tiree), An Cruairtean *or*
An Cruadh Ghoirtean
The English name is "flat farm" or
"holy farm", from Norse. The first
Gaelic name is an abbreviation of
the second, meaning "hard field".
Heylipol Church is *Eaglais na
Mòintich*, "Moss Church", named
after a neighbouring township.

Hielum (Sutherland), Huilleum
This may be "hound holm", from
Norse.

High Borve (Lewis), Am Baile Àrd
The Gaelic name is "the high
township", its full name being *Baile
Àrd Bhuirgh*, "high township of
Borve".

Highbridge (Inverness), An Drochaid
Bhàn
The Gaelic name is "the white bridge".

High Corrie (Arran), An Coire Àrd
"The high corrie." North High
Corrie is *Guala Bàn*, "white shoulder
or ridge".

Highfield (Ross), Ciarnaig
The "high field" referred to in English
is absent from the Gaelic which is
unclear in meaning, which may
contain an element meaning "dark".

Highlands, A' Ghàidhealtachd
The Gaelic name for the "high
lands" is "Gaeldom", meaning the
area occupied by indigenous Gaelic
speakers. These terms are, accurately
speaking, not co-terminous, but the
usage is established. Gaelic uses *air
a' Ghàidhealtachd* for "in the
Highlands".

Hill of Fearn (Ross), Baile an Droma
The Gaelic name is "the township
on the ridge".

Hilton (Bute), Taigh na Beinne
The Gaelic name is "the house on
the hill".

Hilton of Cadboll (Ross), Baile a'
Chnuic
The Gaelic name is "the township on
the hill". Because of local people's
connection to the fishing industry,
they were known as *dubhain*, "hooks".

Hoebeg (North Uist), Na Hogha
Bheag
"The small rocky mound", from
Norse/Gaelic.

Hogharry (North Uist), Hòigearraidh
"Field at a rocky mound", from
Norse.

Holm (Inverness), An Tolm *or* An
Tuilm; (Lewis), Tolm
The Inverness name refers to a river
meadow from English, while the

Lewis name is "islet", from Norse. The Laird of Holm in Inverness was known as *Fear an Tuilm*. Facing the Lewis village of Holm are the rocks known as *Biastan Thuilm*, "Beasts of Holm", on which the *Iolaire* troopship sank after World War I.

Holmisdale (Skye), Holmasdal
"Holm valley", from Norse.

Holoman (Raasay), Holman
"Small islet", from Norse but apparently with a Gaelic diminutive.

Holy Island (Arran), Eilean MoLaise *or* An t-Eilean Àrd
This is "dear St Laisren's island" or "the high island" in Gaelic.

Home Farm (Arran)
See **Mossend**.

Hope (Sutherland), Hób
"Bay", from Norse. The ferry here was known as *Coit Hób*, "the Hope boat".

Hopeman (Moray), Hudaman
This appears to be of Norse origin and may refer to an islet in a bay.

Horgabost (Harris), Torgabost
"Farm at the worship place", from Norse.

Horisary (North Uist), Hórasaraidh
"Grave sheiling", from Norse.

Horneval (Skye), Hornabhal
"Horn mountain", from Norse.

Horsaclete (Harris), Horsacleit
"Horse cliff", from Norse.

Horse Island (Ross), Eilean nan Each
"The island of the horses."

Horve (Barra), Na Horgh
"Cairn", from Norse.

Hosh (Perth), A' Chòis
"The cavern or crevice."

Hosta (North Uist), Hòmhsta
"Hogni's dwelling", from Norse.

Hough (Tiree), Hogh
"Rocky mound", from Norse. A local term for a detour is *Rathad Hogh do Haoidhnis*, "via Hough to Hynish".

Househill (Nairn), Baile an Tuim
"The farm at the hillock."

Houston (Renfrew)
"Hugh's town." This was formerly known as Kilpeter, from Gaelic *Cill Pheadair*, "St Peter's Church".

Howbeg (South Uist), Togh Beag
"Small rocky mound", from Norse/Gaelic.

Howe of Alford (Aberdeen), Lagan Athfuirt
"Hollow of Alford."

Howe of the Mearns (Kincardine), Lag na Maoirne
"The hollow of the steward's territory."

Howmore (South Uist), Togh Mór
"Large rocky mound", from Norse. The old church was called *An Teampall Mór*, "the big chapel".

Hoy (Orkney), Eilean Thothaigh
The Gaelic name was used in north Sutherland and is a gaelicisation of the Norse name which is "high island".

Hughstown (Ross), Cnocan Cruaidh
"Hugh's town", from English although the Gaelic name is "hard hillock".

Hughton (Inverness), An Éipheit
The Gaelic name is "Egypt" which was a nickname given to the place because of the number of biblical first names people had.

Humberstone (Ross), Cill Duinn Uachdrach
The English name, which is that of a family of landowners, replaced the older Gaelic name of "upper Kildun". See **Kildun**.

Hungladder (Skye), Hùnagladair
The first part of this Norse name may come from a personal name based on *húna*, "bear cub". The second element in the name is unclear but may be a plural form. The related name *Ru Hunish/Rubha Hùinis* is nearby.

Hunter's Quay (Argyll), Camas Rainich
The older English name was

Camusronich, from the Gaelic name, which means "bracken bay".

Huntingtower (Perth), Caisteal Ruadhainn
The Gaelic name is "Ruthven castle".

Huntly (Aberdeen), Hunndaidh *or* Srath Bhalgaidh
The English name was imported from England and the first Gaelic name is an adaptation of it. The second Gaelic name is the same as that of the surrounding area of Strathbogie. Huntly Market was *Féill Srath Bhalgaidh*.

Husabost (Skye), Hùsabost
"House farm", from Norse.

Hushinish (Harris), Hùisinis
"House headland", from Norse.

Hynish (Tiree), Haoidhnis
"High headland", from Norse. West Hynish is *na Cùiltean*, "secluded spots", the full name being *Cùiltean Haoidhnis* or *Cùiltean Bhaile a' Phuill*, "secluded spots of Hynish" and "of Balephuil". The old church-yard in Hynish was called *An Cladh Beag*, "the small churchyard".

Hysbackie (Sutherland), Heillsbacaidh
"Flat bank" or "cave bank", from Norse.

I

Ibert (Perth, Stirling)
"Offering", relating to church lands, from Ìobairt.

Ichrachen (Argyll), Ìochdrachann
"Bottom or lower place."

Idrigill (Skye), Ìdrigil
"Outer ravine", from Norse.

Imachar (Arran), An Iomachar *or* An t-Iomachar
Folk etymology has it that this is *iomadh char*, "many turns", and refers to rowing. However this probably refers to ploughed land. Local people were nicknamed *faoileagan*, "seagulls".

Immeroin (Perth), Iomaire Eóghainn
"Ewen's rigg."

Inaltrie (Moray)
"Pasture land", from Gaelic *Ionaltraidh*.

Inch (Midlothian)
"Meadow", from Gaelic *innis* which can also mean "island".

Inchadnie (Perth), Innis Chailtnidh
"Meadow at the hard water."

Inchaffray (Perth), Innis Aifrinn
"Meadow of the offering."

Incharvie (Fife)
"Meadow at the boundary wall", fromn *Innis na h-Airbhe*.

Inchbae (Ross), Innis Beithe
"Birch meadow."

Inchbare (Angus)
This may be "St Barr's meadow", from Gaelic *Innis Bharra*.

Inchbelly (Dunbarton)
"Broom meadow", from *Innis Bealaidh*.

Inchberry (Inverness), Innis a' Bhàiridh; (Moray)
The Inverness name is "the hurling meadow", while the Moray name is possibly "St Bearach's meadow", from *Innis Bhearaigh*. People from Inchberry in Inverness-shire were known as *donais*, "devils".

Inchcailloch (Stirling), Innis Cailleach
"Nuns' island", showing the old form of the genitive plural.

Inchcolm (Fife)
"St Columba's island", from *Innis Choluim*.

Inchdryne (Inverness), Innis Droighinn
"Thorn meadow."

Incheril (Ross), Innis a' Choiril
The defining element of this meadow name is unclear, but may be the name of the saint commemo-rated in the church at **Roybridge**.

Inchgall (Fife)
"Island of non-Gaels", from *Innis Gall*, which would be *Innis Ghall* in modern Gaelic.

Inchgarvie (West Lothian)
"The island of the rough place" or
"Garbhach's island", from *Innis
Gharbhaidh*.

Inchgowan (Ross), Innis a' Ghobhann
"The smith's meadow."

Inchgrundle (Angus)
This is probably "meadow of the low
haugh", from *Innis Ghrunndail*.

Inchina (Ross), Innis an Àtha
"The meadow by the ford."

Inchinnan (Renfrew), Innis Fhìonain
"St Finnan's meadow."

Inchkeith (Fife)
Possibly "the island of the wood",
from Gaelic *innis* and Brythonic
coed, giving *Innis Chéith*.

Inchkenneth (Mull), Innis Choinnich
"St Cainneach's island."

Inchkinloch (Sutherland), Innis
Ceann an Locha
"The meadow at the head of the
loch."

Inchlaggan (Inverness), Innis an
Lagain
"The meadow of Laggan."

Inchlumpie (Ross), Innis Lombaidh
"The meadow at the bare place."

Inchmahome (Perth), Innis
MoCholmaig
"St Colman's island" in the Lake of
Menteith, which is in Gaelic *Loch
Innis MoCholmaig*.

Inchmarnoch (Aberdeen), Innis
Mhearnaig
"St Ernoc's or M'Ernoc's meadow."

Inchmarnock (Bute)
See **Inchmarnoch**.

Inchmartin (Perth)
"Martin's meadow", from *Innis
Mhàrtainn*, possibly commemorat-
ing St Martin.

Inchmichael (Perth)
"Michael's meadow", from *Innis
Mhìcheil*, possibly commemorating
St Michael.

Inchnadamph (Sutherland), Innis
nan Damh
"The meadow of the stags."

Inchnairn (Ross), Innis an Fheàrna
"The meadow of the alder tree."

Inchnavie (Ross), Innis Neimhidh
"The meadow at the sacred
lands."

Inchree (Inverness), Innis an Ruighe
"The meadow at the slope."

Inchrory (Banff, Inverness), Innis
Ruairidh
"Roderick's meadow."

Inchtavannach (Dunbarton)
This is commonly said to derive
from *Innis Taigh a' Mhanaich*, "the
island of the monk's house", but may
have originated as *Innis
DoBheannain*, "St Bannan's
island".

Inchture (Perth), Innis Tùir
"The meadow with a tower."

Inchtuthil (Perth)
"Tuathal's meadow", from *Innis
Thuathail*.

Inchvannie (Ross), Innis
Mheannaidh
"The meadow at the kids' place."
Heights of Inchvannie is *Bràigh
Innis Mheannaidh*.

Inglesmaldie (Kincardine)
"St Màilidh's Church", from *Eaglais
Mhàilidh*, as seen in an older
anglicised form, Eglismaldie. See
Dalmally and **Kilmallie**.

Inishail (Argyll), Innis Fhàil
The name of this island can have
two meanings. *Fàl* can refer to a
dyke or earth wall construction but
also mean "destiny", as in *Lia Fàil*,
the Gaelic name of the Stone of
Destiny.

Inishglass (Ross), An Innis Ghlas
"The grey-green meadow."

Inistrynich (Argyll), Innis
Droighnich
"Thorny meadow."

Innercochill (Perth), Inbhir Cochaill
or Inbhir Chochall
This is the name of a river mouth,
but it is unclear what the name of
the river means.

Innergeldie (Perth), Inbhir Gheallaidh
"The mouth of the bright river." This is similar to **Abergeldie** except that the latter contains the Brythonic *aber* rather than Gaelic *inbhir*.

Innergellie (Fife)
See **Innergeldie**.

Innerhadden (Perth), Inbhir Chadain
"The mouth of the Caddon", which is "warlike river".

Innerleithen (Peebles), Inbhir Liteann
"The mouth of the Leithen."

Innermessan (Wigtown)
"The mouth of the fruit river", from *Inbhir Mheasain*.

Innerourie (Banff)
This may be "mouth of the river", with the Gaelic element *dobhar*, "water", giving *Inbhir Dhobharaidh*, but this is not certain.

Innerpeffray (Perth), Inbhir Pheafraidh
"The mouth of the bright river", related to the river name in the Gaelic names of Dingwall (Inbhir Pheofharain) and Strathpeffer (Srath Pheofhair).

Innisabhaird (Ross), Innis a' Bhàird
"The poet's meadow." However, *bàrd* is also found as "field" in Ross, and it may be the case that *innis* was added after *bàrd* had gone out of popular use to mean "field".

Innis a'Chro (Ross), Innis a' Chrò
"The meadow at the enclosure", referred to in the song about *Crò Chinn Tàile*.

Innisbhuidhe (Ross), An Innis Bhuidhe
"The yellow meadow."

Insch (Aberdeen), Innis
"Meadow." This was earlier *Innis MoBheathain*, "St Bean's meadow".

Insh (Inverness), Am Baile Ùr
The Gaelic name is "the new village" and is a short form of *Baile Ùr Sgìre Innis*, "the new village of Insh district".

Inshes (Inverness), Na h-Innseagan
"The little meadows."

Insh Island (Luing), An Innis
This is "the island" with English "island" added.

Inshore (Sutherland), An Innis Odhar
"The dun-coloured meadow", the name also attached to the nearby loch.

Inver (several), An t-Inbhir
"The river mouth." The full name of Inver in Aberdeen is *Inbhir Àrdair*, "the mouth of the Arder"; in Easter Ross it is *Inbhir Loch Slinn*, "the river mouth at Loch Slin", and in Wester Ross it is *Inbhir Earradail*, "the river mouth at Erradale".

Inverailort (Inverness), Inbhir Ailleart
"The river mouth at Loch Ailort." The old Gaelic name for this place was *Cinn a' Chreagain*, "the end of the little rock".

Inveraldie (Angus)
"The river mouth at the rocky place", from Gaelic *Inbhir Alltaidh*.

Inveralivaig (Skye), Inbhir Àlabhaig
A Gaelic/Norse name containing "river mouth" and either "eel bay" or "deep river bay".

Inverallan (Banff), Inbhir Ailein
This looks like "Alan's river mouth" but is a corruption, possibly of *Inbhir Alain*, "mouth of the Allan", as suggested by older forms.

Inveralligin (Ross), Inbhir Àiliginn
"The mouth of the Alligin stream." This is also known in English as Easter Alligin.

Inverallochy (Aberdeen), Inbhir Aileachaidh
"The river mouth at the rocky place."

Inveralmond (Perth), Inbhir Amain
"The mouth of the Almond."

Inveran (Ross, Sutherland), Inbhirean
"Small river mouth."

Inveraray (Argyll), Inbhir Aora
"The mouth of the Aray." The entrance gate at Inveraray is

deemed one of the wonders of Scotland, as shown in the saying *Tobair Ghlinn Iucha, Cluig Pheairt, Geata Inbhir Aora 's a' chraobh a tha a' fàs an gàrradh na Ceapaich*, "The wells of Linlithgow, the bells of Perth, the gate of Inveraray and the tree that grows in the garden of Keppoch".

Inverardran (Perth), Inbhir Àrdrain
"The mouth of the high water."

Inverarish (Raasay), Inbhir Àrais
"River mouth", containing both the Gaelic and Norse elements for the same feature.

Inverarity (Angus)
"Mouth of the slow river", from *Inbhir Aradaidh*.

Inverarnan (Dunbarton), Inbhir Àirnein
The meaning of the second element is unclear, although it might refer to some kidney-shaped topographical feature.

Inverasdale (Ross), Inbhir Àsdail
"The river mouth in the aspen valley", from Gaelic and Norse. Brae of Inverasdale is *Bràigh Inbhir Àsdail*, "the upper part of Inverasdale". Coast of Inverasdale is *Eirtheaire Inbhir Àsdail*.

Inveraven (Banff), Inbhir Athainn
"The mouth of the very bright river." In earlier literature the Gaelic name was given as *Inbhir Athfhinn*.

Inveravon (West Lothian)
"The mouth of the river", with the Celtic element for a river found as *abhainn* in Gaelic and Irish and as *afon* in Welsh.

Inverbeg (Dunbarton), An t-Inbhir Beag
"The small river mouth."

Inverbervie (Kincardine), Inbhir Biorbhaigh
"The mouth of the boiling river." The old name of Haberberui shows how Gaelic *inbhir* replaced Brythonic *aber* in some instances.

Inverboyndie (Banff)
"The mouth of the eternal river." See **Boyndie**.

Inverbreakie (Ross), Inbhir Breacaidh
"The river mouth at the speckled place." See **Invergordon**.

Inverbroom (Ross), Baile an Lòin
The English name refers to Loch Broom, while the Gaelic one is "farm at the wet meadow". Inverbroom House, also called Foy Lodge, is *Taigh na Fothaidh*, "house with the lawn".

Inverbrough (Inverness), Inbhir Bruachaig
"The river mouth at the small bank."

Invercannich (Inverness), Inbhir Chanaich
"The mouth of the River Cannich."

Invercannie (Kincardine), Inbhir Chanaidh
This may be the same as **Invercannich**.

Invercarnaig (Ross), Inbhir Cheatharnaig
"The mouth of the little warrior river."

Invercassley (Sutherland), Inbhir Charsla
"The mouth of the castle place river."

Invercauld (Aberdeen), Inbhir Call *or* Inbhir Callaidh
"Hazel estuary." The Laird of Invercauld was *Tighearna Inbhir Call*.

Inverchaolain (Argyll), Inbhir Chaolain
"The mouth of the narrow stream."

Invercharron (Ross), Inbhir Charrann
"The mouth of the Carron."

Inverchoran (Ross), Inbhir Chòmhrainn
"The mouth of the Coran", which is "high oozing stream".

Inverchroskie (Perth), Inbhir Chrosgaidh
"The river mouth at the crossing place."

Inverclyde (Renfrew), Inbhir Chluaidh
"The mouth of the Clyde."

Invercoe (Argyll), Inbhir Chomhann
"The mouth of the Coe."

Inverdruie (Inverness), Inbhir Dhrùidh
"The mouth of the Druie."

Inverebrie (Aberdeen)
"The river mouth at the marshy place", from *Inbhir Eabraigh*.

Inveredrie (Perth), Inbhir Eadrain
"The mouth of the between-river."

Invereen (Inverness), Inbhir Fhinn
"The mouth of the fair river."

Inverenzie (Banff), Inbhir Fhionnaidh
"The river mouth at the fair place." The pronunciation collected by Diack (1944) suggests a spelling such as *Inbhir Fhinnidh*, although that would probably not change the meaning of the name.

Inverernie (Inverness), Inbhir Fheàrnaidh
"The mouth of the alder stream" or "the river mouth at the alder place".

Invereshie (Inverness), Inbhir Fhéisidh
"The mouth of the river in the boggy haugh."

Inveresk (Angus, Midlothian), Inbhir Easg
"The mouth of the river", containing the Brythonic water element *esk* which is cognate with Gaelic *uisge*, "water". The Gaelic form of the Angus name was recorded by Diack (1944), and the Midlothian name is the same.

Inveresragan (Argyll), Inbhir Easragain
"The mouth of the Esragan."

Inverewe (Ross), Inbhir Iùbh
"The mouth of the yew river." Inverewe House is *Taigh na Plucaird*, "house at the lump promontory", often over-corrected to *Taigh nam Pluc Àrd*, "house of the high lumps".

Inverey (Aberdeen), Inbhir Eidh
"The mouth of the Ey." Local people distinguished between *Inbhir Eidh Bheag* and *Inbhir Eidh Mhór* (little and big Inverey).

Inverfarigaig (Inverness), Inbhir Fairgeag *or* Inbhir Faragaig
"Mouth of the Farigaig", a river name connected with *fairge*, "ocean". Nearby Stratherrick (*Srath Fharagaig*) is named after the same river. The old church near Inverfarigaig was called *Cill MoLuaig*, "St MoLuag's Church".

Invergarry (Inverness), Inbhir Gharadh
"The mouth of the Garry."

Invergelder (Aberdeen), Inbhir Ghealdair
"The mouth of the white water."

Invergloy (Inverness), Inbhir Ghlaoidh
"The mouth of the gluey or viscous river."

Invergordon (Ross), An Rubha *or* Inbhir Ghòrdain
"The point" or "Gordon's river mouth", named after Sir Alexander Gordon. In Gaelic, "in Invergordon" is expressed by *air an Rubha*, "on the point". An older and more complete name was *Rubha Nach Breacaidh*, "the point on the high speckled moor". Invergordon ferry left from *Port Nach Breacaidh*, "the port of the high speckled place", an abbreviation of *Port Aonach Breacaidh*.

Invergowrie (Perth), Inbhir Ghobharaidh
"The river mouth of Gowrie."

Invergroin (Dunbarton), Inbhir Dhroighinn
"The mouth of the thorny river."

Inverguseran (Inverness), Inbhir Ghùiseirein
The defining element in this river name is unclear.

Inverhaggernie (Perth), Inbhir Chagarnaidh
"The mouth of the whispering river."

Inverharity (Angus), Inbhir h-Eara-
daidh
This may be "the river mouth at the
division". The Gaelic form was
recorded by Diack (1944) using his
own phonetic transcription.

Inverherive (Perth), Inbhir h-Eirbhe
"The river mouth at the boundary
wall."

Inverhope (Sutherland), Inbhir Hób
"The river mouth at Hope", from
Gaelic but featuring the Norse
word for "bay", which is the origin
of *Hób*.

Inverie (Fife); (Inverness), Inbhir
Aoidh
In Fife this is "estuary place", from
Inbhiridh, earlier *Inbhirin*. In
Inverness-shire, this may be "the
river mouth at the isthmus", from
Gaelic/Norse.

Inverinate (Ross), Inbhir Ìonaid
"The mouth of the brown river",
from the earlier *Inbhir Dhuinnid*.
The surrounding area is known as
Lèitir Choill, "hazel slope".

Inverinian (Perth), Inbhir Inneoin
"The mouth of the anvil stream",
which itself is known as *Allt Inneoin*.

Inverkeillor (Angus), Inbhir Chìolair
The meaning of the second element
is unclear.

Inverkeithing (Fife), Inbhir Chéitinn
This may be "the mouth of the wood
river or wood place", with the
second element based on Brythonic
coed, "a wood".

Inverkeithney (Banff)
This may be similar to
Inverkeithing, or alternatively may
contain the element *Cé* referring to
a Pictish district or tribe.

Inverkip (Renfrew), Inbhir Chip
"The river mouth at the stump",
containing Gaelic *ceap*.

Inverkirkaig (Sutherland), Inbhir
Chirceig
"The river mouth at church bay",
from Gaelic/Norse.

Inverlael (Ross), Inbhir Lathail
"The river mouth in the low
hollow", from Gaelic/Norse.

Inverlaidnon (Inverness), Inbhir
Laidirean
The defining element in this name is
unclear.

Inverleith (Midlothian), Inbhir Lìte
"The mouth of the Leith", a name
from Brythonic denoting wetness.

Inverlochlarig (Perth), Inbhir Lòch
Làirig
"The river mouth at the dark pass."

Inverlochy (Inverness), Inbhir
Lòchaidh
"The mouth of the Lochy."
Inverlochy Castle was known as
Caisteal Thìr Lunndaidh or *Caisteal
Thòrr Lunndaidh*, "Torlundy Castle".

Inverlussa (Argyll, Jura), Inbhir Lusa
"The mouth of the bright river",
from Gaelic/Norse.

Invermark (Argyll)
"The mouth of the horse river",
containing Gaelic *marc*.

Invermarkie (Aberdeen), Inbhir
Mharcaidh
"The mouth of the horse river."

Invermoriston (Inverness), Inbhir
Moireasdan
"The mouth of the Moriston", which
is often taken to mean "great water"
but is unclear in meaning.

Invermuick (Aberdeen), Inbhir
Muice
"The mouth of the pig stream."

Invernahyle (Inverness), Inbhir na
h-Aidhle
"The river mouth at the adze", referring to the shape of a piece of land.

Invernauld (Sutherland), Inbhir nan
Allt
"The mouth of the streams."

Invernaver (Sutherland), Inbhir
Nabhair
"The mouth of the Naver."

Inverneill (Argyll), Inbhir Néill
This appears to mean "Neil's river
mouth".

Invernenty (Perth), Inbhir
Leanntaidh
"The mouth of the Nettle River."

Inverness (Inverness), Inbhir Nis
"The mouth of the Ness." Inverness-
shire is *Siorrachd Inbhir Nis* and the
western part is *na Garbh Chrìochan*,
"rough bounds", in full *Garbh
Chrìochan Chloinn Raghnaill*, "rough
bounds of Clanranald".

Inveroran (Argyll), Inbhir Dhobhrain
"The mouth of the little water."

Inverpeffer (Angus)
"The mouth of the bright river",
from *Inbhir Pheofhair*. See
Strathpeffer and **Dingwall**.

Inverpolly (Ross), Inbhir Pollaidh
"The mouth of the Polly."

Inverquharity (Angus)
This may mean "twin river mouth"
and contain *càraid*, "twin" or
"couple".

Inverroy (Inverness), Inbhir Ruaidh
"The mouth of the red-brown river."

Inversanda (Argyll), Inbhir Sannda
"Mouth of the sand river", from
Gaelic/Norse.

Inversheil (Ross), Inbhir Sheile
"The mouth of the Sheil."

Invershin (Sutherland), Inbhir Sin
"The mouth of the old river."
Locally this was also known as
Inbhir Sìn and *Port na Lic*, "port at
the flagstone".

Inversnaid (Stirling), Inbhir Snàthaid
"The mouth of the needle stream",
which is known as *Allt na Snàthaid*.

Invertote (Skye), Inbhir Thobhta
This hybrid Gaelic/Norse name is
"the river mouth at the house site".

Invertrossachs (Perth)
See **Drunkie**.

Inverugie (Aberdeen, Moray), Inbhir
Ùigidh
"The mouth of the Ugie." *Inbhir
Ùigidh* is the name of Peterhead in
eastern Gaelic dialects.

Inveruglas (Dunbarton), Inbhir
Dhùghlais

"Mouth of the Douglas", which
itself is "black stream".

Inverurie (Aberdeen), Inbhir Uaraidh
This may be "the mouth of the landslip river".

Invervack (Perth), Inbhir a' Bhac
It is unclear what the second part
means.

Invervar (Perth), Inbhir Bharra
This may mean "the mouth of the
top river".

Inverveigh (Argyll), Inbhir Bheithe
"The mouth of the birch stream."

Inverwick, Inbhir Bhuic (Inverness);
Inbhir Mhuice (Perth)
The Inverness name is "the mouth of
the buck river" while in Perth it is
"the mouth of the pig river". The fair
held at Inverwick in Perthshire was
An Fhéill Mhuice, "the pig fair",
which is probably a play on words
given the place's Gaelic name.

Invery (Kincardine)
This is "estuary place", from
Inbhiridh, earlier *Inbhirin*.

Iochdar (South Uist), An t-Ìochdar
"The bottom." The English is still
occasionally spelled as "Eochar".

Iona (Iona), Ì, Ì Chaluim Chille *or*
Eilean Idhe
The English name comes from a
misreading of *Ioua* which may be
"yew island". The Gaelic name Ì is
generally lengthened to avoid confusion, to *Ì Chaluim Chaluim*, "St
Columba's Iona", or *Eilean Idhe*, "the
isle of Iona". A native of Iona is an
Idheach, and the island was known as
Ì nam ban bòidheach, "Iona of the
beautiful women".

Irongath (West Lothian)
"Portion of the marsh land", from
Earrann Gaoithe.

Irvine (Ayr), Irbhinn
This river name has been attached to
the town and may be related to a
similar name in Wales.

Isay (Skye), Ìosaigh
"Ice island", from Norse.

Islandfinnan (Argyll), Eilean
Fhìonain
"St Finnan's island."

Island MacNeil (Bute), Eilean
MhicNéill
It is unclear who the MacNeil was
who is commemorated in this name.

Islay (Islay), Ìle
If this is a Gaelic name it may be
"flank shaped". Islay is known as
Eilean uaine Ìle, "green isle of Islay",
and has a number of distinct areas.
The Rinns of Islay are *Roinn Ìle, Na
Roinn Ìleach* and *Na Ranna*, all of
which refer to division. A person
from the Rinns is a *Rannach*. The
north-east of the island is *Na
Hearadh*, which is another word for
"division" also found in "Harris",
while the south-west peninsula of
Oa is *an Obha*, "headland", where
the local people were nicknamed
cuthagan, "cuckoos". A native of Islay
is an *Ìleach*, a name shared with the
people of Glen Isla and Strath Isla.
A number of sayings and expres-
sions concern Islay. *Nuair a thréigeas
na dùthchasaich Ìle, beannachd le sìth
Albainn*, "When the natives leave
Islay, farewell to the peace of
Scotland", is a fairly ominous warn-
ing. Less ominous is *Muileach is
Ìleach is deamhan, An triùir as miosa
air an domhain. Is miosa am Muileach
na an t-Ìleach, Is miosa an t-Ìleach na
an deamhan*, "A Mull person, an
Islay person and the devil, The three
worst in the world. The Mull one is
worse than the Islay one, The Islay
one is worse than the devil". This is
contradicted by *Nam b' eileanach mi,
gum b' Ìleach mi, nam b' Ìleach mi, bu
Rannach mi*, "If I were an islander,
I'd want to be from Islay; if I were
from Islay, I'd want to be from the
Rinns". Islay's placenames are
mentioned in a saying which
includes the line, *Tha ceithir busaichean fichead an Ìle*, "There are

twenty-four *buses* in Islay", which
shows how Norse names from
bólstaðr, which when gaelicised
usually become *-bost*, end in *-bus* in
Islay. A more complete version
mentions *Ceithir busacha fichead an
Ìle, ceithir àirdeacha fichead an Diùra,
's ceithir màmanna fichead am Muile*,
"Twenty-four *buses* in Islay, twenty-
fours *ards* in Jura and twenty-four
màms in Mull". Islay was traditionally linked with Bute and Arran, as
shown in the saying *Bód is Ìle is
Arainn*.

Isle Martin (Ross), Eilean Mhàrtainn
"Martin's island."

Isle of Loch Tay (Perth), Eilean nam
Bannaomh
The Gaelic name is "island of the
female saints". In Kenmore one of the
fairs was called *Féill nam Bannaomh*,
"the fair of the female saints".

Isle of Whithorn (Wigtown), Port
Rosnait
The Gaelic name is "port at the
small promontory". See **Whithorn**.

Isleornsay (Skye), Eilean Iarmain
The alternative version of the name
of the village, *Eilean Dhiarmaid*,
"Diarmid's island", was commonly
heard in Skye. The nearby island
with the same name in English is
Eilean Orasaigh, the second element
from Norse, meaning "tidal island".
Local people were known by the
nickname *eireagan*, "pullets".

Isle Ristol (Ross), Eilean Ruisteil
"Island with the horse valley", from
Gaelic/Norse.

Islivig (Lewis), Ìslibhig
"Ice slope bay", from Norse.

J

Jamestown (Dumfries, Dunbarton,
Ross)
Jamestown in Ross is in Gaelic *Baile
Sheumais* or *Baile Shiamais*, "James's
village", the latter spelling showing
the distinctive local pronunciation.

Janetstown (Caithness), Baile
Seònaid
The Gaelic version is a translation
from the English.

John O' Groats (Caithness), Taigh
Iain Ghròt *or* Taigh Eathain Ghrót
"Jan de Groot's house" in memory of
the Dutch merchant who built the
first house here. The second Gaelic
form is the one used in north-coast
Gaelic. A couple of rather deroga-
tory Gaelic sayings relate to John O'
Groats, *Taigh Iain Ghròt ort!*, "John
O' Groats to you" and *Cuiridh mi a
Thaigh Iain Ghròt thu!*, "I'll send you
to John O' Groats".

Jordanhill (Glasgow), Cnoc Iòrdain
This is a biblical reference.

Jura (Jura), Diùra
"Deer island", from Norse. The
island's byname is *An t-Eilean Bàn*,
"the blessed island", where *bàn* has
had its usual meaning of "fair" or
"white" extended. A local person is a
Diùrach, but would also have been
known by the nickname *each*,
"horse".

K

Kallin (Grimsay), Na Ceallan
"The cells", as inhabited by hermits.

Kames (Argyll), Camas nam
Muclach; (Bute), Camas
In Argyll this is "the bay of the
pig places". In Bute the name is
simply "bay", but is divided into
two parts. Easter Kames is *Camas
Mór*, "big Kames", while Wester
Kames is *Camas Beag*, "small
Kames".

Katewell (Ross), Ciadail
"Cattle fold valley", from Norse.

Keanculish (Ross), Ceann a' Chaolais
"The head of the strait."

Kearstay (Harris), Cearstaigh
"Hart island", from Norse.

Kebbock Head (Lewis), A' Chàbag
"The kebbuck (of cheese)." This may
refer to the headland's shape.

Keil (Argyll), A' Chill
"The cell or church."

Keill (Muck), A' Chill
See **Keil**.

Keills (Argyll), Cill Mhic Ó Carmaig;
(Islay), A' Chill
The Argyll name is "cell or church of
the son of O'Cormack", while the
Islay name is "the cell or church".

Keiloch (Aberdeen), An Caolach
"The narrow place."

Keils (Argyll, Jura), A' Chill
"The cell or church", with an
English plural attached.

Keir (Dumfries, Stirling)
"Fort." In Dumfriesshire this prob-
ably comes from Brythonic, while in
Stirlingshire it may be either
Brythonic or Gaelic *cathair*.

Keiss (Caithness), Céis
This Norse name may indicate
either a promontory or a rounded
ridge.

Keistle (Skye), Ceasdail *or* Ciosdal
This Norse name may mean "low
valley".

Keith (Banff), Baile Chéith
This seems to be from Brythonic
coed, "wood", but a local Pictish
territorial division was *Cé*, and the
name may be related to this. The
Gaelic name is prefixed by *baile*,
"town". The town used to be known
as Kethmalruf (*Céith Maol Rubha*),
"St Maol Rubha's Keith", this saint's
name later becoming confused with
that of St Rufus.

Keithick (Perth)
"Small wood", based on Brythonic
coed with a Gaelic diminutive ending
suggesting *Céitheag*.

Keithmore (Banff), Céith Mhór
"Large Keith", from an original
Brythonic *coed* with Gaelic *mór*
affixed.

Keithock (Angus)
See **Keithick**.

Kellas (Angus, Moray), Ceallas
"Church place."

Kelso (Roxburgh), Cealsaidh *or*
Cealso
"Chalk heugh", from English.

Keltneyburn (Perth), Allt
Chailtnidh
"Stream of the hard river."

Kelty (Fife); (Perth), Cailtidh
In Perthshire this is "hard place",
from the element found in river
names such as *Caladar* and
"Calder". The Fife name may be the
same.

Kenary (Grimsay), Ceann Àirigh
"Sheiling end."

Kendibig (Harris), Ceann Dìbig
"Head of the deep bay", from
Gaelic/Norse.

Kendram (Skye), Ceann Droma
"Ridge end."

Kendrum (Perth), Ceanndruim
"Head ridge."

Kenknock (Perth), Ceannchnoc
"Head hill."

Kenmore (Argyll, Ross), A'
Cheannmhor; (Perth), An
Ceannmhor
"Big headed place." In Ross, people
from Kenmore are known as *ceann-
phollain*, "tadpoles". In Perthshire,
one of the fairs held at Kenmore was
known as *Féill nam Bannaomh*, "the
fair of the female saints", echoing
the Gaelic name of nearby Isle of
Loch Tay, which is *Eilean nam
Bannaomh*, "island of the female
saints".

Kennacraig (Argyll), Ceann na
Creige
"The end of the rock."

Kennacreggan (Inverness), Ceann
nan Creagan
"The end of the rocks."

Kennoway (Fife), Ceannachaidh
Old forms of the name such as
Kennochin and Kennoquhy suggest
a Gaelic origin from *ceann*, "end" or
"head", while the latter part of the
name is unclear but may simply be a
locative form.

Kenovay (Scalpay, Tiree), Ceann a'
Bhàigh
"The head of the bay." The old
church in Kenovay in Tiree is
Teampall Fhìonain, "St Finnan's
Chapel".

Kensaleyre (Skye), Ceann Sàil Eighre
"The head of the inlet at the beach",
from Gaelic/Norse.

Kensalroag (Skye), Ceann Sàil
Ròdhag *or* Ceann an t-Sàile
"The head of Roag inlet." Gaelic also
has the shorter name, "the head of
the inlet".

Kentallen (Argyll), Ceann an t-Sàilein
"The head of the small inlet."

Kentangaval (Barra), Ceann
Tangabhail
"Head of the hill at the sharp point",
from Gaelic/Norse.

Kentra (Argyll, Ross), Ceann Tràgha
"Beach end."

Kentulavaig (Lewis), Ceann
Tùlabhaig *or* Ceann Thùlabhaig
"The head of the rocky bay", from
Gaelic/Norse.

Kenvar (Tiree), Ceann a' Bhara
"The head of the cliff", from Gaelic/
Norse. The old church here was
Teampall Phàraig, "St Patrick's
Chapel".

Keoldale (Sutherland), Cealldail
This may be "keel valley", from
Norse.

Keose (Lewis), Ceòs
"Hollow", from Norse. Keose Glebe
is *Glìb Cheòis*.

Keppanach (Inverness), Ceapanach
"Arable land."

Keppoch (Inverness, Ross), A'
Cheapach
"The tillage land." Back of
Keppoch is *Cùl na Ceapaich* and
Keppoch Muir is *an Sliabh
Ceapanach*, "the moor of the tillage
land".

Kernsary (Ross), Cearnasair
"Sheiling on good land", from
Norse.

Kerrera (Kerrera), Cearrara
"Copse island", from Norse. A
Kerrera person is a *Cearrarach*, also
nicknamed an *eireag*, "pullet", and a
saying about Kerrera people is, *Tha
trì casan deiridh air na h-eireagan an
Cearrara*, "The pullets in Kerrera
have three back legs".

Kerrowdown (Inverness), An
Ceathramh Donn
"The brown quarter-land."

Kerrowgair (Inverness), An
Ceathramh Geàrr
"The short quarter-land."

Kerry (Argyll), An Ceathramh
Comhalach; (Ross), Cearraidh
In Argyll the name means "the
Cowal quarter-land", an inhabitant
of which is known as a *Ceathrach*.
This word also appears in *An Caol
Ceathrach*, "the Kerry strait" or West
Kyle of Bute. In Ross the name may
be "copse river", from Norse.

Kerrycroy (Bute), An Ceathramh
Cruaidh
"The hard quarterland."

Kerrysdale (Ross), A' Chathair Bheag
The English name may be "copse
valley", from Norse, while the Gaelic
one is "the little fort".

Kersavagh (North Uist), Cearsabhagh
This may be "copse bay", from
Norse.

Kershader (Lewis), Ceairseadar
"Copse dwelling" or "deer farm",
from Norse.

Kessock (Inverness), Ceasag
This is named after the saint associ-
ated with the Lennox area. See
North Kessock and **South
Kessock**.

Kettle (Fife)
"Cat place", from *Catail*.

Khantore (Aberdeen), Ceann Tòrr
"Hill end."

Kiel (Argyll), A' Chill
"The cell or church." The full name
of Kiel in Morvern is *Cill Chaluim
Chille*, "the church of St Columba"

while Kiel Crofts in Benderloch is
Croit na Cille, "the croft at the
church".

Kilanallen (Mull), Cill an Àilein
"The church in the meadow."

Kilarrow (Islay), Cill A Rubha
"St Maol Rubha's Church." The *A* in
the Gaelic name is not a definitive
article but a contraction of *Maol*.
Another church in the area was
called *Cill Chaluim Chille*, "St
Columba's Church".

Kilaulay (South Uist), Cill Amhlaigh
"Amhlaigh's Church." There is no
Gaelic saint of this name
recorded, so the name may be an
old dedication to a Norse Olaf,
of which *Amhlaigh* is a
gaelicisation.

Kilbarchan (Renfrew)
"St Bearchan's Church", from *Cill
Bhearchain*.

Kilberry (Argyll), Cill Bheiridh *or*
Cill Bhearaigh
"St Bearach's Church."

Kilbirnie (Ayr), Cill Bhreannain
"St Brendan's Church." St Brennan's
Fair was held here each year.

Kilblain (Bute), Cill Bhlàthain
"St Blane's Church."

Kilblane (Argyll), Cill Bhlàthain
See **Kilblain**.

Kilblean (Argyll), Cill Bhlàthain
See **Kilblain**.

Kilbowie (Argyll, Dunbarton)
Although the anglicised form
suggests "yellow church", older
forms point to *A' Chùilt Bhuidhe*,
"the yellow nook or back". It appears
that the Argyll name was transferred
from Dunbartonshire.

Kilbrandon (Argyll, Islay, Mull), Cill
Bhrianainn
"St Brendan's Church."

Kilbrare (Sutherland), Cill nam
Bràthair
"Church of the brothers."

Kilbrennan (Mull), Cill Bhrianainn
"St Brendan's Church."

Kilbride (Argyll, Arran), Cille Bhrìghde
"St Bridget's Church."

Kilbridemore (Argyll), Cille Bhrìghde Mhór
"Big Kilbride."

Kilbryde (Perth), Cill Bhrìghde
See **Kilbride**.

Kilbucho (Peebles)
This may be "St Beagha's Church", named after a little known 7th-century Irish nun.

Kilcalmonell (Argyll), Cill Cholmain Eala
"St Colman Eala's Church", a saint also commemorated in Colmonell in Ayrshire.

Kilchattan (Argyll, Bute, Colonsay, Luing), Cille Chatain
"St Catan's Church." In Colonsay there are Lower Kilchattan and Upper Kilchattan. Lower Kilchattan comprises both *Baile Ìochdarach*, "lower farm", and *Baile Uachdrach*, "upper farm". Upper Kilchattan is *Baile Mhoire* in Gaelic, "St Mary's farm".

Kilcheran (Lismore), Cill Chiarain
"St Ciaran's Church."

Kilchiaran (Bute, Islay), Cill Chiarain
See **Kilcheran**.

Kilchoan (Argyll, Inverness, Islay), Cille Chomhghain
"St Comhghan's Church." The Gaelic name can also be seen spelled *Cill a' Chòthain* which sounds similar but is meaningless.

Kilchoman (Islay), Cill Chomain
"St Coman's Church."

Kilchousland (Argyll), Cill Chuisilein
"St Constantine's Church."

Kilchrenan (Argyll), Cill Chrèanain
Although there is no saint recorded as *Crèanan*, there is a Kilmacrenan in Donegal, which may refer to a son or devotee of a saint of this name.

Kilchrist (Argyll, Mull, Ross, Skye), Cille Chrìosd
"Christ's Church."

Kilchurn (Argyll), Caol a' Chùirn
"The strait at the cairn."

Kilconquhar (Fife)
"St Dúnchadh's or St Conchadh's Church", from *Cill Dúnchaidh* or *Cill Chonchaidh*.

Kilcoy (Ross), Cùil Challaidh
"Secluded spot at the hazel place."

Kildalton (Islay), Cill Daltain
There is no saint of this name and here the word *daltan* refers to a foster son. The local church was dedicated to St John the Evangelist, and another old church in the area was dedicated to St Columba and called *Cill Chaluim Chille*.

Kildary (Ross), Caoldaraigh
"Narrow plain."

Kildavaig (Argyll), Cill Damhaig
"St Damhóc's Church."

Kildavannan (Bute), Cill DoBheannain
"St Bannan's Church."

Kildavie (Argyll), Cill Dà Bhì
"St Dà Bhì's Church." *Dà Bhì* or *DoBhì* was a byname of Bearchan, who is commemorated in Kilbarchan.

Kildermorie (Ross), Cille Mhuire
"St Mary's Church." Kildermorie Forest is *Frìth Chille Mhuire*.

Kildonan (several), Cill Donnain
"St Donnan's Church." The Kildonan area of Sutherland is *Sgìre Ilidh*, "district of the Ilidh or Helmsdale River". An old saying is, *Cill Fhinn, Cill Duinn 's Cill Donnain, na trì cilltean as sine an Albainn*, "Killin, Kildun and Kildonan, the three oldest cells in Scotland". A person from the Kildonan area in Sutherland, where the fair was known as *Féill Donnain*, is an *Ileach*, which is distinct from *Ìleach*, which refers to someone from Glenisla, Strathisla or Islay.

Kildrochit (Wigtown)
"Bridge end", from an original *Ceann Drochaid*.

Kildrummy (Aberdeen), Cionn Droma
"Ridge end." The fair held here was known as *Fèill Mhoir* or *Fèill Mhoire*, "St Mary's fair".

Kildun (Ross), Cill Duinn
"Brown church." See **Kildonan**.

Kilduncan (Fife)
This appears to be "St Donnchadh's Church", from *Cill Donnchaidh* or *Cill Donnchain*.

Kilduthie (Kincardine)
"St Duthac's Church", from *Cill Dubhthaich*.

Kilerivagh (Benbecula), Cill Éireabhagh
This Gaelic/Norse name may mean "church at the bay with a beach".

Kilfeddar (Wigtown), Cill Pheadair
"St Peter's Church."

Kilfinan (Argyll), Cill Fhìonain
"St Finnan's Church."

Kilfinnan (Inverness). Cill Fhìonain
See **Kilfinan**.

Kilfinnichen (Mull), Cill Fhionnchain
"St Fionnchan's Church." A local saying describing a detour was *Rathad Mhóirnis do Chill Fhionnchain*, "via Mornish to Kilfinnichen".

Kilhenzie (Ayr)
See **Kilkenneth**.

Kilkenneth (Tiree), Cill Choinnich
"St Cainnech's Church."

Kilkenzie (Argyll, Ayr), Cill Choinnich
"St Cainnech's Church." The English form of the Argyll name is pronounced as "Kilkenny". In Ayrshire, the Gaelic name was formerly *Cill MoChainnich*, showing a diminutive, affectionate form of the saint's name.

Kilkerran (Argyll, Ayr), Cill Chiarain
"St Ciaran's Church."

Killallan (Renfrew)
"St Fillan's Church", from *Cill Fhaolain*.

Killanaish (Argyll), Cill Aonghais
"St Angus's Church."

Killandrist (Lismore), Cill Anndrais
"St Andrew's Church."

Killean (Argyll, Islay, Lismore), Cill Eathain
"St John's Church." In Islay, Lower Killean is *Cill Eathain Ìochdrach* and Upper Killean is *Cill Eathain Uachdrach*.

Killearn (Stirling), Cill Earrainn
This was originally *Cinn Earrainn*, "the end of the portion of land", but has changed to a *cill* name, possibly by analogy with other names. AÀA recommend *Cill Earn*.

Killearnan (Ross), Cill Iùrnain
"St Iotharnan's Church." Killearnan parish is *Sgìre Iùrnain*.

Killegray (Harris), Ceileagraigh
"Island of the burial place", from Norse.

Kilellan (Argyll), Cill Fhaolain
"St Fillan's Church."

Killen (Ross), Cill Annaidh *or* Cill Fhannaidh
It is not clear which saint is commemorated in this name.

Kilennan (Islay), Cill Fhìonain
"St Finnan's Church."

Killeonan (Argyll), Cill Eónain *or* Cill Eódhanain
"St Adamnan's Church."

Killernandale (Jura), Cill Earnadail *or* Cill Earradail
"The valley of St Ernan's Church", a Gaelic/Norse name where an earlier Gaelic name had Norse *dalr* attached.

Killernie (Fife)
"End of the alder or sloe place", from *Cinn Fheàrna* or *Cinn Àirne*. Originally this name was formed with *ceann/cinn*, "end", rather than *cill*, "church".

Killichonan (Perth), Cille Chonnain
"St Connan's Church."

Killiechassie (Perth), Cill Chasaidh
"St Casan's Church."

Killiechonate (Inverness), Cille Chonaid
"St Conaid's Church."

Killiechronan (Mull), Coille Chrònain
"The wood of the murmuring sound." Old Killiechronan is *An Seann Bhaile*, "the old farm".

Killiecrankie (Perth), Coille Chreithnich *or* Coille Chneagaidh
"Aspen wood" or possibly "the wood at the knobbly place". The site of the Battle of Killiecrankie is known as *Raon Ruairidh*, "Roderick's field".

Killiehangie (Perth), Cille Chaomhaidh
This may be "St Kevin's Church".

Killiehuntly (Inverness), Coille Chunndainn
"Wood at the confluence."

Killiemacuddican (Kirkcudbright)
"St MoChuda's Church", showing a diminutive form of the saint's name from *Cille MoChudagain*.

Killilan (Ross), Cill Fhaolain
"St Fillan's Church."

Killin (Inverness, Perth), Cill Fhinn; (Sutherland), Cill Eathain
In Inverness-shire and Perthshire the name means "white church", while in Sutherland it is "St John's Church". The fair held at Killin in Perthshire was known as *Fèill Faolain*, "St Fillan's Fair", dedicated to the saint named in nearby Strathfillan. People from Killin were known as *mionnasgan*, "minnows". See **Kildonan**.

Killinaig (Mull), Cill Fhionnaig
"St Fionnag's Church."

Killochan (Wigtown)
"St Onchu's Church", from *Cill Onchon*.

Killundine (Argyll), Cill Fionndain
"St Fintan's Church."

Kilmachalmaig (Bute, Ross), Cill MoChalmaig
"St MoChalmag's Church" showing an affectionate form of the name of St Colman.

Kilmachellaig (Argyll), Cill MoCheallaig
"St MoCheallag's Church."

Kilmacolm (Renfrew), Cill MoCholuim
This was originally a church name dedicated either to St Columba or another saint named Colum.

Kilmadock (Perth), Cill MoDog
"St Cadog's Church."

Kilmaglass (Argyll)
This may be the "church of Glas's son", from *Cill Mac Glais*.

Kilmahoe (Argyll), Cill MoChotha
"St MoChotha's Church."

Kilmahog (Perth), Cill MoChùg
"St MoChùg's Church." The fair held here each November was known as *Fèill MoChùg*, "St MoChùg's Fair". This may be an affectionate form of the name of the saint known as *Cuaca*.

Kilmahumaig (Argyll), Cill MoChumaig
"St MoChumag's Church."

Kilmaichlie (Banff), Cill Mhèichlidh *or* Cinn Mheachlainn
This may be a corrupted form of the name of the saint *Maol Sheachlainn*, as found in the pass of *Làirig Mheachlainn* in Perthshire. *Cinn Mheachlainn* contains *ceann*, "end or head", rather than *cill*, "church", but this may not be significant. The English form of the name is also found as "Kilnmaichlie".

Kilmain (Sutherland), Cill Mheadhain
"Middle church", situated between the churches at Killin and Kilbrare.

Kilmallie (Inverness), Cill Mhàilidh
This church name is unclear, but Kilmaley in Co. Clare is *Cill Mháille*, which seems to contain the same personal name as in *Ó Máille* (O'Malley). See **Culmaily** and **Dalmally**.

Kilmannan (Stirling)
This may be "the church of Manau", from *Cill Mhanainn* or *Cill Mhanann*. See **Clackmannan**.

Kilmany (Fife)
See **Kilmeny**.

Kilmarie (Skye), Cill Ma Ruibhe
"St Maol Rubha's Church."

Kilmarnock (Argyll, Ayr), Cill Mhearnaig
"St Ernoc's or M'Ernoc's Church."

Kilmaronag (Argyll), Cill MoChrònaig
"St Crònan's Church."

Kilmaronock (Dunbarton)
"St Ronan's Church", from *Cill MoRònaig*.

Kilmartin (Argyll, Ayr), Cille Mhàrtainn
"St Martin's Church." In Argyll local people were nicknamed *coilich*, "cockerels", and Kilmartin Glen is *Srath Sgeotanais*.

Kilmaveonaig (Perth), Cill MoMh'Eónaig *or* Cill MoBheònaig
This is either "St Adamnan's Church" or "St Beoghna's Church", both derivations showing a diminutive form of the respective names.

Kilmelford (Argyll), Cill Mheallaird
This may be "church at the lumpy headland", although a Norse source is likely for the second part of the name, possibly meaning "gravelly sea loch".

Kilmeny (Islay), Cill Mheinidh
"St Eithne's Church", from an affectionate form of the name.

Kilmichael (Argyll, Arran), Cill Mhìcheil
"St Michael's Church."

Kilminning (Fife)
This may be "St Maoineann's Church", from *Cill Mhaoininn*

Kilmodan (Argyll), Cill Mhaodhain
"St Modan's Church."

Kilmoluag (Skye, Tiree), Cille MoLuaig *or* Cill MoLuaig
"St MoLuag's Church."

Kilmolymock (Moray)
Older forms of the name, such as Kilmalaman and Kilmalemnock from *Cill MoLomain* and *Cill MoLomanaig*, suggest that St Loman may be commemorated here.

Kilmonivaig (Inverness), Cill MoNaomhaig
"St Naomhan's Church."

Kilmorack (Inverness), Cill Mhóraig
"St Moroc's Church." The Gaelic version suggests the name *Mórag* but the dedication is to *Moroc*. The area of East Kilmorack is known as *Leathair nam Manach*, "the monks' slope", while the Falls of Kilmorack are *an t-Eas Ruadh*, "the red-brown waterfall".

Kilmore (Argyll, Skye), A' Chille Mhór
"The big church." The manse at Kilmore in Skye was known as *An Taigh Bàn* for its pale colour.

Kilmorich (Argyll, Perth), Cill Mhuirich
"St Muireadhach's Church."

Kilmory, Cille Mhoire (Argyll, Rum), Cill Mhuire *or* Cill Mhoire (Arran)
"St Mary's Church."

Kilmote (Sutherland), Baile na h-Àtha
The English name suggests a church dedication to St Mayota from an older Gaelic name including *cill*, while the Gaelic name is "the farm with the stable".

Kilmuick (Banff), Cill Mhuice
This name suggests "pig church", and may refer to a nearby river or stream.

Kilmuir, Cill Mhoir (Ross), Cille Mhoire (Skye)
"St Mary's Church."

Kilmun (Argyll), Cill Mhunna
"St Munna's Church" using an affectionate byname of St Fintan.

Kilmure Easter (Ross), Sgìre Mhoire Shìos
The English name refers to the eastern part of Kilmure, while the

Gaelic name is "lower parish of St Mary".

Kilnaughton (Islay), Cill Neachdain "St Nechtan's Church."

Kilnave (Islay), Cill Néimh "St Ném's Church."

Kilninian (Mull), Cill Naoinein It is unclear which saint is commemorated in this name but it is unlikely to be Ninian, who is mainly associated with the south of the country. Another church in the area was dedicated to St Columba and called *Cill Chaluim Chille*.

Kilninver (Argyll), Cill an Inbhir This name appears to mean "church by the river mouth", however, an older form of *Cill Fhionnbhair*, "St Finbar's Church", appears together with an earlier version of *Cill M'Fhionnbhair*, "Dear St Finbar's Church".

Kiloran (Colonsay), Cill Odhrain "St Oran's Church."

Kilpatrick (Ayr); (Arran), Cill Phàraig, Cill Pheadair *or* Cill Phàdair; (Mull), Cill Phàdraig "St Patrick's Church." The Arran names show the confusion between the names *Pàdraig* and *Peadar* in that the former is translated into English as both Patrick and Peter. The Ayrshire name is from *Cill Phàdraig*.

Kilpheder (South Uist), Cille Pheadair "St Peter's Church."

Kilphedir (Sutherland), Cill Pheadair "St Peter's Church."

Kilpunt (West Lothian) This probably originated as Brythonic *pen pont*, "bridge end", with Brythonic *pen*, "end, head", changing to Gaelic *ceann*, which in turn became *cill*, "church". This gaelicisation of Brythonic names also appears in **Kirkintilloch** and **Kinneil**.

Kilquhockadale (Wigtown) This name is "St Cuaca's Church", from Gaelic *Cill Chuaca* to which Norse *dalr*, "valley", was added. A similar naming process is found in **Killernandale**.

Kilravock (Nairn), Cill Ràthaig "Church at the small circular fort."

Kilrenny (Fife) This seems to be "St Ethernan's Church", from *Cill Eatharnain*.

Kilry (Angus), Caol Ruigh "Narrow slope."

Kilrymonth (Fife), Cill Rìmhinn See **St Andrews**.

Kilslevan (Islay), Cill Sléibheainn "St Slevan's Church."

Kilspindie (Perth) "St Pensandus's Church", from a lost Gaelic form.

Kilsyth (Dunbarton), Cill Saidh This may be "St Sadhbh's Church" although a number of earlier Gaelic forms may suggest alternative interpretations, e.g. *Cill Saoif, Cil Saithe* and *Cill Saighdhe*.

Kiltarlity (Inverness), Cill Taraglain "St Talorcan's Church." The Gaelic name is similar that of the old name of Portree in Skye. The settlement now called Kiltarlity was earlier *Allt Feàrna*, "alder burn", and is known locally as "Allarburn". The wider Kiltarlity area is known as *Bràigh na h-Àirde*, "the upper part of Aird".

Kiltearn (Inverness), Cill Tighearn "The Lord's Church." Kiltearn parish is *Sgìre Thighearn*.

Kilvaxter (Skye), Cille Bhacastair This appears to be a Gaelic/Norse name meaning "the church at the settlement on the bank".

Kilvean (Inverness), Cill Bheathain "St Bean's Church." The same saint is also commemorated in the name of nearby Torvean.

Kilvickeon (Mull), Cill Mhic Eóghainn "Church of Eóghann's son."

Kilwhannel (Ayr)
"St Conall's Church", from *Cill Chonaill*.

Kilwhipnach (Argyll)
This may be "St Coidhbeannach's Church", from *Cill Choidhbeannaich*.

Kilwinning (Ayr), Cill Dingeain
"St Finian's Church", the Gaelic showing an affectionate if rare form of St Finian's name which was recorded in Arran. However, AÀA recommend *Cill D'Fhinnein* which shows the derivation more clearly.

Kinaldie (Aberdeen)
"Head of the rock", from *Cinn Allaidh*.

Kinaldy (Fife)
See **Kinaldie**.

Kinbeachie (Ross), Cinn a' Bheathchaidh
"The head of the birch wood."

Kinblethmont (Angus)
This name may be "the head of the blossom or smooth moor", from *Ceann Bhlàth Mhon*.

Kinbrace (Sutherland), Ceann a' Bhràist
This may be "the head of the upland", including a form of *bràigh*, "upland".

Kincaldrum (Angus)
"The end of the hazel ridge", from *ceann, coll* and *druim*. This name is very similar to that of **Kingoldrum**.

Kincardine (Fife, Kincardine); (Ross), Cinn Chàrdainn
"The head of the copse", including the Brythonic/Pictish word *carden*, "copse". Kincardineshire is *Siorrachd Chinn Chàrdainn*, the older name of which was the **Mearns**.

Kincardine O'Neil (Kincardine), Cinn Chàrdainn
See **Kincardine**. The "O'Neil" part of the name probably stems from the barony of Oneil, which encompassed the surrounding area. An older name for this place was *Eaglais Iarach*, "Iarchadh's Church".

Kinclaven (Perth), Ceann Cliathain *or* Cionn Clìobhain
"The end of the hurdle."

Kincorth (Aberdeen), Ceann na Coirthe
"The head of the standing stone."

Kincraig (Fife, Inverness), Ceann na Creige
"The head of the rock."

Kincraigie (Perth), Cionn Chnagaidh
This may be "the end of the knobbly place".

Kindallachan (Perth), Ceann Daileachain
"The end of the little valley."

Kindeace (Ross), Cinn Déis
The meaning of this is unclear although it contains *ceann*, "end or head", and possibly *dias*, "corn".

Kindrochit (Aberdeen)
"Bridge end", from *Ceann Drochaid*.

Kindrogan (Perth), Ceann Drogain
This appears to mean "dragon head", and may have referred to a river, stream or other topological feature.

Kineddar (Moray)
"Between headland", from *Ceann Eadar*.

Kinell (Angus), Ceann an Fhàil
"The end of the dyke."

Kingairloch (Argyll), Cinn a' Gheàrrloch
"The head of the short loch." Local people were known as *buic*, "bucks".

Kingarth (Bute), Ceann Garadh
"The end of the den", showing a very old name possibly gaelicised from an earlier Brythonic name. AÀA recommend *Ceann a' Ghàrraidh*, which would be "the end of the dyke or wall".

Kingask (Fife)
"The end of the projecting ridge", from *Ceann Ghaisg*.

King Edward (Aberdeen)
This name is from the same origin as **Kineddar**, but was adapted to render it meaningful to English speakers.

Kinghorn (Fife)
"End of the marsh", from *ceann* and *gronn*, an earlier English spelling of the name being Kyngorn.

Kinglass (West Lothian)
This is "green head or end", from *Ceann Glas*.

Kinglassie (Fife)
This may be "the church at the stream", from *Cill Ghlaise*.

Kingoldrum (Angus), Cionn Colldruim *or* Druim Cionn Coill
The English name and the first Gaelic name suggest "the end of the hazel ridge", but the second Gaelic name means "the ridge at the end of the (hazel)wood". Both Gaelic names are noted in Diack (1944) as coming from speakers of eastern dialects.

Kingsburgh (Skye), Cinnseborg *or* Cinnseaborg
This may be "king's castle", from Norse.

Kingscavil (West Lothian)
This may be "headland of the fish catching creel", from *Ceann Cabhail*.

Kingscross (Arran), Rubha na h-Àirde
The English name appears to be from Gaelic *Cinn a' Chrois*, "end of the crossing place", but earlier forms point to *Peighinn a' Chrois*, "penny-land at the crossing place". The modern Gaelic name is "point of the headland".

Kingsmuir (Fife)
This may be the "king's moor", referred to as *rìgh mhonadh*, which became contracted to *rìmhinn* in such names as Balrymonth and the Gaelic name of St Andrews.

Kingseat (Perth), Suidhe an Ruighe
"Seat of the slope." Gaelic *ruigh*, "slope", sounds similar to *rìgh*, "king", and in several names such as Kingsridge and Portree, *ruigh* has been superseded by *rìgh*.

Kingshouse (Argyll), Taigh an Rìgh
Both English and Gaelic names refer to an inn on the king's highway.

Kingussie (Inverness), Ceann a' Ghiuthsaich *or* Cinn a' Ghiuthsaich
"The end of the pine wood."

Kinharvie (Dumfries)
This suggests "the end of the boundary wall", from *Ceann na h-Eirbhe*.

Kiniegallin (Perth), Cinn a' Ghealainn
"The end of the white land."

Kininmonth (Aberdeen, Fife)
"The end of the white moor", from *Ceann Fhionn Mhon*.

Kininvie (Banff)
This appears to be "the end of the fair plain", from *Ceann Fhionn Mhuighe*.

Kinkell (Aberdeen, Perth), Ceann na Coille; (Ross), Cinn a' Choille
"The end of the wood." In Ross, Bishop Kinkell is *Cinn a' Choille an Easbaig*.

Kinloch (Lewis), Ceann an Loch; (Barra, Perth), Ceann Loch; (Rum, Skye), Ceann Locha; (Sutherland), Ceann Loch an Reidhinidh
"Loch head." *Reidhinidh* is unclear but may derive from *reidhneach*, "cow yielding no milk".

Kinlochard (Perth), Ceann Loch na h-Àirde
"The head of the loch of the promontory."

Kinlochbeoraid (Inverness), Ceann Loch Bheòraid
"The head of Loch Beoraid."

Kinlochbervie (Sutherland), Ceann Loch Biorbhaigh
This may be "the head of the loch of boiling water", if the second element is related to that in Inverbervie. However if the second element is of Norse origin, which is likely given its location, it may be "the head of the loch of the rock river". A native

of the area between Kinlochbervie and Rhiconich is known as a *Slisearnach*.

Kinlocheil (Inverness), Ceann Loch Iall
"The head of the thong loch."

Kinlochetive (Argyll), Ceann Loch Éite
"The head of the loch of the foul one", referring to *Éiteag*, a water spirit.

Kinlochewe (Ross), Ceann Loch Iubh
"The head of the yew loch."

Kinlochgair (Argyll), Ceann Locha Giorra
"The head of the short loch."

Kinlochlaggan (Inverness), Ceann Loch an Lagain
"The head of the loch of Laggan."

Kinlochleven (Argyll, Inverness), Ceann Loch Lìobhann
"The head of the loch of Leven."

Kinlochmoidart (Inverness), Ceann Loch Mhùideart
"The head of the loch of Moidart."

Kinlochmorar (Inverness), Ceann Loch Mhórair
"The head of the loch of Morar."

Kinlochmore (Inverness), Ceann Loch Mór
"The big head of the loch."

Kinlochourn (Inverness), Ceann Loch Shùirn *or* Ceann Loch Shubhairne
"The head of the loch of the berry gap."

Kinlochquoich (Inverness), Ceann Loch Chuaich
"The head of the loch of the hollow."

Kinloch Rannoch (Perth), Ceann Loch Raineach
"The head of the loch of Rannoch."

Kinlochroag (Lewis), Ceann Locha Ròg
"The head of the loch of Roag."

Kinlochsheil (Ross), Ceann Loch Seile
"The head of the loch of Sheil."

Kinlochspelve (Argyll), Ceann Loch Spéilbhidh
"The head of Loch Spelve."

Kinlochteagus (Argyll), Ceann Loch Tiacais
"The head of Loch Teagus."

Kinloid (Inverness), Ceann an Leothaid
"The end of the slope."

Kinloss (Moray), Cinn Lois
"Herb headland."

Kinmont (Dumfries)
"Head moor", from *ceann* and *monadh*, giving a hypothetical *Ceann Mhòn*.

Kinmundy (Aberdeen)
"St Munna's Church", from *Cill Mhunna*, using a byname for St Fintan.

Kinmylies (Inverness), Ceann a' Mhilidh
"The head of the warrior." Locally this is known as *Ceann a' Mhìle*, "mile end".

Kinnaber (Angus)
"Marsh end", from *Ceann* and *eabar*.

Kinnabus (Islay), Cionnabus *or* Cinneabus
This Norse name may be "lady's farm" and is one of the places referred to in *Tha ceithir busaichean fichead an Ìle*, "there are twenty-four *buses* in Islay", *bus* being a shortened form of Norse *bólstaðr*, "farm".

Kinnahaird (Ross), Ceann na h-Àirde
"The end of the high point."

Kinnaird (Aberdeen)
"High headland", from *Ceann Àrd*.

Kinneil (West Lothian), Ceann an Fhàil
"The end of the dyke" located at the end of the Antonine Wall.
Originally this name was *Penfahel* containing Brythonic *pen*, "end", rather than Gaelic *ceann*. See also **Kilpunt**.

Kinnell (Angus), Ceann an Fhàil; (Perth), Cinn Alla
The Angus name is "the end of the

dyke", the same as Kinneil in West
Lothian. The Perthshire name is
"the end of the rock".

Kinnettes (Ross), Ceann Iteais
This may be "the head of the corn
place".

Kinnettles (Angus)
The Gaelic pronunciation of this
was recorded by Diack (1944) as
"kynn-nettel", and although it
contains *ceann*, "head" or "end", the
second element is unclear.

Kinnordy (Angus)
This appears to be "the end of the
round-hilled place", from *Ceann
Òrdaigh*.

Kinnoull (Perth)
"The head of the rock", from *Cinn
Alla*.

Kinnudie (Nairn), Cinn Iùdaidh
The meaning of this name is unclear.

Kinrive (Ross), Ceann Ruighe
"Slope end."

Kinross (Kinross), Ceann Rois *or*
Cinn Rois
"Wood end." Kinross-shire is
Siorrachd Cheann Rois or *Siorrachd
Chinn Rois*.

Kinrossie (Perth), Cinn Rosaidh
"The end of the wood place."

Kintail (Ross: Gairloch), Ceann an
t-Sàil; (Ross: Loch Duich), Cinn
Tàile; (Sutherland) Ceann Tàile *or*
Cinn Tàile
"Head of the inlet." The full name of
Kintail by Loch Duich is *Cinn Tàile
MhicCoinnich* or *Cinn Tàile
MhicRath* , "MacKenzie's Kintail" or
"MacRae's Kintail". A saying goes,
*Cho fad's a bhios monadh an Cinn
Tàile, cha bhi MacCoinnich gun àl sa
Chrò*, "as long as there is moorland
in Kintail, MacKenzie will have
stock in the pen". Another saying
refers to *Cinn Tàile nam bodach's
nam bò*, "Kintail of the old men and
the cows". Kintail Church is *Clachan
Dubhthaich* or *Cill Dubhthaich*,
"Duthac's Church or churchyard". A

native of the area is a *Sàileach* or
Tàileach, from which may come the
surname "Tallach". In Sutherland
the full name is *Cinn Tàile
MhicAoidh*, "MacKay's Kintail".

Kintarvie (Lewis), Ceann Tarabhaigh
This compound Gaelic/Norse name
is "head of seaweed bay".

Kintillo (Perth)
"The end of the green hills", from
Ceann Tulach.

Kintore (Aberdeen), Ceann Tòrr
"Hill end."

Kintra (Argyll, Islay), Cinn Tràgha;
(Mull), Ceann na Tràgha
"The head of the beach." People
from Kintra in Islay were known as
feannagan, "crows".

Kintradwell (Sutherland), Clìn Trolla
"St Triduana's slope."

Kintrae (Moray)
See **Kintra**.

Kintyre (Argyll), Cinn Tìre
"Land's end." The older name was
Sàil Tìre, "heel of land". A native of
Kintyre is a *Tìreach* or *Cainntireach*,
but local people were nicknamed
eich, "horses".

Kinuachdrach (Jura), An Ceann
Uachdrach
"The upper end."

Kinveachy (Inverness), Ceann a'
Bheithich
"End of the birch wood."

Kippen (Stirling)
"Small stump", from *ceapan.*

Kippo (Fife)
"Tillage land", from *Ceapach.*

Kirivick (Lewis), Cirbhig
"Quiet bay", from Norse.

Kirkaboll (Tiree), Circepol
"Church farm", from Norse. There
were two graveyards here at one
time, *Cladh Odhrain*, "St Oran's
Churchyard", and *An Cladh Beag*,
"the small churchyard".

Kirkandrews (Kirkcudbright)
"St Andrew's Church." A group of
placenames in the south-west

beginning with "Kirk-" and ending in a saint's name may originally have been created in Gaelic with *Cill*, then adapted into Scandinavian or English, as many of the saints commemorated are of the Gaelic Church, and the word order is Celtic rather than Germanic. On the other hand, Scandinavian *kirkja* may have been adopted into the local Gaelic as a common noun in place of *cill*, "church".

Kirkbean (Kirkcudbright)
"St Beathan's Church."

Kirkblane (Dumfries)
"St Blane's Church."

Kirkbride (Ayr)
"St Bridget's Church."

Kirkbuddo (Angus)
"St Buite's Church", commemorating a saint who visited Nechtan's court nearby.

Kirkcaldy (Fife), Cair Chaladain
This may be "Caled's enclosure", probably first coined in Brythonic then adapted to Gaelic then English phonology. The word *cair*, "enclosure", is different from *cathair*, "seat or fort", but the two have fallen together as a result of their closeness in pronunciation.

Kirkcarswell (Kirkcudbright)
"St Oswald's Church."

Kirkcolm (Wigtown)
Although this name in its current English form appears to be "St Colum's Church", in memory of St Columba, older sources show this to be "St Cuimein's Church", dedicated to the saint mentioned in the Gaelic name of **Fort Augustus**.

Kirkconnel (Dumfries)
"St Conall's Church."

Kirkcudbright (Kirkcudbright), Cill Chuithbeirt
"St Cuthbert's Church."
Kirkcudbrightshire is *Siorrachd Chill Chuithbeirt*.

Kirkebost (Bernera, North Uist), Circebost
"Church farm", from Norse.

Kirkettle (Midlothian)
"Kettil's or Ketill's cairn", created originally in Gaelic, perhaps as *Càrn Cheatail* featuring a Norse personal name.

Kirkfield (Inverness), Achadh na h-Eaglais
"Church field."

Kirkhill (Inverness), Cnoc Odhar *or* Cnoc Mhoire
While the English name is "church hill", the Gaelic ones are "dun-coloured hill" and "St Mary's hill". The old name was *Dul Bachlach*, which may be "crozier haugh". Kirkhill parish is *Sgìre Mhoire*, "St Mary's parish" and *Sgìre Cnoc na Gaoithe*, "Windhill parish". A local oath or saying was *Air Moire sa Chnoc*, "By Mary in Kirkhill".

Kirkiboll (Sutherland), Circeabol
"Church farm", from Norse.

Kirkinner (Wigtown)
"St Cainnear's Church."

Kirkintilloch (Dunbarton), Cair Cheann Tulaich
"Fort at the end of the green hill." This was originally a Brythonic name, *Caerpentaloch*, which was adapted to Gaelic phonology but carried the same meaning. The word *cair*, "enclosure", is different from *cathair*, "seat", but the two have fallen together as a result of their closeness in pronunciation.

Kirklauchline (Wigtown)
"Lachlann's quarterland", from *Ceathramh Lachlainn*.

Kirkmabreck (Kirkcudbright)
"St Broc's Church", from *MoBhruic*, a byform of the saint's name.

Kirkmadrine (Ayr)
"St Draighne's Church", from *MoDhraighne*, a byform of the saint's name.

Kirkmahoe (Dumfries)
"St Cua's chuch", from *MoChua*, a byform of the saint's name.

Kirkmaiden (Ayr)
"St Etain's Church", from *M'Éadain*, a byform of the saint's name.

Kirkmartin (Wigtown)
"St Martin's Church."

Kirkmichael (Ayr, Banff, Perth), Cille Mhìcheil
"St Michael's Church." Kirkmichael parish in Banff is *Sgìre Eaglais Mhìcheil*, "the parish of St Michael's Church".

Kirkmirran (Kirkcudbright)
"St Mirren's Church."

Kirkoswald (Ayr)
"St Oswald's Church."

Kirkpatrick (Dumfries, Kirkcudbright)
"St Patrick's Church."

Kirksheaf (Ross), A' Chroit Mhór
The Gaelic name is "the big croft". A 16th-century form of the English name, "Kerskeith", suggests a Gaelic origin, "hawthorn seat".

Kirkton (several)
"Churchyard" or "village with a church". In Raasay the Gaelic name is *an Clachan*, "the churchyard" or "the village with a church", while in Perth and Sutherland it is *Baile na h-Eaglais* and in Argyll *Baile na h-Eaglaise*, "village of the church". Kirkton of Glenisla is *Baile na h-Eaglais Ghlinn* Ìl', "the village with the church in Glenisla". Kirkton of Lochalsh is *an Clachan Aillseach*, "the Lochalsh clachan". Kirkton of Skene is *Clachan Sgàin*, and Kirkton of Strathfillan is *Clachan Shraithibh*.

Kirkton Glen (Perth), Làirig Eibhreannach
"Pass of the castrated goats." This name has been understood to include the word *Éireannach*, "Irishman", given that the original word, *eibhreannach*, is obscure.

Kirriemuir (Angus), Cearan Mhoire
"St Mary's quarter-land."

Kirtomy (Sutherland), Ciortamaidh *or* Ciurtamaidh
This name is unclear.

Kiscadale (Arran), Cisteal
This name came from Norse *kistudalr*, "coffin valley". North Kiscadale is *Cisteal Bheag*, while Mid and South Kiscadale collectively are *Cisteal Mhór*.

Kishorn (Ross), Ciseorn
"Large bulky headland."

Kisimul (Barra), Cìosamul
"Castle island." This is the castle referred to in *Bàgh a' Chaisteil*, "Castlebay".

Klibreck (Sutherland), Cleithbrig
Although the second element of this name is clearly Norse *brekkr*, "stream", the first is obscure.

Knapdale (Argyll), Cnapadal
"Knob valley", from Norse. The area was known as *Cnapadal a' bhuntàta mhóir*, "Knapdale of the great potatoes", and local people were nicknamed *crodh maol*, "hornless cattle", by residents of other areas and *caoraich dhubh*, "black sheep", by themselves.

Knapp (Perth)
"Lump", from *cnap*.

Kneep (Lewis), Cnìp *or* Crìp
"Cliff edge", from Norse.

Knock (several), An Cnoc
"Hill." The full name of Knock in Inverness-shire is *Cnoc na h-Àirde*, "hill of the Aird". In Lewis, Knock near Carloway is *Cnoc Chàrlabhaigh*, "the hill of Carloway", while Knock in Point is *Cnoc na h-Aoidhe*, "the hill of the Eye isthmus". Knock in Skye is *an Cnoc Uaine*, "the green hill", or *Cnoc a' Chamais*, "the hill at the bay", and in Mull is *Cnoc Tìr Mhàrtainn*, "the hill on Martin's land".

Knockaird (Lewis), An Cnoc Àrd
"The high hill."

Knockan (Sutherland), An Cnocan
"The hillock."

Knockando (Moray), Cnoc Cheannachd
"Market hill."

Knockandon (Arran), An Cnocan Donn
"The brow hillock."

Knockandu (Banff), An Cnocan Dubh
"The black hillock."

Knockanduie (Lewis), Cnoc Iain Duibh
"Black John's hill."

Knockaneorn (Banff)
"The barley hill", from *Cnoc an Eòrna*.

Knockankelly (Arran), Cnoc a' Choiligh
"The hill of the cock", referring to a nearby rock.

Knockantivore (Mull), Cnoc an Taigh Mhóir
"The hill at the big house."

Knockbain (Ross), An Cnoc Bàn
"The fair hill."

Knockban (Ross), An Cnoc Bàn
"The fair hill."

Knockbreck (Skye), An Cnoc Breac
"The speckled hill."

Knockbrex (Kirkcudbright)
"Speckled hill", from *Cnoc Breac*, to which an English plural has been added.

Knockcuien (North Uist), Cnoc Cuidhein *or* Cnoc Uithein
"Cuidhean's hill."

Knockdamph (Sutherland), Cnoc Dhamh
"Stag hill."

Knockdon (Islay), An Cnoc Donn
"The brown hill."

Knockentiber (Ayr)
"The hill at the well", from *Cnoc an Tiobair*.

Knockespock (Aberdeen)
"The bishop's hill", from *Cnoc an Easbaig*.

Knockfarrel (Ross), Cnoc Fearralaidh *or* Cnoc Fearghalaigh
"The hill of the high cliff" or "Fearghal's hill".

Knockfrink (Banff, Moray), Cnoc Fraing
According to Diack's transcription (1944), this seems to be "Frank's hill".

Knockhill (Fife)
This name is an example of where an original name coined in one language has had the name word added in the superseding language as the original element ceased to be understood by the population. In this case Gaelic *cnoc*, "hill", has had English "hill" added to it in order to explain the name after Gaelic had died out and been replaced in Fife by English.

Knockinreoch (Bute), An Cnocan Riabhach
"The brindled hillock."

Knockintorran (North Uist), Cnoc an Torrain
"The hill at the little hillock."

Knockline (North Uist), Cnoc an Lìn
"The flax hill."

Knockmore (Ayr, Fife), An Cnoc Mór
"The big hill."

Knocknamonie (Benbecula), Cnoc na Mòna
"The peat hill."

Knocknavie (Ross), Cnoc Neimhidh
"Hill of the sacred lands."

Knockrioch (Argyll), An Cnoc Riabhach
"The brindled hill."

Knockrome (Jura), An Cnoc Crom
This appears now to mean "the crooked hill", but the second element may have been simplified through the years and have originally meant something different.

Knockvologan (Mull), Cnoc Mhaolagain
"Maolagan's hill." *Maolagan* means "little tonsured one", denoting a monk.

Knoydart (Inverness), Cnòideart
"Knut's firth", from Norse. Local people were known as *gobhair*, "goats".

Kyle (Ayr), Cuil
This area is named after Coel, a ruler of the Britons locally around 400 AD and immortalised in the rhyme, "Old King Cole". The same person is also named in **Coylton**.

Kyleakin (Skye), Caol Àcain
"Haakon's strait."

Kyle of Lochalsh (Ross), An Caol *or* Caol Loch Aillse
"The strait" or "the strait of Lochalsh". Local people were known as *steàrnairean*, "terns".

Kylerhea (Skye), Caol Reatha
"The narrows at the current." A popular story surrounding this name is that *Reatha*, a member of the legendary band of warriors known as the *Fianna*, drowned here.

Kyles (Argyll), Na Caoil; (Harris), Caolas Stiadar
The Argyll name is "the kyles or straits", referring to the *Na Caoil Bhódach*, "the Kyles of Bute". The Harris name in English is "the strait", while in Gaelic in full it is "the strait of Stiadar".

Kyles Flodday (Benbecula), Caolas Fhlodaigh
"The strait of Flodday", a Gaelic/ Norse name.

Kyles Knoydart (Inverness), Caolas Chnòideart
"The strait of Knoydart."

Kylesku (Sutherland), An Caolas Cumhang
"The narrow strait."

Kyles Morar (Inverness), Caolas Mhórair
"The strait of Morar."

Kyles Scalpay (Harris), Caolas Sgalpaigh
"The strait of Scalpay."

Kyles Stockinish (Harris), Caolas Stocainis
"The strait of Stockinish", a Gaelic/ Norse name.

Kylestrome (Sutherland), Caol Sròim
"The strait of the current", a Gaelic/ Norse name.

Kyllachy (Inverness), Coileachaigh
"Woodcock place."

Kynachan (Perth), Coinneachan
"Meeting place" or "junction".

L

Labost (Lewis), Làbost
"Muddy farm", from Norse.

Lackalee (Harris), Leacan Lì
This appears to be a Gaelic/Norse name meaning "slab or slabs at the slope".

Laga (Argyll), Làga
"Low island", from Norse.

Lagavellie (Arran), Lag a' Bhile
"The hollow of the rim or edge."

Lagavulin (Islay), Lag a' Mhuilinn
"The hollow of the mill."

Lagg (Arran, Ayr, Jura), An Lag
"The hollow."

Laggan (Arran, Inverness), An Lagan
"The little hollow." The full name of Laggan in Badenoch is *Lagan Choinnich*, "Cainneach's little hollow", while in the Great Glen it is *Lagan Achaidh Droma*, "hollow at the field of the ridge".

Lagganallachie (Perth), Lagan Aileachaidh
"The hollow at the rock place."

Laggan Bridge (Inverness), Ceann Drochaid; (Islay), An Drochaid Mhór
The Gaelic name in Inverness is "bridge end", while in Islay it is "the big bridge".

Lagganlia (Inverness), An Lagan Liath
"The grey-green hollow."

Lagganmore (Argyll), An Lagan Mór
"The big hollow."

Laggantygown (Inverness), Lagan Taigh Ghobhainn
"The hollow at the smith's house."

Lagganulva (Mull), Lagan Ulbha
"The little hollow of Ulva."

Laggmore (Arran), An Lag Mór
"The big hollow."

Laich of Moray (Moray), Machair
Mhoireibh
"The plain of Moray."

Laid (Sutherland), An Leathad
"Slope." A native of this area is
known as a *Cròbach*.

Laide (Ross), An Leathad
See **Laid**. Local people are known as
caoraich mhaola, "Cheviot sheep". Coast
of Laide is *Eirtheaire an Leothaid* or
simple *an t-Eirtheaire*, "the coast".

Laig (Eigg), Lathaig
This is possibly "muddy bay", from
Norse.

Laight (Wigtown), Leac Ailpein
This was originally "Alpin's grave",
and the English name has kept only
the "grave" part. See **Glenapp**.

Lairg (Sutherland), Luirg
"Shank."

Lalathen (Fife)
"Broad half or share", from *Leth
Leathann*.

Lamancha (Peebles)
Grange of Romanno was thus
renamed in the 18th century by
Admiral Cochrane in memory of
the Spanish province. See
Romanno.

Lambhill (Arran), Cnoc nan Uan
"The hill of the lambs."

Lamigo (Sutherland), Lamaigeo
"Lamb ravine", from Norse.

Lamlash (Arran), Eilean MoLaise,
An t-Eilean *or* An t-Eilean Àrd
The Gaelic names are "the island of
dear St Laisren", "the island" and
"the high island". The English name
is a contraction of *Eilean MoLaise*
which is the name recommended by
AÀA and which refers to Holy
Island.

Lanark (Lanark, Perth), Lannraig
"Clearing", from Brythonic *lanerc*.
Lanarkshire is *Siorrachd Lannraig*.

Land, The (Tiree), Lag an t-Seagail
The Gaelic name is "the rye hollow".

Langal (Argyll), Langal
"Long hill", from Norse.

Langamull (Mull), Langamul *or*
Langabhail
"Long ridge" or "long field", from
Norse.

Langass (North Uist), Langais
"Long ridge", from Norse.

Langay (Harris), Langaigh
"Long island", from Norse.

Langley Park (Angus)
This name was given by a landlord
to replace an earlier name derived
from Gaelic *Eaglais Eòin*, "St John's
Church".

Langwell (Caithness, Ross,
Sutherland), Langail
"Long field", from Norse.

Lanrick (Perth), Laraig
"Clearing", from Brythonic *lanerc*.
An earlier Gaelic form was *Lanraig*,
showing the derivation more clearly.

Larachantivore (Ross), Làrach an
Taigh Mhóir
"The site of the big house."

Larachbeg (Argyll), An Làrach Bheag
"The small site."

Largie (Argyll), An Learg
"The slope."

Largiemore (Bute), An Leargaidh
Mhór
"The big slope-place."

Largieside (Argyll), Taobh na
Leargaich
"The side or area of the sloping
place."

Largo (Fife), Leargach
"Slope place." Nearby Largo Law
was earlier known as *Knocklargauch*,
suggesting a Gaelic form of *Cnoc
Leargach*, "the hill of Largo".

Largs (Ayr), An Leargaidh Ghallda
The Gaelic original is "the Lowland
sloping place", while the English
form is based only on "sloping place".

Largy (Argyll), An Leargaich;
(Arran), Leargaidh
"Slope place." To express "in Largy"
with reference to the place in Argyll,

Gaelic uses *air an Leargaich*, "on Largy". Largybeg in Arran is *Leargaidh Beag*, "little Largy"; Largymeanoch is *Leargaidh Meadhanach*, "middle Largy"; and Largymore is *Leargaidh Mór*, "big Largy".

Laroch (Argyll), An Làrfhaich
"The bottom lawn or green."

Lary (Aberdeen), Làiridh *or* Làraidh
This may be "bottom place".

Lasgair (South Uist), Laisgeir
This Norse name may be "low skerry".

Latheron (Caithness), Latharan *or* Lathairn
"Muddy place." This is believed by some to be from the same origin as *Latharna*, "Lorne".

Latheronwheel (Caithness), Latharan a' Phuill *or* Lathairn a' Phuill
"Latheron by the pool."

Lathrisk (Fife)
This name appears to derive from *lios* and *riasg*, giving "boggy enclosure".

Laudale (Argyll), Labhdal
"Low valley", from Norse.

Laurencekirk (Kirkcardine), Eaglais Labhrainn
"St Laurence's Church." Locally this is known as "Lowrin", a form of the saint's name found as *Labhrann* in Gaelic. The older name of the parish was Conveth from *Coinmheadh*. See **Conveth**.

Lawers (Perth), Labhar
"Talkative one", referring to a stream. East Lawers is *Labhar Shìos*, "lower Lawers", West Lawers is *Labhar Shuas*, "upper Lawers", and Mid Lawers is *Labhar na Craoibhe*, "Lawers of the tree". Lawers church-yard is *Cladh Magh Thuaim*, "the graveyard of Machuim".

Laxay (Lewis), Lacasaigh
"Salmon river", from Norse.

Laxdale (Lewis), Lacasdal
"Salmon valley", from Norse.

Laxford (Sutherland), Lusard
"Salmon firth", from Norse.

Leachcan (Harris), Na Leacainn
"The broad hillsides."

Leachkin (Inverness), An Leacainn
"The broad hillside." The small area known as Pig Row is *Sràid nam Muc*, "street of the pigs".

Leachonich (Ross), An Leachanaich
"The sloping hill face."

Leacnasaide (Ross), Leac nan Saighead
"The flat rock of the arrows."

Leadburn (Midlothian), Leac Bhearnaird
"The grave or flat rock of Bernard." An older form of the name was Leckbernard.

Lealt (Jura, Skye), Leathallt
"Stream with one high bank."

Lealty (Ross), Leathalltaidh
"Place of the stream with one high bank." Wester Lealty is *Leathalltaidh Shuas*, "upper Lealty".

Leanach (Inverness), An Liathanaich
This may be "the grey-blue place".

Leanachan (Inverness), An Lèanachan
"The little meadow."

Leanaig (Ross), Lianaig
"Meadow."

Leanish (Barra), Lèanais
This may be "slope headland", from Norse.

Leargybreck (Jura), An Leargaidh Bhreac
"The speckled slope."

Lebhall (Aberdeen), An Leth Bhaile
"The half farm."

Lecht (Aberdeen, Banff), An Leac
"The flat rock." The more complete name in Gaelic is *Leac a' Ghobhainn*, "the flat rock of the smith".

Leckfurin (Sutherland), Leac Bheòirn
"Bjorn's stone."

Leckie (Perth, Ross), Leacaidh
"Flat rock place."

Leckmelm (Ross), Leac Mhailm
"The slab of Mailm", possibly a
personal name and referring to a
gravestone.

Ledaig (Argyll), Leideag; (Barra), An
Leideag
"The small slope." In Argyll, North
Ledaig is *Leideag a Tuath* and South
Ledaig is *Leideag a Deas.*

Ledbeg (Sutherland), An Leathad Beag
"The small slope."

Ledgowan (Ross), Leathad
Ghobhainn
"The smith's slope."

Ledlanet (Kinross)
This may be "elm slope", from
Leathad Leamhnach.

Ledmore (Sutherland), An Leathad
Mór
"The big slope."

Lednagullin (Sutherland), Leathad
nan Giullan
"The boys' slope."

Leirable (Sutherland), Lìreabol
"Muddy farm" or "tern farm", from
Norse.

Leirinbeg (Sutherland), An Leithrinn
Bheag
"The small peninsula."

Leirinmore (Sutherland), An
Leithrinn Mhór
"The big peninsula."

Leith (Midlothian), Lìte
The origin of this name is from a
Brythonic element signifying
wetness or dampness, and may also
be found in "Lithlithgow". Leith
Links was known as *Feighdean Lìte*
with the same meaning.

Lemlair (Ross), Leum na Làir *or* An
Leum
"The mare's leap." This is also known
as "the leap", in Gaelic. The old
churchyard here is *Cladh MoBhrìgh*,
"St Brìgh's graveyard".

Lemreway (Lewis), Leumrabhagh
This Norse name contains *vágr*,
"bay", but the first element is
unclear.

Lendrick (Angus, Kinross, Perth)
See **Lanark**.

Lenihall (Bute)
"Cathal's half-pennyland", from
Leth-pheighinn Chathail.

Lenihuline (Bute)
"Half-pennyland of the holly", from
Leth-pheighinn a' Chuilinn.

Lenimore (Arran)
See **Thundergay**.

Lennox (Dunbarton, Stirling), An
Leamhnachd *or* Leamhnachd
"The elm land." The Lord of Lennox
is *Morair Leamhnach* or *Morair
Leamhna*, also known in earlier
times as *Rìgh Bealaigh*, "the King of
Balloch". A native of the area is a
Leamhnach.

Leny (Perth), Lànaigh
The meaning of this name is unclear.
The Pass of Leny is *Cumhang
Lànaigh* and Brae Leny is *Bràigh
Lànaigh*. The old castle of Leny is
known as *An Caisteal Briste*, "the
broken (ruined) castle".

Lenzie (Dunbarton), Lèanaidh
This appears to be a locative form of
lèana, "wet meadow".

Leochel (Aberdeen)
"Dark place", from *lòchail* or *lòicheil.*

Lephin (Skye), An Leth-pheighinn
"The half pennyland."

Lerwick (Shetland), Léiruig
"Mud bay", from Norse.

Lesmahagow (Lanark), Lios
MoFhéige
"Dear St Féichín's enclosure", showing an affectionate form of the
saint's name.

Lesmurdie (Ayr, Moray)
"Murdoch's enclosure", from *Lios
Mhuirich.*

Lethen (Nairn), Leathan Dubhthaich
"Duthac's broad slope." The Laird of
Lethen is *Tighearn Leathan
Dubhthaich.*

Lethendy (Perth)
"Place of the broad slope", from
Leathandaidh.

Letter (Arran), Leitir
"Gentle slope." The full name used
to be *Leitir nan Canach*, "gentle
slope of the canons".

Letterewe (Ross), Leitir Iubh
"The gentle slope of the Ewe."

Letterfearn (Ross), Leitir Fheàrna
"Gentle alder slope."

Letterfinlay (Inverness), Leitir
Fhionnlaigh
"Finlay's gentle slope."

Lettermorar (Inverness), Leitir
Mhórair
"The gentle slope of Morar."

Letters (Ross: Loch Broom), An
Leitir; (Ross: Easter Ross), Na
Leitrichean
These names are "the gentle slope"
and "the gentle slopes" respectively.

Lettoch (Perth, Ross), An Leathdach
"The half davoch", from *leth* and
dabhach.

Leuchars (Fife, Moray)
"Reeds", from Gaelic *luachair* with
an English plural suffixed.

Leurbost (Lewis), Liùrbost
"Ljúfa's farm", from Norse. Other
interpretations have been suggested
for the origin of this name.

Level, The (Moray)
"The half farm", from *An Leth
Bhaile*.

Leven (Fife), Inbhir Liobhann
"The mouth of the Leven." The
older English name was Innerleven.

Levencorrach (Arran), An Leth-
pheighinn Corrach
"The uneven half pennyland."

Leverburgh (Harris), An Tòb *or* An
t-Òb
The Gaelic name is "the bay", from
Norse *hóp*. The English name used
to be Obbe until it was renamed by
the proprietor, Lord Leverhulme.

Levishie (Inverness), Lìbhisidh
This name is unclear, but might be
"smooth meadow place".

Lewis (Lewis), Leódhas
One explanation is that this name

came from Norse *ljóðahús*, "song
house", which was then applied to
the entire island. A native of Lewis
is a *Leódhasach*, also nicknamed a
biorach, "dogfish". The island is
known as *Eilean Fraoich* or *Eilean an
Fhraoich*, "heather island".

Lewiston (Inverness), Blàr na Maigh
The English and Gaelic names are
unrelated, the Gaelic being "the field
on the plain".

Leys (Inverness), An Leigheas
This name is unclear.

Lhanbryde (Moray), Lann Brìghde
"St Bridget's Church."

Li (Inverness), Lì
"Slope", from Norse.

Liddesdale (Roxburgh); (Argyll),
Lìdeasdal
In Roxburghshire this is the name
of the valley through which the
River Leader flows. In Argyll the
name appears to be from Norse and
may represent a valley named after
an individual.

Lienassie (Ross), Lianaisidh
"Place of the wet meadow."

Lierinish (North Uist), Lìoranais
"Muddy headland", from Norse.

Lietrie (Inverness), Liathdoire
"Grey-blue grove." This name is
surprising in that the *d* did not
become *dh* after *liath*.

Lighthill (Lewis), Cnoc an t-Solais
"Hill of the light."

Likisto (Harris), Liceasto
"Body harbour", from Norse, possibly a place from which bodies were
ferried for burial.

Limelands (Fife)
The older name of this place is from
Innis Cailc, "chalk meadow".

Lindores (Fife)
The first part of this name seems to
be *linn*, "pool", or *lann* in the sense
of a church, while the second may
be *dubhros*, "dark point" or "dark
wood", or maybe *doras* in the sense
of a pass.

Lingay (Barra, Harris, South Uist), Lingeigh
"Heather island", from Norse.

Lingerabay (Harris), Lingearabhagh
"Heather bay" or "heather beach bay", from Norse.

Liniclete (Benbecula), Lianacleit *or* Lìonacleit
"Flax rock" or "flax hill", from Norse.

Linicro (Skye), Lianacro
"Flax land", from Norse.

Liniquie (South Uist), Lianacuidh
"Flax enclosure", from Norse.

Linlithgow (West Lothian), Gleann Iucha
"Lake by the wet hollow", from Brythonic. The Gaelic name seems to contain *gleann*, "valley", but this was a rationalisation on the part of Gaelic speakers to give the name meaning for them. The name occurs in a number of Gaelic sayings such as *Trì iongantasan na h-Alba: drochaid Obar Pheallaidh, tobraichean Ghlinn Iucha is cluig Pheairt*, "The three wonders of Scotland: Aberfeldy bridge, the wells of Linlithgow and the bells of Perth", and *tomhas Ghlinn Iucha*, "a Linlithgow measure", one of the weights and measures which disappeared after 1707.

Linshader (Lewis), Lìseadar *or* Linnseadar
"Flax township", from Norse.

Linsidemore (Sutherland), Lianasaid Mhór
"Large flax township", from Norse/ Gaelic.

Lintrathen (Angus)
This name was recorded by Diack (1944) from speakers of Perthshire Gaelic as *lan-tréin* and *lyann-tré-an*. This suggests that the first element is Brythonic or Gaelic for "church" or "pool", but the second element is unclear and may also be Brythonic. The name would be written in Gaelic as either *Lann Tréithean* or *Linn Tréithean*.

Lintrose (Angus)
An older form of the name suggests "shelving slope by the wood", from *fothair* and *ros*.

Lionel (Lewis), Lìonail
"Flax field", from Norse.

Lismore, Liosmór
"Big enclosed garden." A native of Lismore is a *Liosach*, also nicknamed an *othaisg*, "yearling sheep" or "hog".

Little Bernera (Lewis), Beàrnaraigh Beag

Little Colonsay (Mull), Colbhasa Beag

Little Cumbrae (Cumbrae), Cumaradh Beag

Little Daan (Ross), Dathan Bhig
"Small davoch."

Little Dunkeld (Perth), Baile a' Mhuilinn
The Gaelic name is "the farm with the mill".

Little Ferry (Sutherland), Am Port Beag
The Gaelic name is "the little harbour".

Little Lude (Perth), Leòid Bheag

Littlemill (Nairn), Am Muileann Beag
"The little mill."

Little Sand (Ross), Sannda Bheag
See **Sand**.

Little Scatwell (Ross), Sgatail Beag
See **Scatwell**.

Little Struy (Inverness), Sruthaidh Beag
See **Struy**.

Liveras (Skye), Laoras
The meaning of this is unclear, but it appears in part of a poem, *bidh cnàmhan nam fear móra air tràigh bhàn Laorais*, "the bones of the big men will be on the fair beach of Liveras".

Livingston (West Lothian), Baile Léibhinn *or* Baile DhùnLéibhe
"Leving's village." The Gaelic name *Baile DhùnLéibhe* is common but erroneous as it is based on the

surname *MacDhùnLéibhe*, "Livingstone", which is unconnected with the name of the town.

Lix (Perth), Lic
"Slab place" or "hard slope". Easter Lix is *Lic Ìochdrach*, Mid Lix is *Lic Meadhanach* and Wester Lix is *Lic Uachdrach*. Easter Lix is also known as *Toll Lic*, "the hole at Lix".

Loandhu (Ross), An Lòn Dubh
"The black wet meadow."

Loanreoch (Ross), An Lòn Riabhach
"The brindled wet meadow."

Loanroidge (Ross), An Lòn Roid
"The wet meadow of bog myrtle."

Lochaber (Inverness), Loch Abar
"Muddy or swampy loch." A native of the area is an *Abrach*. A Gaelic equivalent of "carry coals to Newcastle" is *fiodhrach a thoirt a Loch Abar*, "to take wood to Lochaber".

Lochailort (Inverness), Loch Ailleart *or* Ceann Loch Ailleart
"(Head of) Lochailort." This Gaelic/Norse name contains both languages' elements for "sea loch", but the defining Norse element is unclear. The second Gaelic name was used to refer to the settlement rather than the loch, but has been superseded in recent years by the first name.

Lochainort (South Uist), Loch Aoineart
"Isthmus loch", from Norse with *loch* added. North Lochainort is *Taobh a Tuath Loch Aoineart*, "the north side of Lochainort", and South Lochainort is *Taobh a Deas Loch Aoineart*.

Lochaline (Argyll), Loch Àlainn
"Beautiful loch", although one would expect the definite article in a simple name of this sort. The second element may originally have been a slightly different word rationalised as *àlainn*.

Lochalsh (Ross), Loch Aillse
Possibly "loch of spume". Lochalsh parish is *Sgìre Chomhghain*, "St Comhghan's parish". A native of Lochalsh is an *Aillseach*. Various villages in the area and their inhabitants appear in the ditty, *Steàrnairean a' Chaoil, faoileagan Abhairnis, taighean dubha Réaraig, pàilisean Bhaile Mac Ara, Diùranais an eòrna, clòbhair Ach nan Darach, Druim Buidhe nan deargannan, Earbarsaig nan con clomhach*, "terns from Kyle, gulls from Avernish, black houses in Reraig, palaces in Balmacara, Duirnish of the barley, clover in Achindarach, Drumbuie of the fleas, Erbusaig of the scabby dogs".

Lochardil (Inverness), Loch Àrdail
"The loch at the high place."

Lochawe (Argyll), Loch Obha
"Loch of the water." The old church here was *Caibeal Chiarain*, "St Ciaran's Chapel". Natives of the area were nicknamed *liath-chearcan*, "heath hens". This place appears in a number of sayings such as *Cha leithne Loch Obha null na nall*, "Loch Awe is no wider over than back"; *Eireachdas mnathan Loch Obha, am bréid odhar a thionndadh*, "the ingenuity of the Loch Awe women, to turn the dun-coloured cloth"; *Is fad an éigh o Loch Obha is cobhair o Chlann Ó Duibhne*, "It's a far cry from Loch Awe and help from the Campbells".

Lochbay (Skye), Loch a' Bhàigh
"The loch of the bay." Lochbay House was known as *am Bàgh*, "the bay", which suggests that the name of Lochbay refers to the house rather than a generic bay.

Lochboisdale (South Uist), Loch Baghasdail
"Baegi's loch", containing a Norse personal name. North Lochboisdale is *Taobh a Tuath Loch Baghasdail*, "the north side of Lochboisdale", and South Lochboisdale is *Taobh a Deas Loch Baghasdail*.

Lochbroom (Ross), Loch Bhraoin
"The loch of water." A native of the area is a *Braonach* also nicknamed a *clamhan*, "hawk". Locals from the Little Loch Broom area were known as *crodh*, "cattle".

Loch Buie (Inverness), An Loch Buidhe
"The yellow loch."

Lochbuie (Mull), Locha Buidhe
"Yellow loch."

Lochcarnan (South Uist), Loch a' Chàrnain
"The loch of the little cairn."

Lochcarron (Ross), Loch Carrann
"Loch of the rough water." A native of the area is a *Carrannach*, also nicknamed a *fitheach dubh*, "black raven". The old name of the village was *Tòrr nan Clàr*, "hill of the flat slabs", and changes of name are recorded in the rhyme, *Faire, faire, Tòrr nan Clàr, Baile Sèine th' ort an-dràst'. Chan eil taigh air an tèid fàd, nach bi similear air no dhà*, "Alas Tòrr nan Clàr, now you're called Janetown. Every house burning peat will have a chimney on it or two". The parish church here is *Clachan Ma Ruibhe*, "the Church of St Maol Rubha".

Lochcroistean (Lewis), Loch Croistean
The second part of the name is unclear.

Lochdonhead (Mull), Ceann Loch Dona
"The head of the bad loch", referring to the loch's tendency to dry up.

Lochearnhead (Perth), Ceann Loch Éireann *or* Ceann Loch Éir
"Head of the loch of Ireland." The old church here was called *Caibeal Bhlàthain*, "St Blane's Chapel".

Lochend (Inverness), Ceann Loch
This settlement was known by two earlier names, *An Dabhach Dearg*, "the red davoch", and *Dabhach na Creige*, "the davoch by the rock",

both now moribund. The churchyard here is *Cladh Churadain*, "St Curadan's Churchyard".

Locheport (North Uist), Loch Euphort
"Loch at the isthmus port", from Gaelic/Norse.

Locheye (Ross), Loch na h-Ùidhe
"The loch of the isthmus."

Lochgair (Argyll), Loch Giorra
"Short loch."

Lochganvich (Lewis), Loch a' Ghainmhich
"The sandy loch."

Lochgelly (Fife), Loch Gheallaidh
"Loch of the white water."

Lochgilphead (Argyll), Ceann Loch Gilb
"Head of the chisel loch", referring to its shape. A native is a *Gilbeach* and the parish is called *Cill Fhionnbhair*, "St Finbar's Church".

Lochgoilhead (Argyll), Ceann Loch Goibhle
This appears to be "the head of the loch of the fork", possibly referring to the split in Loch Long of which Lochgoil is an arm. Locally the name was pronounced *Ceann Loch Gaodhail*. The church here is *Cill nam Bràithrean*, "the church of the brothers".

Lochindorb (Moray), Loch nan Doirb
"The loch of the minnows."

Lochinver (Moray, Sutherland), Loch an Inbhir
"The loch at the river mouth."

Lochletter (Inverness), Lòch Leitir
"Dark hillside."

Lochluichart (Ross), Loch Luinncheirt
"The loch of the encampment."

Lochmaben (Dumfries)
"Maban's or Maponos's loch", referring to the Gaelic equivalent of Apollo.

Lochmaddy (North Uist), Loch nam Madadh
"The loch of the wolves", referring

to rocks in the bay known as *Na Madaidhean*. West Lochmaddy is *An Rubha Iar*, "the west point".

Lochnabo (Moray)
"The loch of the cows", from *Loch nam Bó*.

Lochnaw (Wigtown)
"The loch of waters", from an old form *Loch n-Abha*, or "the loch of the water", from *Loch an Abha*, the former being more likely.

Lochnellan (Moray), Loch an Eilein
"The loch with the island."

Lochore (Fife)
This name appears to have been formed by using the English "ore", given that the loch and then settlement are located in a mining area.

Lochportan (North Uist), Loch Portain
"Crab loch."

Lochranza (Arran), Loch Raonasa
"Loch of the Rowan River", a Gaelic/Norse name. The village used to be known as *Ceann Loch Raonasa*, "head of Lochranza".

Lochs (Lewis), Na Lochan
"The lochs." The inhabitants are referred to in *Sùlairean sgìre na h-Aoidhe, 's muinntir aoigheach nan Loch*, "The gannets from the Eye district, and the hospitable people from Lochs". South Lochs contains the district of Park, known as *A' Phàirc* or *A' Phàirc Leòdhasach*. To express "in Lochs", Gaelic uses *air na Lochan*, "on Lochs".

Lochskiport (South Uist), Loch Sgioport
"Ship loch", from Norse, with *loch* added.

Lochslin (Ross), Loch Slinn
"The loch of the weaver's sleye", referring to its shape.

Lochtreighead (Inverness), Ceann Loch Tréig
"The head of the loch of death."

Lochuisge (Argyll), Loch Uisge
"Freshwater loch."

Logan (Ayr)
"Hollow", from *lagan*.

Loggie (Ross), An Lagaidh
"Place of the hollow."

Logie (Moray), Lagaidh
"Place of the hollow."

Logie Almond (Perth)
"The place of the hollow by the Almond", from *Lagaidh Amain*.

Logie Buchan (Aberdeen), Lagan Talargaidh
The Gaelic name is "Talorcan's hollow", while the English name is from *lagaidh*, "place of the hollow".

Logie Coldstone (Aberdeen), Lògaidh
The English name contains *lagaidh*, "place of the hollow", while the second part is said to come from *comhdhail*, "tryst", which was held at a particular stone marker. The current Gaelic name comes from the anglicised pronunciation of "Logie".

Logie Easter (Ross), Lagaidh
The Gaelic name is "place of the hollow", while English distinguishes between this place and Logie Wester.

Logie Mar (Aberdeen), Lògaidh Mhàrr
"The place of the hollow in Mar." See **Logie Coldstone**.

Logierait (Perth), Lagan *or* Lagan Ràit
"The hollow at the circular fort", although most recently this place was known simply as *Lagan*, "hollow". An older name was *Lagan MoChoid*, "St MoChuda's hollow".

Logie Wester (Ross), Lagaidh Bhrìghde
The Gaelic name is "St Bridget's Logie", while English differentiates between this place and Logie Easter.

Loinveg (Aberdeen), Loinn Bheag
"Small enclosure." An alternative derivation is *Loinn nam Fiodhag*, from older *Loinn na bhFiodhag*, meaning "the enclosure of the bird-cherry trees".

Lonach (Aberdeen), Lònag
"Small wet meadow." The rivalry
between Mar and Lonach is shown
in the Mar saying *Olc air mhath le
Lònag*, "whether Lonach likes it or
not". A native of Lonach is a
Lònagach.

Lonbain (Ross), An Lòn Bàn
"The fair wet meadow." Local people
are nicknamed *bodaich bhiorach an
Lòin Bhàin*, "the sharp old men of
Lonbain".

Londubh (Ross), An Lòn Dubh
"The black wet meadow."

Lonemore (Ross, Sutherland), An
Lòn Mór
"The large wet meadow."

Longa (Ross), Longa
"Ship island", from Norse.

Longannet (Fife)
This may be "the churchyard at the
small church", from *lann* and *annaid*.
See **Achnahannet**.

Longay (Ross), Longaigh
See **Longa**.

Longforgan (Perth), Forgann
The Gaelic name is "the place above
the bog", while the English form
has "long" prefixed.

Longformacus (Berwick)
"Macas's camp", from *Longphort
Mhacais*, a personal name also found
in **Maxton**.

Longman (Inverness), An Longman
This name is unclear in either
English or Gaelic, but may be of
Norse origin and refer to a long islet.
The *-man* ending is also found in
the name of **Hopeman** several miles
east along the coast.

Longmorn (Moray)
This could be "the church at the
marsh", from *lann* and *morgrann*,
although a personal name *Morgrunn*
also existed.

Longridge (West Lothian)
"Clearing", from Brythonic *lanerc*.

Longrigg (Argyll), An t-Iomaire Fada
"The long rigg."

Lonmay (Aberdeen)
This may be *Lòn a' Mhaigh*, "wet
meadow on the plain".

Lonmore (Skye), An Lòn Mór
"The big wet meadow."

Lorgill (Skye), Lobhairgil *or*
Lobhargail
The full meaning of this Norse
ravine name is unclear.

Lorne (Argyll), Latharna
"Loarn's land", referring to the
leader of one of the groups of
Dal Riada. A person from the
area is a *Latharnach*, also nicknamed as a *losgann*, "frog". The
nicknames applied to inhabitants
of various parts of Lorne are
found in the rhyme, *Fithich
dhubha Chreiginis, coilich Chille
Mhàrtainn, liath chearcan taobh
Loch Obha 's coin-odhar an Àtha*,
"Black ravens from Craignish,
cocks from Kilmartin, heath hens
from Loch Awe-side and otters
from Ford". Upper Lorne is
Bràigh Latharna while Nether
Lorne is *Latharna Ìochdarach*.
The String of Lorne is *An
t-Sreang Latharnach*.

Lossiemouth (Moray), Inbhir
Losaidh
"The mouth of the herb river."

Loth (Sutherland), Loth
"Mud." Locals are known as
Lothaich. Lothbeg is *Loth Beag* while
Lothmore is *Loth Mór*.

Lothian (West Lothian, East
Lothian, Midlothian), Labhdaidh *or*
Lodainn
This name is apparently of
Brythonic origin and the area was
also known as *Machair Labhdaidh*,
"plain of Lothian". The Perthshire
surname "Lothian" is *Labhdain* or
Loudin in Gaelic but is not of Gaelic
origin.

Loudon (Ayr), Lughdun
"Lugh's fort", referring to a pre-
Christian deity.

Lovat (Inverness), A' Mhormhoich

The English name comes from a Gaelic source suggesting rotting or putrefaction, as reflected in a local name for the place, *Lòbhait*. The Gaelic name is "the carse" or "sea plain". Lovat Bridge is *Drochaid nam Manach*, "the monks' bridge".

Lowlands, A' Ghalldachd

"Non-Gaeldom." The Lowlands are also known as *Am Machaire Gallda* or *A' Mhachaire Ghallda*, "the Lowland plain". *Gall* originally meant any non-Gaelic foreigner but eventually became restricted to mean only a non-Gaelic Lowlander.

Lubcroy (Ross), An Lùb Chruaidh

"The hard bend."

Lubinvullin (Sutherland), Lùban a' Mhuilinn

"The little bend at the mill."

Lubreoch (Perth), An Lùb Riabhach

"The brindled bend."

Ludag (South Uist), An Lùdag

"The little finger", referring to a headland.

Lude (Perth), Leòid

"Slope place." A person from here is a *Luidneach*.

Lugar (Ayr)

This name was originally that of a river, formerly called Lugdour and meaning "bright water", from *Lughdhobhar*, later *Lughar*.

Luib (Perth, Ross, Skye), Lùib

"Bend." The full name of Luib in Ross is *Lùib a' Ghargain*, "the bend at the little rough place or stream". The inn at Luib is mentioned in a ditty, *'S e taigh-òsta Chailein a dh'fhàg mo phòcaid falamh, 'S iomadh stòp is gloinne chuir mi 'n tarraing ann*, "Colin's inn has left my pocket empty, I had many a stoup and glass there".

Luibchoinnich (Ross), Lùib a' Chòinnich

"The bend of the moss."

Luing (Luing), Luinn

This is probably a pre-Gaelic name of unclear meaning. A native of the island is a *Luinneach*, also nicknamed a *piocach*, "coalfish".

Lumbo (Fife)

"Bare place", from *Lomach*.

Lumphanan (Aberdeen), Lann Fhìonain

"St Finnan's Church."

Lumphinnans (Fife)

See **Lumphanan**. The dedication here may have been to *Faolan* (Fillan) rather than *Fìonan* (Finnan).

Luncarty (Perth), Longartaidh

"Encampment place", referring to the camping place of a Danish fleet unable to pass the rapids at Murthly. The Danes are also commemorated in nearby Denmarkfield.

Lundale (Lewis), Lunndail

"Roller valley", referring to rollers used to launch ships.

Lundavra (Inverness), Lunn Dà Bhrà

The name has drawn many attempts at interpretation but none satisfactory. The term *lunnd*, "marsh", may be the origin.

Lundie (Angus, Perth)

"Marshy place", from *Lunndaidh*.

Lundin (Fife)

This may come from *Lunndan*, "small marsh".

Lundy (Inverness), An Lanndaidh

"The marshy place."

Lunga (Argyll, Luing, Mull), Lunga

"Ship river", from Norse.

Lurg (Fife)

"Shank", from *lurg*, referring to a shank-shaped piece of land.

Luskentyre (Harris), Losgaintir

This name is unclear.

Luss (Dunbarton), Lus

"Vegetation."

Lussa Bridge (Skye), Drochaid Lusaidh

"The bridge over the bright river", a Gaelic/Norse name.

Lussagiven (Jura), Lusa Dhìomhain
"Lazy bright river", from Gaelic/Norse.

Lusta (Skye), Lusta
"Bright farm", from Norse.

Lybster (Caithness), Liabost
This Norse name may be "slope farm".

Lynachork (Banff), Lainn a' Choirce
"The enclosed field of oats."

Lynchat (Inverness), Lainn a' Chait *or* Baile a' Chait
"The enclosed field of the cat" or "the village of the cat".

Lynedale (Skye), Lianadail
"Flax valley", from Norse.

Lyngarrie (Inverness), Lainn Gharaidh
"The enclosed field in the den."

Lynwilg (Inverness), Lainn a' Bhuilg *or* Baile a' Bhuilg
"The enclosed field of the bellows" or "the village of the bellows".

Lyrabus (Islay), Liurabus
This may be of the same origin as **Leurbost**. People from Lyrabus were nicknamed *coilich dhubha*, "black cocks".

M

Maaruig (Harris), Màraig
"Sea mew ridge", from Norse.

Macallan (Moray)
This appears to be "St MoChailean's or St Mac Ailein's parish", possibly from *Sgìre MoChailein* or *Sgìre Mac Ailein*, although no record exists of saints with these names.

Macduff (Banff)
The Duff family were prominent landowners locally but the village was earlier known as Doune from *dùn*, "hill" or "hill fort", named after nearby Doune Hill or *An Dùn* in Gaelic. AÀA recommend *Dùn MhicDhuibh* as the Gaelic name of the town.

Machair Illeray (North Uist), Machair Iolaraigh
"The machair of Illeray."

Macharioch (Argyll), Am Machaire Riabhach
"The brindled machair." The old name was *Am Baile Sear*, "the east village".

Machars of Galloway (Wigtown), Machair Ghall-ghàidheil
"The plain of the foreign Gaels", a term attached to Gaelic speakers of Scandinavian origin.

Machrie (Arran), Am Machaire *or* Macharaidh
"The machair" or "machair place".

Machrihanish (Argyll), Machaire Shanais
"The machair of Sanas" *or* possibly "the machair of the old meadow".

Machrins (Colonsay), Na Machraichean
"The machairs."

Machuim (Perth), Magh Thuaim
"The plain of the tomb."

MacLean's Nose (Argyll), An t-Sròn Mhór
In Gaelic this headland is called "the big nose or point".

Maggieknockater (Banff), Magh an Fhùcadair
"The plain of the fuller or waulker."

Malaclete (North Uist), Màlacleit
This Norse name may be "small rock or cliff".

Maligar (Skye), Màileagar
This Norse name may be "small bays".

Mallaig (Inverness), Malaig
This Norse name may be "small bay".

Mallaigmore (Inverness) Malaig Mhór
"Big Mallaig."

Mallaigvaig (Inverness), Malaig Bheag
"Little Mallaig."

Mambeg (Dunbarton), Am Màm Beag
"The small mountain gap."

Mandally (Inverness), Manndalaigh *or* Meanndailidh
This may be "place of the kids' haugh".

Mangersta (Lewis), Mangartaigh
"Monk place" or "peddler's place".
Local pronunciation collected by
Oftedal (1954) suggests *Mangartadh*
at an earlier period.

Manish (Harris), Mànais
"Sea mew headland", from Norse.

Mannel (Tiree), Manal
This Norse name is said to mean
"man field".

Mar (Aberdeen), Màrr
This may be from a Brythonic personal
name. The divisions of the area are
Braemar or *Bràigh Mhàrr*, "the upland
of Mar", Cromar or *Crò Mhàrr*, "the
enclosure of Mar", and Midmar or *Mic
Mhàrr*, which may be the "the bog of
Mar". Mar Lodge is *An Dail Mhóir*,
"the big haugh", and used to be known
in English as Dalmore. The Forest of
Mar is *Frìth Mhàrr*. A native of Mar is
a *Màrnach*, from which comes the
surname, Marnoch.

Marble Lodge (Perth), Taigh a'
Mharbail
"The marble house" in Gaelic.

Marchmont (Berwick, Midlothian)
This may be "horse hill", from
Brythonic.

Margadale (Islay), Margadal
This Norse name may be "merkland
valley".

Marganaish (Arran), Marg an Eis
"The merkland by the stream or
waterfall", a merkland being an area
of land equivalent to the value of a
merk in the old Scottish currency
which was abolished in 1707.

Margmonagach (Argyll), Marg
Mòineagach
"The peaty merkland."

Margnaheglish (Arran), Marg na
h-Eaglais
"The merkland of the church."

Marishader (Skye), Mairiseadar
"Sea village", from Norse.

Markinch (Fife) Marc Innis
This is "horse meadow", and similar
to "Merkinch" in Inverness.

Marrel (Sutherland), Maraill
"Sea field", from Norse.

Marvig (Lewis), Marabhaig
"Sea bay", from Norse.

Marybank (Ross: Logie Easter), An
Lagaidh; (Ross: Urray), Bruach
Màiri
The English name in Logie Easter
commemorates Mary Ross of
Balnagowan, while the Gaelic name
is "the place of the hollow". The
English and Gaelic names in Urray
mean the same as each other and
the Gaelic is probably a translation
from English.

Maryburgh (Ross), Baile Màiri
"Mary's village."

Maryculter (Kincardine)
"St Mary's Culter." See **Culter**.

Marykirk (Kincardine), Obar
Luathnait
The English name is "St Mary's
Church", while the Gaelic name is
"mouth of the swift river".

Masterton (Fife)
This is "master's farm" but was
known earlier as Lethmacdungal
from *Leth Mac Dhùghaill*, "the
slope of the sons of Dùghall or
Dùngal".

Mauchline (Ayr), Machlainn
This name may be "field of the
pool", from *magh* and *linn*, and
AÀA recommend *Maghlinn* as the
Gaelic name. According to legend it
was the site of one of the wonders of
Scotland, a miraculous underground
quern which worked constantly
except on Sundays. Near to
Mauchline is Achenbrain or
Auchenbrain, "the field of the
quern", from Gaelic *Achadh na
Bràthann*.

Maud (Aberdeen), Màd
This may be "meeting place", from
Gaelic *Mòd*, but AÀA recommend
Màd.

Mauld (Inverness), Màld
The meaning of this name is unclear.

Mause (Perth), Meallaibh
"Lump-shaped hills."

Mawhill (Kinross), Magh Chuaich
The Gaelic name is "the plain of the hollow", while the English name implies the opposite.

Maxton (Roxburgh)
"Macas's farm", from English but featuring a Gaelic personal name, which shows Gaelic settlement in the Borders area. See **Longformacus**.

Maybole (Ayr)
"Maidens' dwelling", from English. Gaelic *beag* and *mór* were later added to the older "Meibothel" to distinguish two separate places of which there is now no trace.

Mayen (Banff)
This is probably from *maighean*, "small plain".

Mayish (Arran), A' Mhàis
This may be from Brythonic *maes*, "field", or from the Gaelic equivalent *magh*, "plain", with the -*ais* ending indicating "place".

Mayne (Moray)
See **Mayen**.

Meadale (Skye), Miadal
"Narrow valley", from Norse.

Meadowside (Arran), Baile Uachdrach; (Inverness), Coille an t-Suidhe
The English name is self-explanatory, while the Gaelic name in Arran is "upper farm" and in Inverness is "the wood by the seat". The place in Arran is known also as Baluagra in English.

Mealista (Lewis), Mealasta
"Bent-grass place", from Norse. Mealista island is *Eilean Mhealasta*.

Mearns (Kincardine, Renfrew), A' Mhaoirne *or* A' Mhaorainn
"Territory of the steward" or "stewartry". A native of Kincardineshire is a *Maoirneach*.

Meavaig (Harris), Miabhaig
"Narrow bay", from Norse. Meavaig

in South Harris has the full name, *Miabhaig nam Bàgh*, "Meavaig in Bays", while in North Harris the full name is *Miabhaig nam Beann*, "Meavaig in the mountains".

Meddat (Ross), Meitheid
"Soft or spongy place."

Meggernie (Perth), Migearnaidh
"Boggy place."

Megstone (Inverness), Clach Mhairearad
"Margaret's stone."

Meigle (Ayr); (Perth), Mìgeil
In Perthshire this is "boggy haugh" and the Ayrshire name may be the same.

Meikle Daan (Ross), Dathan Mhór
"Big davoch."

Meikle Ferry (Sutherland), Port a' Choltair
"Big ferry", known in Gaelic as "the port of the coulter", a coulter being part of a plough.

Meikleour (Perth)
"Big yew", from English "meikle" and Gaelic *iubhar*. There was also a "Littleour" in the vicinity.

Melbost (Lewis), Mealabost
"Bent-grass farm." The full name of *Mealabost Bhuirgh*, "Melbost of Borve", distinguishes Melbost on the west side of Lewis from Melbost near Point. The old graveyard in Melbost on the west side is called *Cladh Bhrìghde*, "St Bridget's churchyard".

Melgarve (Inverness), Am Meall Garbh
"The rough lump-shaped hill."

Mellon Charles (Ross), Meallan Theàrlaich *or* Na Meallan
"Charles's lump-shaped hill" or "the lump-shaped hills". Local people were known as *rodain*, "rats".

Mellongaun (Ross), Meallan a' Ghamhna
"The lump-shaped hill of the stirk." This place is also known as Stirkhill in English.

Mellon Udrigle (Ross) Meallan
Ùdraigil *or* Na Meall'
"The lump-shaped hill of Udrigle"
or "the lump-shaped hill".

Melness (Sutherland), Taobh
Mhealainis
"Bent-grass headland." The Gaelic
name is the same with *taobh*, "side or
district", attached. Locally this was
also pronounced *Meinleas* and
Taobh Mheinleas. The area is nicknamed *an t-Seich* which may be "the
pelt or hide" and a local person is
called a *Seichear*.

Melrose (Banff, Selkirk), Maol Ros
In Banffshire this name is "blunt or
bare promontory", from Gaelic,
while in Selkirkshire it may be "bald
moor", from Brythonic or may mean
the same as the Banffshire name,
given old Melrose's location on a
bend of the Tweed.

Melvaig (Ross), Mealbhaig *or*
Mealabhaig
"Bent-grass bay", from Norse. The
village is also known by the nickname *A' Bhoilc* and a person from
Melvaig is a *Boilceach or boc*, "buck".
A saying concerning Melvaig is *'S
fhada bhon lagh Dìobaig, 's fhaide na
sin sìos Mealbhaig*, "Diabaig is far
from the law, and Melvaig even
further".

Melvich (Sutherland), A'
Mhealbhaich *or* Mealbhaich
This may be "bent-grass bay", from
Norse. To express "in Melvich",
Gaelic uses *air a' Mhealbhaich*, "on
Melvich". The ferry at Melvich was
known as *Coit Healadail*, "the
Halladale boat".

Menteith (Perth), Tèadhaich *or* Srath
Thèadhaich
This name is from that of the River
Teith and the second Gaelic name
defines the area as a "strath". The
English form appears to be from an
older Gaelic one containing *mon*,
"moor or upland", which in turn

may be from Brythonic. The Braes
of Teith is *Bràigh Thèadhaich*, "the
upper part of Menteith". A native of
the area is a *Tèadhach*. Local
pronunciation suggests that
Tèamhaich or *Tèamhaich* might be a
more accurate spelling.

Meoble (Inverness), Meobal *or* Miabol
"Narrow farm", from Norse.

Merkadale (Skye), Margadal
This Norse name may be "merkland
valley".

Merkinch (Inverness), Marc Innis
"Horse meadow", and similar to
"Markinch" in Fife.

Merkland (Arran), Am Marg
"The merkland." Merkland Point is
Rubha Shalach, "dirty point" or
"willow point".

Methil (Fife), Meadhchill
This may be "middle or mid church",
from an early Gaelic form *Meadh
Chill*.

Methven (Perth), Meadhainnigh *or*
Meithinnigh
"Middle stone", from Brythonic. The
Gaelic name was believed to derive
from *meadhan*, "middle". Methven
Wood was known as *Coille
Mheadhain*, while the high moor-
land north of the village is *Sliabh
Mheadhainnigh*. The Battle of
Methven in Gaelic is *Blàr Monadh
Carno*, "the battle of Carno Moor".

Miagro (Sutherland), Mèathgro *or*
Miagro
"Narrow river pit", from Norse.

Mial (Ross), Mitheall
"Narrow field or hill", from Norse.

Mianish (Tiree), Mianais
"Narrow headland", from Norse.

Miavaig (Lewis), Miabhaig
"Narrow bay", from Norse. Local
pronunciation as collected by
Oftedal (1954) suggests a preferable
spelling of *Mitheabhag*.

Micras (Aberdeen), Miagra
This may be "boggy circular fort".
The English name was originally

"Micra", with the plural added to reflect the place's division into two parts, Easter Micras being *Miagra Shìos* and Wester Micras *Miagra Shuas.*

Mid Argyll (Argyll), Dal Riada *or* Meadhan Earra-Ghàidheal
The middle part of Argyll was where the Scots' first settlement took place. They brought with them the name of the area in Ireland from which the settlers came, *Dal Riada*, "Riada's territory".

Midcalder (West Lothian)
Calder is "hard water", from *Caladar*, a common river name throughour Scotland. Midcalder is part of a larger area along with East Calder and West Calder, and by analogy with the names of the other two places would be *Caladar Meadhanach* in Gaelic.

Middlequarter (North Uist), An Ceathramh Meadhanach
"The middle quarter-land."

Middle Quarter (South Uist), Na Meadhanan
"The middle lands" in Gaelic, situated between Boisdale to the south and Iochdar to the north.

Middleton (Inverness), Baile Mheadhain; (Tiree), Am Baile Meadhanach
"The middle farm."

Mid Fearn (Ross), Feàrna Meadhanach
"Middle alder place."

Midfield (Sutherland), Achadh Mheadhanach *or* An t-Achadh Meadhanach
"Middle field."

Mid Lawers (Perth), Labhar na Craoibhe
"Lawers by the tree."

Mid Lix (Perth), Lic Meadhanach
"Middle Lix."

Midlothian (Midlothian), Meadhan Labhdaidh *or* Meadhan Lodainn
"The middle of Lothian."

Midmar (Aberdeen), Mic Mhàrr
This may be "the bog of Marr".

Mid Ross (Ross), Ros Meadhanach
"Middle Ross."

Midstrath (Aberdeen), Mig Srath
"Boggy strath."

Midtown (Ross), Am Baile Meadhain; (Sutherland), Am Baile Meadhanach
"Middle farm."

Midtown of Duntelchaig (Inverness), Bail Shìos
The Gaelic name is "lower or easter farm".

Migdale (Sutherland), Migein
The English name is "boggy valley", while the Gaelic is "little bog".

Migger (Perth), Migear
"Boggy place."

Migvie (Aberdeen), Migeaghaidh; (Inverness), Mìgibhidh
"Boggy hill face."

Mile End (Inverness)
See **Kinmylies**. This was formerly known as Balachlan or *Baile Lachlainn*, "Lachlann's farm".

Millbuie (Aberdeen), Am Maol Buidhe
"The yellow rounded hill."

Millbuies (Moray)
See **Millbuie**. In this case an English plural has been attached to the basic name.

Millburn (Inverness, Sutherland), Allt a' Mhuilinn
"The stream of the mill."

Millcraig (Ross), Muileann na Creige
"The mill by the rock."

Milleur Point (Wigtown)
This may be "dun-coloured headland", from *Maol Odhar*, or "yew headland", from *Maol Iubhar*.

Millfield (Arran), Achadh a' Mhuilinn *or* Achd a' Mhuilinn
"Field of the mill."

Millhouse (Argyll), Taigh a' Mhuilinn
"The house of the mill."

Mill of Sterin (Aberdeen), Muileann Stairein
"Mill at the stepping stones."

Millpark (Raasay), Pàirc na Muilne
"Field by the mill."

Millport (Cumbrae), Port a' Mhuilinn
"The port at the mill."

Milnafua (Ross), Maol nam Fuath
"Rounded hill of the ghosts."

Milngavie (Dunbarton), Muileann
Ghaidh
There are a number of interpretations of this name, such as "Davie's
mill", from Gaelic *Muileann
Dhàibhidh* (although *Muileann
Dàibhidh* might be expected),
"windmill", from Gaelic *Muileann
Gaoithe* and "windy or boggy
rounded hill", from Gaelic *Maol na
Gaoithe*. AÀA concede that the
recommended form contains an
obscure second element.

Milovaig (Skye), Mìolabhaig
This Norse name may be "bay at the
narrow field". Lower Milovaig is
Mìolabhaig Ìseal and Upper
Milovaig is *Mìolabhaig Àrd*.

Milton (several)
There are many places with this
name, which means a farm with a
mill (milltown). Normally the
Gaelic equivalent is *Baile a'
Mhuilinn*, as in Applecross and
Wick, but this is not always the case.
Milton in Easter Ross is known by
the full name of *Baile Mhuilinn
Anndra*, "Andrew's milltown", while
in South Uist Milton is known as
Gearra-bhailteas, "fertile land by the
river mouth", from Norse.

Milton Eonan (Perth), Baile
Mhuilinn Eónain
"Adamnan's milltown."

Milton of Campsie (Dunbarton),
Baile Mhuilinn Chamaisidh
"The milltown of Campsie."

Milton of Clova (Angus), Baile
Mhuilinn Chlàbhaidh
"The milltown of Clova."

Milton of Culloden (Inverness),
Baile Mhuilinn Chùil Lodair
"The milltown of Culloden."

Milton of Kincraigie (Perth), Baile a'
Mhuilinn
"The milltown."

Milton of Roro (Perth), Baile
Mhuileann Ruadh Shruth
"The milltown of Roro."

Minard (Argyll), Mionaird
"Tiny headland."

Mingarry (Argyll), Mìogharraidh;
(South Uist), Mingearraidh
"Main field or pasture land", from
Norse.

Minginish (Skye), Minginis
"Main headland."

Mingulay (Barra), Miughalaigh
This Norse name may be "main hill
island" or "narrow hill island".

Minigaig (Perth), Miongag
"Little cleft."

Minish (North Uist), Midhinis
"Narrow headland", from
Norse.

Minishant (Ayr)
This may mean "sacred shrubbery",
from *Muine Sianta*.

Minmore (Banff), A' Mhon Mhór
"The big moor."

Miodar (Tiree), Am Mìodar
This Norse name may mean "narrow
valley".

Mishnish (Mull), Misinis
This Norse name is "goat
headland".

Modsarie (Sutherland), Modsairidh
This Norse sheiling name may
include a personal name or "meeting" as its first element.

Moidart (Inverness), Mùideart
This Norse name probably means
"narrow sea loch". A native of the
area is a *Mùideartach*.

Moine (Sutherland), A' Mhòine
"The peat bog." West Moine is
Us-mhòine, "upper Moine".

Molinginish (Harris), Mol Linginis
"Shingle beach by the heather headland", a Gaelic/Norse name.

Moll (Skye), Am Mol
"The shingle beach."

Monachylemore (Perth), Monachul
The meaning of this name is unclear. The English name is "big Monachyle" containing Gaelic *mór* and suggesting that at one time there was a *Monachul Beag* or "small Monachyle".

Monaltrie (Aberdeen), Mòine Ailtridh
The first part of the name is "peat moss", while the second may be "rocky place".

Monamore (Arran)
This is either *Am Monadh Mór*, "the big hill-range" or *A' Mhòine Mhór*, "the big peat bog".

Moncrieff (Perth)
"Hill or moor of the tree", from Gaelic *Mon(adh) Craoibhe*.

Moniack (Inverness), Mon Itheig
The first part of the name is "upland" or "moor", while the second is unclear.

Monifeith (Angus)
This may contain elements suggesting moor or upland and ownership or property, and might be realised as *Monadh Fotha* in today's Gaelic.

Monimail (Fife)
This may be "bald or exposed moor", from Gaelic *Monadh Maol*, but may be from a cognate Brythonic/Pictish source meaning the same.

Monklands (Lanark), Bad nam Manach
The English name is "land of the monks", while the Gaelic form is "spot or clump of the monks".

Monkstadt (Skye), Mogastad
"Monk village", from Norse. A saying about the hard work involved in harvesting the land around Monkstadt, *Cha do thuig thu a dhol a bhuain a Mhogastad*, "You didn't realise what harvesting in Monkstadt entailed", is a way of expressing that one has bitten off more than one can chew.

Monorgan (Perth)
"Peat moss on land above a marsh", from *Mòine Fhorgrainn*.

Monquhitter (Aberdeen)
The first part of the name suggests Gaelic *mon(adh)*, "upland" or "moor", while the second is unclear but may be related to a form of the second element in **Balquhidder**, giving a conjectural form of *Mon Chuidir*.

Monreith (Wigtown)
This may be "level moor", from *Mon(adh) Réidh*, or of Brythonic origin.

Montgarrie (Aberdeen)
This may be "the hill of the den", from *Mon(adh) a' Gharaidh*.

Montgreenan (Ayr)
"Hill at the sunny place", from Brythonic and/or Gaelic, *Mon(adh) a' Ghrianain*.

Montrose (Angus), Mon Rois, Monadh Rois *or* Montròsa.
"The moor by the wood." The third Gaelic form is a gaelicised borrowing from the English form. A native of Montrose and the east coast of Angus and the Mearns generally is a *Tròsach*. The east coast of Angus and the Mearns is *an Taobh Tròsach*, "the Montrose side/area".

Monymusk (Aberdeen), Monadh Musga
The present Gaelic name is probably a gaelicisation of the English, which is in turn from a Gaelic original. Given this place's location the generic is probably *mòine*, "peat", rather than *monadh*, "upland, hills". The second element may refer to dampness or moisture.

Monyquil (Arran), Mon a' Choill
"The hill of the hazel tree."

Monzie (Perth: Strathearn), Magh Eadh; (Perth: Atholl), Mon Fhiadh
Magh Eadh is "corn field" and *Mon Fhiadh* is "deer moor".

Monzievaird (Perth), Magh Bhàird
The Gaelic name is "poet's field",
while the English name has
amended the first part of the name
to link it to "Monzie".

Moor of Dinnet (Aberdeen), Sliabh
Muileann Dùnaidh
The Gaelic name is "moor of Dinnet
mill".

Morangie (Ross), Móraistidh
"Large meadow." Morangie Forest is
Frìth Mhóraistidh.

Morar (Inverness), Mórar
"Great water." North Morar is
Mórar MhicShimidh, "Lovat's
Morar"; South Morar is *Mórar
MhicDhùghaill*, "MacDougall's
Morar". Someone from Morar is a
Mórarach. Nearby Loch Morar or
Loch Mhórair is said to be home to a
monster called *Mórag* or *a' Mhórag*,
whose relationship to *an Niseag* on
the other side of the country is
unclear.

Moray (Moray), Moireibh *or*
Moireabh
"Sea settlement." The area was
known in north-coast Gaelic as *An
Taobh Moireach*, "the Moray side or
district". The Laich of Moray is
Machair Mhoireibh, while Braemoray
is *Bràigh Mhoireibh*. A native of
Moray is a *Moireach*, which gives the
surname Murray.

Morefield (Ross), A' Mhór Choille
The English name is a corruption of
the Gaelic "the big wood".
Morefield Cottage is *An Ceanna
Chruinn*, "the round head", possibly
referring to a headland.

Morenish (Perth), Móirnis
"Big meadow."

Morile (Inverness), Móirl
This may be Brythonic/Pictish,
meaning "big clearing".

Mornish (Mull), Móirnis
This may be Norse for "sea headland". An alternative Gaelic derivation would be "great meadow", but

this place's location suggests a more
likely Norse origin. A local saying
denoting a detour is *Rathad
Mhóirnis do Chill Fhionnchain*, "via
Mornish to Kilfinichen".

Morsgail (Lewis), Morsgail
This Norse name may be "sea
house".

Mortlach (Banff), Mórthlach
"Big green hill."

Morvern (Argyll), A' Mhorbhairne
"The sea gap." This was first applied
to Loch Sunart, and Morvern itself
was known as *Cineal Bhaodain*,
"Baodan's tribe". Lower Morvern is
An Leathair Mhorbhairneach, "the
Morvern slope", and Mull and
Morvern together are *An Dreòllainn*.
A Morvern person is a
Morbhairneach.

Morvich (Ross), A' Mhormhoich
"The carse."

Moss (Argyll), A' Mhòinteach;
(Tiree), A' Mhòinteach Ruadh
In Argyll this is "the mossy moor",
in Tiree, "the red-brown mossy
moor".

Mossat (Aberdeen)
This may be "stale damp place", from
Musaid.

Mossend (Arran), Ceann na Mòine
"The end of the peat moss", also
known as Home Farm.

Moss Farm (Arran), An Sliabh
"The moor."

Motherwell (Lanark), Tobar na
Màthar
"The well of the mother", referring
to St Mary.

Moulin (Perth), Maoilinn
"Smooth round hill." Moulin is
known for its good weather, as in
*Cur is cathadh am Bealach Dearg,
sneachd is reòthadh an Càrn a' Bhalg,
cùl ri gaoith air Làirig Bhealaich,
grian gheal am Maoilinn*, "Drifts and
storms at Bealach Dearg, snow and
frost at the Cairnwell, back to the
wind at Lairig Bhealaich, bright

sunshine at Moulin". Moulin fair was called *Féill MoCholmaig*, "St Colman's Fair", to whom the parish church was dedicated.

Moulinearn (Perth), Maol an Fheàrna
"The round hill of the alder."

Mound, The (Sutherland), A' Mhùnd
The English name of this artificial mound was adopted into Gaelic.

Mount Alexander (Inverness), Mùrbhlagan *or* Mùrlagan
While the English name refers to a landlord, the Gaelic name is "rounded little inlet".

Mountblairy (Banff)
This may be "dappled hill", from *Mon(adh) Blàraigh.*

Mounteagle (Ross), Cnoc na h-Iolaire
"The eagle hill."

Mountgerald (Ross), An Claon
The English name refers to a local notable, while the Gaelic name is "the slope".

Mountrich (Ross), Cill Chomhghain
The English name is a 19th-century creation replacing Kilchoan, which is from the Gaelic name, "St Comhghan's Church".

Moy (Inverness), A' Mhòigh; (Ross), A' Mhuaigh; (Sutherland), A' Mhuigh
"The plain."

Moy Bridge (Ross), Drochaid Mhuaigh *or* Drochaid Port Mhuaigh
The two names mean "the bridge of Moy" and "the bridge of the port of Moy" respectively.

Moyle (Ross), A' Mhaoile
"The bare hill."

Moy Lodge (Mull), Taigh na h-Abhainn
The Gaelic name is "the house by the river".

Moyness (Nairn), Muighnis
"Meadow on the plain."

Mualich (Perth), Muthalaich
This may be "gentle green hill".

Mualaichbeg is *Muthalaich Beag*, "small Mualich", and Mualichmore is *Muthalaich Mór*, "big Mualich".

Muasdale (Argyll), Muasdal
This Norse name may be "moss valley".

Muck (Muck), Eilean nam Muc
Although this name appears to mean "the island of the pigs" it is actually "the island of the whales", from Gaelic *muc*, "pig", a short form of *muc-mhara*, "whale". A native of the island is a *Mucanach* also nick-named a *piatan*, "pet lamb". The island is also known by the byname *Tìr Chràine*, "the land of the sow".

Muckairn (Argyll), Mucàrna
The meaning is unclear although the old form, *Bo-càrna*, suggests *both*, "hut". Muckairn churchyard is *Cladh an Easbaig Earaild*, "the graveyard of Bishop Harold". The character of local people was referred to in the term *iongantas muinntir Mhucàrna*, "the unusualness of the people of Muckairn". Local people were known as *gearra-ghobaich Mhucàrna*, "the sharp-tongued people of Muckairn", for their quick-wittedness.

Muckernich (Ross), A' Mhucarnaich
"The swine place."

Muckersie (Perth)
This is a diminutive form of the name found in "Muckross", as suggested by the old anglicised form "Mucrosin", possibly from *Mucrosan*, "small swine wood".

Muckhart (Clackmannan)
"Swine point", from *Mucaird*. AÀA recommend *Muc-Àird*, which has the same meaning.

Muckovie (Inverness), Mucamhaigh
"Swine plain."

Muckrach (Inverness), Mucrach
"Swine place."

Muckraw (West Lothian)
This may be "swine fort", from *Mucrath.*

Muckross (Fife)
"Swine wood", from *Mucros*.

Mucomir (Inverness), Magh Comair
"Plain of the confluence."

Mudale (Sutherland), Modhudal
"Valley of the muddy river", from Norse.

Mugeary (Skye), Mùigearraidh
"Narrow field", from Norse.

Muie (Sutherland), A' Mhuigh
"The plain."

Muieblairie (Ross), Muigh Bhlàraigh
"Dappled moor."

Muir of Aird (Benbecula), Sliabh na h-Àirde
"The moor of the headland."

Muir of Fairburn (Ross), Blàr Fharabraoin
"Moor of Fairburn."

Muir of Ord (Ross), Am Blàr Dubh
"Ord" is a rounded hill from Gaelic *òrd*. The Gaelic name is "the black moor". The Ord Arms Hotel is on the site of *an Taigh Bhàn*, "the white house".

Muir of Tarradale (Ross), Blàr Tharradail
"The moor of Tarradale."

Muirshearlich (Inverness), Muir Sìorlaich
"Plain of the broom rape." Gaelic *muir* means "sea" but the original name was *Magh Sìorlaich*, which became corrupted.

Muirtown (Inverness), Baile an Fhraoich; (Ross), Mórdun
While the English name is "moor farm", the Gaelic name in Inverness is "heather village", and in Ross may be "great fort".

Mulben (Banff), Am Muileann Bàn
"The white mill."

Muldoanich (Barra), Maol Dòmhnaich
"The blunt headland of the Lord."

Mulhagery (Lewis), Mol Chadha a' Ghàrraidh
"The shingle beach at the pass by the enclosure."

Mull, Muile
This name is pre-Gaelic, and has no connection with the names of headlands such as "Mull of Kintyre". Poetically Mull is known as *Muile nam Mór Bheann*, "Mull of the great mountains". The coastland of Mull opposite Morvern is *An Leathair Mhuileach*, "the Mull slope", while Mull and Morvern were jointly known as *An Dreòllainn*. The placenames of Mull are mentioned in the saying *Ceithir busaichean fichead an Ìle 's ceithir àrdacha fichead am Muile*, "Twenty-four *buses* in Islay and twenty-four *ards* in Mull". It is worth noting that many basically similar sayings varied in their detail from place to place. A native of Mull is a *Muileach* but local people were also nicknamed *Doideagan*, after a witch said to live in the island. The alleged nature of Mull people is referred to in a number of sayings, such as *Shob am Muileach is sgròbaidh e thu, sgròb am Muileach is shobaidh e thu*, "Stroke the Mull person and he'll scratch you, scratch the Mull person and he'll stroke you" and *Muileach is Ìleach is deamhan, An triùir as miosa air an domhain. Is miosa am Muileach na an tÌ-leach, Is miosa an t-Ìleach na an deamhan*, "A Mull person, an Islay person and the devil, The three worst in the world. The Mull one is worse than the Islay one, The Islay one is worse than the devil". It is likely that the latter saying did not originate in Mull, and that it also varies from area to area.

Mullinloan (Inverness), Muileann an Lòine
"The mill at the pond."

Mull of Cara (Gigha), Maol Chara
"The rounded headland of Cara."

Mull of Galloway (Wigtown), Maol Ghall-ghàidheil *or* Maol nan Gall
"The rounded headland of the foreign Gaels" or "the rounded headland of the non-Gaels".

Mull of Kintyre (Argyll), Maol Chinn Tìre
"The rounded headland of Kintyre."

Mull of Logan (Wigtown), Maol Logain
"The rounded headland by the hollow."

Mull of Oa (Islay), Maol na h-Obha
"The rounded headland of the Oa."

Mulreesh (Islay), Am Maol Ris
The second part of this headland name is unclear.

Multovie (Ross), Multabhaidh
"Wedder plain."

Mundurno (Aberdeen)
This may be "pebbly hill or moor", from *Mon(adh) Dòrnach*.

Mungasdale (Ross), Mùngasdal
"Monk's valley", from Norse.

Munlochy (Ross), Poll Lòchaidh
The English name is "the mouth of the dark water", from an older Gaelic name *Bun Lòchaidh*. The modern Gaelic name is "the pool of the dark water".

Murlaggan (Inverness), Mùrbhlagan *or* Mùrlagan
"Rounded sea inlet."

Murriel (Aberdeen)
This was formerly "Rathmurriel", from *Ràth Muirghil*, "the round fort of Muriel".

Murthly (Perth), Mórthlaich
"Large green hill."

Musall (Sutherland), Musal
"Moss field", from Norse.

Musdale (Argyll), Mùsdal
This may be "moss valley", from Norse.

Mussadie (Inverness), Musadaidh
"Stale damp place."

Muthil (Perth), Maothail
This may be "gentle place". The Roman camp at Ardoch was known as *Cathair Mhaothail*, "Muthil fort".

N

Naast (Ross), Nàst
This may be "boat place", from Norse.

Nairn (Nairn), Inbhir Narann
"Mouth of the Nairn." The town's nickname was *Baile Spealtaig*, "splinter town". Nairnshire is *Siorrachd Inbhir Narann*.

Narrachan (Argyll), An Arthar
These names are unclear.

Nask (Barra), An Nasg
If this name is of Gaelic origin, it means "the link" or "connection".

Navar (Angus)
"The sacred lands of St Barr", from *Neimheadh Bharra*.

Nave Island (Islay), Eilean Néimh
"St Ném's island."

Navidale (Sutherland), Neimheadal
"Valley of the sacred lands", from Gaelic/Norse.

Navitie (Fife)
See **Navity**.

Navity (Ross), Neamhaididh
"Place of sacred lands."

Neave Island (Sutherland), Eilean na Neimhe
"The island of the sacred place." This is also known as Coomb Island, in memory of St Columba.

Nedd (Sutherland), An Nead
"The nest." Local people were known as *eòin*, "birds".

Neist (Skye), An Éist
"The horse", from Norse. A more full name is *An Éist Fhiadhaich*, "wild Neist". Neist Point is *Rubha na h-Éist* or *Gob na h-Éist*.

Nereabolls (Islay), Nèarabus
The first element of this Norse farm name is unclear.

Ness (Lewis), Nis
"Headland", from Norse. A native of Ness is a *Niseach* nicknamed a *guga*, "gannet".

Nether Lorne (Argyll), Latharna Ìochdarach
"Lower Lorne."

Nethybridge (Inverness), Cinn Drochaid
The Gaelic name is "bridge end".

Nevie (Banff), Neimheadh Chrìosda
"Sacred lands." The Gaelic name is
"the sacred lands of Christ".

New Aberdour (Aberdeen), Obar
Dobhair
"Mouth of the water." *New* in the
English name distinguishes this
place from its namesake in Fife.

Newbigging (Aberdeen, Angus,
Lanark)
"New building." The Gaelic name of
Newbigging in Mar is *Coire Laoigh*,
"the corry on the Lui", but this
name does not apply to any of the
other Newbiggings.

Newburgh (Aberdeen), Baile Ùr
Fobharain; (Fife), Am Borgh Ùr
The Gaelic name of the village in
Aberdeenshire is "the new village of
Foveran", while in Fife it is "the new
burgh".

New Deer (Aberdeen), Achadh Reite
The English name distinguishes this
place from Old Deer. The Gaelic
name contains *achadh*, "field", but
the second part is unclear. It is
found anglicised as Auchreddy.

Newe (Aberdeen)
"Sacred lands", from *Neimheadh*.

New Kelso (Ross), Eadar Dhà
Charrann, Cealsaidh *or* Cealso Ùr
The English name was given by a
farmer who settled here from Kelso.
The original name, *Eadar Dhà
Charrann*, is "between two Carrons".
Cealsaidh is a gaelicisation of
"Kelso", and *Cealso Ùr* is "New
Kelso". The fair held here was
known as *Féill Chealsaidh*, "Kelso
Fair".

Newlands (Sutherland), An Fhearann
Ùr
"The new land."

New Luce (Wigtown), Baile Ùr
Ghlinn Lus
The Gaelic name is "the new village
of Glen Luce".

Newmills (Ross), Am Muileann Ùr
The Gaelic name is "the new mill".

Newmore (Ross), An Neo Mhór
"The large sacred lands."

Newpark (Lewis), Gearraidh Sgor
The English name is self-explanatory, while the Gaelic is "fertile land
by the wood", from Norse.

New Pitsligo (Aberdeen)
"Pitsligo" contains Pictish *pett*,
"share" or "lands", while the second
element is Gaelic *sligeach*, which
refers to shells.

New Street (Lewis), Am Poileagan
The Gaelic name is unclear.

Newton (several)
"New village or farm." The are a
variety of Gaelic names for the
different Newtons throughout the
country. Newton in Argyll is *An
Fhadhail Dhubh*, "the black ford".
Newton in Arran is *Baile Nodha*,
"new farm", which is sub-divided
into North Newton or *Cùl a'
Bhaile*, "back of the farm", and
South Newton, which is simply
Baile Nodha. Nearby Newton Point
is *Rubha a' Chùirn*, "the headland
by the cairn". In Lewis, Newton is
Ionacleit, "brow cliff", from Norse,
and the people were nicknamed
fithich dhubha, "black ravens". In
North Uist, Newton is *Baile
MhicPhàil*, "MacPhail's farm". In
Ross and Tiree, Newton is *Am
Baile Nodha*, "the new farm or
village".

Newtonferry (North Uist), Port nan
Long
The English name is "the ferry at
Newton", while the Gaelic one is
"harbour of the ships". Local people
are *faoileagan*, "seagulls".

Newtonmore (Inverness), Baile Ùr an
t-Sléibh *or* An Sliabh
"The new village of the moor."
Gaelic also has the shorter name
"the moor".

Newton Stewart (Wigtown), Baile
Ùr nan Stiùbhartach
"The new town of the Stewarts."

New Valley (Lewis), An Gleann Ùr
"The new valley."

Nigg (Aberdeen); (Ross), Neig *or* An Uig
"The notch." The second Gaelic name is that used locally in Easter Ross. In Ross, the Sands of Nigg are *An Oitir*, "the long low promontory", and Nigg Links is *Machair Neig.*

Nithsdale (Dumfries), Srath Nid
"The valley of the Nith." An older English name is "Stranit", showing the connection to the Gaelic name.

Nonach (Ross), Nònach
"Foam or spume place", the current Gaelic form having assimilated the definite article into the name, which may originally have been similar to *Omhanaich* (Onich).

Nonakiln (Ross), Neo na Cille
"The sacred lands of the church."

North Ballachulish (Inverness), Seann Bhaile a' Chaolais
The Gaelic name is "Old Ballachulish".

Northbay (Barra), Am Bàgh a Tuath
"The north bay."

North Berwick (East Lothian), Bearaig a Tuath
"North" distinguishes this place from Berwick in England, which for a time was termed South Berwick. See **Berwickshire**.

North Cuan (Seil), Cuan Saoil
The English name distinguishes this place from South Cuan, while the Gaelic name is "Cuan of Seil", *cuan* here meaning "bay" rather than the normal meaning of "ocean".

North Kessock (Ross), Ceasag a Tuath
The older name is *Aiseag Cheasaig*, "the ferry of Kessock". See **Kessock**.

North Queensferry (Fife), Port na Banrighinn
The English name distinguishes this place from South Queensferry. The Gaelic name is simply "the port of the queen".

North Rona (Lewis), Rònaigh
The English name distinguishes this island from the other Rona near Raasay. The name means "rough island", from Norse. It is also known as *Rònaigh an Daimh*, which appears to be "Rona of the stag" but may in fact be *Rònaigh an Taibh*, "Rona of the Atlantic", containing the old word *tabh*, "ocean", from Norse.

Northton (Harris), An Taobh Tuath
The English name is "north farm" while the Gaelic name is "the north side".

North Uist (North Uist), Uibhist a Tuath
See **Uist**. North Uist is also known locally as *an Ceann a Tuath*, "the north end", and is nicknamed *Tìr an Eòrna*, "the land of barley". A native of North Uist is a *Tuathach*, "northerner".

Noss Head (Caithness), Rubha Nòis
"The headland of the river mouth", from Gaelic/Norse. This name was originally *Rubha an Òis* but became contracted.

Noster (Harris), Nostair
"North farm", from Norse.

Nostie (Ross), Ceann na Mòna
The English name is from *Nòsdaidh*, which in turn is from *òst-thaigh*, "inn", but the current Gaelic name is "the end of the peat bog". Nostie Bridge is *Drochaid Nòsdaidh*, retaining the older Gaelic name.

Novar (Ross), Taigh an Fhuamhair
"The house of the giant."

Nuide (Inverness), Noid
"Green place."

Nunton (Benbecula), Baile nan Cailleach
"The village of the nuns." Nunton graveyard is *Cladh Mhoire*, "graveyard of St Mary".

O

Oa (Islay), An Obha
"The headland." Local people were nicknamed *cuthagan*, "cuckoos".

Oape (Ross), An t-Òb
"The bay", from Norse.

Oban (Argyll), An t-Òban
"The little bay." The full name is *An t-Òban Latharnach*, "little bay of Lorne". A Gaelic equivalent of "When in Rome ..." is *Ma tha thu san Òban, dèan mar an t-Òban*, "If you're in Oban, do as Oban does".

Obsdale (Ross), Òbasdal
"Bay valley", from Norse.

Ochtavullin (Argyll), Ochdamh a' Mhuilinn
"The octave, or eighth-land, at the mill."

Ochtermuthil (Perth)
"The top of Muthil", from *Uachdar Mhaothail*.

Ochtertyre (Perth), Uachdar Thìre
"The top of the land."

Ochtofad (Argyll), An t-Ochdamh Fada
"The long octave, or eighth-land."

Ochtomore (Argyll), An t-Ochdamh Mór
"The big octave, or eighth-land."

Ochtow (Sutherland), An t-Ochdamh
"The octave, or eighth-land."

Ockle (Argyll), Ocal *or* Ochdal
This Norse name is unclear but may contain either *dalr*, "valley", or *vǫllr*, "field".

Octofad (Islay), An t-Ochdamh Fada
See **Ochtofad**.

Octomore (Islay), An t-Ochdamh Mór
See **Ochtomore**.

Octovulin (Islay), Ochdamh a' Mhuilinn
"The eighth-land of the mill."

Oldany (Sutherland), Alltanaigh
"Fruit island", from Norse. Oldany Island is *Eilean Alltanaigh*.

Old Croggan (Mull)
There is no Gaelic equivalent of this name as Gaelic distinguishes between Old Croggan's two parts, *Baile Geamhraidh*, "winter farm", and *Baile nan Seabhag*, "the hawks' farm",

considering them as two separate places.

Old Deer (Aberdeen), Déir
The English name uses "Old" to distinguish this from New Deer. The Gaelic name was believed to be from *deur*, "a tear", but this is unclear. The earliest examples of written Scottish Gaelic are in *Leabhar Dhéir*, "the Book of Deer".

Old Kilpatrick (Dunbarton)
"Old" is used to distinguish this place from New Kilpatrick at Bearsden. Kilpatrick itself is *Cill Phàdraig*, "St Patrick's Church".

Oldshore (Sutherland), Àisir
"Path or pass", from Norse. Oldshorebeg is *Àisir Bheag* with Gaelic *beag*, "small", added, while Oldshoremore is *Àisir Mhór*, with *mór*, "big", attached. A native of the area extending from Oldshore to Sheigra is known as an *Àisireach*.

Oldtown (Inverness, Ross), An Seanbhaile
"The old settlement."

Ollach (Skye), An t-Òlach
This may be "the rank grass". Upper Ollach is *An t-Òlach Shuas*.

Onich (Inverness), Omhanaich
This is thought to mean "froth place", possibly referring to a frothy beach.

Opinan (Ross), Na h-Òbaidhnean
"The little bays." There are two places with this name, the first, near Gairloch, also known as *Òbaidhnean Gheàrrloch* and the second, near Laide, known as *Òbaidhnean an Leothaid* or *Òbaidhnean an Uillt Bheithe*, "the little bays of Laide" or "the little bays of Aultbea".

Orbost (Skye), Orabost
This Norse name may be "Orri's farm" or "seal farm".

Orchill (Perth), Urchoill
"Wood side."

Ord (Skye), An t-Òrd
"The rounded hill."

Ordie (Aberdeen)
"Place of the rounded hill", from Òrdaigh.

Ord of Caithness (Caithness), An t-Òrd Gallach
"The Caithness rounded hill."

Orinsay (Lewis), Orasaigh
"Ebb island", from Norse.

Orkie (Fife)
"Pig place", from *Orcaidh*, earlier *Orcan*.

Orkney (Orkney), Arcaibh
"Land of the swine or whale people", a tribal name. An Orcadian is an *Arcach*. The Pentland Firth is *An Caol Arcach*, "the Orcadian Sound".

Ormaclete (South Uist), Ormacleit
"Shale rock or hill."

Ormidale (Argyll), Ormadal
"Shale valley."

Ormiscaig (Argyll), Ormasgaig
This may be "shale strip of land" or "Orm's strip of land", from Norse.

Ormsaigbeg (Argyll), Ormsaig Bheag
"Shale bay" or "Orm's bay", from Norse with Gaelic *beag*, "small".

Ormsaigmore (Mull), Ormsaig Mhór
"Shale bay" or "Orm's bay", from Norse with Gaelic *mór*, "large".

Ormsary (Argyll), Ormsaraidh
"Orm's field" or "shale field", from Norse.

Ormscaig (Ross), Ormasgaig
See **Ormiscaig**.

Oronsay (Colonsay), Orasa; (Skye), Orasaigh
See **Orinsay**.

Orosay (South Uist), Orasaigh
See **Orinsay**.

Orsay (Islay), Orasa *or* Orasaigh
See **Orinsay**.

Osdal (Skye), Òsdal
"River mouth valley", from Norse.

Ose (Skye), Òs
"River mouth", from Norse.

Osedale (Ross), Òsdal
See **Osdal**.

Oskaig (Raasay), Ósgaig
"Strip of land at a river mouth", from Norse.

Oskamull (Mull), Osgamul
This may be "ox island", from Norse.

Osmigarry (Skye), Osmaigearraidh
"Asmund's field or pasture land", from Norse.

Osnaburgh (Fife)
This appears to include the same first element as in Osnabrück in Germany. This place is also known as Dairsie, which is "oak stance", from *dair* and *fasadh*, giving *Darfhasaidh*.

Ospisdale (Sutherland), Usdal
This Norse valley name is unclear, although the English form suggests a personal name as the first element. The Gaelic form is much reduced and the vowel quality suggests it does not mean the same as **Osdal** or **Osedale**.

Ostaig (Skye), Ostaig
"East bay", from Norse.

Ostem (Harris), Ostam
"East islet", from Norse.

Otter Ferry (Argyll), An Oitir *or* Port na h-Oitrich
"The long low promontory" or "the harbour at the long low promontory".

Otternish (North Uist), Odarnais
"Sharp point headland."

Outend (Scalpay), An Ceann a-Muigh
"The outside end."

Overscaig (Sutherland), Ofarsgaig
"Over-strip of land."

Ovie (Inverness), Ubhaidh
This is said to be from *uabhaidh*, "terrible", but may actually refer to some oval-shaped feature from Gaelic *ugh*, "egg".

P

Pabay (Harris), Pabaigh
"Priest island", from Norse. A native of Pabay was a *Pabach* or *cathan*, "barnacle goose".

Pabbay (Barra, Skye), Pabaigh
See **Pabay**.

Paible (North Uist), Paibeil
"Priest village", from Norse. A
saying warns, *Na toir bó á Paibeil, 's
na toir bean á Boighreigh*, "Don't take
a cow from Paible or a wife from
Boreray".

Paiblesgarry (North Uist),
Paiblisgearraidh
"Fertile pasture land of Paible", from
Norse.

Pairc (Lewis), A' Phàirc
"The park." The full name is *A'
Phàirc Leódhasach*, "the Lewis Park".

Paisley (Renfrew), Pàislig
"Basilica", from Latin.

Palascaig (Ross), Feallasgaig
"Hilly strip of land", from Norse.

Palnure (Kirkcudbright)
This may be "the pool by the yew
tree or trees", from *Poll an Iubhair* or
Poll nan Iubhar, but also see
Achanalt.

Panbride (Angus), Pann Brighde
"St Bridget's hollow" with Brythonic
pant, "hollow", or a gaelicised
version. The Gaelic name was
recorded by Diack (1944).

Panmuir (Angus)
"Large hollow" or "St Mary's
hollow", from Brythonic *pant* or a
gaelicised version such as *pann*, and
Gaelic *mór* or *Moire*.

Pannanich (Aberdeen), Pananaich
"Place of hollows" with a Brythonic
origin. Pannanich Wells is *Fuaran
Phananaich*.

Papadil (Rum), Pàpadal
"Priest valley", from Norse.

Park (Lewis), A' Phàirc
"The park", also known as *A' Phàirc
Leódhasach*, "the Lewis Park", which
is in the southern part of the area
known as Lochs.

Parkend (Lewis), Ceann nam
Buailtean
The Gaelic name is "the end of the
folds".

Parks (Eriskay), Na Pàirceannan
"The parks or fields."

Partick (Glasgow), Pearthaig *or* Partaig
"Little copse", from Brythonic. The
term *cho luath ri muileann Phearthaig*
means "as fast as Partick mill". The
Gaelic form *Partaig* has probably
come into use under the influence of
the English name.

Patt (Ross), A' Phait
"The lump." The full name is *A'
Phait Mhonarach*, "the Monar lump".

Paulfield (Ross), Am Bàrd
It is unclear who is referred to in the
English name, but the Gaelic name
is "the meadow".

Pearsie (Angus), Parsaidh
This may be "copse place", from
Brythonic or Pictish.

Peebles (Peebles), Na Puballan
This may be "pavilions", from
Brythonic *pebyll* with English and
Gaelic plurals. Peeblesshire is
Siorrachd nam Puballan.

Peinaha (Skye), Peighinn na h-Àtha
"The pennyland of the kiln."

Peinchorran (Skye), Peighinn a'
Chorrain
"The pennyland at the narrow
headland".

Peingown (Skye), Peighinn a'
Ghobhainn
"The pennyland of the smith."

Peinlich (Skye), Peighinn an Lighiche
"The pennyland of the doctor."

Peinmore (Skye), Am Peighinn Mór
"The large pennyland."

Peinness (Skye), Peighinn an Easa
"The pennyland by the waterfall or
stream."

Penbreck (Ayr)
"Speckled pennyland", from
Peighinn Breac.

Penick (Nairn)
This may be "small pennyland", from
Peighinneag.

Penifiler (Skye), Peighinn nam
Fìdhleir
"The pennyland of the fiddlers."

Peninerine (South Uist), Peighinn nan Aoireann
"The pennyland at the raised beaches."

Peninver (Argyll), Peighinn an Inbhir
"The pennyland at the river mouth."

Pennycraig (Islay), Creagan na Peighinne
"The small rock at the pennyland."

Pennycross (Mull), Peighinn na Croise
"The pennyland of the cross", the cross in question being *Crois an Ollaimh*, "the doctor's cross", known as "Beaton's Cross" in English.

Pennyfuir (Argyll), Peighinn a' Phùir
"The pennyland of the pasture."

Pennyghael (Mull), Peighinn a' Ghàidheil
"The pennyland of the Gael."

Penrioch (Arran), A' Pheighinn Riabhach
"The brindled pennyland."

Pensoraig (Skye), Peighinn Sòraig
"Pennyland by the muddy bay", from Gaelic/ Norse.

Pentaskill (Angus)
"Land of the gospel", from Pictish *pett* and Gaelic *soisgeul*.

Persabus (Islay), Pearsabus
"Priest's farm", from Norse.

Persie (Perth), Parasaidh *or* Parsaidh
See **Pearsie**.

Perth (Perth), Peairt
"Copse", from Brythonic/Pictish. The term *bho Pheairt gu Hiort*, "from Perth to St Kilda", was used to delineate the extent of the Gaelic-speaking area of Scotland from east to west. According to another saying *Tatha mhór nan tonn, bheir i sgrìob lom air Peairt*, "Great Tay of the waves will cut a swathe through Perth". The town is also mentioned in the saying *Trì iongantasan na h-Alba: drochaid Obar Pheallaidh, tobraichean Ghlinn Iucha is cluig Pheairt*, "The three wonders of Scotland: Aberfeldy bridge, the wells of Linlithgow and the bells of Perth". Perthshire is *Siorrachd Pheairt*, and a Perth person is a *Peairteach*. The southern part of Perthshire is known as *a' Mhachair*, "the plain".

Peterburn (Ross), Alltan Phàdraig
"Peter's little stream."

Peterculter (Aberdeen), Cùltair
In English this is "Peter's Culter", but simply "Culter" in Gaelic. Usually Peterculter is known in English simply as **Culter**.

Peterhead (Aberdeen), Ceann Phàdraig *or* Inbhir Uigidh
"Peter's headland." The name *Ceann Phàdraig* is a fairly recent translation from English. The town was known as *Inbhir Uigidh*, "mouth of the Ugie", in the eastern Gaelic-speaking areas. Inverugie itself is located nearby.

Petersport (Benbecula), Port Pheadair
"Peter's port."

Petley (Ross), Am Maol Buidhe
The English name comes from the surname of the wife of a previous proprietor. The Gaelic name is "the yellow rounded hill".

Pettensier (Moray)
"The farm of the joiners", with Pictish *pett* and Gaelic *saor*.

Petty (Inverness), Peitidh
"Piece of land", from Pictish *pett* with a Gaelic locative ending.

Phantassie (East Lothian, Fife)
This may mean " damp gentle slope", from *Fàn Taise*.

Philiphaugh (Roxburgh), Filiopfach
"Philip's haugh", from English. The gaelicised name appears in the poetry of Iain Lom.

Phoineas (Inverness, Ross), Foinnis
"Under-meadow." Phoineas in Ross is also known as *Fothairis*.

Phoness (Inverness), Fothairis
See **Phoineas**.

Pien (Arran), A' Pheighinn
"The pennyland."

Pinhannet (Ayr)

This appears to be "the pennyland of the small church", from *Peighinn na h-Annaid*. See **Achnahannet**.

Pinmore (Ayr)

This may be "large pennyland", from *Peighinn Mór*.

Pinwherrie (Ayr)

This may be "pennyland of the corrie", from *Peighinn a' Choire*.

Piperhill (Nairn), Tom a' Phìobair

"The piper's hillock."

Pirnmill (Arran), Am Muileann *or* A' Mhuilinn

"Mill of the pirns." The Gaelic name is "the mill", the full name being *Am Muileann Iteachan*, "the pirn mill". Another name, *Muileann nam Piùirneachan*, "mill of the pirns", suggests that the English name came first and was later translated into Gaelic.

Pitagowan (Perth), Baile a' Ghobhainn

"The smith's farm." As is the case in so many names containing Pictish *pett*, while the anglicised form of the name has retained *pett* as "pit", the Gaelic name has changed this to *baile*. Usually the second element of "pit" names is a Gaelic word which, together with other evidence, suggests that prior to changing to *baile*, Gaelic used *pett* in the form of *peit* as a common noun referring to a farm or settlement in the previously Pictish areas.

Pitarrick (Perth), Baile an Tarraig

"Farm of the pulling", possibly referring to the steep hill road above it.

Pitcairn (Fife)

"Farm at the cairn", from *peit* and *càrn*.

Pitcalnie (Ross), Baile Chailnidh *or* Cuilt Eararaidh

"Farm at the hard place." The second Gaelic name is "secluded spot of the parching". The Strath of Pitcalnie is *Srath Chuilt Eararaidh*.

Pitcalzean (Ross), Baile a' Choillein

"Farm by the small wood."

Pitcaple (Aberdeen)

"Farm of the horses", from *Peit/Baile Capall*.

Pitcarden (Moray)

"Farm by the thicket", from Pictish *Peit Chàrdainn*.

Pitcarity (Angus), Pit Charadaidh

The second element of this farm name suggests "pair" or "twin", and may refer to its location at the confluence of two rivers.

Pitcarmick (Perth), Baile Charmaig

"Cormac's farm."

Pitcastle (Perth), Baile a' Chaisteil

"The farm at the castle."

Pitchaish (Banff)

This may be "steep farm", from *Peit/Baile Chais*.

Pitchroy (Moray)

"Hard farm", from *Peit/Baile Chruaidh*.

Pitconochie (Fife)

"Duncan's farm", from *Peit/Baile Dhonnchaidh*.

Pitcorthie (Fife)

"The farm of the standing stone", from *Peit/Baile Coirthe*.

Pitcorthy (Aberdeen)

See **Pitcorthie**.

Pitcruive (Perth), Peit Chraoibh

"The farm at the tree." Unusually, the Gaelic form of the name has retained Pictish *pett* rather than amending it to Gaelic *baile*.

Pitfaed (Ross), Baile Phàididh

"Paddy's farm."

Pitfichie (Aberdeen)

This may be "raven farm" or "farm at the raven place", from *Peit/Baile Fithichidh*.

Pitfodels (Aberdeen)

"The copse at the section of land", from *Bad Fodail*.

Pitfour (Perth, Ross), Baile Phùir

"The farm at the pasture."

Pitfuir (Ross), Pit Fhùir

See **Pitfour**. Interestingly, Gaelic

has retained *pit* rather than change it to *baile*.

Pitfure (Sutherland), Baile Phùir
See **Pitfour**.

Pitgaveny (Moray)
"The farm of the stirk", from *Peit/Baile a' Ghamhna*.

Pitglassie (Banff), Baile Glasaidh; (Ross), Baile a' Ghlasaich
"The farm by the grassy land."

Pitgrudie (Sutherland), Baile Ghrùididh
"The farm by the gravelly river."

Pithogarty (Ross), Baile Shogartaidh
"Farm at the priest's place."

Pitilie (Perth), Baile na Mòine
The English name comes from an older Pictish/Gaelic farm name, possibly referring to the stream now called "Pitilie Burn", while the Gaelic name is "farm of the peat moss".

Pitkeathley (Perth)
"Cathalan's farm", from *Peit/Baile Chathalain*.

Pitkennedy (Angus)
"Kennedy's farm", from *Peit/Baile a' Cheanadaich*.

Pitkenny (Fife)
"Cainneach's farm", from *Peit/Baile Chainnigh*.

Pitkerrald (Inverness), Baile Chaoraill
"Caorall's farm."

Pitkerrie (Ross), Baile Chéirigh
This name may contain a form of *ciar*, "dark", giving "farm at the dark place".

Pitlochie (Fife)
This farm name referred originally to a stone, *clach*, rather than a loch.

Pitlochrie (Angus), Baile Chloichrigh
"The farm at the stony place."

Pitlochry (Perth), Baile Chloichrigh
"The farm at the stony place." This used to be known as *Both Chloichrigh*, "the hut at the stony place". The fair held here in October was *An Fhéill Sràide*, "the street fair". See **Atholl**.

Pitmachie (Aberdeen)
This is said to be "Maol Fheichin's farm", from *Peit/Baile Mhaol Fheichin*.

Pitmackie (Perth), A' Mhacaig
This name is unclear.

Pitmaduthy (Ross), Baile MhicDhuibh *or* Peit MhicDhuibh
"MacDuff's farm."

Pitmedden (Aberdeen)
"Middle farm", from *Peit/Baile Meadhain*.

Pitmurchie (Aberdeen)
"Murchadh's farm", from *Peit/Baile Mhurchaidh*.

Pitnacree (Perth), Baile na Craoibhe
"The farm with the tree." The Pitnacree fair was called *Féill Baile a' Mhuilinn*, "Milton fair".

Pitnellie (Ross), Baile an Eunlaith
"The farm of the poultry."

Pitourie (Inverness), Baile Odharaidh
"The farm at the dun-coloured place."

Pittencrieff (Fife)
"Farm at the tree or trees", from *Peit/Baile na Craoibhe* or *Peit/Baile nan Craobh*.

Pittendreich (Moray, Perth), Baile an Dreich
"The farm at the hill face."

Pittentaggart (Aberdeen)
"The farm of the priest", from *Peit/Baile an t-Sagairt*.

Pittentrail (Sutherland), Baile an Tràill *or* Bad an Tràill
"The farm of the serf." This is also known locally as *Bad an Tràill*, "the spot of the serf", but Gaelic *bad* may have been substituted for Pictish *peit* as they sound quite similar.

Pittenweem (Fife), Peit na h-Uaimhe
"The farm by the cave."

Pitteuchar (Fife)
"Farm at the river bank" using *eochair*, "edge, bank", as found in "Yoker".

Pittyvaich (Banff)
"The farm with the byre", from *Peit/Baile a' Bhàthaich*

Pityoulish (Inverness), Baile
Gheollais
"The farm at the bright place."

Pladda (Arran), Plada
"Flat island", from Norse.

Plocrapol (Harris), Plocrapol
This Norse name contains *bólstaðr*,
"farm", but the first part is unclear.

Plockton (Ross), Am Ploc
"The pimple." The English name has
"town" attached. The full Gaelic
name is *Ploc Loch Aillse*, "the pimple
of Lochalsh", nicknamed *baile nam
bochd*, "the village of the poor".

Pluscarden (Moray)
Although the first part of the name
is unclear, the second is "thicket",
from Pictish *carden*.

Point (Lewis), An Rubha
"The headland." A native of Point is
a *Rubhach* also nicknamed a *sùlaire*,
"gannet", or *turnag*, "duck", the last
name imitating the Point accent.

Point of Sleat (Skye), An Rubha *or*
Rubha Shléite
"The headland" or "headland of Sleat".

Point of Stoer (Sutherland), Rubha
an Stòir
"The headland of Stoer."

Polbain (Ross), Am Poll Bàn
"The white pool."

Poldrait (West Lothian)
"The pool at the bridge", from *Poll
na Drochaid*.

Polglass (Ross), Am Poll Glas
"The grey-green pool."

Polin (Sutherland), Pòlain
"The farm", from Norse.

Polkemmet (West Lothian)
If this is a Gaelic name, it may be
"pool at the crooked place", from
Poll Camaid.

Polla (Sutherland), Am Polladh
"The pool" or "pool river", from
Norse.

Pollagharrie (Ross), Poll a'
Ghearraidh
"The pool of the cut", referring to a
land feature.

Polloch (Argyll), Poll Loch
"Mud loch."

Pollochar (South Uist), Poll a'
Charra
"The pool by the standing stone."

Pollosgan (Skye), Poll Losgann
"Frog pool."

Polmaddie (Argyll), Poll a' Mhadaidh
"The pool of the wolf."

Polmadie (Glasgow)
This appears to be "the pool of the
son of God", from *Poll Mac Dé*.

Polmont (Stirling)
This may be "muddy moor" or "pool
moor", from *Poll Mhon(adh)*, or a
cognate Brythonic source.

Polnessan (Ayr)
"The pool of the stream or waterfall", from *Poll an Easain*.

Polvinister (Argyll), Poll a' Mhinisteir
"The minister's pool."

Poniel (West Lothian)
"Neil's pool or stream", from *Poll
Néill*.

Poolewe (Ross), Poll Iubh *or* Abhainn
Iubh
"The pool on the Ewe River." The
second Gaelic name is "River Ewe".
The coast from Poolewe to Cove is
known as *An Slios*, "the side".

Porin (Ross), Pòrainn
"Pasture (place)." Porin Churchyard
is *Cladh Phòrainn* but used to be
known as *Cladh Mèinn*, "churchyard
of Mid Strathconon".

Port an Righ (Ross), Port an Draoidh
"The druid's harbour." The English
name, which looks like "the king's
harbour" in Gaelic, results from a
misunderstanding of the Gaelic
name.

Port Appin (Argyll), Port na
h-Apann *or* Port na Croise
"The port of Appin" or "the port of
the cross". An older name is *Achadh
a' Bhirlinn*, which appears to mean
"the field of the galley", although
one would usually expect *Achadh na
Birlinn*.

Port Askaig (Islay), Port Asgaig
"The harbour at ash bay", from
Gaelic/Norse.

Portavaddie (Wigtown)
See **Portavadie**.

Portavadie (Argyll), Port a' Mhadaidh
"The harbour of the wolf."

Portban (Tiree), Am Port Bàn
"The white or fair harbour."

Port Bannatyne (Bute), Port
MhicEamailinn
"Bannatyne's harbour." The old
name is *Baile a' Chamais*, "the village
on the bay".

Port Charlotte (Islay), Port Sgioba *or*
Sgioba
The English name is from the
mother of Frederick Campbell of
Islay. The Gaelic names are "harbour
at the ship river" or simply "ship
river", from Norse.

Portclare (Inverness), Port Chlàir
"The harbour at the plain."

Port Dundas (Glasgow), Am Port
The English name commemorates
the Dundas family, while the Gaelic
name is simply "the port".

Port Ellen (Islay), Port Ìlein
This is named after the wife of
Frederick Campbell of Islay. The old
name is *Leòdamas*, "Leòd's farm",
from Norse.

Portessie (Banff)
This may be "the harbour at the
stream place", from *Port Easaidh*.
The local name is "the Sloch", from
sloc, "pit".

Portfield (Mull), Achadh a' Phuirt
"The field by the port."

Port Glasgow (Renfrew), Port
Ghlaschu
"The port of Glasgow."

Portgordon (Banff), Port Ghòrdain
"The port of the Gordons."

Port Henderson (Ross), Portaigil *or*
Portaigin
The Gaelic names mean "port
ravine", from Norse. Locals are
known as *cnùdanan*, "gurnards".

People from outside the village
call it *Port an Sgùmain*, the
second element referring to
something gathered or skimmed
together.

Portinisherrich (Argyll), Port na
Searaich
This was earlier *Port Innis Shearaich*,
which appears to be a reference to
an eastern meadow or island.
Locally the name was said to be
from *Port Innis Sia Ràmhaich*, "the
port of the island of the six-oar
galley".

Portknockie (Banff), Port Chnocaidh
"Harbour at the hilly place."

Portlethen (Kincardine), Port
Leathain
This may be "port at the slope".

Port Logan (Wigtown), Port an
Neasaig
The English name commemorates
the Logan family, while the older
Gaelic name is "the port at the little
isthmus".

Portmahomack (Ross). Port
MoCholmaig
"St Colman's harbour."

Portmoak (Kinross)
"St Mayota's village", from *Port
M'Aodhaig*.

Portmoluag (Lismore), Port
MoLuaig
"St MoLuag's harbour."

Port Mor (Tiree), Am Port Mór
"The big harbour."

Portmore (Peebles); (Muck), Am Port
Mór
In Muck the name means "the big
harbour", but in Peebles it is probably "the big village".

Portnacon (Sutherland), Port nan
Con
"The harbour of the hounds."

Portnacraig (Perth), Port na Creige
"The village at the rock."

Portnacroish (Argyll)
"The harbour of the cross", from
Port na Croise.

Portnadoran (Inverness), Port nan Dobhran
"The port of the otters."

Portnaguran (Lewis), Port nan Giùran
"The harbour of the barnacles."

Portnahaven (Islay), Port na h-Abhainne
"Harbour at the river." There is an argument that this may be a gaelicisation of a name originally including Norse *höfn* (harbour) rather than Gaelic *abhainn* (river). The Gaelic name of neighbouring Port Charlotte is of Norse origin.

Portnaheile (Ross), Port na h-Éile
The defining element of this name is unclear.

Portnalong (Skye), Port nan Long
"The harbour of the ships."

Port nam Murach (Inverness), Port na Mùraich
"Port of the sandhill."

Portnellan (Perth), Port an Eilein
"The harbour of the island."

Port of Menteith (Perth), Port Loch Innis MoCholmaig *or* Am Port
"The port of the Lake of Menteith" or "the port".

Port of Ness (Lewis), Port Nis *or* Am Port
"The harbour of Ness", or simply "the harbour" in Gaelic. The village's old name was *Calaigmhol*, from Norse.

Port Patrick (Wigtown), Port Phàdraig
"Patrick's harbour." This was earlier known as *Port Rìgh*, "king's harbour".

Port Ramsay (Lismore), Port Ramasa *or* Port Ramasaigh
The second part of this name is Norse for "raven island" and the island in question, *Eilean Ramasa*, is just offshore.

Portree (Skye), Port Rìgh
"King's harbour." This is said originally to have been *Port Ruighe*,

"slope harbour". An earlier name was Kiltaraglan, from *Cill Targhlain*, "St Talorcan's Church", also found in **Kiltarlity**.

Portskerra (Sutherland), Port Sgeireach
"Skerry harbour."

Portsonachan (Argyll), Port Samhnachain
"The port of the river trout" or "the port at the sorrel place".

Portsoy (Banff), Port Saoidh
This may be "saithe, or coalfish, harbour".

Portuairk (Argyll), Port Uairce *or* Port Uaraig
This may be "Ualraig's harbour".

Portvasco (Sutherland), Port Bhaisgea *or* Am Port
The longer name is "the port of Vasco or *Bhaisgea*", which appears to comprise the Norse elements for "current" and "ravine". The place is locally known as *Am Port*, "the harbour".

Portvoller (Lewis), Port Mholair
This may be "port by the field", from Norse.

Port Wemyss (Islay), Bun Othan
The Wemyss family are commemorated in the English name, but the Gaelic name means "river mouth".

Pottie (Mull), Poit Ì *or* Poit Idhe
"The pot of Iona."

Poulouriscaig (Sutherland), Poll Aoraisgeig *or* Poll Éirisgeig
This Gaelic/Norse name may be "pool at the gravel beach strip of land" or even "pool at Erik's bay".

Poyntzfield (Ross), An Àrdach
A family name is used in the English name, but the Gaelic name is "the high place".

Prabost (Skye), Pràbost
This name is said to have been *Bréabost* originally, which is "broad farm", from Norse.

Prescaulton (Moray)
"Hazel thicket", from *Preas Calltainn*.

Presnerb (Angus), Preas na h-Earb
"Thicket of the roe deer."

Proncycroy (Sutherland), Prannsaidh Cruaidh
"Hard tree place", including what appears to be a Brythonic or Pictish element for "tree".

Pubil (Perth), Puball
"Pavilion" or "tent".

Purin (Fife)
"Pasture place", from *Pòran*. See **Porin**.

Q

Quaish (Tiree), Cu-dhéis
See **Cuigeas**.

Quarryfield (Ross), Taigh an Rothaid
The Gaelic name means "the road house".

Quarryhill (Ross), Cnoc an t-Sabhail
The Gaelic name means "the hill at the barn".

Queebec (Ross), Muileann Luathaidh
The English name commemorates Quebec, while the Gaelic name means "waulk mill".

Quidinish (Harris), Cuidinis
"Cattle fold headland", from Norse.

Quier (Lewis), Cuidhir
"Cattle folds", from Norse.

Quinish (Mull), Cuidhinis
"Cattle fold headland", from Norse.

Quothquan (Lanark)
This may be "common land", from *Coitcheann*.

R

Raarem (Harris), Ràiream
"Islet with a nook", from Norse.

Raasay (Raasay), Ratharsair *or* Ratharsaigh
"Roe deer island", from Norse. The island also has the byname of *Eilean nam Fear Móra*, "the island of the great men". Raasay House is *Taigh Mór a' Chlachain*, "big house of Churchtown". A Raasay person is a *Ratharsach*, nicknamed *saoidhean*, "saithe". A saying lists the various

wells of Raasay, *Tobar na Creachainn an Ósgaig, Tobar an Dòmhnaich sa Ghleann, Tobar an Fhìona aig Tobhtagan, Tobar nam Bioran an Glaic nan Curran, 's an Tobar Mór an Suidhisnis.*

Raddery (Ross), Radharaidh
"Arable land not in use."

Raemoir (Kincardine)
This may be from *Ràth Mór*, "large circular fort".

Raffin (Sutherland), An Ràthan
"The small circular fort."

Rafford (Moray), Ràthard *or* Ràthfard
This name in connected to a circular fort.

Rahoy (Argyll), Rathuaidhe
This may be "northern circular fort", from an earlier *Ràth Thuaidhe*.

Raigbeg (Inverness), (An) Ràthaig Bheag
"Small place of the circular fort."

Raigmore (Inverness), (An) Ràthaig Mhór
"Large place of the circular fort."

Rairaig (Mull), Réaraig
"Reed bay", from Norse.

Raith (Fife)
"Circular fort", from *Ràth*.

Raitts (Inverness), Ràt *or* Ràta
"Circular fort." See **Atholl**.

Ralia (Inverness), An Ràth Liath
"The grey circular fort."

Ramasaig (Skye), Ramasaig
"Raven bay", from Norse.

Ramorgan (Fife)
This is said to be "Morgan's circular fort", from *Ràth a' Mhorganaich*.

Ramornie (Fife)
See **Ramorgan**.

Ranish (Lewis), Rànais *or* Radhairnis
"Roe deer headland", from Norse.

Rannagulzion (Perth), Ruigh nan Cuileag
"The sheiling of the flies".

Rannoch (Perth), Raineach
"Bracken." Rannoch Moor is *Mòinteach Raineach* or *Madagan na Mòine* (locally *Madaigein na Mòin*).

The north side of Loch Rannoch is *An Slios Mìn*, "the smooth slope", while the south side is *An Slios Garbh*, "the rough slope", and contains *An Giuthsach*, "the Black Wood of Rannoch". Rannoch was known poetically as *Raineach nam bó*, "Rannoch of the cows", and appears in the saying, *Trì gearastain na h-Albann – Dùn Breatann, Dùn Chailleann is Madaigein na Mòin*, "Three fortresses of Scotland – Dumbarton, Dunkeld and Rannoch Moor".

Rarichie (Ross), Ràth Riachaidh
"Circular fort at the scratching place." Easter Rarichie is *Ràth Riachaidh Shìos*, "lower Rarichie", Wester Rarichie is *Ràth Riachaidh Shuas*, "upper Rarichie", and Lower Rarichie is *Baile a' Phuill*, "farm by the pool".

Rascarrel (Kirkcudbright)
This may be "Cearbhall's headland", from an original *Ros Cearbhaill*, which would be *Ros Chearbhaill* in today's Gaelic.

Ratagan (Ross), Ràtagan
"Small circular fort."

Rathelpie (Fife)
"Alpin's circular fort", from *Ràth Ailpein*.

Rathillet (Fife)
This may be "circular fort of the Ulstermen", from *Ràth Uladh*.

Ratho (Midlothian), Ràthach
"Circular fort place."

Rattray (Perth), Raitear *or* Baile Raiteir
"Fort place" or "village of the fort place".

Rayne (Aberdeen)
"Division", from *Rann*.

Reay (Caithness), Meadhrath *or* Ràth
"Mid fort" or "fort". The poet Rob Donn MacKay spelled this name as *Mìodhrath* or *Mìodhradh*.

Reay Forest (Sutherland), Dùthaich MhicAoidh *or* Frìth
This deer forest is "MacKay's country" or "deer forest" in Gaelic.

Rechullin (Ross), An Ruigh Chuilinn
"The holly slope."

Redburn (Inverness), An t-Allt Ruadh
"The red-brown stream."

Redcastle (Ross), An Caisteal Dearg *or* An Caisteal Ruadh
"The red castle." Gaelic has two words for "red", *dearg* is the bright crimson to scarlet colour while *ruadh* is more russet or red-brown. The old name of this place was *Eadar Dà Dhobhar*, "between two waters" or Edradour.

Redcliff (Skye), An Uamh Ruadh
"The red-brown cave" in Gaelic.

Redfield (Ross), An Raon Dearg
"The red plain."

Redgorton (Perth), Ruigh a' Ghartain
"The sheiling by the enclosed field."

Redkirk Point (Dumfries), Rinn Phàdraig
"Point of the red church." The old name in English is Reynpatrick, from the Gaelic name for "Patrick's headland".

Redpoint (Ross), An Rubha Dearg
"The red headland." The north end of the village is *Am Baile Shìos*, while the southern end is *Am Baile Shuas*. The old name of Redpoint is *An Rubha Lachdann*, "the swarthy, or dun-coloured, headland".

Reef (Lewis), An Riof; (Tiree), An Ruighe
In Lewis the name means "the reef", from Norse, while in Tiree it appears to mean "the slope" but may originally have been from Norse also.

Regoilachy (Ross), Ruigh Ghobhlachaidh
"Slope at the forked field."

Rehourie (Nairn), An Ruigh Shamhraidh
"The summer sheiling."

Reiff (Ross, Sutherland), An Rif
"The reef", from Norse.

Reinakyllich (Perth), Raon nan Coileach
"The field of the cockerels."

Reisgill (Sutherland), Rìdhisgil
"Brushwood gully", from Norse.

Relugas (Moray), Ruigh Lùgais
"Slug slope or sheiling."

Remony (Perth), An Réidh Mhuin
"The level hill."

Renfrew (Renfrew), Rinn Friù
"The headland of the current", from Brythonic. Renfrewshire is *Siorrachd Rinn Friù* while East Renfrewshire is *Siorrachd Rinn Friù an Ear*.

Renish Point (Harris), Rubha Réinis
This may be "reed headland", from Gaelic/Norse.

Reraig (Ross), Réaraig
"Reed bay", from Norse.

Resaurie (Ross), Ruigh Samhraidh
"Summer sheiling."

Rescobie (Angus)
This may be "the wood of splinters or thorns", from *Ros Sgolban*, as an old form of the anglicised name "Roscolbyn" suggests.

Resipol (Argyll), Réiseapol
This may mean "brushwood farm", from Norse.

Resolis (Ross), Ruigh Solais *or* Ruigh Sholais
"Bright slope." Resolis parish is *Sgìre Ruigh Sholais* or *Sgìre Mhàrtainn*, the latter meaning "St Martin's parish".

Restenneth (Angus)
This may be "wood of fire", from Brythonic or Gaelic *Ros Teine*.

Reudle (Mull), Raodal *or* Raoghadal
This may be the same name as **Rodel**.

Revack (Moray), Ruigh a' Bhaic
"The sheiling at the hollow."

Reyran (Argyll), Radharan
This may refer to an unused patch of arable land.

Rhegreannoch (Ross), An Ruigh Ghrianach
"The sunny slope."

Rheindown (Ross), Ruigh an Dùin
"The slope of the fort."

Rhelonie (Ross), Ruigh an Lòin
"The slope of the wet meadow."

Rhenetra (Skye), Réineatra
This may be "rowan township", from Norse.

Rhenigadale (Harris), Réinigeadal
This may be "rowan bay valley", from Norse.

Rhian (Sutherland), An Ruighean
"The little slope."

Rhianbreck (Sutherland), An Ruighean Breac
"The speckled little slope."

Rhicarn (Sutherland), Ruigh nan Càrn
"The slope of the cairns."

Rhiconich (Sutherland), (An) Ruigh Cóinnich
"(The) mossy slope." A native of the area between Kinlochbervie and Rhiconich is known as a *Slisearnach*.

Rhicullen (Ross), Ruigh a' Chuilinn
"The slope of the holly."

Rhidorroch (Ross), An Ruigh Dhorch
"The dark slope."

Rhiedorroch (Perth). An Ruigh Dhorch
See **Rhidorroch**.

Rhifail (Sutherland), An Ruigh Fàil
"The hedge or dyke slope."

Rhigolter (Sutherland), Ruigh a' Ghalldfhir *or* Ruigh a' Ghalldair
This is said to be "the slope of the lowland man" but the second element may be Norse.

Rhilochan (Sutherland), Ruigh an Lochain
"The slope of the small loch."

Rhiloisk (Sutherland), An Ruigh Loisgte
"The burnt slope."

Rhinns of Galloway (Wigtown), Ranna Ghall-ghàidheil *or* Na Rannaibh
"The divisions of Galloway" or "the divisions".

Rhireavoch (Ross), An Ruigh Riabhach
"The brindled slope."

Rhitongue (Sutherland), Ruigh
Thunga
"The slope of Tongue."

Rhives (Ross: Black Isle), Na
Ruighean *or* Ruigheas; (Ross: Easter
Ross), Na Ruighean *or* Na
Ruigheanan; (Sutherland), An
Ruigheach
In the Black Isle, Rhives is *Na
Ruighean*, "the slopes", or
Ruigheas, "slope place"; in Easter
Ross, it is *Na Ruighean* or *Na
Ruigheanan*, "the slopes"; in
Sutherland, it is *An Ruigheach*,
"the slope place".

Rhu (Dunbarton, Inverness), An
Rubha
"The headland."

Rhubain (Eriskay), An Rubha Bàn
"The fair headland."

Rhubodach (Bute), An Rubha
Bódach
"The Bute headland." An older
name was *Rubha an t-Snàimh*, "the
headland of the swimming", which
reflects its location opposite *Caol an
t-Snàimh* or Colintraive, "the
narrows of the swimming".

Rhughasinish (South Uist), Rubha
Ghaisinis
"The headland of goose point", from
Gaelic/Norse.

Rhunahaorine (Argyll), Rubha na
h-Aoireann
"The headland of the raised beach."

Rhuvanish (Berneray), Rubha
Mhànais
"Magnus's headland."

Rhynamarst (Banff), Ruigh nam
Mart
"The slope or sheiling of the cattle."

Rhynd (Fife); (Perth), Rinn
Dealgros
In Perthshire this is "the point of
the thorny wood". The name in Fife
is simply from *Rinn*, "point".

Rhynettan (Inverness), Ruigh an
Aitinn
"The sheiling of the juniper."

Rhynie (Aberdeen), Roinnidh; (Ross),
Ràthan
The Aberdeenshire name means
"division place", and the Ross name
is "small circular fort".

Ribigill (Sutherland), Rìbigil *or*
Ruibigil
"Lady's farm", from Norse. The old
name in English was Regebol.

Rigg (Skye), Ruig
"Ridge", from Norse.

Rimsdale (Sutherland), Rumasdal
"Roaring stream", from Norse.

Rinaittin (Aberdeen), Ruigh an
Aitinn
"Juniper sheiling."

Rinanuan (Inverness), Ruigh nan
Uan
"The sheiling of the lambs."

Rinavey (Perth), Rinn a' Bheithe
"The point at the birch."

Rinavie (Sutherland), Roinnimhigh
"Point plain."

Ringdoo Point (Kirkcudbright)
"Black point", from *Rinn Dubh*.

Rinloan (Aberdeen), Ruigh an Lòin
"The sheiling at the wet meadow."

Rinns of Islay (Islay), Na Ranna, Na
Roinn Ìleach *or* Roinn Ìle
"The divisions" or "the division of
Islay". A native of the Rhinns is a
Rannach. There is a saying, *Nam b'
eileanach mi, gum b' Ìleach mi; Nam b'
Ìleach mi, bu Rannach mi*, "If I were
an islander, I'd want to be from Islay; If
I were from Islay, I'd want to be
from the Rinns".

Rintoul (Kinross)
"The slope, or sheiling, at the barn",
from *Ruigh an t-Sabhail*.

Risga (Argyll), Riosga
This originally Norse island name
may contain *hrís*, "brushwood".

Rispond (Sutherland), Ruspainn
"Copse place."

Roag (Skye), Ròdhag
This may be "deer bay", from Norse.
Roag people were known as *coilich*,
"cockerels", and their ability to make

use of odds and ends is recorded in the saying, *Chan eil maide cam no dìreach nach fhaigh feum ann an Ròdhag*, "There isn't a stick, bent or straight, that can't be made use of in Roag". In Lewis, the name of *Loch Roag* is *Locha Ròg* and is said to derive from a Norse loanword for a shag.

Robostan (Skye), Na Ròbostan *or* Na Ròbostanaich
This name is unclear but may contain Norse *bólstaðr*, "farm".

Rockall (Harris), Ròcal
This Norse name may contain *fjall*, "mountain". Rockall may have been the origin of the mythical *Ròcabarra*, as in the saying, *Nuair thig Ròcabarra ris, 's ann a théid an saoghal sgrios*, "When Rocabarra appears, the world will be destroyed".

Rockfield (Ross), A' Chreag *or* Creag Tarail Bheag
The Gaelic names are "the rock" and "the small rock of Tarrel".

Rodel (Harris), Ròdal *or* Roghadal
"Rood valley", from Norse. Rodel Church is *Eaglais Chliamhain*, "St Clement's Church".

Rogart (Sutherland), Sgìre Raoghaird *or* Sgìr' Raoird
The *Raoghard* or "Rogart" element is "great enclosed field". The Gaelic name contains *sgìre*, "district", and the "Rogart" element is never used on its own in Gaelic.

Rogie (Ross), Ròagaidh *or* Rothagaidh
This may mean "great hill face". A local ditty describes the people from a number of places in Ross, east and west, *Daoine beaga Ròagaidh 's crogaichean Thairbhidh; Buic Srath Ghairbh, meanbhlaich Srath Bhrainn; Fithich dhubh Loch Carrann 's clamhanan Loch Bhraoin*, "Little men from Rogie and crocks from Tarvie; Bucks from Strath Garve, runts from Strath Bran; Black ravens from

Lochcarron, hawks from Loch Broom".

Rohallion (Perth), Ràth Chailleann
"The circular fort of the Caledonians."

Romanno (Peebles)
This may be "the circular fort of the monks", from *Ràth Manach* in earlier Gaelic, now *Ràth Mhanach*. Nearby Lamancha was previously known as Grange of Romanno.

Rome (Angus, Perth), Ruam
"Graveyard", from Latin *Roma*, "Rome", which became restricted in meaning to "graveyard".

Romesdale (Skye), Ròmasdal
"Giant's valley", from Norse.

Ronachan (Argyll), Roinneachan
This may mean "small division".

Rona Lodge (Raasay), Taigh Mór na h-Acarsaid
In Gaelic the name is "the big house at the anchorage" referring to Acairseid Mhór on the island of South Rona.

Ronay (Grimsay), Rònaigh
"Rough island", from Norse.

Rora (Aberdeen)
This may be "great circular fort", from *Ròrath*.

Rora Head (Orkney), Ceann Thothaigh
The Gaelic name translates as "Hoy Head" and was used in north coast Gaelic.

Roro (Perth), Ruadh Shruth
"Red-brown stream."

Roroyeare (Perth), Ruadh Shruth Gheàrr
"Short red-brown stream."

Roscobie (Fife)
See **Rescobie**.

Rosebank (Ross), Cùil Choinnich
The Gaelic name is "Kenneth's secluded spot".

Rosehall (Sutherland), Innis nan Lìon
The English name is "horse field", from Norse, while the Gaelic name is "the flax meadow".

Rosehaugh (Ross), Peit Dhonnchaidh
The Gaelic name is "Duncan's land
or farm" and is unusual in that it has
retained Pictish *pett* rather than
changing it to Gaelic *baile*.

Rosehearty (Aberdeen), Ros
Àbhartaich
"Àbhartach's headland."

Rosemarkie (Ross), Ros Mhaircnidh
"Headland of the horse stream."

Roshven (Argyll), Roisbheinn
"Horse mountain", from Norse/
Gaelic.

Rosinish (Benbecula, Eriskay),
Roisinis
"Horse headland", from Norse.

Roskeen (Ross), Ros Cuithne
This may mean "antler headland".

Roskill (Ross), An Roisgeil; (Skye),
Roisgil
"Horse gully", from Norse.

Rosneath (Dunbarton), Ros
Neimhidh
"The point of the sacred lands." The
old name was simply *Neimheadh*,
"sacred lands".

Ross (Berwick, Kirkcudbright, Perth);
(Ross), Ros
The Kirkcudbrightshire and
Perthshire names are "headland"
and would probably have been *An
Ros* in Gaelic locally. The name in
Berwickshire appears from its loca-
tion to be of the same origin. The
Ross-shire name is probably "forest"
but may be "headland" referring
either to the Black Isle or Tarbat
Ness. The divisions of Ross are
Easter Ross, *Ros an Ear* or
commonly *Taobh Sear Rois*; Wester
Ross, *Ros an Iar* or *Taobh Siar Rois*;
and Mid Ross, *Ros Meadhanach*.
North-east Ross is *Machair Rois*,
"the plain of Ross" and the Black
Isle is *an t-Eilean Dubh*. The area
between Tain and Edderton is *A'
Mhorbhaich* or *A' Mhormhoich*, "the
carse". The east side of Ross and
Inverness-shire was known as *a'*

Mhachair to the inhabitants of the
west coat. Ross-shire is *Siorrachd
Rois* and Ross and Cromarty is *Ros
is Cromba*. A native of Ross is a
Rosach.

Rossal (Mull), Rosal; (Sutherland),
Rasail
"Horse field", from Norse.

Rossdhu (Dunbarton), Ros Dubh
"Black headland." Locally the definite article was not used in this
name although it would be
expected.

Rossie (Perth), Ros nan Cléireach
"The headland of the clerics" in
Gaelic, while the English form is
"headland", possibly with a Gaelic
locative attached, suggesting that
locally the place may have been
called in Gaelic simply *Rosaidh*.

Ross of Mull (Mull), An Ros
Mhuileach
"The Mull headland."

Rosyth (Fife), Ros Fhìobh, Ros
Fhìobha *or* Ros Saidh
The first two Gaelic names are "the
headland of Fife" or "the Ross of
Fife" and the first is the form
recommended by AÀA. The third
Gaelic name is one which is fairly
current and based on a folk etymology suggesting "headland of saithe".

Rothes (Moray), Ràthais
"Circular fort place."

Rothesay (Bute), Baile Bhóid
The English name appears to be a
Norse island name possibly featur-
ing a personal name. The Gaelic
name is "the town of Bute".
Rothesay's old church was *Cille
Bhruic*, "St Broc's Church" and the
parish was known as *Sgìreachd
Bhruic*, "St Broc's parish". The fair
held here in May was *Féill Bhruic*.

Rothiemay (Aberdeen), Ràt a'
Mhaigh
This may be "the circular fort on the
plain", from a possible older *Ràth a'
Mhaigh*.

Rothiemurchus (Inverness), Rata
Mhurchais
"Murchas's circular fort."

Rothienorman (Aberdeen)
This may be "the Normans' circular
fort".

Rotmell (Perth), Rathad a' Bhile *or*
Ràit a' Mhilidh
The two Gaelic forms have been
recorded and sound similar, the first
being "the road by the rock edge"
and the second "the circular fort of
the warrior".

Rottearns (Perth), Ràth Éireann
"The circular fort of the Earn." The
English name has a plural attached.

Rovie (Ross), Ròmhaigh
"Great plain."

Rowardennan (Stirling), Rubha Àird
Eónain
"Point on the headland of
Adamnan."

Roxburgh (Roxburgh), Rosbrog
"Roch's burgh", from English.
Roxburghshire is *Siorrachd Rosbrog*.

Roybridge (Inverness), Drochaid
Ruaidh
"The bridge over the Roy." The old
name was *A' Cheapach*, "the tillage
plot", and the church is *Cille Choireil*
or Cille Choirill, "St Caireall's Church".

Ruaig (Tiree), Ruthaig
"Clearing bay", from Norse.

Ruantallain (Jura), Rubha an t-Sàilein
"The headland at the small inlet."

Ruarach (Ross), An Ruadhrach
"The red-brown place."

Rubha Ardvule (South Uist), Rubha
Àird a' Mhaoile
"The point of the blunt headland."

Rubha Bhoisinnis (Berneray), Rubha
Bhoisinis
"The headland of Bhoisinis", from
Gaelic/Norse. *Bhoisinis* itself is
"current point".

Rubha a' Chumhainn Bhig (Jura),
Rubha a' Chumhaing Bhig
"The headland at the small narrow
place."

Rubha Mhic 'ille mhaoil (Jura),
Rubha MhicIllemhaoil
"MacMillan's headland."

Rubha Reidh (Ross), Rubha Réidh
"Level point." The old and local
name for this headland is *An*
t-Seann Sgeir, "the old skerry", and
Rubha Reidh lighthouse is known
as *Taigh-solais na Seann Sgeir*.

Rudhadubh (Grimsay), An Rubha
Dubh
"The black headland."

Ru Hunish (Skye), Rubha Hùinis
This Gaelic/Norse name contains
both languages' words for "headland", but the first Norse element
may be from a personal name based
on *húna*, "bear cub". The related
name of "Hungladder" or
Hùnagladair, is nearby.

Rum (Rum), Rùm
This is a pre-Gaelic name, and
unclear. A part of Rum is known
as *Na Hearadh Rumach*, "Rum
division", using the term *Na*
Hearadh, also found in Harris and
Islay. The Cuillins of Rum are
known as *An Cuiltheann Rumach*.
A native of Rum is a *Rumach*,
also nicknamed a *ròcas*, "rook".
The island was known by the
byname *Rìoghachd na Forraiste*
Fiadhaich, "the kingdom of the
wild forest".

Rummond (Fife)
"The circular fort of Manau",
from *Ràth Mhanainn* or *Ràth*
Mhanann.

Runavey (Perth), Ruigh nam Fiadh
"The slope of the deer." This is now
known as Westerton of Runavey.

Runroy (Perth), An Raon Ruadh
"The red-brown field."

Runtaleave (Angus)
This may be "the plain at two moor-
lands", from *Raon Dà Shliabh*.

Rushgarry (Berneray), Ruisigearraidh
"Fertile pastureland of the horse",
from Norse.

Ruskie (Perth)
This may be "marshy place", from *Rùsgaidh*.

Russel (Ross), Riseail
"Mare field", from Norse.

Rutherglen (Lanarkshire), An Ruadh Ghleann
"The red-brown valley."

Ruthven (Aberdeen, Angus, Banff, Berwick, Inverness), Ruadhainn
In Aberdeenshire, Angus, Banffshire and Inverness-shire this is "red-brown place". The Berwickshire name may be of the same origin or more likely have been planted there in commemoration of another Ruthven further north. The upper part of Ruthven in Inverness-shire is *Bràigh Ruadhainn*.

Ryefield (Ross), Ach an t-Seagail
"The field of rye." The Gaelic name was pronounced locally as *Ach an t-Siugaill*.

Ryluachrach (Inverness), An Ruigh Luachrach
"The reedy sheiling."

Rynechtera (Inverness), Ruigh an Eachdra
It is unclear what this sheiling or croft name means.

Rynuie (Inverness), Ruigh an Naoimh
Although said locally to be "sheiling or croft of the saint", the second part may have had a different origin.

Ryvoan (Inverness), Ruigh a' Bhothain
"The sheiling or croft with the hut." The Pass of Ryvoan is *An Slugan Shìos*, "the eastern defile".

S

Saddell (Argyll), Saghadal
"Saw valley", from Norse.

Salen (Argyll, Mull), An Sàilean
"The small inlet." The full name of Salen in Argyll in *an Sàilean Suaineartach*, "Salen of Sunart", while in Mull it is *Sàilean Dubh Chaluim Chille*, "black Salen of St Columba".

Saligo (Islay), Sàiligeo
This Norse name may be "sheep ravine".

Saline (Fife)
This appears to be "small barn", from the old diminutive *sabhailín*.

Sallachy (Ross, Sutherland), Saileachaidh
"Willow place" or "willow wood".

Sallochy (Stirling), Salachaidh
See **Sallachy**.

Saltburn (Ross), Alltan an t-Salainn
"The little stream of salt."

Saltcoats (Ayr), Baile an t-Salainn *or* Baile Salainn
The English name is "salt cotts", while the Gaelic version, used in Arran and Argyll, is "salt town".

Saltpans (Argyll), Na Coireacha Salainn
"The salt pans", where salt was gathered.

Salum (Tiree), Sathalum
This Norse name may mean "sheep islet".

Samadalan (Inverness), Samh nan Dailichean
This appears to mean "the tidal surge by the haughs".

Samala (North Uist), Samhla
This Norse name may be "sheep isle".

Sand (Ross), Sannda
"Sand river", from Norse. Sand in Gairloch is known in full as *Sannda Gheàrrloch* while Sand near Laide is *Sannda an Leothaid*. People from Sand in Gairloch are known as *eich*, "horses". Big Sand is *Sannda Mhór* while Little Sand is *Sannda Bheag*.

Sanda (Argyll), Àbhainn *or* Eabhainn
The English name is "sand island", from Norse. The Gaelic name is pre-Gaelic. See **Ailsa Craig**.

Sandaig (Inverness), Sanndaig
"Sand bay", from Norse.

Sandaveg (Eigg), Sannda Bheag
"Little Sanda", from Norse *Sanda*, "sand river".

Sandavore (Eigg), Sannda Mhór
"Big Sanda", from Norse *Sanda*,
"sand river".

Sanday (Canna), Sanndaigh
"Sand island", from Norse.

Sandbank (Argyll), Taigh a'
Chladaich; (Mull), An t-Aoineadh
Beag
The Gaelic name of Sandbank in
Argyll is "the house by the shore".
An older form of the English
name was Claddyhouse, showing
that the local Gaelic was *Taigh a'
Chladaigh*, with the older form of
the genitive singular rather than
the standard form given above. See
Acharanny. In Mull the Gaelic
name means "the small steep
promontory".

Sandray (Barra), Sanndraigh
"Sand island", from Norse.

Sandside (Sutherland), Sanndasaid *or*
Sannsaid
"Sand dwelling", from Norse.

Sandwick (Lewis, South Uist),
Sanndabhaig
"Sand bay", from Norse. Lower
Sandwick in Lewis is *Mol
Shanndabhaig*, "the shingle beach of
Sandwick".

Sandwood (Sutherland), Seannabhad,
Sannabhad *or* Salabhad
Both the English and Gaelic names
are misleading in that the name's
origin appears to be Norse "sand
water".

Sangobeg (Sutherland), Saingea Beag
"Small sandy ravine", from Norse.

Sangomore (Sutherland), Saingea
Mór
"Large sandy ravine", from Norse.

Sanna (Argyll), Sanna
"Sand river", from Norse. Sanna
Point is *Rubha Shanna*.

Sannaig (Jura), Sannaig
"Sand bay", from Norse.

Sannox (Arran), Sannaig
"Sand bay", from Norse. The English
version has a plural form.

Sanquhar (Dumfries, Moray), An
t-Seanchair
"The old stone fort."

Sartle (Skye), Sartail
This may be "muddy valley", from
Norse.

Sasaig (Skye), Sàsaig
"Cask bay", from Norse.

Satran (Skye), Sàtran
This name is unclear.

Sauchieburn (Stirling), Allt a' Phuill
Sheilich
The English name is "willow wood
stream" and the Gaelic is "stream of
the willow pool". The Battle of
Sauchieburn is *Blàr Allt a' Phuill
Sheilich*.

Saundaig (Tiree), Sanndaig
"Sand bay", from Norse.

Savalbeg (Sutherland), Sàbhal Beag
This is from Norse for "high mountain", with Gaelic for "small"
attached.

Savalmore (Sutherland), Sàbhal Mór
See **Savalbeg**, but in this case the
Gaelic attachment is "large".

Savary (Argyll), Samharaidh
This appears to be "sorrel sheiling".

Scadabay (Harris), Sgadabhagh
This Norse name may be "tax bay".
Local people were nicknamed *cait*,
"cats".

Scalan (Banff), An Sgàilean
"The little shelter."

Scalasaig (Colonsay, Inverness),
Sgalasaig
"Skali's bay", from Norse.

Scaliscro (Lewis), Sgealascro
This Norse name may mean "Skali's
river pit".

Scalladale (Harris), Sgaladal
"Valley of soft rock", from Norse.

Scallasdale (Argyll), Sgalasdal
"Skali's valley", from Norse.

Scallastle (Mull), Sgalasdal
See **Scallasdale**.

Scalpay (Harris, Skye), Sgalpaigh
"Ship island", from Norse. Scalpay
by Harris is also *Sgalpaigh Na*

Hearadh and Scalpay near Skye is
Sgalpaigh an t-Sratha, "Scalpay of
Strath". Someone from Scalpay is a
Sgalpach.

Scalpsie (Bute)
This is a Norse name but the meaning is unclear. It may contain *eid*,
"isthmus", and refer to a place where
ships could be dragged overland.
However, it might equally be taken
to be "ship coast". The name would
be written as *Sgalpasaidh* in Gaelic.

Scamadale (Inverness), Sgamadal
This Norse name denotes a valley
but the first part of the name is
unclear.

Scaniport (Inverness), Sganaphort
"Ferry by the cleft."

Scaravay (Harris), Sgarabhaigh
"Cormorant island", from Norse.

Scarba (Jura), Sgarba
"Cormorant island", from Norse.

Scardroy (Ross), Sgàrd Ruaidh
"Red-brown swathe of land."

Scarinish (Tiree), Sgairinis
"Notch headland", from Norse. The
old church here is *Caibeal Thòmais*,
"St Thomas's Chapel".

Scarista (Harris), Sgarastadh
"Township of the notch or cut",
from Norse. Scaristavore is
Sgarastadh Mhór, "big Scarista".

Scarp (Harris), An Sgarp
"Barren", from Norse.

Scatwell (Ross), Sgatail
"Tax field", from Norse.

Scolpaig (North Uist), Sgolpaig
"Ship bay", from Norse.

Scone (Perth), Sgàin
This may mean "cleft".

Sconser (Skye), Sgonnsar
The meaning of this name is not
clear.

Scoonie (Fife)
"Place of the lumpy hill", from
Sgonnaidh, which was earlier
Sgonnan.

Scoraig (Ross), Sgoraig
"Rift bay", from Norse. An

uncomplimentary saying about
Scoraig claims, *Sgoraig sgreachach, 's
dona beag i – àite gun dìon, gun fhasgadh, gun phreas no coille*, "Repulsive
Scoraig, small and no good – a place
without protection, shelter, bush or
wood". Local people were known as
coin, "dogs".

Scorguie (Inverness), Sgòr Gaoithe
"Windy hill."

Scotasay (Harris), Sgotasaigh
"Scots' island", from Norse.

Scotsburn (Ross), Allt nan
Albannach
"Stream of the Scots." An older
name from Norse was *Uladal*, "Ulli's
valley".

Scotscalder (Caithness), Caladal nan
Gall *or* Cal nan Gall
The English name is "Calder of the
Scots" while the Gaelic name is
"Calder of the non-Gaels", which is
an interesting distinction.

Scotstown (Argyll), A' Mhèinn
The Gaelic name is "the mine",
referring to the mining which began
in the area in the 18th century.

Scottas (Inverness), Sgotas *or* Sgòiteas
The meaning of this name is unclear.

Scotven (Grimsay), Sgotbheinn
This name is unclear, but may be
Norse/Gaelic for "tax mountain" or
"Scots' mountain".

Scourie (Sutherland), Sgobharaidh
"Shed sheiling." Scouriemore is
Sgobharaidh Mhór, "large Scourie".
The area was called *Sgobharaidh na
Beurla* because of the spread of
English here.

Scrabster (Caithness), Sgrabastal
This may be "cormorant farm", from
Norse.

Scudiburgh (Skye), Sgudabrog
This name contains Norse for
"castle" but the first part is unclear.

Scullamus (Skye), Sgùlamus
"Skúli's moss or farm", from Norse.
The upper part of Scullamus is
Bràigh Sgùlamuis.

Scurrival Point (Barra), Rubha Sgoireabhail
"Headland of the wooded hill", from Gaelic/Norse.

Seabeg (Kincardine, Stirling)
"The small seat", from *An Suidhe Beag*.

Seaboard Villages (Ross), Bailtean na Mara *or* Na Trì Port Mara
"The villages by the sea" or "the three sea ports", referring to Cadboll, Shandwick and Hilton.

Seafield (Ross), Rubha Nòis
The Gaelic name is "the headland of the river mouth", from Gaelic/Norse. See **Noss Head**.

Seaforth Head (Lewis), Ceann Loch Shìophort
"The head of Loch Seaforth."

Seaforth Island (Harris, Lewis), Eilean Shìophort
"The island of Seaforth."

Seamore (Stirling)
"The large seat", from *An Suidhe Mór*.

Second Coast (Ross), An t-Eirtheaire Shuas
The Gaelic name is "the upper coast". This place also had the alternative names of *an t-Eirtheaire Donn*, "the brown coast", and *an t-Eirtheaire Bhos*, "the coast here".

Seil (Seil), Saoil
This is probably a pre-Gaelic name. A Seil person is a *Saoileach*.

Seilebost (Harris), Seilebost
"Shell farm", from Norse.

Selkirk (Selkirk), Sailcirc
This is a church name from English. Selkirkshire is *Siorrachd Shailcirc*.

Severie (Perth), Suidhe Bhrith'
"The judge's seat", from *Suidhe a' Bhritheimh*.

Sgodachail (Ross), Sguit Chathail
"Cathal's croft."

Shader (Lewis), Siadar
"Village", from Norse. Shader in Point, also known as "Shulishader" in English, is *Siadar an Rubha*. Lower Shader near Barvas is *Siadar*

Iarach and Upper Shader is *Siadar Uarach*. Local pronunciation collected by Oftedal (1954) suggests a preferable spelling of *Siadair*.

Shagarry (Skye), Seoigearraidh
The first element of this Norse name referring to pasture land may represent "sea".

Shalunt (Bute)
This is a Norse name originally *sjáland* or *sjálundr*, "sea land" or "sea wood" respectively, which came into English via Gaelic *Sialannd*.

Shandwick (Ross), Seannduaig
"Sand bay", from Norse. Local people were known as *seanndlairean*, "chandlers", and *slaiteirean*, a word related to *slat*, "fishing rod" which also suggests a tall, thin person.

Shannochie (Arran), Sean Achaidh
"Old field."

Shannochill (Perth)
"Old church", from *Seann Chill*.

Shanquhar (Aberdeen)
"Old stone fort", from *Seann Chathair*. See **Sanquhar**.

Shanrie (Banff), An t-Seann Ruigh
"The old sheiling."

Shantullich (Ross), An t-Sean Tulaich
"The old green hill."

Shanwell (Moray)
"Old village or farm", from *Seann Bhaile*.

Shawbost (Lewis), Siabost
"Sea farm", from Norse. New Shawbost is *Pàirc Shiaboist* "Shawbost park" or *A' Phàirc*, "the park". North Shawbost is *Siabost a Tuath* (*Siabost bho Thuath* on roadsigns) and South Shawbost is *Siabost a Deas* (*Siabost bho Dheas* on roadsigns).

Sheader (Skye), Siadar
"Village", from Norse.

Shebster (Caithness), Sèabastal
This may be "valley of the sea farm", from Norse.

Shedog (Arran), Seideag
The meaning of this name is unclear.

Shegarton (Dunbarton), Sìth-Ghartan
"Fairy field."

Sheil Bridge (Ross), Drochaid Sheile
"The bridge of the Sheil." The old name was *An Taigh Bàn*, "the white house", while the old burial ground is called *Cill Fhearchair*, "St Fearchar's Church".

Sheildaig (Ross), Sìldeag
"Herring bay", from Norse. People from Sheildaig by Applecross were known as *gathan dubha*, which may refer to beards of oats or barley. Sheildaig in Gairloch is known in full as *Sìldeag Ghearrloch*.

Sheildinish (Lewis), Sìldinis
"Herring headland", from Norse.

Sheilfoot (Argyll), Bun na h-Abhann
The English name is "mouth of the Sheil" but the Gaelic name is simply "the mouth of the river".

Shenval (Banff, Inverness), An Seann Bhaile
"The old farm."

Sheriffmuir (Perth), Sliabh an t-Siorraim *or* Monadh an t-Siorraim
"The moor of the sheriff." The Battle of Sheriffmuir is known as *Blàr Sliabh an t-Siorraim*.

Sheshader (Lewis), Seiseadar
"Sea village", from Norse.

Shetland (Shetland), Sealtainn
These names are an anglicisation and a gaelicisation of Norse *Hjaltland*, which is said to mean "hilt land", referring to the resemblance of the Shetland mainland to a downturned sword. A Shetlander is a *Sealtainneach*. The old Gaelic name for Shetland was *Innse Cat*, "islands of the Cat people", which is a reference to the tribal name of the people who also inhabited **Caithness** and **Sutherland**.

Shian (Argyll), An Sìthean
"The fairy hill." North and South Shian are *An Sìthean a Tuath* and *An Sìthean a Deas* respectively.

Shian Ferry (Argyll), Port an t-Sìthein
"The harbour at the fairy hill."

Shiant Islands (Lewis), Na h-Eileanan Móra
The Gaelic name is "the big islands". The English name comes from an older Gaelic one, *Na h-Eileanan Sianta*, "the charmed or holy islands".

Shillay (North Uist), Sileigh
"Herring island", from Norse.

Shinagag (Perth), Sionagag
"Old gap", which was one of the old roads from Atholl to Strathardle.

Shinness (Sutherland), Sìnnis
This may be "old meadow", from *seann innis*. West Shinness is *Seann Sìnnis*, "old Shinness".

Shirrabeg (Inverness), Siorrath Beag
"Little Shirra", an unclear name which may contain *ràth*, "circular fort".

Shirramore (Inverness), Siorrath Mór
"Big Shirra." See **Shirrabeg**.

Shiskine (Arran), An t-Seasgann
"The boggy or sedgy place."

Shona (Argyll), Eilean Seona
This may be "sea island", from Norse. The Gaelic name also has "island" attached. The old Gaelic name for the island was *Arthràigh*, "foreshore island", similar to that of Erraid.

Shoretown (Ross), Baile a' Chladaich
"The village by the shore."

Shulishader (Lewis, Skye), Siùiliseadar
"Village at the sea slope", from Norse. The village in Lewis is more commonly known as *Siadar an Rubha*, "Shader in Point".

Shulista (Skye), Siùlasta
"Place at the sea slope", from Norse.

Shuna (Argyll), Siùna
This may be "sea island", from Norse.

Sidinish (North Uist), Saighdinis
This Norse name may be "slope headland".

Skallary (Sutherland), Sgalaraidh
"Field of soft rock", from Norse.

Skeabost (Skye), Sgeubost
"Skiði's farm", from Norse.

Skelbo (Sutherland), Sgeireabol
"Rock farm", from Norse.

Skelpick (Sutherland), Sgeilpig
This may be "rock bay", from Norse.

Skelpie (Fife)
Old forms of the name show this to
derive from *Gasg Ailpein*, "the
projecting ridge of Ailpean".

Skene (Aberdeen), Sgàin
This may mean "cleft" and may be
the same name as found in "Scone".

Skerinish (Skye), Sgeirinis
"Skerry headland", from Norse.

Skerray (Sutherland), Sgeirea *or*
Sgeara
This may be "skerry river". A local
person is known as a *Sgeireach* or
Sgearach.

Skerricha (Sutherland), Sgeir a'
Chadha
"The skerry at the pass."

Skiag Bridge (Sutherland), Drochaid
Sgiathaig
"The bridge at the winged place or
river."

Skiary (Sutherland), Sgiatharaidh
The meaning of this name is unclear,
but might be "winged field or sheiling", from Norse.

Skiberscross (Sutherland),
Sìobarsgaig
"Syborg's piece of land", from Norse.

Skibo (Sutherland), Sgìobal
"Shell farm", from Norse. This was
known as *Sgìobal nan ùbhlan*, "Skibo
of the apples".

Skigersta (Lewis), Sgiogartaigh
"Skeggi's place", from Norse.

Skillymarno (Aberdeen), Sgàilean
Mearnaig
"St Ernoc's or M'Ernoc's shelter."

Skinidin (Skye), Sgianaidean
The meaning of this name, which is
a plural, is unclear but may derive
from Norse *skjóna*, "dappled horse".

Sgianailt in Lewis is "rough hill
ground of the dappled horses", and
this may be related.

Skinnertown (Ross), Baile nan
Sginnearach
"The village of the Skinners."

Skinnet (Sutherland), Sgianaid
See **Skinidin**.

Skipness (Argyll), Sgibinis
"Ship headland." Skipness House is
Tùr an t-Sagairt, "the priest's tower".

Skirinish (Skye), Sgeirinis
"Skerry headland", from Norse.

Skulamus (Skye), Sgùlamus
See **Scullamus**.

Skullomie (Sutherland), Sgulamaidh
This may be "Skuli's farm", from
Norse. The place is known as
*Sgulamaidh chreagach nam bealach 's
nam beàrn*, "rocky Skullomie of the
passes and gaps".

Skye (Skye), An t-Eilean Sgitheanach
This may be "the indented island".
An alternative form of the name is *an
t-Eilean Sgiathanach* which points to
sgiath, "wing", as the root of the
name. A poetic name of the island is
Eilean a' Cheò, "island of the mist". A
Skye person is a *Sgitheanach*.

Skye of Curr (Inverness), Sgiath
Churr
"The wing (of land) at the pit."

Slackbuie (Inverness), An Slag
Buidhe
"The yellow hollow." Upper
Slackbuie was known as *Cnoc na
Circe*, "hill of the hen", or
Knocknakirk in English. *Slag* as
opposed to *lag* was the usual term
locally to denote a hollow.

Slaggan (Ross), An Slagan Odhar
The Gaelic name is "the dun-
coloured little hollow", whereas the
English name is only "hollow".

Slamannan (Stirling)
"The moor of Manau", from *Sliabh
Mhanann* or *Sliabh Mhanainn*.

Slatich (Perth), Slàtaich
"Rod place."

Slattadale (Ross), Sléiteadal
"Smooth valley", from Norse.

Sleach (Aberdeen), An Sliabhach
"The moor place", formerly "Easter
Sleach" in English.

Sleat (Skye), Sléite or Sléibhte
This is from Norse *sléttr*, "smooth".
A native of Sleat is a *Sléiteach*, also
nicknamed a *coileach*, "cockerel". At
least three sayings exist concerning
the women of Sleat – a visit that
lasts too long is called *céilidh nam
ban Sléiteach*, "a visit from Sleat
women"; Sleat was compared to
neighbouring Strath in *Clachan an
t-Sratha's mnathan Shléite*, "the stones
of Strath and the women of Sleat";
and the area is also known as *Sléite
rìomhach nam ban bòidheach*, "lovely
Sleat of the beautiful women".

Sletell (Sutherland), Sléiteil
"Smooth field", from Norse.

Sliddery (Arran), Slaodraidh
This name has connotations of trail-
ing or dragging.

Sligachan (Skye), Sligeachan
"Small shell place."

Sligo (Aberdeen)
"Shell place", from *Sligeach*.

Sligrachan (Argyll), Sligreachan
This may mean the same as
Sligachan.

Slockavullin (Argyll), Sloc a'
Mhuilinn
"The hollow by the mill."

Sluggans (Skye), Na Sluganan
"The hollows."

Slumbay (Ross), Slumba
"Slim bay", from Norse.

Sma' Glen (Perth), An Caol Ghleann
"The narrow glen." The full name is
Caol Ghleann Ghlinn Amain, "the
narrow glen of Glen Almond".

Small Isles (Canna, Eigg, Muck,
Rum), Na h-Eileanan Tarsainn;
(Jura), Na h-Eileanan Beaga or Na
h-Eileanan Caola
The Small Isles of Canna, Eigg,
Muck and Rum are called "the cross

islands", referring to their situation
between Morar on the mainland
and Uist in the west. In Jura, the
Gaelic names are "the small islands"
and "the narrow islands".

Smaull (Islay), Smeidheal or Smeall
This may be "narrow field", from
Norse.

Smerclete (South Uist), Smeircleit
This may be "butter rock or hill",
from Norse.

Smiorasair (Ross), Smiorasair
"Butter sheiling", from Norse.

Smirasary (Inverness), Smiorasaraidh
See **Smiorasair**.

Smithstown (Ross), Baile a'
Ghobhann
"The village of the smith."

Smithton (Inverness), Baile a'
Ghobhainn
"The village of the smith."

Smoo (Sutherland), Smudha or Smó
"Cave", from Norse. This is the location of Smoo Cave or *Uaimh Smó*.

Snishival (South Uist), Snaoiseabhal
This Norse name may mean "snowy
sea mountain".

Snizort (Skye), Sniothasort
"Snow firth", from Norse.

Soay (Skye, St Kilda), Sòaigh or
Sòthaigh
"Sheep island", from Norse.

Soilshan (Inverness), An Soillsean
"The bright place."

Soilzarie (Perth), Soillearaidh
"Light place." The name of this place
between Strathardle and Glenshee is
opposite in meaning to "Dollerie" in
Strathearn.

Soletote (Skye), Sòlatobht
"Toft of the solan goose", from
Norse.

Sollas (North Uist), Solas
This name is unclear. *Solas* means
"light" in Gaelic but is unlikely to
mean that here. Sollas contained
two chapels close by each other,
Caibeal Mhoire, "St Mary's Chapel",
also known as *Caibeal nan*

Dòmhnallach, "the MacDonalds' chapel", and *Caibeal Ultain*, "St Ultan's Chapel". The churchyard was known as *Cladh Pheadair*, "St Peter's Churchyard".

Sonachan (Inverness), Na Sanndaichean
"The sands", from Norse.

Sorisdale (Coll), Sórasdal
"Mud valley", from Norse.

Sorn (Ayr)
"Kiln", from Gaelic *sorn*.

Soroba (Argyll), Soroba
"Muddy village", from Norse.

Soroby (Tiree), Sóiribidh
See **Soroba**.

South Cuan (Luing), Cuan Luinn
The English name distinguishes this place from **North Cuan**. The Gaelic name is "Cuan of Luing".

Southend (Argyll), Ceann mu Dheas
This village is at the south end of Kintyre and the wider Southend area is called *An Ceann Shiar*, "the western end".

South Kessock (Inverness), Ceasag a Deas
The older name is *Port Cheasaig*, "the port of Kessock". See **Kessock**.

South Obbe (Skye), An t-Òb a Deas
"The south inlet or bay."

South Queensferry (West Lothian), Cas Chaolas *or* Cas Faoileas
The Gaelic name is "steep strait". "South" in the English name distinguishes this place from North Queensferry in Fife; this was the royal crossing point as opposed to Earlsferry further east.

South Rona (Raasay), Rònaigh
The Gaelic name is "rough island". "South" in the English name distinguishes this island from North Rona to the north of Lewis.

South Uist (South Uist), Uibhist a Deas
See **Uist**. South Uist is also known as *an Ceann a Deas*, "the south end" and *Tìr a' Mhurain*, "the land of

marram grass". A person from South Uist is a *Deasach*.

Soval (Lewis), Sóbhal
"Sheep mountain", from Norse.

Soyal (Ross), Saoidheal
"Sheep meadow", from Norse.

Spean Bridge (Inverness), Drochaid Aonachain
The English name refers to the River **Spean**. The Gaelic name is "the bridge at the market place". The old name was *Aonachan*, "market place", which survives in "Unachan".

Speyside (Banff, Moray), Fàn Spé
The Gaelic name is "the gentle slope of the Spey". The river itself is mentioned in the saying, *Spé, Dé is Tatha, na trì uisge as motha fon adhar*, "Spey, Dee and Tay, the three greatest rivers under the sun".

Spinningdale (Sutherland), Spainnigeadal
This Norse name contains *dalr*, "valley", but the first element is unclear.

Spittal of Glenshee (Perth), An Spideal *or* Spideal Ghlinn Sìth
"The hospice" or "the hospice of Glenshee".

Sponish (North Uist), Spònais
This Norse name contains *nes*, "headland", but the first element is unclear.

Springfield (Ross), Achadh an Fhuarain
"The field of the spring."

Spynie (Moray)
This may be "thorny place", and related to the name of the River **Spean**.

Sronphadruig (Perth), Sròn Phàdraig
"Patrick's nose", referring to a nose-shaped topographical feature.

Stack Island (Eriskay), Eilean an Staca
"Island of the pillar rock", from Gaelic/Norse.

Staffa (Mull), Stafa
"Staff island", from Norse.

Staffin (Skye), An Taobh Sear *or* Stafainn

The English and second Gaelic names come from Norse and may contain the word for "staff" or be based on *stamh*, a type of seaweed. The first Gaelic name means "the east side". Staffin Island is *Eilean Stafainn*.

Stair (Ayr), An Stair

"The stepping stones" or "the causeway".

St Andrews (Fife), Cill Rìmhinn

This is the place to which St Andrew's relics were said to have been brought. The Gaelic name was originally *Cinn Rìmhinn*, "end of the royal moor" and the present form gave rise to Kilrymonth, which is nearby. The latter part of the name is a contraction of *rìghmhonadh*, "king's moor", referring to a moor said to have been given by King Aonghas to St Andrew. Kingsmuir is in the area.

Star (Fife)

See **Stair**.

St Catherines (Argyll), Cill Chaitrìona

"St Catherine's Church."

St Cyrus (Angus), Eaglais Chiric

"St Cyricius's Church." This place used to be known in English as Ecclesgreig.

Steall (Inverness), Steall

"Waterfall."

Stein (Skye), Steinn

"Stone", from Norse. Brae Stein is *Bràigh Steinn*, "Upper Stein".

Steinish (Lewis), Steinnis

"Stone headland", from Norse.

Stenschol (Skye), Steinnseal

"Stone hill or field", from Norse.

Stewarton (Argyll, Ayr), Baile nan Stiùbhartach

"Town of the Stewarts."

Stewartry (Kirkcudbright), An Stiùbhartachd

"Stewarded lands." This is the old name for Kirkcudbrightshire.

St Fergus (Aberdeen), Peit Fhearghais

The English name commemorates the Church of Fergus whereas the Gaelic name is "Fergus's farm", containing Pictish *pett*, "lands or farm".

St Fillans (Perth), Am Port Mór

The Gaelic name is "the big port or village".

St George's Head (Orkney), Ceann Sheórais

The Gaelic form was used on the north coast and is a translation from English, referring to the headland on the island of Hoy.

Stilligarry (South Uist), Stadhlaigearraidh

"Rocky fertile land", from Norse.

Stirkhill (Ross), Meallan a' Ghamhna

See **Mellongaun**.

Stirling (Stirling), Sruighlea

This is said to be a Brythonic name meaning "dwelling place of Melyn", which led to the older English form, Strivelin. Stirlingshire is *Siorrachd Shruighlea*.

Stix (Perth), Na Stuiceannan

"The stumps."

St Katherines (Aberdeen)

An older name of the place, "Raitt", is from *Ràt*, "circular fort".

St Kilda (St Kilda), Hiort

Neither the English nor Gaelic names are clear but the English name is thought to refer to a well while the Gaelic name may contain an old word for "death". A number of sayings refer to St Kilda, such as *bho Pheairt gu Hiort* or *eadar Peairt is Hiort*, "from Perth to St Kilda", which signifies the former extent of the Gaelic speaking areas from east to west across Scotland. *B' fheàrr leam gun robh e ann an Hiort*, "I wish he were in St Kilda", is said of someone one wishes to be rid of. A *pòsadh Hiortach*, "a St Kilda wedding", means a wedding between close relations. A threat to a badly behaved child is *Cuiridh mi a Hiort thu air muin mairt*, "I'll send you to St Kilda on a cow's back". A native of St Kilda was a *Hiortach*.

St Monans (Fife), Cill Mhaoininn
"St Maoineann's Church." The old name was Abercrombie from *Obar Chrombaidh*, "mouth of the crooked river".

St Ninians (Inverness), Slios an Trinnein
The Gaelic name is "St Ninian's slope", from an older *Slios Shant Rinnein*.

St Ninian's Point (Bute)
This name was recorded in Gaelic as *Rudh-an-t-Sninian*, indicating *Rubha Shant Ninian* or *Rubha Shant Rinnein*, of which the English is a translation.

Stobo (Peebles)
This may be "stump place", from *Stobach*.

Stockay (North Uist), Stocaigh
"Chasm island", from Norse.

Stockinish (Harris), Stocainis
"Chasm headland", from Norse.

Stoer (Sutherland), An Stòr
"Large", from Norse. A local saying is '*S fhada Dùn Éideann bhon fhear a tha ag éirigh san Stòr*, "Edinburgh is far from the man who rises in Stoer".

Stonefield (Argyll: Knapdale; Skye), Achadh na Cloiche; (Argyll: Muckairn), Taigh an t-Sratha
"The field of the stone" in the meaning of the name in Knapdale and Skye but in Muckairn the Gaelic name is "the house in the strath".

Stoneybridge (South Uist), Staoinibrig
"Stony slope", from Norse.

Stoneyfield (Inverness), Sgrìodan-Sgràd; (Lewis), Buaile na Cloich; (Ross), Féith nan Clach
In Inverness the name refers to a stony ravine, but the second element is unclear. In Lewis, the name is

"enclosure by the stone", while in Ross it is "the stony bog channel".

Stoneykirk (Wigtown)
"Stony field", from Norse.

Stormyhill (Skye), Cnoc na Gaoithe
The Gaelic name is "the windy hill".

Stormont (Perth)
"Moor with stepping stones", from *stair* and *monadh*, as shown in an old form of the name, Starmunth.

Stornoway (Argyll, Lewis), Steòrnabhagh
"Rudder bay" or "steering bay", from Norse. The inhabitants of various parts of Stornoway in Lewis are mentioned in the rhyme, *Fithich dhubha Ionacleit, shogairean shìos a' bhaile, daoine uasal Ceann a' Bhàigh, spàgairean Ghiùrseadair*, "Black ravens from Newton, sneaks from down the town, noble folk from Bayhead, clumsy folk from Guershader".

Stotfield (Argyll), Achadh nan Daimh
The English name refers to "stoats" while the Gaelic name is "field of the stags or oxen".

Straad (Bute)
See **Straid**.

Strabane (Arran), Srath Bàn
"Fair or white river haugh."

Stracathro (Angus), Srath Chatara
The first part of this name is "strath", but the second is unclear although said to be "mossy", from *càtharach*. However, it would be unusual for *càtharach* to become *chatara*.

Strachur (Argyll), Srath Chura
"Strath of the pit."

Straid (Perth, Bute)
"Street", from *sràid*. The locally used name is likely to have been *An t-Sràid*, "the street".

Straloch (Aberdeen, Perth), Srath Locha
The Perthshire name is "strath of the loch", and the Aberdeenshire name may be of the same origin.

Stranraer (Wigtown), An t-Sròn
    Reamhar
    "The broad headland."

Strath (Ross, Skye), An Srath
    "Strath." The full name of Strath in
    Ross is *Srath Gheàrrloch*, "strath of
    Gairloch", and in Skye *Srath
    MhicFhionghain*, "MacKinnon's
    Strath", which is contrasted with
    Sleat in the saying, *Clachan an
    t-Sratha 's mnathan Shléite*, "the
    stones of Strath and the women of
    Sleat". People from Strath in Skye
    were nicknamed *faochagan*, "whelks".

Strathaird (Skye), Àird an t-Sratha
    "The headland of Strath." Strathaird
    House was earlier known as
    Circeabost. See **Kirkibost**.

Strathallan (Perth), Srath Alain
    "The strath of the Allan."

Strathan (Sutherland), Srathan *or* An
    Srathan Shìos
    "Little strath (strathan)" or "lower
    Strathan". Strathan West is *(An)
    Srathan Shuas*, "upper Strathan".

Strathanbeg (Sutherland), (An)
    Srathan Beag
    "Little Strathan."

Strathanmore (Sutherland), (An)
    Srathan Mór
    "Big Strathan."

Strathardle (Perth), Srath Àrdail
    "The strath of the Ardle."

Strathaven (Lanark)
    This is probably the same as **Strath
    Aven**, and is given in Gaelic as *Srath
    Athainn*.

Strath Aven (Banff), Srath Athainn
    or Srath Thàmhainn
    "The strath of the Aven", which in
    turn refers to a bright river, previ-
    ously rendered in Gaelic spelling as
    athfhinn. The second name appears
    to be different but may only repre-
    sent a corrupted form of the original
    name, affected by local Scots or
    English pronunciation, as often
    happened in areas where Gaelic was
    being replaced by Scots or English.

Strathbeg (Aberdeen)
    "Small strath", from Gaelic *Srath
    Beag*.

Strathblane (Stirling), Srath
    Bhlàthain
    "Blane's strath."

Strathbogie (Aberdeen), Srath
    Bhalgaidh
    "The strath of the Bogie." See
    Huntly.

Strathbraan (Perth), Srath
    Freamhainn
    "The strath of the Braan." The name
    of the river is *Breamhainn*.

Strathbran (Ross), Srath Brain *or*
    Srath Brainn
    "The strath of the Bran." People
    from the area were nicknamed
    meanbhlaich, "runts".

Strathbrora (Sutherland), Srath
    Bhrùra
    "The strath of the River Brora." This
    strath contains seven churches, *Cill
    nam Bràthair, Cill Pheadair Bheag,
    Cill Pheadair Mhór, Cill Chaluim
    Chille, Cill Eathain, Cill Mhearain*
    and *Cill Ach Breanaidh*.

Strathcarron (Ross), Srath Carrann
    "The strath of the Carron." People
    from the wider area are known as
    Carrannaich.

Strathclyde (Dunbarton, Lanark,
    Renfrew), Srath Chluaidh
    "The strath of the Clyde."

Strathconon (Ross), Srath Chonainn
    "The strath of the Conon." A rhyme
    shows that the names of the straths
    and rivers in this area do not always
    coincide, *Abhainn Mìg tre Srath
    Chonainn, Abhainn Chonainn tre
    Srath Bhrainn, Abhainn Dubh-
    chuileagach tre Srath Ghairbh, trì
    aibhnichean gun tairbh iad sin*, "River
    Meig through Strathconan, River
    Conon through Strathbran, river of
    the black flies through Strathgarve,
    three unprofitable rivers." The area
    of Mid Strathconon is known as
    Mèinn.

Strathdearn (Inverness), Srath
  Éireann
  "The strath of the Findhorn." There
  is a saying comparing the five divisions of Strathdearn (which means
  "the strath of Ireland", referring to
  the Findhorn River) with those of
  Ireland, *Tha cóig cóigimh an Éirinn 's
  tha cóig cóigimh an Srath Éireann,
  ach 's fheàrr aon chóigeamh na
  h-Éireann na cóig cóigimh Srath
  Éireann*, "There are five fifths in
  Ireland and five fifths in the strath
  of Ireland, but one fifth of Ireland
  is better than five fifths of the
  strath of Ireland". The fifths or divisions of Strathdearn are *Cóig na
  Feàrna, Cóig nan Sgàlan, Cóig na
  Sìthe, Cóig a' Mhuilinn* and *Cóig
  nam Fionndaraich*. The distinctive-
  ness of Strathdearn's placenames is
  commented on in another saying,
  *Tha cóig bothan an Loch Abar, cóig
  gasgan ann am Bàideanach 's cóig
  cóigean ann an Srath Éireann*,
  "There are five boths in Lochaber,
  five gasgs in Badenoch and five
  cóigs in Strathdearn". See
  Strathearn.
Strathdee (Aberdeen, Kincardine),
  Srath Dhé
  "The strath of the Dee." See
  Deeside.
Strath Dionard (Sutherland), Srath
  Dìonaird
  "The strath of the Dionard."
Strathdon (Aberdeen), Srath
  Dheathain
  "The strath of the Don."
Strathearn (Perth), Srath Éireann
  "The strath of the Earn." *Éire*, the
  Gaelic original of "Earn", is one of a
  group of poetic bynames for Ireland,
  including *Eilg, Banbh* and *Fótla*,
  which were applied to places in
  Scotland. See **Strathdearn**.
Strathendrick (Stirling), Srath
  Eunaraig
  "The strath of the Endrick."

Stratherrick (Inverness), Srath
  Fhairgeag *or* Srath Fharagaig
  "The strath of the Farigaig."
Strathfillan (Perth), Na Sraithibh *or*
  Srath Chinn Fhaolain
  The English name commemorates
  St Fillan. The first Gaelic name is
  "the straths" and the second is "the
  strath of the church of St Fillan",
  from an earlier *Srath Chill
  Fhaolain*. Strathfillan churchyard is
  Clachan Shraithibh, and to express
  the phrase "in Strathfillan", Gaelic
  uses *air na Sraithibh*, "on the
  straths".
Strathfleet (Sutherland), Srath
  Fleòid
  "The strath of the Fleet."
Strathgartney (Perth), Srath
  Ghartain *or* Srath Ghartnaidh
  "Gartan's or Gartnait's river haugh."
  Earlier forms of the anglicised name
  suggest that *sròn*, "promontory",
  rather than *srath* may have been the
  original generic element.
Strathgarve (Ross), Srath Ghairbh
  "The strath of Garve." Local people
  were nicknamed *buic*, "bucks".
Strathgirnock (Aberdeen), Srath
  Goirneig
  "The strath of the Girnock."
Strathglass (Inverness), Srath Ghlais
  "The strath of the Glass." *Glas*
  itself can mean "grey-green". A
  local person is known as a
  Glaiseach.
Strathgryfe (Renfrew)
  "The strath of the Gryffe", possibly
  from *Srath Ghrìobha*. This is the old
  name of Renfrewshire.
Strath Halladale (Sutherland), Srath
  Healadail
  "The strath of the Halladale."
Strathisla (Banff), Srath Ìle
  "The strath of the Isla."
Strathkanaird (Ross), Srath
  Chainneart
  "The strath of the Can Firth", from
  Gaelic/Norse.

Strathkyle (Ross, Sutherland), Srath
a' Chaoil
"The strath at the strait", referring to
an Caol Catach, "Kyle of
Sutherland". The old name was *Slios
a' Chaolais*, "the slope at the strait".

Strathlachlan (Argyll), Srath
Lachainn *or* Srath Lachlainn
"Lachlann's strath." The first Gaelic
name is that used locally.

Strathmartine (Angus)
"Martin's strath", from Gaelic *Srath
Mhàrtainn*.

Strathmashie (Inverness), Srath
Mhathaisidh
"The strath of the good haugh."

Strathmiglo (Fife)
"Boggy strath" or "boggy river
holm", from *Srath Mioglach*.

Strathmore (several), An Srath Mór
"The big strath." Strathmore in
Angus and Perthshire was known as
A' Mhachair, "the plain", to speakers
of Perthshire Gaelic.

Strathnairn (Inverness, Nairn), Srath
Narann
"The strath of the Nairn."

Strathnaver (Sutherland), Srath
Nabhair
"The strath of the Naver." Locally,
people were said to live *air Srath
Nabhair*, "on Strathnaver", and local
people were *dhe Srath Nabhair*, "from
Strathnaver", using an unusual
construction in Gaelic. Both forms
were used for a number of straths in
north Sutherland.

Strathnoon (Inverness), Srath Nìn
In this case *srath* is a river holm, but
the second element is unclear.

Strath of Applecross (Ross), Srath
Mhaol Chaluim
The large strath in Applecross is "the
strath of the devotee of St Columba"
in Gaelic.

Strath of Kildonan (Sutherland),
Srath Ilidh
The English name refers to
Kildonan, but the Gaelic name is

"the strath of the Helmsdale River".
A local person is known as an *Ileach*,
to be distinguished from *Ìleach*,
which is applied to someone from
Glenisla, Islay or Strathisla.

Strath of Pitcalnie (Ross), Srath
Chuilt Eararaidh
See **Pitcalnie**.

Strathore (Fife)
"The strath of the River Ore."

Strath Ossian (Inverness), Srath
Oisein
"The strath of Ossian."

Strathoykel (Sutherland), Srath
Òiceall
"The strath of the Oykel."

Strathpeffer (Ross), Srath Pheofhair
"The strath of the bright river."

Strathrannoch (Ross), Srath
Raineach
"Bracken strath."

Strathrory (Ross), Srath Uaraidh
"The strath of the Rory."

Strathrusdale (Ross), Srath Rùsdail
"The strath of Rusdale."

Strathspey (Inverness, Moray), Srath
Spé
"The strath of the Spey."

Strathtay (Perth), Srath Tatha
"The strath of the Tay." A native of
the area is known as a *Tathach*, "Tay
person".

Strath Tirry (Sutherland), Srath
Tìridh
"The strath of the Tirry."

Strath Tongue (Sutherland), Srath
Thunga
"The strath of Tongue."

Strathtummel (Perth), Srath Teimhil
"The strath of the Tummel."

Strath Vagastie (Sutherland), Srath
Bhàgastaidh
The meaning of the Norse part of
this strath name is unclear, although
it may be "watching place".

Strathwhillan (Arran), Srath Chuilinn
Although the current name is "holly
strath", this place was first called *Tìr
Chuilinn*, "holly land".

Strathy (Ross), An t-Srathaidh; (Sutherland), Srathaidh
The Ross name is "the little strath", while the Sutherland name either means the same or "strath place". Strathy Point in Sutherland is *Rubha Shrathaidh.*

Strathyre (Perth), An t-Iomaire Riabhach *or* An t-Iomaire Fada (village); Srath Eadhair (district)
"The brindled rigg" or "the long rigg", both names applying to the village only, the old English name of which was Immerioch. The valley of Strathyre is *Srath Eadhair*, "the strath of the corn land".

Streens of Findhorn (Nairn), Na Srianan
"The restraints", referring to narrows in the River Findhorn.

Street of Kincardine (Inverness), An t-Sràid
The Gaelic name is simply "the street".

Strichen (Aberdeen), Srath Eichin
The second part of this strath name is unclear. The old name of the village was Mormond, from Gaelic *Mòr Mhon(adh)*, "large hill".

Stroanpatrick (Kirkcudbright)
"Patrick's point", from *Sròn Phàdraig.*

Strollamus (Skye), Stròlamus
"Stúrli's moss or farm", from Norse.

Stroma (Caithness), Stròma
"Current island", from Norse.

Stromay (North Uist), Sròmaigh
See **Stroma.**

Strombane (North Uist), An Sròm Bàn
"The fair stream."

Strome (Ross), An Sròm (Carrannach); (South Uist), An Sròm Dearg
The Ross name is "the (Carron) current", from Norse. Strome is divided into several parts on the north side of Loch Carron opposite Stromeferry, with Stromemore being

An Sròm Mór, "big Strome", Mid Strome being *An Sròm Meadhanach* and North Strome being *An Sròm a Tuath*. In South Uist the name is "the red stream".

Stromeferry (Ross), Port an t-Sròim
"The port at the current."

Stronachlachair (Perth), Sròn a' Chlachair
"The mason's point."

Stronachullin (Argyll), Sròn a' Chuilinn
"The holly point."

Stronafyne (Dunbarton), Sròn na Fine
"Point of the clan", referring to the inner circle of the clan.

Stronchreggan (Argyll), Sròn a' Chritheagain
This may be "the point of the little aspen".

Stronchrubie (Sutherland), Sròn Chrùbaidh
"The point at the bent place."

Strond (Harris), Srannda
"Beach", from Norse.

Strone (Argyll, Inverness, Jura, Perth), An t-Sròn
"The point." Strone in Inverness-shire is in full *Sròn a' Chaisteil*, "the point of the castle", referring to nearby Urquhart Castle, which is known as *Caisteal na Sròine*, "the castle at Strone". Strone Glen in Argyll is *Gleann na Sròine*, "the glen of the headland". Strone near Callander in Perthshire had the more complete name of *Sròn Gharbh Allt*, "promontory on the Garbh-allt stream".

Stroneba (Inverness), Sròn na Bà
"The point of the cow."

Strone of Cally (Perth), Sròn Challaidh
"The point at the hazel place or river."

Strone Point (Argyll), Rubha Sroigheann; (Inverness), Sròn a' Chaisteil

The Argyll name is "Striven Point", while the Inverness name is "the point of the castle". See **Strone**.

Stronlossit (Inverness), Sròn Losaid
"The point on the Lossit."

Stronmilchan (Argyll), Sròn Mhialachain
This name refers to a nose-like point of land, but the second element is unclear.

Strontian (Argyll), Sròn an t-Sìthein
"The point at the fairy hill."

Stronuich (Perth), Sròn Iubhaich
"The point at the yew place."

Stronyre (Perth), Sròn Eadhair
"The point at the corn land."

Struan (North Uist), An Sruthan Ruadh; (Perth), Srùthan; (Skye), An Sruthan
In North Uist this is "the red-brown stream", while in Perthshire and Skye it is "stream" or "the stream".

Struanmore (Skye), An Sruthan Mór
"The big stream."

Struie (Ross), An t-Srùigh
"The stream place." The Struie Road is *Rathad na Srùigh*.

Strumore (North Uist), An Sruth Mór
"The big current."

Struy (Inverness), Sruthaidh
"Stream place." Little Struy is *Sruthaidh Beag*. The churchyard here is *Cladh Churadain*, "St Curadan's Churchyard".

Stuartfield (Aberdeen), Craichidh
This is "Stuart's field" in English, but the older English name was Crechie, from *Craichidh* or *Creichidh*, "shaking place", as in **Crathie**.

Stuckindroin (Dunbarton), Stùc an Droighinn
"Thorn hill."

Stylemouth (Perth), Cùil nan Cnàimh
The English name is "mouth of the Style", while the Gaelic one is "nook of the bones".

Succoth (Argyll), An Socach
"The sow place."

Suddie (Ross), Suidhe
"Seat." Easter Suddie is also covered by the same Gaelic name.

Suie (Banff, Perth), An Suidhe
"The seat." The full name in Banff is *Suidhe Artair*, "Arthur's seat", while in Perth it is *Suidhe Fhaolain*, "St Fillan's seat", where *Deòr a' Bheàrnain*, the keeper of St Fillan's bell lived.

Suisgill (Sutherland), Sìdhisgil
"Seething gully", from Norse. Suisgill Lodge is *Achadh na Feannaig*, "the field of the crow or lazybed".

Suishnish (Raasay, Skye), Suidhisnis
"Seething headland", from Norse.

Suledale (Skye), Sùladal
"Sea slope valley", from Norse.

Sule Skerry (Sutherland), A' Chleit
The English name is "gannet rock", from Norse while the Gaelic name is "the rock or cliff", also of Norse origin.

Sulishader (Skye), Sùlaiseadar
"Sea slope place", from Norse.

Summer Isles (Ross), Na h-Eileanan Samhraidh
"The islands of summer."

Sunadale (Gigha), Sunadal
This may be "Svein's dale", from Norse.

Sunart (Argyll), Suaineart
"Svein's firth", from Norse, known poetically as *Suaineart Ghorm nan Darach*, "verdant Sunart of the oaks". The rivalry between Sunart and neighbouring Ardnamurchan is recorded in the saying, *Sùrd le Suaineart! Chaidh Àird nam Murchan a dholaidh!*, "Let Sunart rejoice! Ardnamurchan has been ruined!". Pre-Norse, Loch Sunart was called *A' Mhorbhairne*, "the sea gap", a name which has since been transferred to the district of Morvern. A native of Sunart is a *Suaineartach*.

Sunderland (Islay), Sionarlann
This may be an imported name with the Gaelic form merely representing local pronounciation.

Sunipol (Argyll), Suaineapol
"Svein's farm", from Norse.

Sunisletter (Inverness), Suainisleitir
"Svein's level land", from Norse.

Sutherland (Sutherland), Cataibh
The English name is "southern land", from the point of view of the Norse while the Gaelic name is "Cat people's land", referring to the tribe also mentioned in the name of Caithness and in the old Gaelic name of **Shetland**. East Sutherland is *Machair Chat,* "plain of Sutherland", and the hilly area behind it is *Bràigh Chat,* "upland of Sutherland". The central part of the county is *Dìthreabh Chat,* "wilderness of Sutherland", and north Sutherland or the Reay Forest is *Dùthaich MhicAoidh,* "MacKay's country". South-east Sutherland between Bonar Bridge and Dornoch is *Fearann Coscraigh,* "Coscrach's land". The area in the north of the county called the Flow Country is known locally as *Na Flobhachan,* which is a modern name adopted from English. A Sutherland person is a *Catach.* Historically, Sutherland did not include *Dùthaich MhicAoidh* or Assynt.

Sutors of Cromarty (Ross), Na Sùdraichean
"The tanners", two headlands facing each other across the mouth of the Cromarty Firth. Diack (1944) also recorded the name as *Creag Cromba* or *Creag Chromba* ("Cromarty rock") and *Beul Chromba* ("the mouth of Cromarty"), although this last name suggests the opening of the Cromarty Firth rather than the Sutors themselves.

Swainbost (Lewis), Suaineabost
"Svein's farm", from Norse.

Swordale (Lewis, Ross, Skye), Suardal
"Grassy valley", from Norse.

Swordle (Argyll), Suarsdal *or* Na Suarsdailean
This may be the same as **Swordale** but the second Gaelic form is a plural.

Swordly (Sutherland), Suardailigh *or* Suardlaidh
"Grassy slope", from Norse.

Sydera (Sutherland), Siara
See **Cyderhall**.

Syre (Sutherland), Saghair
This may stem from Norse *saurr,* "marsh".

T

Taagan (Ross), Na Tathagan
"The in-fields", from Norse.

Tahay (North Uist), Tathaigh
"High island", from Norse.

Tain (Ross), Baile Dhubhthaich
The English name comes from the river name. The Gaelic name is "St Duthac's town" where the sanctuary was *Comraich Bhaile Dhubhthaich.* The main Tain fair was *Féill Dubhthaich,* "St Duthac's fair", and the fair at Lammas was *Féill Bearchain* or *Féill Bhearchain,* "St Barchan's fair". The area between Tain and Edderton is *A' Mhorbhaich* or *A' Mhormhoich,* "the carse". Tain is linked with places further north in the rhyme, *Baile Dhubhthaich bòidheach, Dòrnach na goirt; Sgìobal nan ùbhlan 's Bil an arain choirc'; Earabol nan coileagan, Dùn Robain a' chàil; Goillspidh nan sligean dubh 's Druim Muighe a' bhàrr,* "Beautiful Tain, Dornoch of the starvation; Skibo of the apples and Bil of the oatcakes; Embo of the cockles, Dunrobin of the kail; Golspie of the mussels and Drumuie of the cream".

Talisker (Skye), Talaisgeir
"Sloping rock", from Norse.

Tallabheith (Perth), Tall a' Bheithe
"The rock at the birch."

Talladale (Ross), Tealldhadal
"Ledge valley", from Norse. Loch
Maree Hotel was known as *Taigh-
òsta Thealldhadal*.

Talmine (Sutherland), Tealamainn
This Norse name appears to contain
"ledge" but the second part of the
word is unclear. Upper Talmine is
Tealamainn Uthard and Lower
Talmine is *Tealamainn Stàn*. Upper
Talmine is known locally as *An
Leathad Glas*, "the grey-green slope".

Tamavoid (Perth), Tom a' Mhòid
"Hillock of the meeting place."

Tambowie (Dunbarton)
"The yellow hillock", from *Tom
Buidhe*.

Tamdhu (Moray), An Tom Dubh
"The black hillock."

Tamnavay (Lewis), Tamnabhaigh
"Harbour bay", from Norse.

Tanera (Ross), Tannara
"Harbour island", from Norse.
Tanera Beg is *Tannara Bheag* and
Tanera More is *Tannara Mhòr*.

Tangusdale (Barra), Tangasdal
"Valley of the sharp ridge", from
Norse.

Tannach (Caithness)
"Green field", from Gaelic
Tamhnach.

Tannadice (Angus), Tanachais
This may be from *tamhnach*, "green
field". The church here was known
as *Cill Earnain*, "St Ernan's Church".

Tannochside (Lanark)
This contains Gaelic *tamhnach*,
"green field" with English "side"
attached.

Tannock (West Lothian)
See **Tannach**.

Taransay (Harris), Tarasaigh
"Taran's island", from Norse. The old
church and graveyard were known
respectively as *Teampall Ché* and
Cladh Ché, apparently dedicated to a
saint named *Cé* or Keith, while
another old church was *Teampall
Tharain*, "St Taran's Chapel", with

the accompanying graveyard called
Cladh Tharain.

Tarbat (Ross), Tairbeart
"Isthmus or portage." Tarbat
Church and parish are respectively
Cill MoCholmaig and *Sgìre
MoCholmaig* dedicated to St
Colman. The parish was also known
as *Sgìre Thairbeirt*, "Tarbat parish".
Nearby is *Port MoCholmaig* or
Portmahomack. Tarbat Ness is
Rubha Thairbeirt.

Tarbert (several), An Tairbeart
"The isthmus or portage." Some of
the places thus named in English
have more complete Gaelic names.
Tarbert on Loch Fyne is *Tairbeart
Loch Fìne*, "the isthmus of Loch
Fyne", or *An Tairbeart Cainntireach*,
"the Kintyre Tarbert", where locals
were referred to by terms such as
fithich dhubha, "black ravens",
ducairean, "guillemots" and
gallachan, "bitches". In Harris,
Tarbert is *Tairbeart Na Hearadh*,
"the isthmus of Harris", while East
Tarbert is simply *an Tairbeart* and
West Tarbert is *an Taobh Siar*, "the
west side". To say "in Tarbert"
Gaelic uses *air an Tairbeart*, "on the
Tarbert".

Tarbet (several), An Tairbeart
"The isthmus or portage." The full
name of Tarbet on Loch Lomond is
Tairbeart Loch Laomainn, "the isth-
mus of Loch Lomond", or *An
Tairbeart Laomainneach*, "the
Lomond isthmus". Tarbet at Loch
Nevis is *Tairbeart Loch Nibheis*, "the
isthmus of Loch Nevis".

Tarbrax (West Lothian)
This may be "speckled hill", from
Gaelic *Tòrr Breac*, with an English
plural.

Tarbreakes (Fife)
See **Tarbrax**.

Tarland (Aberdeen), Turlann
"Bull field", from an older
Tarbhlann. Tarland Church is *Cill*

MoLuaig, "MoLuag's Church" and the fair here was *Fèill Bhrìghd*, "Bridget's Fair". In Aberdeenshire Gaelic a saying used to denote an unlikely event mentioned Tarland, *Theagamh gum faic mise thu fhathast an Turlann's muc dhubh air do chroit*, "Maybe I'll see you in Tarland with a black pig on your back".

Tarlogie (Ross), Tàrlagaidh
This is thought to be a Pictish name meaning "white brow".

Tarradale (Ross), Tarradal
This Norse name may be "peat valley".

Tarrel (Ross), Tarail
"Over-cliff." A saying mentions *Tarail Mhór is Tarail Bheag is Tarail fon a' chreig*, "Big Tarrel, Little Tarrel and Tarrel under the rock".

Tarrnacraig (Arran), Tòrr na Creige
"The hill of the rock."

Tarskavaig (Skye), Tarsgabhaig
"Cod bay", from Norse.

Tarves (Aberdeen), Tarbhais
"Bull place."

Tarvie (Perth, Ross), Tairbhidh
"Bull place." Local people in Tarvie in Ross were known as *crogaichean*, "crocks". The name of the place in Perthshire might be *Tarbhaidh* rather than *Tairbhidh*, but with the same meaning.

Tarvit (Fife)
This may be "bull place", from *Tarbhaid*.

Tavool (Mull), Tàbol
"High farm", from Norse.

Taychreggan (Argyll), Taigh a' Chreagain
"The house by the little rock".

Tayinloan (Argyll, Skye), Taigh an Lòin
"The house by the pond."

Taymouth (Perth), Bealach
"Pass." The full name is *Bealach nan Laogh*, "the pass of the calves". Taymouth Castle is *Caisteal Bhealaich*.

Taynish (Argyll), Taighnis
This may be "high headland", from Norse.

Taynuilt (Argyll), Taigh an Uillt
"The house by the stream."
Taynuilt proper was known as *Taigh an Uillt a' Bhràighe*, "Taynuilt of the upper part", to distinguish it from *Taigh an Uillt an t-Sratha*, "Taynuilt of the strath", near Achnacloich.

Tayport (Fife), Port na Creige
This harbour on the Tay used to be known as Portincraig, "the port at the rock".

Tayside (Angus, Perth), Taobh Tatha
The river itself occurs in the saying *Spé, Dé is Tatha, na trì uisge as motha fon adhar*, "Spey, Dee and Tay, the three greatest rivers under the sun". The north side of Loch Tay is *Deisear*, "south-facing land", while the south side is *Tuathar*, "north-facing land".

Tayvallich (Argyll), Taigh a' Bhealaich
"The house at the pass."

Tayvullin (Islay), Taigh a' Mhuilinn
"The house at the mill."

Teafrish (Inverness), Taigh a' Phris
"The house at the bush."

Teagate (Inverness), Taigh a' Gheata
"The house at the gate."

Teanacoil (Inverness), Taigh na Coille
"The house at the wood."

Teanamachar (North Uist), An t-Seana Mhachair
"The old machair."

Teanassie (Inverness), Taigh an Easa; (Ross), Taigh an Fhasaidh
In Inverness-shire this is "the house at the waterfall" and in Ross "the house at the stance".

Teangue (Skye), An Teanga
"The tongue" or "spit of land". Upper Teangue is *Bràigh na Teanga*, "the upper part of Teangue".

Teaninich (Ross), Taigh an Aonaich
"The house on the moor."

Teavarran (Inverness), Taigh a' Bharain
"The baron's house." An older form of the name was *Làrach Taigh a' Bharain*, "the site of the baron's house".

Teawig (Inverness, Ross), Taigh a' Bhuic
In Ross this is "the house of the buck", but the Inverness-shire name is less clear and may contain *ùig*, "a nook".

Teilesnish (Harris), Teilisnis
"Cave headland", from Norse.

Temple (Midlothian), Baile nan Trodach
This name commemorates the Knights Templar. The old name in English was Ballentroddoch, "the farm of the combatants".

Tenandry (Perth), An t-Seanaontachd
"The old leased land."

Tenga (Mull), An Teanga
See **Teangue**.

Terreagles (Dumfries)
"Village with a church", from Brythonic *tref yr eglwys* and not the Gaelic cognate *treamhar eaglaise*.

Tersets (Aberdeen)
This may be "crossing path", from *Tarsaid*.

Texa (Islay), Teacsa *or* Teugsa
This Norse island name is unclear.

Thornbush (Inverness), Am Preas Draighinn
The name means the same in both languages.

Three Arch Bridge (Jura), An Drochaid Mhór
The Gaelic name is "the big bridge".

Thundergay (Arran), Tòrr a' Ghaoth
"The windy hill." North Thundergay, known also as Lenimore, is *Lèanaidh Mór* or *Lèanaidh Mhór*, "big meadow". South Thundergay is *Achadh Mór*, "big field", also known as Auchamor in English.

Thurso (Caithness), Inbhir Theòrsa
The English name is the name of

the river while the Gaelic name is "mouth of the Thurso". The July fair held here was known as *Fèill Peadair*, "St Peter's Fair", while the September one was *Fèill Moire*, "St Mary's Fair".

Tibbermore (Perth)
"Big well", from Gaelic *Tiobar Mór*.

Tigharry (North Uist), Taigh a' Gheàrraidh
"The house on the fertile land."

Tighnabruaich (Argyll), Taigh na Bruaich
"The house on the bank." The Tighnabruaich area is known as Kerry or *An Ceathramh Comhalach*, "the Cowal quarterland", and a native of the area is a *Ceathrach*.

Tighnafiline (Ross), Taigh na Faoilinn *or* Taigh na Fadhlainn
"The house by the shore field."

Tighphuirst (Argyll), Taigh a' Phuirt
"The house at the port."

Tillydrine (Aberdeen), Tulach an Droighinn
"The green hill of thorns."

Tillydrone (Aberdeen), Tulach an Droighinn
"The green hill of thorns."

Tillyfour (Aberdeen)
"The green hill of the pasture", from *Tulach a' Phùir*.

Tillyfourie (Aberdeen)
"The green hill at the pasture place", from *Tulach Phùiridh*.

Tillytarmont (Aberdeen)
"The green hill of the sanctuary", from *Tulach an Tèarmainn*.

Timsgarry (Lewis), Tuimisgearraidh
The first part of this Norse field name may be a personal name.

Tipperty (Aberdeen)
"Place of wells", from *Tiobartaidh*.

Tirandrish (Inverness), Tìr an Dris
"The land of the briars."

Tirarragan (Mull), Tìr Fheargain
"Feargan's land."

Tirarthur (Perth), Tìr Artair
"Arthur's land."

Tiree, Tiriodh
"Corn land." The island is known as *Tiriodh ìosal an eòrna*, "low Tiree of the barley". East Tiree is known as *an Cinn t-Sear*, "east end", and the west part is known as *an Cinn t-Siar*, "west end". A Tiree person is a *Tiristeach*.

Tirfergus (Argyll), Tìr Fhearghais
"Fergus's land."

Tirfuir (Lismore), Tìr a' Phùir
"The land of the pasture."

Tirghoil (Mull), Tìr a' Ghoill
"The land of the non-Gael."

Tirinie (Perth), Tìr Ìngnidh
"The land of the claw place." A saying maintains, *Cha bhi Tòiseach air Tìr Ìngnidh, 's cha bhi Tìr Ìngnidh gun Tòiseach*, "Tirinie will never have a master, and Tirinie will never be without a master". This saying depends on the ambiguity of *tòiseach* which means "leader" or "master", but also "Macintosh".

Tiroran (Mull), Tìr Odhrain
"St Oran's land."

Tiumpan Head (Lewis), Ceann an Tiùmpain *or* Rubha an Tiùmpain
"The headland of the drumming." A variant spelling, *Ceann an t-Siùmpain*, is also seen.

Tobermory (Mull), Tobar Mhoire
"St Mary's well." This was formerly known as *Tobar Maol Rubha*, "St Maol Rubha's well".

Toberonochy (Luing), Tobar Dhonnchaidh
"Duncan's well."

Tobson (Bernera), Tòpsann
"Sound or head of the bay", from Norse.

Tochineal (Banff)
The Gaelic form of this name was recorded by Diack (1944) and appears to represent *Teochaigh Niall*, "Neil's small house".

Toe Head (Harris), Gob an Tobha
"The peak at the grassy point", from Gaelic/Norse.

Tokavaig (Skye), Tòcabhaig
"Tóki's bay", from Norse.

Toldunie (Perth), Tail Dùnaidh
This may be "haugh of the fort place".

Tollie (Ross), Tollaidh
"Place of holes."

Tolmachan (Harris), An Tolmachan
"The little knoll."

Tolsta (Lewis), Tolastadh
"Tholf's place", from Norse. New Tolsta is *Am Baile Ùr*, "the new village" and North Tolsta is *Tolastadh bho Thuath*. Tolsta Head is *Ceann Tholastaidh*.

Tolstacholais (Lewis), Tolastadh a' Chaolais
"Tolsta at the narrows", from Norse/Gaelic.

Tolvah (Inverness), Toll a' Bhàthaidh
"The drowning hole."

Tomacharich (Inverness), Tom a' Charraich
This is said to be "Carrach's hillock", although it is unusual to have a personal name accompanied by the definite article. Another derivation may be *carragh*, "rock".

Tomatin (Aberdeen), An Tom Aitinn; (Inverness), Tom Aitinn
"Juniper hillock." The Aberdeenshire name in Gaelic includes the definite article.

Tombae (Banff)
"The birch hillock", from *An Tom Beithe*.

Tombain (Moray)
"The fair hillock", from *An Tom Bàn*.

Tomchrasky (Inverness), Tom Chrasgaidh
"The hillock at the crossing place."

Tomcrail (Perth), Tom MhicRéIll
"MacNeil's hillock", the spelling showing the local pronunciation of *MacNéill* as *MacRéill*.

Tomdhu (Aberdeen), Na Tuim Dhubh
This place near Mar Lodge is "the black hillocks".

Tomdoun (Inverness), An Tom Donn
"The brown hillock", locally
pronounced *An Toma Donn*.

Tomich (Inverness), Tomaich
"Hillock place."

Tomidhu (Aberdeen), Na Toman
Dubh
"The black hillocks."

Tomintoul (Banff), Tom an t-Sabhail
"The hillock with the barn."

Tomnacross (Inverness), Tom na
Croiche
"The hillock of the gallows."

Tomnahurich (Inverness), Tom 'na
h-Iubhraich
"The hillock of the yew wood."

Tomnamoon (Moray)
"The hillock of the peat", from *Tom
na Mòna*.

Tomnavoulin (Banff), Toman a'
Mhuilinn
"The small hillock at the mill." This
place was also referred to as *Tom
Mhuilinn* locally, which means much
the same.

Tong (Lewis), Tunga
"Tongue" or "spit of land", from
Norse. Possibly under the influence
of English, the locally accepted
name in Gaelic is *Tong*.

Tongadale (Skye), Tungadal
"Tongue valley", from Norse.

Tongue (Sutherland), Ceann Tàile *or*
Ceann an t-Sàil, Tunga *or* Circeabol
The English and second Gaelic
names are "tongue of land", from
Norse. The first Gaelic name is "bay
head" and is an abbreviation of
Ceann Tàile MhicAoidh, "MacKay's
Kintail". The last Gaelic name is
"church farm", from Norse, and in
English is known as Kirkiboll,
which is now part of the settlement
of Tongue. A local person is a
Sàileach, also nicknamed a *bodach*,
"old man".

Torastan (Coll), Torathastan
This may be "Thorir's dwelling",
from Norse.

Torastay (Lewis), Torastaigh
"Torfi's farm", from Norse.

Toravaig (Skye), Tòrabhaig
"Thorir's bay" or "peat bay", from
Norse.

Torbain (Fife)
"Fair hill", from *Tòrr Bàn*.

Torbane (West Lothian)
See **Torbain**.

Torbeg (Arran), An Tòrr Beag
"The small hill."

Torbreck (Inverness), An Tòrr Breac
"The speckled hill."

Torcastle (Inverness), Tòrr a' Chaisteil
"The hill of the castle."

Tore (Ross), An Tòrr
"The hill." *An Todhar*, "the manure
or fertiliser", is now seen on roadsigns. The site of the old Tore Inn is
Cnoc an Acrais, "hunger hill".

Torechastle (Moray)
See **Torcastle** and **Dallas**.

Torgorm (Ross), An Tòrr Gorm
"The green hill." See **Glen Gorm**.

Torgyle (Inverness), Tòrr a' Ghoill
"The hill of the non-Gael." The
settlement of Torgyle Bridge is
Ceann Drochaid, "bridge end".

Torinturk (Argyll), Tòrr an Tuirc
"The hill of the boar."

Torloisk (Mull), Tòrrloisgt *or* An Tòrr
Loisgte
"Burnt hill."

Torlum (Benbecula), Tòrlum
This may be "Thorir's holm", from
Norse.

Torlundy (Inverness), Tòrr
Lunndaidh *or* Tìr Lunndaidh
The English form comes from the
Gaelic name meaning "mound at the
marshy place", but Gaelic has a
second name meaning "land of the
marshy place".

Tormore (Arran, Moray, Skye), An
Tòrr Mór
"The big hill."

Tornapress (Ross), Treamhar nam
Preas
"The settlement of the thickets."

Tornaveen (Aberdeen)
This may be "hill of the Fianna", from *Tòrr na bhFiann*, now written *Tòrr nam Fiann*.

Torness (East Lothian); (Inverness), Tòrr an Eas; (Mull), Tòrr an Easa
In East Lothian the name refers to a headland which is of Norse or Anglian origin. In Inverness-shire and Mull it is "the hill at the waterfall", and the Gaelic names above apply only to the places in Inverness-shire and Mull.

Torphichen (West Lothian), Tòrr Fhéichin
This seems to be "Fechin's hill", from an older *Tòrr Féichin*.

Torphin (Midlothian)
See **Torphins**.

Torphins (Aberdeen), An Tòrr Fionn
"The white hill."

Torrachilty (Ross), Tòrr Àicheallaidh
"The hill of Achilty."

Torrance (Dunbarton), Torranan
"Hillocks", from *Torran* or *Torranan* with an English plural. See **Torrin**.

Torridon (Ross), Toirbheartan
This denotes a place where boats were dragged overland, the word being related to *tairbeart*, "isthmus".

Torrie (Perth)
"Hill place", from *Torraidh*.

Torrin (Skye), Na Torran
"The hills." The local laird was called *Fear nan Tòrr*, which shows the shortening in vowel length when monosyllabic *Tòrr* becomes *Torran*.

Torrincudigan (Sutherland), Clais Torran nan Cudaigean
"The ditch at the hillock of the saithe, or coalfish."

Torrisdale (Argyll), Tórasdail; (Sutherland), Tòrasdal
"Thorir's valley", from Norse.

Torrish (Sutherland), Torrais
"Hill place."

Torrobol (Sutherland), Tòrabol
This may be "Thorir's farm", from Norse.

Torry (Aberdeen, Fife)
"Hill place", from *Torraidh*, earlier *Torran*.

Torrylin (Arran), Tòrr an Linne
"The hill by the pool."

Torsa (Luing), Torsa
"Thorir's island."

Torvean (Inverness), Tòrr Bheathain
"Bean's hill", referring to a saint also commemorated in nearby Kilvean.

Toscaig (Ross), Toghsgaig
"Strip of land at the howe", from Norse.

Totachocaire (Skye), Tobhta a' Chòcaire
"The cook's house site."

Totaig (Ross), An Tobhtaig
"The bay at the house site", from Norse.

Totamore (Coll), An Tobhta Mhór
"The big house site."

Totarder (Skye), Tobhta Àrdair
"The house site on the high water."

Totarol (Bernera), Tobhtarol
"Hill of the house sites", from Norse.

Tote (Skye), An Tobhta
"The house site", from Norse.

Toteronald (Skye), Tobhta Raghnaill
"Ronald's house site."

Totescore (Skye), Tobhta Sgoir
"House site at the wood", from Norse.

Touch (Fife)
"Green hill", from *tulach*.

Tough (Aberdeen, Fife)
See **Touch**.

Tougal (Inverness), Tùigeal
This name is unclear. The local landowner was called *Fear Thùigeal*.

Toulvaddie (Ross), Toll a' Mhadaidh
"The lair of the fox or wolf."

Tournaig (Ross), Tùrnaig
"Rounded hillock."

Toward (Argyll), Tollard
This name appears to be "hole point" or maybe "cave point". Toward Point is *Rubha Thollaird*.

Towie (Aberdeen), Tollaidh *or* Tollaigh
"Hole place."

Tralligill (Sutherland), Tràiligil
"Serf's gully", from Norse.

Tralee (Argyll), Trà Lì *or* Tràigh Lì
This may be "beach at the slope",
from Gaelic/Norse.

Trantlebeg (Sutherland), Tranntail
Beag
"Little Trantle", from Norse for
"Thrond's field", with Gaelic for
"small" added.

Trantlemore (Sutherland), Tranntail
Mór
"Big Trantle." See **Trantlebeg.**

Treaslane (Skye), Triaslainn
The meaning of this name is unclear.

Tree House (Bute), Taigh na
Craoibhe
The English is a translation of the
Gaelic name.

Treshnish (Mull), Treisinis
This Norse headland name is
unclear.

Tressady (Sutherland), Treasaididh
"Battle place."

Trinafour (Perth), Trian a' Phùir
"Third-land of the pasture."

Trinloist (Inverness), An Trian
Loisgte
"The burnt third-land."

Trislaig (Argyll), Trìoslaig *or* Trinnsleig
This Norse name refers to a bay but
the first element of the name is
unclear.

Trochry (Perth), Trochraidh
This may be "trough place".

Trodday (Skye), Tròndaigh
"Thrond's headland", from Norse.
The same personal name appears in
Trotternish.

Troon (Ayr), An Truthail
"The nose-shaped headland", from
Brythonic *trwyn.* The Gaelic name,
"the stream or current", was used in
Arran Gaelic and is a slight corrup-
tion of the original.

Trossary (South Uist), Trosaraidh
"Thrasi's fertile land", from Norse.

Trotternish (Skye), Tròndairnis
"Thrond's headland", a personal
name also found elsewhere.
Trotternish people were nicknamed
coin, "dogs", and known as *stapagaich*,
"stapag people", by their neighbours
in Duirinish. Trotternish itself was
known as *Dùthaich nan Stapag* or *am
Fearann Stapagach*, "the stapag land",
stapag being an oatmeal-based dish.
The northern part of Trotternish is
Ìochdar Thròndairnis, "lower
Trotternish", while Braes is *Bràigh
Thròndairnis*, "upper Trotternish", as
well as *Bràigh Phort Rìgh*, "upper
Portree".

Troup Head (Aberdeen), Ros Cuisne
This headland is "cold headland" in
Gaelic.

Trudernish (Islay), Trudairnis
See **Trotternish.**

Trumisgarry (North Uist),
Truimisgearraidh
"Thrum's fertile land", from Norse.

Trumpan (Skye), Trumpan
The meaning of this name is
obscure.

Tubeg (Sutherland), Taobh Beag
"Small area."

Tulchan (Angus, Moray), Tulachan
"Little green hill."

Tulliallan (Fife)
This *tulach* name may contain the
elements found in **Alloa** and **Alva.**

Tullich (Aberdeen), An Tulach;
(Ross), An Tulaich
"The green hill." Tullich Church in
Aberdeen is *Cill Nachlain*, "St
Nathalan's Church", while the Laird
of Tullich was *Fear an Tulaich.*
Tullich Muir in Ross is *Blàr na
Tulaich.*

Tullichewen (Dunbarton), Tulach
Eóghainn
"Ewen's green hill."

Tullimet (Perth), Tulach Mhait *or*
Tulach a' Mhaid
The second part of the name is
unclear but *tulach* is "green hill".

Tulloch (several), An Tulach
"The green hill."

Tullochbeg (Aberdeen)
"Small green hill", from *Tulach Bheag*.

Tullybanchor (Perth), Tulaich Bheannchair
"The green hill at the horn place."

Tullybardine (Perth), Tulach Bhàirdne
"The green hill of the poet's land."

Tullybelton (Perth), Tulach Bhealltainn
"The green hill of Beltane."

Tullybreck (Fife)
"Speckled green hill", from *Tulach Bhreac*.

Tullyfergus (Perth), Tulach Fhearghais
"Fergus's green hill."

Tullygreig (Aberdeen)
This may be "Ciric's or Giric's green hill", from *Tulach Chiric* or *Tulach Ghiric*.

Tullymurdoch (Perth), Tulach Mhuirich
"Muireach's green hill."

Tummel Bridge (Perth), Drochaid Dubhaig *or* Drochaid Choinneachain
"The bridge over the black stream" or "bridge at the junction".

Tumore (Sutherland), An Taobh Mór
"The large area."

Turriff (Aberdeen), Baile Thurra *or* Turra
This may be "hill place" also "the village of the hill place" in Gaelic. An older form *Turbhruadh* is found in the Book of Deer but is unclear.

Tweeddale (Berwick, Peebles, Selkirk), Srath Thuaidh
"Valley of the Tweed."

Tynayere (Perth), Taigh Neimh Gheàrr
"The house at the short sacred land."

Tyndrum (Inverness), Trian an Droma; (Perth), Taigh an Droma
The Inverness-shire name near

Foyers is "the third-land at the ridge", referring to a unit of land-measurement. In Perthshire the name is "the house on the ridge".

Tynribbie (Argyll), Taigh an Ribe *or* Taigh an Ribidh
The first part of the name means "house" but the final element is unclear.

Tyrie (Aberdeen, Fife)
"Land place", from *Tìridh*.

U

Uachdar (Benbecula), An t-Uachdar
"The top."

Uags (Ross), Na h-Uamhagan *or* An Uamhag
"The little cave(s)." Local people were nicknamed *buic*, "bucks".

Udale (Ross), Uadal
"Yew valley", from Norse.

Ugadale (Argyll), Ugadal
The first element of this Norse valley name is unclear.

Uidh (Vatersay), An Ùidh
"The isthmus", from Norse.

Uig (Coll, Lewis), Ùig; (Ross), An Ùig; (Skye), Ùige
"Bay", from Norse. A native of Uig in Lewis is an *Ùigeach* and the people here were known as *daoine uaisle Ùig*, "the noble folk of Uig".

Uigean (Lewis), Na h-Ùigean
"The bays", from Norse.

Uiginish (Skye), Ùiginis
"Bay headland", from Norse.

Uigshader (Skye), Ùigiseadar
"Bay township", from Norse.

Uiskentuie (Islay), Uisge an t-Suidhe
"The water at the sitting place." Local people were nicknamed *corra-ghrithich*, "herons".

Uiskevagh (Benbecula), Uisgeabhagh
This may be "ox bay", from Norse.

Uist (North Uist, South Uist), Uibhist
This may be "corn island". North Uist is *Uibhist a Tuath* and is also known as *an Ceann a Tuath*, "the north end", and *Tìr an Eòrna*, "the

land of barley". South Uist is *Uibhist a Deas*, also known as *an Ceann a Deas*, "the south end", and *Tìr a' Mhurain*, "the land of marram grass". Uist as a whole comprises the islands linked by causeways extending from Berneray in the north to Eriskay in the south via North Uist, Grimsay, Benbecula and South Uist. A Uist person is an *Uibhisteach*.

Ulladale (Ross), Uladal
"Wool valley", from Norse.

Ullapool (Ross), Ulapul
"Wool farm" or "Ulli's farm", from Norse. Local people were known as *sùlairean*, "gannets", and *crodh*, "cattle".

Ullinish (Skye), Uilinis *or* Uilbhinis
"Wolf headland", from Norse.

Ulva (Mull), Ulbha
"Wolf island", from Norse.

Umachan (Raasay), Iumachan
This name appears to be of Gaelic origin but is unclear.

Unachan (Inverness), Aonachan
"Market place."

Unakille (Skye), Baile Ung na Cille
The Gaelic name has *baile*, "village", attached to "ounce-land of the church".

Unapool (Sutherland), Ùnabol
This Norse farm name may contain "ounceland" as its first element.

Ungeshader (Lewis), Ungaiseadar
This may be "ounce-land township", from Norse. Local pronunciation collected by Oftedal (1954) suggests a preferable spelling of *Ungaiseadair*.

Unish (Skye), Baile an Tàilleir
The English form is from a Norse headland name while the Gaelic name is "the farm of the tailor".

Uphall (West Lothian)
"Up haugh", from English. Uphall parish used to be known as Wester Strathbroc from *Srath Broc*, "strath of badgers", now *Srath Bhroc*. "Easter Strathbrock" is the old name for the parish of Broxburn.

Uppat (Sutherland), Upaid
This Norse name may refer to a "high area" or "high part of an area".

Uragaig (Colonsay), Uragaig
This is "small rubble mound" or "bay at the small rubble mound", from Norse.

Urchany (Ross), Urchanaidh
This is said to mean "place beside the bog cotton".

Urgha (Harris), Urgha
"Rubble mound", from Norse.

Urinbeg (Arran), Uaran Beag
"Small spring." As is seen in several Arran placenames comprising noun and adjective, the definite article is not used although it is the norm elsewhere as well as in Arran itself.

Uroch (Wigtown)
This is "yew place", from *Iubhrach*.

Urquhart (Fife); (Inverness), Urchadan; (Moray), Urchard
"Woodside", from Pictish. Urquhart parish in Inverness is *Urchadan MoChrostain*, "St Drostan's Urquhart". Urquhart Castle in Inverness is *An Caisteal Dubh*, "the black castle", *Caisteal na Sròine*, "the castle of Strone", and *Caisteal Dubh na Sròine*, "the black castle of Strone". Nether Urquhart in Moray was formerly known as *Ìochdar Urchaird*. The name in Fife is most likely the same as that in Moray.

Urrard (Perth), Urrard
"Prominent landmark."

Urray (Ross), Urrath
"Prominent fort."

Urvaig (Tiree), An Urbhaig
"Bay at the rubble place", from Norse.

Ushinish (South Uist), Ùisinis
The first part of this Norse headland name is unclear.

V

Vaitem (Harris), Bhéiteam
"Wet island", from Norse.

Valamus (Lewis), Bhalamus
"Whale farm", from Norse.

Valasay (Bernera), Bhàlasaigh
"Whale island", from Norse.

Vale of Leven (Dunbarton), Magh
Leamhna *or* Srath Leamhna
"Elm plain" or "elm strath". The Vale
of Leven is part of the area of
Lennox which is *Leamhnachd* in
Gaelic. A native of Lennox is a
Leamhnach.

Vallay (North Uist), Bhàlaigh
"Whale island" or "shallow water
island", from Norse, the latter being
appropriate here. The old chapel was
called *Caibeal Odhrain*, "St Oran's
Chapel".

Valtos (Lewis, Skye), Bhaltos
"River mouth", from Norse.

Varkasaig (Skye), Bharcasaig
"Castle bay", from Norse.

Vaternish (Skye), Bhatairnis
"Water headland." Local people
were nicknamed *cait*, "cats".
Vaternish Point is *Rubha
Bhatairnis* and the old church
nearby was *Cill Chonnain*, "St
Connan's Church".

Vatersay (Vatersay), Bhatarsaigh
"Water island." Vatersay village is
Baile Bhatarsaigh and a native of
Vatersay is a *Bhatarsach*.

Vatisker (Lewis), Bhatasgair
"Water skerry", from Norse.

Vatten (Skye), Bhatan
"Water", from Norse.

Vaul (Tiree), Bhalla
"Hill", from Norse. Upper Vaul is
Bràigh Bhalla, "the upper part of
Vaul".

Viewfield (Skye), Goirtean na Creige
The English name is "field with a
view", while the Gaelic is "the
enclosed field by the rock".

Village (Scalpay), Am Baile
"The village."

Votersay (North Uist), Bhoitearsaigh
See **Vatersay**.

Vuia Mor (Bernera), Bhuia Mór
"Large Vuia", or "house island", from
Norse.

W

Wards (Harris), An Rubha Àrd
"The high headland."

Waterloo (Ayr, Perth); (Skye),
Achadh a' Chùirn
In Perthshire, houses were built
especially for veterans of the Battle
of Waterloo. In Skye, the area was
settled by soldiers returning from
Waterloo. The Gaelic name only
applies to Waterloo in Skye and is
"the field at the cairn".

Waternish (Skye), Bhatairnis
See **Vaternish**.

Waterstein (Skye), Bhatairsteinn
"Water stone", from Norse.

Waterton (Ross), Baile nam Fuaran
This is "water farm" in English, but
"the farm of the springs" in Gaelic.

Wauchan (Inverness), Na
h-Uamhachan
"The caves."

Weavers Point (North Uist), Rubha
an Fhigheadair
"Headland of the knitter."

Weem (Perth), Baile a' Chlachain
(village); Uaimh (parish)
The English name is a corruption
of Gaelic *uamh*, "cave", which in
the form *Uaimh* is the name of the
parish. The village has the same
name in English but in Gaelic is
"the village with the churchyard".
Weem Rock is *Creag Uaimhe*
while the cave after which Weem
is named is *Toll nan Trì
Nigheanan*, "cave of the three
girls". Castle Menzies, which is
located nearby, is *Caisteal Uaimh*,
"Weem castle".

Wellhouse (Inverness), An Torran
Bàn
The Gaelic name is "the small fair
hill".

Wemyss (Fife)
This name was earlier written
"Weems" and may stem from *Uaimh*
meaning "cave" and perhaps understood to be a plural form.

Wemyss Bay (Renfrew)
See **Wemyss**, but this name may
stem from the Wemyss family.

West Calder (West Lothian),
Caladair an Iar
Calder is "hard water", from
Caladar, a common river name
throughout Scotland. West Calder is
part of a larger area along with East
Calder and Midcalder.

Westerdale (Caithness), An Dail Shuas
"The upper or wester dale."

Wester Ross (Ross), Ros an Iar
This is also known in Gaelic as
Taobh Siar Rois, "the west side of
Ross", although this is not used
locally.

Westertown of Duntelchaig
(Inverness), Bail Shuas
"Upper or wester farm" at
Duntelchaig.

West Kilbride (Ayr), Cille Bhrìghde
an Iar; (South Uist), Cille Bhrìghde
In the Ayrshire name "West" is
used to distinguish this place
from East Kilbride in
Lanarkshire. In South Uist the
Gaelic name is simply *Cille
Bhrìghde*, "St Bridget's Church",
"West" being used in English to
differentiate it from neighbouring
East Kilbride, which is *Taobh a'
Chaolais*, "beside the sound (of
Barra)", in Gaelic.

West Lothian, Labhdaidh an Iar *or*
Lodainn an Iar
See **Lothian**.

West Side (Lewis), An Taobh Siar
"The west side." A native of the area
is a *Siarach*.

Wheen (Angus)
This is a much reduced form of
earlier "Eglismaqueheyne" recorded
in 1578 and probably deriving from
Eaglais MoChomhghain, "St
Comgan's Church".

Whistlefield (Argyll), Taigh na Fead
The Gaelic name is "whistle
house".

Whitebridge (Inverness), An
Drochaid Bhàn
"The white bridge."

Whitefarland (Arran), An Aoirinn
"White headland" is the English
name but the Gaelic name is "the
raised beach". Whitefarland Point is
Rubha na h-Aoireann.

Whitefield (Arran), Srath Bhàn;
(Inverness), An t-Achadh Geal
In Arran, the name is "white river-
holm", but in Inverness it is "the
white or bright field".

Whitehouse (Argyll), An Taigh Bàn
or An Taigh Geal
Both Gaelic names mean "the white
house". The place was earlier known
as *Glac a' Mhuilinn*, "the hollow at
the mill".

Whiteness (Ross), Rubha na hInnse
Móire
The English name is "white headland", from Norse and the Gaelic
name is "the headland at the big
meadow".

Whithorn (Wigtown), Taigh
Mhàrtainn
The English name is "white house",
from English and the Gaelic name
is "Martin's house". Earlier Gaelic
names for this place were *Rosnat*,
"small promontory", and *Futarna*, a
gaelicised version of the Latin
form of the English name. This was
the site of *Candida Casa* of St
Ninian.

Whiting Bay (Arran), Am Bàgh *or*
Am Bàigh
The Gaelic names are "the bay". The
village used to be known as *Eadar
Dhà Rubha*, "between two
headlands".

Wiay (Benbecula), Bhuia *or*
Fùidheigh
"House island", from Norse.

Wick (Caithness), Inbhir Ùige
The English name is "bay", from
Norse and the Gaelic is "the mouth of
the Wick river", from Gaelic/Norse.

The fair held at Wick was called *Féill Fhearghais*, "St Fergus's Fair".

Wigtown (Wigtown), Baile na h-Ùige
"Town on the bay", from Norse/English, of which the Gaelic version is a translation. Wigtownshire is *Siorrachd Bhaile na h-Ùige*.

Wilkhaven (Ross), Port nam Faochag
"The harbour of the whelks."

Windhill (Ross), Cnoc na Gaoithe
"The hill of the wind."

Woodend (Argyll, Skye), Ceann na Coille; (Islay), Cnoc na Coille
In Gaelic in Argyll and Skye this is "the end of the wood", but in Islay it is "the hill at the wood".

Woodlands (Ross), An Claon Uachdrach
"Land of the wood" in English, but this is "the upper slope" in Gaelic.

Woodside (Ross), Ceann na Coille
The Gaelic name is "the end of the wood".

Wyvis (Ross), Coire Bhacaidh
The English name comes from the mountain name *Beinn Uais*, "mountain of terror", or Ben Wyvis. The Gaelic name is "corrie of the ghost". Wyvis Forest is *Frith Uais*.

Y

Yellow Wells (Ross), Am Fuaran Buidhe
The Gaelic is "the yellow spring".

Yoker (Glasgow), An Eochair
"The river bank."

Lochs and Sea Areas

A

Airds Bay (Argyll), Bàgh nan Àird
"The bay of the headlands."

Alness Bay (Ross), Camas Alanais
The Gaelic and English names both mean the same.

Annat Bay (Ross), Am Poll Mór *or* Linne na h-Annaid
The first Gaelic name is "the big pond", the local name of the bay. The second Gaelic name is "the firth of Annat".

Ardlussa Bay (Jura), Tràigh an Airgid
The Gaelic name is "the silver beach".

Atlantic Ocean, An Cuan Siar
The Gaelic name is "Western Ocean". In Argyll and islands this is known as *An Cuan Mór*, "the great ocean". In poetry the Atlantic was known as *An Tabh*, from Norse.

Avoch Bay (Ross), Camas Abhach
The Gaelic and English names both mean the same.

B

Beauly Firth (Inverness, Ross), Linne Fharair *or* Poll an Ròid
This arm of the Moray Firth is known in Gaelic as "the firth of the Farrar" and as "the pool of the rood", referring to a cross erected on a small island in the 13th century.

Broad Bay (Lewis), An Loch a Tuath
The "broad bay" may originally have been named by the Norse as there is a village on the bay named *Bréibhig* from the Norse for "Broad Bay". The Gaelic name is "the north loch".

C

Cambuscurrie Bay (Ross), Camas Curaidh
The Gaelic name is "coracle bay". The English name has duplicated *camas* by adding "bay" to the original.

Campbeltown Loch (Argyll), Loch Chille Chiarain
The Gaelic name is "the loch at St Ciaran's Church". This loch was known in English by an anglicised form of the Gaelic name until that was superseded by the present English name following the foundation of the planned town of Campbeltown.

Corryvreckan (Argyll), Coire Bhreacain
"Breacan's cauldron", referring to the whirlpool here. A saying claims that, *Ge b' e nach stiùir coire a' bhrochain, cha stiùir Coire Bhreacain,* "He who cannot manage the porridge cauldron, will never manage Breacan's cauldron".

Craig Bay (Ross), Lùb na Creige
"The bay of Craig."

Cromarty Bay (Ross), Camas Chrombaigh
The Gaelic and English names both mean the same.

Cromarty Firth (Ross), Linne Chrombaigh
The mouth of the Cromarty Firth between the Sutors is *Caolas Chrombaigh*, "the Cromarty strait", and also *Beul Chromba*, "the mouth of Cromarty", as recorded by Diack (1944).

Crom Loch (Ross), An Crom Loch
"The crooked loch."

Crowlin Sound (Ross, Skye), An
Linne Chròlaigeach *or* An Linne
Chròlainneach
The Gaelic name is "the Crowlin
Firth".

Cuillin Sound (Rum, Skye), An
Linne Sgitheanach
The Gaelic name is "the Skye Firth".

D

Dornoch Firth (Ross, Sutherland),
Caolas Dhòrnaich
The Gaelic name is "the strait of
Dornoch".

Dorus Mor (Argyll), An Doras Mór
"The great doorway", leading out
into the Atlantic from the shelter of
the Argyll islands.

E

East Kyle of Bute (Argyll, Bute), An
Caol an Ear
The Gaelic name is "the east
sound".

Eilean Tigh Sound (Raasay), Caolas
Eilean Taighe
The Gaelic and English names both
mean the same.

F

Fairy Loch (Dunbarton), An Lochan
Uaine
The Gaelic name is "the small green
loch".

Firth of Clyde (Argyll, Arran, Ayr),
An Linne Ghlas; (Argyll, Bute,
Renfrew), Linne Chluaidh, Uisge
Fìne
The Firth of Clyde south of the
northern tip of Arran is known as
An Linne Ghlas, "the grey-blue firth".
Linne Chluaidh, "the firth of the
Clyde", extends from Arran up to
Inverclyde. North of Arran and west
of Bute, the area is known as *Uisge
Fìne*, "the river of Fyne". In the
Gaelic of Arran, the Firth of Clyde

between Arran and Ayrshire was
called *Caol an Eilein*, "the island
strait".

Firth of Forth (Fife, East Lothian,
West Lothian, Midlothian), Linn
Giùdain *or* Muir Giùdain
The English name refers to the
River Forth. The Gaelic name is not
entirely clear, although *linn* or *linne*
denotes a firth or sea loch and *muir*
refers to the sea. *Giùdain* may be
related to Gododdyn, the name of
the Brythonic people who inhabited
the Lothians prior to the arrival of
the Scots and Angles.

Firth of Lorne (Argyll), An Linne
Latharnach
"The Lorne firth" in Gaelic.

Firth of Tay (Angus, Fife, Perth),
Linne Tatha *or* Loch Tatha
The Gaelic names are "the firth of
the Tay" and "the loch of the Tay".
The latter name was used in
Perthshire Gaelic and is also the
name applied to Loch Tay.

Flowerdale Bay (Ross), Ceann an
t-Sàil *or* Òb Cheann an t-Sàil
The English name refers to the
settlement name of Flowerdale,
while the Gaelic names are "the
head of the inlet" and "the bay at the
head of the inlet".

G

Gairloch (Ross), Geàrrloch
"Short loch."

Gareloch (Argyll, Dunbarton), An
Geàrr Loch
"The short loch."

Gunna Sound (Coll, Tiree), Am Bun
Dubh
This sound which surrounds the islet
of Gunna between Coll and Tiree is
known as "the black mouth" in
Gaelic.

H

Holy Loch (Argyll), An Loch Sianta
"The sacred or holy loch."

Horse Bay (Ross), Caolas Eilean nan Each
The Gaelic name differs from the English in that it means "strait of the island of the horses".

Horseshoe Bay (Ross), Crudh an Eich
The Gaelic name is simply "the horseshoe".

I

Inner Sound (Raasay, Ross), An Caolas Ratharsach *or* An Linne Ratharsach
The English name uses "inner" to signify that this sound links Raasay to the mainland. The Gaelic name of the Inner Sound is "the Raasay strait or firth". The Sound of Raasay is another sea area linking Raasay with Skye, but with the same Gaelic name. Slightly north of Raasay the sea area called *An Lighe Rònach*, "the Rona flood", separates South Rona from Applecross, while *Lighe Phort Rìgh*, "the flood of Portree", separates South Rona from Skye.

K

Kerry Bay (Ross), Inbhir Chearraidh
The English name refers to the bay into which the Kerry River flows, while the Gaelic name is "the mouth of the Kerry".

Kilbrannan Sound (Argyll, Arran), An Caolas Brandanach, An Caolas Srandanach, Caol a' Bhrannaidh *or* Caol Bhrannain
This is "St Brendan's strait", known by a variety of names in the areas surrounding it.

Kilchoan Bay (Argyll), Bàgh Chille Chomhghain
The Gaelic and English names both mean the same.

Kyle Akin (Skye), Caol Àcain
"Haakon's narrows", referring to a Norse king.

Kyle More (Raasay, Skye), An Caol Mór
"The big narrows."

Kyle of Durness (Sutherland), Caolas Dhiùirnis *or* Caolas Dhiùranais
"The strait of Durness." The Kyle of Durness ferry was known as *Aiseag Taobh a' Phairbh*.

Kyle of Lochalsh (Ross, Skye), Caol Loch Aillse
"The narrows of Lochalsh."

Kyle of Sutherland (Ross, Sutherland), An Caol Catach
"The Sutherland narrows."

Kyle of Tongue (Sutherland), Caolas Thunga
"The narrows of Tongue." The Kyle of Tongue ferry was known as *Aiseag Chinn an t-Sàil'*.

Kyle Rhea (Inverness, Skye), Caol Reatha
"The narrows at the current." See **Kylerhea**.

Kyle Rona (Raasay), An Caol Rònach
"The Rona narrows", referring to the island of South Rona.

Kyles Flodday (Benbecula), Caolas Fhlodaidh
"The strait of Flodday."

Kyles Knoydart (Inverness), Caolas Chnòideart
"The strait of Knoydart."

Kylesku (Sutherland), An Caolas Cumhang
"The narrow strait."

Kyles Morar (Inverness), Caolas Mhórair
"The strait of Morar."

Kyles of Bute (Argyll, Bute), Na Caoil Bhódach
"The Bute narrows." The East Kyle is *An Caol an Ear*, while the West Kyle is *An Caol an Iar* or *An Caol Ceathrach*, "the Kerry sound".

Kyles Scalpay (Harris, Scalpay), Caolas Sgalpaigh
"The strait of Scalpay."

Kyles Stockinish (Harris), Caolas Stocainis
"The strait of Stockinish."

L

Laggan Bay (Islay), Bolg na Tràgha Móire
The Gaelic name appears to be "the bag of the large beach", as *balg/bolg* ("bag") appears in other names with reference to the sea. See **Murlaggan**.

Lake of Menteith (Perth), Loch Innis MoCholmaig *or* Loch a' Phuirt
The Gaelic names do not refer to the district of Menteith but to the island and "the port", meaning Port of Menteith. The island is *Innis MoCholmaig*, "St Colman's island".

Lamlash Bay (Arran), Loch an Eilein *or* A' Bhàigh
"The loch with the island" referring to Holy Island. Local people simply used *a' Bhàigh*, "the bay".

Little Loch Broom (Ross), An Locha Beag *or* Loch Bhraoin Beag
This arm of Loch Broom is also known as "the small loch" in Gaelic.

Little Minch (Benbecula, North Uist, Skye), An Cuan Sgìth
This is an extension of the main Minch, and the Gaelic name is "the Skye ocean".

Loch Achilty (Ross), Loch Àicheallaidh
"The loch of Achilty."

Loch Achonchie (Ross), Loch Achadh Dhonnchaidh
"The loch at Duncan's field."

Loch Affric (Inverness), Loch Afraic
"The loch of the Affric."

Loch Ailort (Inverness), Loch Ailleart
See **Lochailort**.

Loch Ainort (Skye, South Uist), Loch Aoineart
See **Lochainort**.

Loch Aline (Argyll), Loch Àlainn
See **Lochaline**.

Loch Alsh (Ross), Loch Aillse
See **Lochalsh**.

Loch Ard (Perth), Loch na h-Àirde
"The loch with the headland."

Loch Arkaig (Inverness), Loch Airceig
"Loch of the difficult river."

Loch Arklet (Stirling), Loch Aircleid
"Loch at the difficult slope."

Loch Ashie (Inverness), Loch Athaisidh
"Loch at the bare meadow."

Loch Assynt (Sutherland), Loch Asainte
"The loch of Assynt."

Loch Avich (Argyll), Loch Abhaich
"The loch at the water place."

Loch Awe (Argyll), Loch Obha
"The loch of fresh water." See **Lochawe**.

Loch Bee (South Uist), Loch Bì
The meaning of the Norse second element of this name is unclear.

Loch Beneveian (Inverness), Loch Beinn a' Mheadhain
"The loch of the middle mountain."

Loch Bervie (Sutherland), Loch Biorbhaigh
This might be "loch of boiling water", but in its location a Norse derivation might be likely such as "the head of the loch of the rock river".

Loch Boisdale (South Uist), Loch Baghasdail
See **Lochboisdale**.

Loch Bracadale (Skye), Loch Bhràcadail
"The loch of Bracadale."

Loch Brittle (Skye), Loch Breadail
"The loch at the broad valley", from Gaelic/Norse.

Loch Broom (Perth), Loch a' Bhraoin; (Ross), Loch Bhraoin
"The loch of water."

Loch Buie (Mull), Locha Buidhe
"Yellow loch."

Loch Carron (Ross), Loch Carrann
"Loch of the rough water." See **Lochcarron**.

Loch Cluanie (Ross), Loch Chluainidh
"The loch of Cluanie."

Loch Coruisk (Skye), Loch a' Choir' Uisge
"The loch at the fresh water corrie."

Loch Coulter (Inverness), Loch Caoldair
"The loch of the narrow water."

Loch Creran (Argyll), Loch Creurain
The meaning of this name is unclear.

Loch Dochfour (Inverness), An Eadarloch
"The between-loch", between Loch and River Ness.

Loch Duich (Ross), Loch Dubhthaich
"St Duthac's loch."

Loch Duntelchaig (Inverness), Loch Dhùn Deilcheig
"The loch of Duntelchaig."

Loch Dunvegan (Skye), Loch Dhùn Bheagain
"The loch of Dunvegan."

Loch Earn (Perth), Loch Éireann *or* Loch Éir
"The loch of the Earn." The second Gaelic name reflects local pronunciation.

Loch Eck (Argyll), Loch Aic
The meaning of this name is unclear. It is alleged to mean "the loch of the notch", but this seems unlikely.

Loch Eil (Argyll, Inverness), Loch Iall
"Thong loch", referring to its long thin shape.

Loch Eilt (Inverness), Loch Aoillt
The meaning of this name is unclear.

Loch Eishort (Skye), Loch Eiseort
This is a Norse loch name.

Loch Eport (North Uist), Loch Euphort
"Isthmus loch", from Norse.

Loch Eriboll (Sutherland), Loch Éireabuil
"Beach farm loch." The ferry here was known as *Aiseag Loch Éireabuil.*

Loch Ericht (Perth), Loch Eireachd
"Assembly loch."

Loch Erisort (Lewis), Loch Eireasort
"Harris firth", from Norse.

Loch Errochty (Perth), Loch Eireachdaidh
"Loch at the assembly place."

Loch Etchachan (Aberdeen), Loch Éiteachain
This may be "loch of the little foul one".

Loch Etive (Argyll), Loch Éite
"Loch of the foul one", referring to *Éiteag*, a spirit said to live in the waters.

Loch Ewe (Ross), Loch Iubh
"Yew loch."

Loch Eynort (Skye), Loch Aoineart
"Isthmus loch", from Norse.

Loch Fad (Bute), An Loch Fada
"The long loch."

Loch Fannich (Ross), Loch Fainich
This is of pre-Gaelic origin and may refer to surging waves.

Loch Farraline (Inverness), Loch Farralainn
The meaning of this name is unclear.

Loch Finlaggan (Islay), Loch an Eilein
The English form appears to come from Gaelic *Fionn Lagan*, "white or fair hollow", which became corrupted to *Loch Bhìollagain*, a name by which the loch used to be known in Gaelic. The present Gaelic name is "the loch with the island" referring to *Eilean na Comhairle*, where *Comhairle nan Eilean*, comprising the main clan chiefs, used to gather.

Loch Fleet (Sutherland), Loch Fleòid
"Loch of the current", from Gaelic/Norse. This is one of the few instances on the east coast of *loch* being used to designate a firth or sea loch rather than a freshwater inland loch.

Loch Frisa (Mull), Loch Phrìosa
The Norse element of this name contains á, "river", but the rest is unclear.

Loch Fyne (Argyll), Loch Fìne, Uisge Fìne
"Loch of wine" or "water of Fyne". *Uisge Fìne* extends from Loch Fyne southward past Bute to the northern tip of Arran. People from the surrounding area were nicknamed *mucan biorach*, "porpoises".

Loch Garve (Ross), Loch Maol Fhinn
This loch near Garve is known in Gaelic as "the loch of Fionn's devotee".

Loch Garry (Inverness), Loch Garadh
"Copse loch."

Loch Gelly (Fife), Loch Gheallaidh
"Loch of the white water."

Loch Gilp (Argyll), Loch Gilb
"Chisel loch", referring to its shape.

Loch Glass (Ross), Loch Ghlais
"Loch of the stream."

Loch Goil (Argyll), Loch Goibhle
"The loch of the fork." See **Lochgoilhead**.

Loch Hope (Sutherland), Loch Hób
"Loch of the bay", from Gaelic/Norse.

Loch Hourn (Inverness), Loch Shùirn *or* Loch Shubhairne
"Loch of the berry gap."

Loch Inchard (Sutherland), Loch Uinnseort
"Loch of the meadow firth", from Gaelic/Norse.

Lochindaal (Islay), Loch an Dàil
This is said to be "loch of the delay" but this may only be a folk etymology.

Lochindorb (Moray), Loch nan Doirb
"Loch of the minnows."

Loch Katrine (Perth), Loch Caiteirein
This may refer to a dark or gloomy location.

Loch Killisport (Argyll), Loch Caolasport
This is a Norse firth name, but the specifying element is unclear.

Loch Laggan (Inverness), Loch an Lagain
"Loch of Laggan."

Loch Lamlash (Arran), Loch an Eilein *or* A' Bhàigh
See **Lamlash Bay, Holy Island** and **Lamlash**.

Loch Langavat (Lewis), Loch Langabhat
"Long fresh water loch", from Norse.

Loch Lee (Angus), Loch Lìgh
It is unclear what this name means, although *lighe* can refer to a flood or strong current.

Loch Leven (Argyll, Inverness, Kinross), Loch Lìobhann
"Loch of the smooth water."

Loch Linnhe (Argyll, Inverness), An Linne Dhubh *and* An Linne Sheileach
The English name has used Gaelic *linne*, "firth", as a specifying element here. The first Gaelic name is "black firth" and refers to the upper part of Loch Linnhe inside the narrows at Corran. The second name is "brackish firth" and is applied to the part of Loch Linnhe beyond Corran towards the open sea.

Loch Loch (Perth), Loch Lòch
"Dark loch." Locally it is said that this loch is so-called because it was so big it was named twice.

Loch Lochay (Perth), Loch Lòcha *or* Loch Lòchaidh
"Loch of the dark river."

Loch Lochy (Inverness), Loch Lòchaidh
"Loch of the dark river."

Loch Lomond (Dunbarton, Stirling), Loch Laomainn
This pre-Gaelic name is thought to mean "beacon", referring in some way to Ben Lomond.

Loch Long (Argyll, Ross), Loch Long
"Loch of ships."

Loch Loyal (Sutherland), Loch Laghail
This name of Norse origin is said to be "law mountain" applied in the first instance to Ben Loyal then transferred to the loch.

Loch Lubnaig (Perth), Loch Lùdnaig
This may mean "finger-shaped loch".

Loch Liuchart (Ross), Loch Luinncheirt
"Encampment loch."

Loch Lyon (Perth), Loch Lìomhann
"Loch of the smooth water."

Loch Maddy (North Uist), Loch nam Madadh
"Loch of the wolves", referring to rocks named *na Madaidhean*, "the wolves".

Loch Mahaick (Perth), Loch MoThathaig
"St MoThatha's loch."

Loch Maree (Ross), Loch Ma Ruibhe
"St Maol Rubha's loch." This loch had two older names, *Loch Feadhail Feas* and *Loch Iubh*.

Loch Moidart (Inverness), Loch Mhùideart
"Narrow firth", from Norse.

Loch Monar (Ross), Loch Mhonair
"Loch at the upland place."

Loch Morar (Inverness), Loch Mhórair
"Loch of the great water." This loch is said to be inhabited by a monster called *Mórag* or *a' Mhórag*.

Loch More (Inverness), An Loch Mór; (Sutherland), Loch an Reidhinidh
The English form is from the Gaelic for "big loch". In Sutherland the name is unclear but may contain *reidhneach*, which is applied to a cow yielding no milk.

Loch Morie (Ross), Loch Mhoire
"St Mary's loch", a northern equivalent of "St Mary's Loch" in Roxburghshire.

Loch Morlich (Inverness), Loch Mhùrlaig
"Loch with the small inlet."

Loch Moy (Inverness), Loch na Mòighe
"Loch on the plain."

Loch Mullardoch (Inverness), Loch Maol Àrdaich
"Loch at the blunt high place."

Loch na Caoidhe (Sutherland), Loch na Cuinge
The English form is from a misreading or mispronunciation of the Gaelic name, which means "loch of the yoke".

Lochnagar (Aberdeen), Loch na Gàire
"Loch of the loud noise."

Loch na h-Uamhachd (Sutherland), Loch na h-Uagha
"Loch of the cave or grave."

Loch na Keal (Mull), Loch nan Ceall
"Loch of the cells."

Loch nan Ceall (Inverness), Loch nan Ceall *or* Loch nan Cilltean
Both names mean "loch of the cells" and the second name is the one used locally.

Loch Naver (Sutherland), Loch Nabhair
This pre-Gaelic name has connotations of swimming.

Loch Nell (Argyll), Loch nan Eala
"Loch of swans." This name may originally have been *Loch n-Eala* meaning "loch of swans" and showing a form of the genitive plural which has been obsolete for many centuries.

Loch Ness (Inverness), Loch Nis
This name is most likely pre-Gaelic, denotes a river and is unrelated to Norse *nes*, "headland". The well-known monster said to inhabit the loch is called *an Niseag*.

Loch Nevis (Inverness), Loch Nibheis
This name was believed to stem from *uabhas*, "terror", but the basis of the name is that of the River Nevis, which comes from an Indo-European root with connotations of wetness.

Loch of Lintrathen (Angus), Linn Tréithean
See **Lintrathen**.

Loch of Strathbeg (Aberdeen)
"Loch at the small strath."

Loch Oich (Inverness), Loch Obhaich
"Loch of fresh water." This name was earlier *Loch Abha*, with the same meaning.

Loch Ouirn (Lewis), Loch Odhairn
The meaning of this name is unclear.

Loch Portan (North Uist), Loch Portain
"Loch with a little harbour."

Loch Quoich (Inverness), Loch Chuaich
"Loch at the hollow."

Loch Rannoch (Perth), Loch Raineach
"Loch of Rannoch."

Loch Riddon (Argyll), Loch Ruadhail
This is said to be "loch at the red place", but see **Glendaruel**.

Loch Roag (Bernera, Lewis), Locha Ròg
See **Kinlochroag**.

Loch Rosque (Sutherland), Loch a' Chroisg
"Loch at the crossing place."

Loch Ruthven (Inverness), Loch Ruadhainn
"Loch at the red-brown place."

Loch Ryan (Ayr, Wigtown), Loch Rìoghaine
This may be "loch of Rian", containing a personal name.

Loch Scavaig (Skye), Loch Sgàbhaig
"Loch at the shaw bay."

Loch Scridain (Mull), Loch Sgrìodain
This appears to be "scree loch".

Loch Seaforth (Harris, Lewis), Loch Shìophort
"Loch of the sea firth", from Gaelic/Norse.

Loch Sheil (Argyll, Inverness), Loch Seile
This may be "brackish loch" or have a much older origin.

Loch Shell (Lewis), Loch Sealg
This name is unclear.

Loch Shin (Sutherland), Loch Sin
This is said to be "loch of the old river" but may be of a pre-Gaelic origin.

Loch Skiport (South Uist), Loch Sgioport
"Ship firth", from Norse with *loch* attached.

Loch Slapin (Skye), Loch Shlaopainn
The meaning of this name is unclear. A saying applied to someone very thirsty or keen on drink is *Dh'òladh e Loch Shlaopainn*, "He would drink Loch Slapin".

Loch Slin (Ross), Loch Slinn
"Loch of the weaver's sleye." This loch has since been drained.

Loch Snizort (Skye), Loch Shnìothasort
"Snow firth", from Norse with *loch* attached.

Loch Spallander (Argyll), Loch Spealadair
"Scytheman's loch."

Loch Spelve (Mull), Loch Spéilbhidh
The meaning of this name is unclear.

Loch Striven (Argyll), Loch Sroigheann
The meaning of this name is unclear.

Loch Sween (Argyll), Loch Suain
"Svein's loch", from Gaelic but containing a Norse personal name. It is also known as *Loch a' Chaisteil*, "loch of the castle".

Loch Tarbert (Argyll, Harris), Loch an Tairbeirt
"Loch at the isthmus or portage."

Loch Tay (Perth), Loch Tatha
This is a pre-Gaelic river name. The same Gaelic name is applied in Perthshire Gaelic to the Firth of Tay.

Loch Teachuis (Argyll), Loch Tiacais
The meaning of this name is unclear.

Loch Treig (Inverness), Loch Tréig
This is said to be "loch of death".

Loch Trool (Ayr), Loch an t-Sruthail
"Loch of the current, or stream."

Loch Truderscaig (Sutherland), Loch Trudarsgaig
The second word is of Norse origin and refers to "Thrond's spit of land", featuring a personal name found also in "Trodday", "Trotternish" and "Trudernish".

Loch Tulla (Argyll), Loch Toilbhe
This name is pre-Gaelic and unclear.

Loch Tummel (Perth), Loch Teimhil
"Loch of the dark river."

Loch Uiskevagh (Benbecula), Loch Uisgeabhagh
"Ox bay", from Norse with *loch* attached.

Loch Ussie (Ross), Loch Ùsaidh
The name is obscure and may be pre-Gaelic.

Loch Varkasaig (Skye), Loch Bharcasaig
"Loch at castle bay", from Gaelic/Norse.

Loch Vatandip (Lewis), Loch Bhatandìob
"Loch of deep fresh water", from Gaelic/Norse.

Loch Venacher (Perth), Loch Bheannchair
"Loch at the horned place."

Loch Veyatie (Ross), Loch Mheathadaidh
This name may contain a reference to a damp or spongy place. See **Meddat**.

Loch Voil (Perth), Loch Bheothail
This is said to mean "lively loch" but the name may have been corrupted through time.

Lynn of Morvern (Argyll, Mull), An Linne Mhorbhairneach
"The Morvern firth."

M

Machrie Bay (Arran), Bàgh a' Mhachaire
"Bay of Machrie."

Minch, A' Mhaoil, An Cuan Leòdhasach *and* An Cuan Sgìth
The English name is similar to *Manche*, the French term for the English Channel. The first Gaelic name refers to the sea area between Lewis and the mainland and is related to the "Moyle" between Scotland and Ireland. In Wester Ross this sea area is called *An Cuan Leòdhasach*, "the Lewis ocean". The second Gaelic name, "the Skye ocean", is applied to the sea between Skye and the Western Isles. The saying, *Tha dà thaobh air a' Mhaoil*, "there are two sides to the Minch", is used to mean that there are two ways of seeing things.

Moray Firth, An Cuan Moireach, Geòb Mhoireibh *or* Linne Mhoireibh
The first Gaelic name is "the Moray ocean", the second is "bight of Moray" and the third and most commonly used is "firth of Moray".

Munlochy Bay (Ross), Òb Poll Lòchaidh
"Bay of Munlochy."

N

Narrows of Raasay (Raasay, Skye), Caol na h-Àirde
The Gaelic name is "sound at the headland".

Nechtansmere (Angus), Linn Garan
The English name is "Nechtan's loch", while the Gaelic is "Garan's pool".

Nigg Bay (Ross), Camas Neig
"Inlet of Nigg."

North Channel, Sruth na Maoile
The Gaelic name is "Moyle channel", referring to the Mull of Galloway or of Kintyre.

North Ford (Benbecula), An Fhadhail a Tuath
"North sea ford." The old name was *Fadhail na Comraich*, "ford of the sanctuary".

North Sea, An Cuan a Tuath
The Gaelic name is "the north
ocean". Earlier the North Sea was
known as *Muir Lochlainn*, "the sea of
Scandinavia". The seas around
Orkney are known as *An Cuan
Arcach*, "the Orcadian ocean".

O

Oban Bay (Argyll), Bàgh an Òbain
"Bay of Oban." Oban itself is "small
bay".

P

Pabbay Sound (Ross, Skye), An
Linne Phabach
The Gaelic name means "the Pabbay
firth" and refers to the sea area
between Pabbay and Kyle of
Lochalsh.

Pentland Firth (Caithness, Orkney),
An Caol Arcach
The English name is from Norse for
"Pictland firth", while the Gaelic
name is "Orcadian narrows".

Port Henderson Bay (Ross), Lùb
Phortaigil
"The bay of Port Henderson."

Portree Loch (Skye), Loch Chaluim
Chille
The Gaelic name is "St Columba's
loch".

R

Redpoint Bay (Ross), Lùb an Rubha
"The bay of the point" in Gaelic.

S

Salen Bay (Argyll), Bàgh an t-Sàilein
"Bay of Salen", which itself means
"small inlet".

Sand Bay (Ross), Lùb Shannd
"The bay of Sand."

Sea of the Hebrides (Barra, Canna,
South Uist), An Cuan Barrach *and*
Cuan Uibhist
The Gaelic names are "the Barra
ocean" and "ocean of Uist", the
former being south of the latter

although this distinction is not
made in English.

Slaggan Bay (Ross), Camas Mór an
t-Slagain
The Gaelic name is "the large bay of
Slaggan".

Solway Firth (Kirkcudbright,
Dumfries, Wigtown)
In older Gaelic this sea area was
known as *Trácht Romra*, "the shore
of the mighty sea", probably realised in modern Gaelic as *Tràchd
Romhra*.

Sound of Barra (Barra, South Uist),
Caolas Bharraigh
"Strait of Barra."

Sound of Bernera (Bernera, Lewis),
Sruth Iarseadair
The Gaelic name is "current of
Earshader".

Sound of Berneray (Berneray, North
Uist), Caolas Bheàrnaraigh
"Strait of Berneray."

Sound of Boreray (North Uist),
Caolas a' Mhòrain
The name of this strait is unclear,
although it may be related to *Àird a'
Bhorrain*, "Ardvorran".

Sound of Canna (Canna, Rum), An
Caol Canach
"The Canna sound."

Sound of Carna (Argyll), Caol
Chàrna
Both names mean the same.

Sound of Eriskay (Eriskay, South
Uist), Caolas Éirisgeigh
"Strait of Eriskay."

Sound of Harris (Berneray, Harris),
Caolas Na Hearadh
"Strait of Harris."

Sound of Iona (Iona, Mull), Caol
Idhe
"Sound of Iona."

Sound of Islay (Islay, Jura), An Caol
Ìleach *or* Caol Ìle
"The Islay sound."

Sound of Jura (Argyll, Jura), An
Linne Dhiùrach *or* An Linne
Rosach

The Gaelic names are "the Jura firth" and "the Ross firth", which refers to a headland. The northern and narrower end of the sound is called *Caol Dhiùra*, "the sound of Jura".

Sound of Longa (Ross), An Caol Beag
The Gaelic name is "small sound".

Sound of Mull (Argyll, Mull), Caol Muile
"Sound of Mull."

Sound of Pabay (Barra), Caolas Phabaigh
"Strait of Pabay."

Sound of Pabbay (Ross, Skye), An Linne Phabach
See **Pabbay Sound**.

Sound of Raasay (Raasay, Skye), An Caolas Ratharsach *or* An Linne Ratharsach
The Gaelic name is "the Raasay sound or firth" and is also applied to the Inner Sound. The strait betweeen Scalpay and Raasay is called *An Caol Mór*, "the big strait", while that between Scalpay and Skye is *An Caol Beag*, "the small strait".

Sound of Sandray (Barra), Caolas Shanndraigh
"Strait of Sandray."

Sound of Scalpay (Harris, Scalpay), Caolas Sgalpaigh
"Strait of Scalpay."

Sound of Scarba (Jura), Bealach a' Choin Ghlais
The Gaelic name is "Pass of the grey dog".

Sound of Shiant (Lewis), Sruth nam Fear Gorm
The Gaelic name is "current of the blue men" who were said to inhabit the Shiant islands.

Sound of Sleat (Inverness, Skye), An Linne Shléiteach
The Gaelic name is "the Sleat firth".

Sound of Vatersay (Barra, Vatersay), An Caolas Cumhang
The Gaelic name is "the narrow strait", which is the same name as that of Kylesku.

South Ford (Benbecula, South Uist), An Fhadhail a Deas
"The south sea ford."

Strait of Corryvreckan (Jura), Coire Bhreacain
"Breacan's cauldron", referring to the whirlpool here. A saying claims that, *Ge b' e nach stiùir coire a' bhrochain, cha stiùir Coire Bhreacain*, "He who cannot manage the porridge cauldron, will never manage Breacan's cauldron".

T

Talmine Bay (Sutherland), Poll Tealamainn
"The pool of Talmine."

U

Udale Bay (Ross), Camas Uadail
"Inlet of Udale."

Ulva Sound (Mull), Caolas Ulbha
"Strait of Ulva."

Uig Bay (Lewis), Camas Ùig
"Inlet of Uig."

V

Vatersay Bay (Vatersay), Bàgh Bhatarsaigh
"Bay of Vatersay."

W

West Kyle of Bute (Argyll, Bute), An Caol an Iar *or* An Caol Ceathrach
The Gaelic names are "the west sound" and "the Kerry sound". See **Kerry**.

Whitefarland Bay (Jura), Bàgh na h-Inbhireach
The Gaelic name is "the bay at the river mouth", and contains no reference to **Whitefarland**.

Rivers

Although English uses the definite article with the names of rivers, e.g. "the Spey, the Tweed", etc., Gaelic – perhaps surprisingly – does not, e.g. "Spé, Tuaidh". Major rivers are referred to in Gaelic using *uisge*, "water", rather than *abhainn*, "river", as in *Uisge Chluaidh*, "River Clyde".

A

Add, Abhainn Athad *or* An Abhainn Fhada
The meaning of this name is unclear. The second Gaelic name is "the long river", but this is not the original but rather an attempt by Gaelic speakers to give the name meaning.

Adder
This pre-Celtic Indo-European name comes from a root meaning "watercourse".

Affrick, Afraic *or* Abhainn Afraic
"Dappled river."

Albany Burn, Allt an Albannaigh
"The Scotsman's stream."

Alder, Eallar *or* Abhainn Eallair
This may be from a Gaelic source meaning "rock".

Aldie Water, Allt Àthaigh
The English name suggests a Gaelic origin from *allt*, "stream", while the Gaelic name is "Eathie stream".

Aldourie Burn, Dobhrag *or* Allt Dobhraig
"Little water."

Ale
This is from a pre-Celtic source meaning "flow" and from the same origin as "Allan".

Allan, Alan *or* Abhainn Alain
See **Ale**.

Allander, Alandar
This appears to be the river name "Allan" or "Alan" with *dobhar*, "water", added.

Almond, Aman *or* Abhainn Amain
This is from a Celtic origin meaning "river".

Alness, Abhainn Alanais
"River of the Alan place." This name includes that of the village of Alness (which means "Alan place") and may originally have been called simply "Alan".

Annan, Anainn *or* Abhainn Anann
This name is said to commemorate a water goddess, Anu.

Annaty Burn, Allt na h-Annaide
"Stream of Annat", which itself means "small church". See **Achnahannet** in the Settlements section.

Aray, Aora
It is unclear what the meaning of this name is, but it may be from a pre-Gaelic source meaning "watercourse".

Arder, Àrdar *or* Abhainn Àrdair
"High water."

Ardle, Àrdail *or* Abhainn Àrdail
"River of the high place."

Arkaig, Airceig *or* Abhainn Airceig
"Difficult river."

Aven, Athainn
"Very bright river." The Gaelic name is sometimes seen in an older spelling, *Athfhinn*. This river was also known as *an t-Uisge Bàn*, "the white river".

Averon, Abharan *or* Abhainn Abharain
This comes from Celtic *abh*, denoting a river.

Avon, Abhann
See **Averon**.

Awe, Abha *or* Uisge Abha
See **Averon**.

Ayr, Àr *or* Abhainn Àir
This may be pre-Celtic Indo-European and mean "watercourse".

B

Balgy, Abhainn Bhalgaidh
"River of Balgy."

Balnagowan, Uaraidh *or* Abhainn Uaraidh
The English form is that of a place through which this river also known as "Strathrory" flows. The Gaelic name has its origins in *uar*, "landslip".

Banavie, Banbhaidh
"Pig river."

Banvie, Banbhaidh
See **Banavie**.

Beauly, Farar, Uisge Farair *or* Abhainn nam Manach
The English name is from the town of Beauly, while the first two Gaelic names are from a pre-Celtic root conveying "wetness". The third Gaelic name is "river of the monks", referring to the monastery at Beauly known as *Manachainn Mhic Shimidh*.

Bervie, Biorbhaigh
"Boiling river."

Blackadder
This is the same as **Adder** but with "black" attached to distinguish it from the Whiteadder.

Black Cart
This is the same as **Cart,** but with "black" attached to distinguish it from the White Cart.

Black Devon, Duibhe
The basic name means "black one", i.e. "black river".

Black Water, An t-Uisge Dubh
"The black water."

Bogie, Balgaidh *or* Abhainn Bhalgaidh
"Bag river", referring to bag-shaped pools.

Boyne, Bòinn *or* Abhainn Bhòinn
Like its counterpart in Ireland, this name may be pre-Gaelic.

Boyndie, Bòinnidh
See **Boyndie** in the Settlements section.

Braan, Breamhainn *or* Abhainn Bhreamhainn
"Bellowing river."

Bran, Bran *or* Abhainn Bhrain
"Raven river."

Brannie, Branaidh *or* Abhainn Bhranaidh
"Raven river."

Brerachan, Briathrachan *or* Abhainn Bhriathrachain
"Small talkative river."

Brora, Brùra *or* Abhainn Bhrùra
"Bridge river", from Norse.

Brothock Burn, Brothag *or* Abhainn Bhrothaig
"River of heat."

Bruar, Bruthar *or* Abhainn Bhruthair
"Bridge river", referring to natural rock formations.

Burn of Brown, Allt Bhruthainn
"Stream of heat."

Burn of Vat, Allt na Dabhaich
"Stream of the vat or davoch."

C

Caddon, Cadan *or* Abhainn Chadain
"Warlike river."

Calder, Caladar *or* Abhainn Chaladair
"Hard water."

Callater, Caladar *or* Abhainn Chaladair
See **Calder**.

Calvie, Cailbhidh *or* Abhainn
Chailbhidh
"Stalk river", possibly referring to
reeds.

Cander
"Fair water", from Brythonic.

Carron, Carrann *or* Abhainn
Charrann
"Rough water."

Cart
This is said to come from a Gaelic
root meaning "to clean", but may be
pre-Celtic.

Cassley, Carsla *or* Abhainn Charsla
"River of the castle place."

Cattie, Cataidh *or* Abhainn Chataidh
"Cat river."

Clova, Clàbha *or* Abhainn Chlàbha
The meaning of this name is unclear.

Clyde, Cluaidh *or* Uisge Chluaidh
This is an unclear pre-Gaelic name.

Coe, Comhann *or* Abhainn
Chomhann
This may be a tribal name attached
to the river.

Cona, Cona *or* Abhainn Chona
This may be "dog river".

Conan, Conann *or* Abhainn
Chonainn
"Dog river."

Conglass, Conghlais *or* Abhainn
Chonghlais
"Dog stream."

Connie, Conaidh *or* Abhainn
Chonaidh
"Dog river."

Conon, Conann *or* Abhainn
Chonainn (Ross), Connan *or*
Abhainn Chonnain (Skye)
The river in Ross is "dog river", but
in Skye is based on *Connan*, the
name of a saint.

Cowie, Collaidh *or* Abhainn
Chollaidh
"Hazel river."

Craig, Abhainn na Creige *or* Abhainn
Bhràigh Thaithisgeail
This is named after "Craig", through
which the river passes. The

alternative Gaelic name is "river of
the upper part of Taithisgeail",
which in turn is a Norse name.

Creed, Abhainn Ghrìde
"Grit or shingle river", from Norse.

Creran, Creuran *or* Abhainn
Chreurain
This name is obscure.

Crombie, Crombaidh *or* Abhainn
Chrombaidh
"Bent river."

D

Daer
This Brythonic name is possibly
related to the Dare or *Dâr* in Wales.

Dee, Dé *or* Uisge Dhé
This Celtic name has connotations
of divinity and is based on the same
word as *dia*, "god".

Deveron, Dubh Éireann
This name is basically the same as
that of the "Earn", namely a
commemoration of Ireland from the
term *Éire*. The Deveron has Gaelic
dubh, "black" attached to give "Black
Earn", perhaps to distinguish it from
the Findhorn or "White Earn",
which although now known in
Gaelic simply as *Éireann* appears
from the English form to have
formerly been preceded by *fionn*,
"white".

Devon, Duibhe *or* Abhainn Duibhe
This Gaelic name connotes
blackness.

Dionard, Dìonard *or* Abhainn
Dìonaird
This is probably from Norse *dyn* and
fjörðr, giving "noisy sea loch".

Divie, Dubhaidh *or* Duibhidh
(Banff), Duibhe *or* Abhainn Duibhe
(Inverness)
See **Devon**.

Dochart, Dochard *or* Abhainn
Dochaird
This name may be related to "Cart",
although with negative connotations
as implied by the prefix *do-*.

Doe, Dotha *or* Abhainn Dotha
This is said be named after *Dotha* or *Dogha*, a water sprite drowned in the River Barrow in Ireland. However, the name may simply mean "bad water".

Doll, An Dòl
This name, the Gaelic form of which was recorded by Diack (1944), is unclear.

Don, Deathain *or* Abhainn Deathain
Like its sister river, the Dee, this name implies divinity although from a different root. The English form of the name appears to have bypassed Gaelic and come directly from Pictish.

Doon
Although believed to represent *Dubh abhainn*, "black river", this is from the same source as **Don**.

Dorback, Dorbag *or* Uisge Dhorbaig
"Minnow river."

Douglas, Dùghlas *or* Abhainn Dùghlais
"Black river."

Dubh Lighe, Dubhailigh *or* Abhainn Dubhailigh
"River of the black rocky place."

Dulnain, Tuilnean *or* Abhainn Tuilnein
"Flood river."

Dye Water, Uisge Dhàidh
It is unclear what this name means. Cairn Dye is known as *Càrn an Tàilleir*, "the tailor's cairn", but if this is the original name of the mountain it is unlikely to be that of this river.

E

Earn, Uisge Éireann *or* Uisge Éir
This is a commemoration of Ireland from the term *Éire*.

Easter Fearn Burn, Allt Fheàrna Àrd
"The stream of Easter Fearn."

Eathie Burn, Allt Àthaigh
"Stream of Eathie." This is also known as the "Aldie Water".

Echaig, Eachag *or* Abhainn Eachaig
"Little horse river."

Edderton Burn, Allt Eadardain
"Stream of Edderton."

Elchaig, Eilcheag *or* Abhainn Eilcheig
This river is said to have been named after a water sprite living in it called *Eilcheag*, but it is more likely that the sprite was named after the river. The name may be related to **Ellachie**.

Ellachie, Eileachaidh *or* Abhainn Eileachaidh
"River at the rocky place."

Elvan
This name may denote "stony", from a Gaelic or other Celtic root.

Endrick, Eunarag *or* Abhainn Eunaraig
"Snipe river", although this name is the subject of ongoing debate.

Ericht, Eireachd *or* Abhainn Eireachd
"River of assemblies."

Errochty, Eireachdaidh *or* Abhainn Eireachdaidh
See **Ericht**.

Esk, Uisge Easg
This is a Celtic term for river found in the Brythonic-speaking areas. The North Esk is *Easg Thuath* and the South Esk is *Easg Dheas* in Aberdeenshire and Perthshire Gaelic.

Esragan, Easragan
"The little river of the waterfalls."

Etive, Éite *or* Abhainn Éite
This name carries implications of foulness and was the abode of *Éiteag*, a water sprite.

Ettrick
The meaning and origin of this name are unclear.

F

Farrar, Farar *or* Uisge Farair *or* Abhainnn nam Manach
See **Beauly**.

Fechlin, Abhainn Feachlainn
This old name is unclear and the
river is also known as the River
Foyers.

Fender, Fionndar *or* Abhainn
Fhionndair
"White water."

Fernate, Feàrnaid *or* Abhainn
Fheàrnaid
"Alder river."

Feshie, Féisidh *or* Abhainn Fhéisidh
"River of the boggy haugh."

Fiddich, Fiodhach *or* Abhainn
Fhiodhaich
"River of the wood place."

Findhorn, Uisge Éire *or* Uisge
Éireann
This name is based on *Éire* in
commemoration of Ireland. The
English form suggests the name
once contained *fionn*, "white",
perhaps to distinguish it from *Dubh
Éireann*, "black Earn", or Deveron.

Finglas, Fionnghlais *or* Abhainn
Fhionnghlais
"White river."

Finlas, Fionnghlais *or* Abhainn
Fhionnghlais
See **Finglas**.

Fintaig, Abhainn Fhionntaig
"Little white river."

Fionn Lighe, Fionnailigh *or* Abhainn
Fhionnailigh
"River at the white rocky place."

Forth, Foirthe *or* Abhainn Foirthe,
For *or* Uisge For; An Abhainn Dubh
This is an unclear name, although it
may be from a Brythonic source as
the form *Gwerid* is found, which is
equivalent to *Foirthe*. *For* was the
form of the name used in Perthshire
Gaelic. The upper stretches of the
Forth are known in Gaelic as *an
Abhainn Dubh*, "the black river".

Fowlis, Foghlais *or* Uisge Foghlais
"Lower river."

Foyers, Abhainn Feachlainn
The English name refers to the
village through which the river flows,

where it is also known as the River
Fechlin. The Gaelic name is unclear.

Fruin, Freòin *or* Abhainn Freòin
This name may be based on Gaelic
freòine, "rage".

Fyne, Fìne *or* Uisge Fìne
"Wine", a name occasionally applied
to good-tasting water.

G

Gadie, Gadaidh *or* Abhainn
Ghadaidh
"Twig river."

Gairn, Garthan *or* Abhainn
Gharthain
"Calling river."

Garnock, Gairneag
"Crying river", the same as Girnaig
and Girnock.

Garry, Garadh *or* Abhainn Gharadh
(Inverness), Gar *or* Abhainn Ghar
(Perth)
"Copse river."

Garve, Abhainn Ghairbh
"River of Garve."

Gaur, Gamhair *or* Uisge Ghamhair
This name carries implications of
winter.

Gelder, Gealdar *or* Abhainn
Ghealdair
"White or bright water."

Geldie, Geallaidh *or* Abhainn
Gheallaidh
"White or bright river."

Girnaig, Goirneag *or* Abhainn
Ghoirneig
See **Garnock**.

Girnock, Goirneag *or* Allt Ghoirneig
See **Garnock**.

Girvan, Garbhan *or* Abhainn
Gharbhain
"Rough river."

Glass, Abhainn Ghlais
"River." Gaelic has attached the
more commonly used *abhainn*,
"river".

Glaster, Glasdar *or* Abhainn
Ghlasdair
"Grey river."

Glen Lochsie Burn, Allt Lòchsaidh
The English form has added "burn" to the name of the glen through which the river flows. The Gaelic name is "stream of the dark river".

Glorat, Glòraid *or* Abhainn Ghlòraid
"Babbling river."

Gloy, Glaoidh *or* Abhainn Ghlaoidh
"Viscous or gluey river."

Golly, Gollaidh *or* Abhainn Ghollaidh
"Blind river", perhaps implying that it is overgrown.

Gormack, Gormag *or* Allt Ghormaig
"Blue river."

Gowrie, Gobharaidh *or* Allt Ghobharaidh
"Goat river."

Grudie, Grùididh *or* Abhainn Ghrùididh
"Gravelly river."

H

Halladale, Abhainn Healadail
This river takes its name from the Norse "hallowed valley" through which it flows.

Helmsdale, Ilidh *or* Abhainn Ilidh
The English name is that of the town at the mouth of the river. The Gaelic name is unclear but also appears in *Srath Ilidh*, the Gaelic name of the Strath of Kildonan through which it flows.

I

Irvine, Irbhinn
This name, with counterparts in Wales, is unclear.

Isla, Uisge Ìle *or* Ìl
This name is unclear. The Gaelic form is the same as that of the name of the island of Islay but it is unclear whether they are from the same origin.

J
Jed
The origin of this name is unclear.

K
Kale, Calan
"Calling river."

Keltney Burn, Allt Chailtnidh
"Stream of the hard river."

Kelty, Cailtidh
"Hard river."

Kerry, Abhainn Chearraidh
"Copse river", from Norse.

Kingie, Cingidh *or* Abhainn Chingidh
"Hero river."

Kymah Burn, Uisge Chìoma
This name is unclear.

L

Lavern, Labharan *or* Abhainn Labharain
"Loud or talkative river."

Lawers, Labhar *or* Uisge Labhair
"Loud river."

Laxford, Lusard *or* Abhainn Lusaird
This Norse name means "salmon firth".

Lednock, Liadnag *or* Abhainn Liadnaig
This name is unclear but may be of Gaelic origin.

Leithen Water, Lìteann *or* Abhainn Lìteann
This Brythonic name has connotations of wetness.

Leven (Dunbarton), Leamhan *or* Uisge Leamhain; (Argyll, Fife, Kinross), Lìobhann *or* Abhainn Lìobhann
The Dunbartonshire name is "elm river" and has given rise to the district name *Leamhnachd*, "Lennox". The other Levens are "smooth river".

Levern, Labharan
"Loud or talkative river."

Linhouse Water, Caladar *or* Uisge Chaladair
The English name is that of a place while the Gaelic is "hard water".

Linn O'Dee, Eas Dhé *or* An Linne
The English form is "pool on the Dee", while the Gaelic names are "Dee waterfall" and "the pool".

Liver, Lìbhir
This may be "smooth river".

Livet, Lìobhaid *or* Uisge Lìobhaid
"Smooth river."

Lochay, Lòcha *or* Uisge Lòcha
"Dark, or black, river." The river which flows into Loch Tay is also known as *Lòcha Albannach*, "Lochay of Alba", to distinguish it from *Lòcha Urchaidh*, "Lochay of Orchy", which flows into the Orchy.

Lochty, Lòchaidh *or* Abhainn Lòchaidh
See **Lochay.**

Lochy, Lòchaidh *or* Abhainn Lòchaidh
"Dark or black river." The short River Lochy which flows into Loch Linnhe is the subject of a sarcastic saying, *Is mòid a' mhuir Lòchaidh*, "The sea is the bigger for the Lochy".

Lossie, Losaidh *or* Uisge Losaidh
"Herb or vegetation river."

Loy, Abhainn Laoigh
"Calf river."

Lugar Water
"Bright river", from a Celtic origin.

Lui, Abhainn Laoigh
See **Loy.**

Luthnot, Luathnait *or* Abhainn Luathnait
"Swift river."

Lyon, Lìomhann *or* Uisge Lìomhann
"Smooth river."

M

Mallie, Màilidh *or* Abhainn Mhàilidh
This is said to be the name of a saint. See **Dalmally** and **Kilmallie.**

Markie, Marcaidh *or* Abhainn Mharcaidh
"Horse river."

Mashie, Mathaisidh *or* Abhainn Mhathaisidh
"River of the good haugh."

May Water, Uisge Méidh
The meaning of this name is unclear.

Meig, Mìg *or* Abhainn Mìg
This may be "boggy river" if a Gaelic name, but its origins may be older.

Milk
This Celtic name has connotations of rotting or putrefaction.

Morar, Mórar *or* Abhainn Mhórair
"Great water."

Moriston, Abhainn Mhoireasdain
This name is often said to mean "great river", presumably by confusing the *mor* part of the river name with *mór*, "great", and thinking that *eas*, "waterfall", meant "river" here. However, the name is from a different origin whose meaning remains unclear.

Mossat, Abhainn Mhusaid
"Stale river."

Mussadie, Abhainn Mhusaididh
See **Mossat.**

N

Nairn, Narann *or* Uisge Narann
This pre-Gaelic name carries connotations of swimming or flowing.

Nant, Abhainn Neannta
"Nettle river."

Naver, Nabhar *or* Abhainn Nabhair
This pre-Gaelic name implies moistness. The ferry across the Naver was known as *Coit Nabhair*, "the Naver boat".

Ness, Nis *or* Abhainn Nis
This Indo-European name denotes a stream or river.

Nethan, Neitheann *or* Abhainn Neitheann
"Pure river."

Nethy, Neithich *or* Uisge Neithich
"Pure river." The Inverness-shire Nethy was said to be inhabited by spirits called *na Neithichean*, and when in spate it was said that, *Tha na Neithichean a' tighinn*, "The Nethy spirits are coming".

Nevis, Nibheis *or* Abhainn Nibheis
This is commonly said to derive from *uabhas*, "terror", but the source is pre-Gaelic with connotations of moistness.

Nith, Nid *or* Abhainn Nid
This may be from Brythonic meaning "new".

Nochty Water, Uisge Nochda
"Naked water."

Noe, Abhainn Nodha
"New river."

North Esk, Easg Thuath
"Esk" is a Celtic term for river found widely in the Brythonic-speaking areas.

North Ugie Water, Fionn Ùige
"White Ugie" which appears to be an unclear pre-Gaelic river name.

O

Oich, Obhaich *or* Abhainn Obhaich
This is based on Celtic *abb*, "river", and was previously *Abha*.

Orchy, Urchaidh *or* Abhainn Urchaidh
"Wood river." Locally the name is *Urcha* or *Abhainn Urcha*.

Orrin, Oirrinn *or* Abhainn Oirrinn *and* Orthainn *or* Abhainn Orthainn
"Offering", a religious term. This river was said to be haunted by *Cailleach na h-Abhann*, "hag of the river".

Oykel, Òiceall *or* Abhainn Òiceill
This is pre-Gaelic for "high river".

P

Pattack, Patag *or* Abhainn Phataig
"Pot river." Because this river does not follow the expected course eastwards into the Spey it is called *Patag dhubh bhalgach an aghaidh uisge Alba*, "Black, bag-like Pattack against the waters of Scotland".

Pean, Peathan *or* Abhainn Pheathain
This pre-Gaelic name is unclear.

Peffery, Peofhar *or* Abhainn Pheofhair
This pre-Gaelic name means "bright".

Peffray
See **Peffery**.

Polly, Pollaidh *or* Abhainn Phollaidh
"Pool river."

Pools of Dee, Lochan Dubh na Làirige
The English name seems to be a fairly recent invention, while the Gaelic one is "the small black loch at the pass", referring to *Làirig Dhrù*, the Lairig Ghru.

Prosen, Pràsag *or* Uisge Phràsaig *and* Pràsan *or* Uisge Phràsain
This may be a personal name of pre-Gaelic origin.

R

Roy, Uisge Ruaidh
"Red-brown river."

Ruchill, Abhainn Rùchaill
This was said locally to stem from *ruadh thuil*, "red-brown flood", but appears to contain *coille*, "forest".

Ruthven, Abhainn Ruadhainn
"River at the red-brown place."

S

Scaddle, Sgadal *or* Abhainn Sgadail
This name comes from a Norse valley name.

Scotsburn, Allt nan Albannach
"Stream of the Scots."

Shee, Sìth *or* Uisge Sìth
"Fairy river."

Sheil, Seile *or* Abhainn Seile
This Indo-European name denotes a stream.

Shin, Sin *or* Abhainn Sin
This may derive from Gaelic *sean*, "old", or be a pre-Celtic Indo-European term for "river".

Shira, Siara *or* Abhainn Siara
"Eternal river."

Skiach, Allt na Sgitheach
"Thorn stream."

South Esk, Easg Dheas
"Esk" is a Celtic term for river widely found in the Brythonic-speaking areas.

South Ugie Water, Dubh Ùige
"Black Ugie", an unclear pre-Gaelic river name.

Spey, Spé *or* Uisge Spé
This is said to be "thorn river" but may be of a pre-Gaelic origin. This river is mentioned in *Spé, Dé agus Tatha – trì uisgeachan as motha fon adhar*, "Spey, Dee and Tay – the three greatest rivers under the sun".

Spean, Spiothan *or* Abhainn Spiothain
This appears to be "small thorn river", a diminutive form of the root of "Spey", but may be pre-Gaelic.

Strathrory, Uaraidh *or* Abhainn Uaraidh
The English form comes from the name of the strath through which this river, also known as "Balnagowan River", flows. The Gaelic name comes from *uar*, "landslip".

Strathrusdale, An Abhainn Dubh
The English form is that of the strath through which the river flows. The Gaelic name is "the black river".

Strathy, Abhainn Shrathaidh
This name refers to the place through which the river flows.

Strone Burn
This stream in the Callander area of Perthshire may originally have been known as *Garbh Allt*, "rough burn".

T

Tain
This comes from an Indo-European root meaning "flow".

Tanar, Tanar *or* Uisge Thanair
This is said to come from *torann*, "thunder".

Tanner Water
See **Tanar**.

Tarf Water, Uisge Thairbh
"Bull river."

Tarff, Abhainn Tairbh
See **Tarf Water**.

Tay, Tatha *or* Uisge Tatha
This may be from the same Indo-European root meaning "flow" as **Tain**. The might of the river is mentioned in the saying, *Tatha mhór nan tonn, bheir i sgrìob lom air Peairt*, "The great Tay of the waves will cut a swathe through Perth".

Teatle, Teatall *or* Abhainn Teataill
This pre-Gaelic name is obscure.

Teith, Tèadhaich *or* Uisge Thèadhaich
This obscure Brythonic name has the same form in Gaelic *Tèadhaich*, the Gaelic name of **Menteith**.

Teviot
This appears to be from an Indo-European root meaning "flow".

Thurso, Abhainn Theòrsa
This Norse name is possibly "Thori's river".

Tilt, Teilt *or* Abhainn Teilt
The meaning of this name is unclear.

Treig, Tréig *or* Abhainn Tréig
This is said to be "river of death".

Tromie, Tromaidh *or* Abhainn Tromaidh
"Elder tree river."

Truim, Abhainn Truim
See **Tromie**.

Tummel, Teimheal *or* Uisge Theimhil
"River of darkness."

Turret, Turraid *or* Uisge Thurraid
"Dry river", meaning one which reduces in size in summer.

Tweed, Tuaidh *or* Uisge Thuaidh
This pre-Gaelic name is unclear, as is its earlier Gaelic form, *Tumaid*.

Tyne
This seems to be from an Indo-European root meaning "flow".

U

Ugie, Ùige *or* Ùigidh
The meaning of this name is unclear and is pre-Gaelic.

Urie, Uaraidh *or* Ùraidh
This may stem from *uar*, "landslip", or may mean "fresh river".

W

Water of Allachy, Uisge Aileachaidh
"River at the stony place."

Water of Leith, Uisge Lìte
  This pre-Gaelic name has connotations of moistness.
Water of Lus, Uisge Lus
  "Herb or vegetation river."
Wells of Dee, Fuaran Dhé
  "Spring of the Dee" in Gaelic.
Wester Fearn Burn, Allt Grùgaig
  The English name contrasts this stream with the Easter Fearn Burn, while in Gaelic the name appears to contain Norse *vík*, "bay".
Whiteadder
  This is the same as **Adder**, but with "White" attached to distinguish it from the "Blackadder".

White Cart
  This is the same as **Cart** but with "White" attached to distinguish it from the "Black Cart".
White Water, An t-Uisge Bàn
  "The white river."
Wick, Abhainn Ùige
  The English name is also that of the town which is of Norse origin. The Gaelic form is a gaelicisation of the same Norse word, *vík*, "bay".

Y
Ythan
  This is from a Celtic root for "talk".

Mountain Passes

A

Am Bealach Buidhe
"Ballochbuie" or "the yellow pass"
near Crathie in Aberdeenshire.

Am Bealach Maol
"Ballochmyle" or "the blunt pass" in
Ayrshire.

Am Bealach Mór
"The large pass" between Loch Awe
and Loch Craignish.

Am Bealach Ruadh
"The red-brown pass" between
Meall Reamhar and Beinn Fuath in
Perthshire.

An Crasg
"Crask" or "the crossing" between
Lairg and Tongue in Sutherland.

An Làirig
"The pass" between Boath and
Glenglass in Ross-shire.

An Làirig Leacach
"The slabbed pass" between
Lianachan and the head of Loch
Treig in Lochaber.

An Sloc
"The Slochd" or "the pit" between
Tomatin and Carrbridge in
Inverness-shire.

B

Bealach a' Bhràigh Bhig
"Pass at the small upland" between
Orval and Glen Shellesdar in Rum.

Bealach a' Chaolais
"Pass at the strait" leading inland
from Kyles Stuley in South Uist.

Bealach a' Chonnaidh
"Pass of the fuel" between Glen
Buckie and Gleann Dubh in
Perthshire.

Bealach a' Ghlinne
"Pass of the glen" north of Fiunary
in Argyll.

Bealach a' Mhorghain
"Shingle pass", at the foot of Ben
Edra in Skye.

Bealach an Dubh-bhràighe, Bealach
an Dubh Bhràighe
"Pass at the black upland" between
Orval and a' Bhrìdeanach in Rum.

Bealach an Fhuarain
"Pass at the spring" between
Ainshval and Trallaval in Rum.

Bealach an Òir
"Pass of gold" between Askival and
Trallaval in Rum.

Bealach an t-Suidhe
"Bellochantuy" or "pass of the
sitting" in Kintyre.

Bealach a' Phosta
"Postman's pass" between Sunart and
Kingairloch.

Bealach Àrnabhal
"Pass of Arnaval" between Arnaval
and Trinival in South Uist.

Bealach Baircmheall, Bealach
Barcabhal
"Pass of Barkeval" between Barkeval
and Hallival in Rum.

**Bealach Carragh Dhòmhnaill
Ghuirm**
"Pass at the rock of blue Donald"
between Benmore and Maola Breac
in South Uist.

Bealach Collaigh
"Pass at the hazel river or place" west
of Ben Wyvis in Ross.

Bealach Coire a' Choin
"The pass of the dog's corrie" near
Cape Wrath in Sutherland.

Bealach Crosgard
"Pass of Crosgard" between
Benmore and Glen Liadale in South
Uist.

Bealach Heileasdail
"Hellisdale pass" between
Benmore and Ben Corodale in
South Uist.

Bealach MhicNéill
"MacNeil's pass" inland from
Kinloch in Rum.

Bealach na Ba, Bealach nam Bó
See **Bealach nam Bó**.

Bealach na Gaoithe
"Windy pass" in Argyll.

Bealach na h-Imriche
"Migration pass" near Dunoon. Also
between Strathbeg and Loch
Dionard in Sutherland.

Bealach nam Bó
"Pass of the cattle" between
Applecross and Kishorn in Wester
Ross. Also the pass south of Loch
Katrine below Ben Venue in
Perthshire.

Bealach nam Bròg
"Pass of the shoes" between Wyvis
Forest and Lochbroom.

Bealach nam Mèirleach
"Pass of the thieves" between
Strathmore and Loch Merkland in
Sutherland.

Bealach nan Àrr
Originally *Bealach nan Àradh*, "pass
of the ladders", this is near
Applecross and Lochcarron.

Bealach nan Cabar
"Pass of the antlers" between
Strathyre and Glen Artney in
Perthshire.

Bealach nan Cabrach
"Pass of the antler places" in Glen
Orchy.

Bealach nan Corr
"Pass of the cranes" south of
Knockfarrel in Ross.

Bealach nan Laogh
"Pass of the calves" at Taymouth in
Perthshire.

Bealach na Sgàirde
"Scree pass" through Glamaig in
Skye.

Bealach Sgrìodain
"Scree pass" between Conaglen and
Glen Hurich in Argyll.

Bealach Sheubhal
"Sheaval pass" between Sheaval and
Trinival in South Uist.

Bealach Sloc an Eich
"Pass at the horses' pit" between
Glen Cribesdale and Kinlochteacuis
in Argyll.

C

Cadha Fionndain, Cadha Fhionntain
"Fintan's path" between Tolly and
the Averon in Ross.

Cadha na Beucaich
"The pass of the bellowing" at
Foinaven in Sutherland.

Creagach Bhealadair
"Pass of Ballater" or "rocky place of
Ballater" in Deeside.

Cumhang a' Bhrannraidh
"Pass of Brander" or "pass at the
obstruction" in Argyll.

Cumhang Dhùghlais
"Pass of Lyon" or "pass at the
black river" at the mouth of Glen
Lyon.

Cumhang Lànaigh
"Pass of Leny" between Callander
and Strathyre.

D

Devil's Staircase, Staidhir an Donais
The name is the same in both
languages.

F

Féith Bhealach
"Boggy channel pass" between
Bealach Heileasdail and Ben
Corodale in South Uist.

Fionn Làirig
"White pass" at Killin in
Perthshire.

L

Làirig Àirnein
"Àirnean's pass" between Inveraray and the foot of Glen Falloch.

Làirig an Lochain
"Pass at the little loch" between Bridge of Balgy and Loch Tay. Also between Strathrusdale and Dibidale in Ross.

Làirig an Tùir
"The tower pass" on the south side of Strath Nairn.

Làirig Bhaile Dhubhthaich
"Lairgs of Tain" or "pass of Tain" between Tain and Edderton.

Làirig Bhreislich
"Pass of confusion" between Bridge of Balgy and Glen Lochay in Perthshire.

Làirig Chalabha
This name is unclear but the route lies between Rannoch and Inverwick.

Lairig Ghru, Làirig Dhrù
"Pass of the Druie." In Braemar this was known as *an Làirig Shuas*, "the upper pass".

Làirig Ghartain
"Gartan's pass" in Glen Etive.

Làirig Ìlidh
"Pass of Isla" between Lochearnhead and the north side of Glen Dochart.

Làirig Luaidhe
"The lead pass" between Glen Lyon and Glen Lochay in Perthshire.

Lairig Lui, Làirig an Laoigh
"Pass at the Lui." In Braemar this was called *an Làirig Shìos*, "the lower pass".

Làirig Mheachdainn
This name is unclear but the pass runs between Loch Tay and Loch Rannoch.

Làirig Mìle Marcachd
"Pass of a mile of riding" between Kenmore and Glen Quaich in Perthshire. This was formerly known as *Làirig Monadh Marcachd*, "pass at the riding hills".

Làirig Mhuice
"Pass of the pig river" between Inverwick and Rannoch.

Làirig nan Lunn
"Pass of the staves" between Pubil and Kenknock in Perthshire.

Làirig Nodha
"Pass of Noe" between Glen Noe and Glen Strae in Argyll.

Làirig Phrasgain
"Pass of the troop", in Glen Almond.

Làirig Thurraid
"Pass of Turret" or "pass of the dry river" at the head of Glen Roy in Lochaber.

M

Màm a' Choire Uidhir
"Gap at the dun-coloured corrie" in Mull.

Màm Beathaig
"Beathag's gap" in Ardgour.

Màm Lìrein
"Lìrean's gap" in Mull.

Màm na Céire
"The wax gap" in Morvern.

Màm Ràtagain
"The Ratagan gap" between Kintail and Glenelg.

P

Parallel Roads, Casan a' Ghlinne, Casan Ghlinne Ruaidh *or* Na Casan
This natural feature is referred to as "path of the glen", "path of Glen Roy" or "the paths" in Gaelic. The generic term here is *casan*, an obsolete singular noun meaning "path" which was understood by Gaelic speakers as a plural.

Pass of Ryvoan, An Slugan Shìos
"The eastern defile" leading into Glen More.

S

String Road, An t-Sreang
"The string", signifying a narrow
pass. This is located between Tullich
Hill and Benreoch in
Dunbartonshire.

The Slochd, An Sloc
"The Slochd" or "the pit", between Tomatin and Carrbridge in Inverness-shire.

The Sluggan, An Slugan Shuas
"The western defile", leading into
Glen More.

Hills and Mountains

Although many hill and mountain names are written in an approximate Gaelic form, the spelling is often divergent from accepted modern norms. In such cases below, the generally used form is in bold followed by the name which adheres to Gaelic orthography and is sometimes identical to the widely used form.

A

A' Bhuidheanach Bheag, A' Bhuidheanach Bheag
"The little yellow hill."

A' Chailleach, A' Chailleach
"The old woman."

A' Chaoirnich, A' Chaorthainnich
This name may be connected with rowan berries.

A' Chioch, A' Chìoch
"The breast."

An Coileachan, An Coileachan
"The little cockerel."

A' Choinneach, A' Chòinneach
"The moss."

A' Chralaig, A' Chràlaig
The meaning of this name is unclear.

A' Ghlas-beinn, A' Ghlas Bheinn
"The grey-green mountain."

Ainshval, Ainiseabhal
"Hill of the rocky ridge."

Airgiod Bheinn, Airgead Bheinn
"Silver mountain."

Am Basteir, Am Baisteir *or* Am Bàsadair
"The baptist" or "the executioner", depending on the name's original form.

Am Bathach, Am Bàthach
"The byre."

Am Bodach, Am Bodach
"The old man."

Am Faochagach, Am Faochagach
"The whelk-like mountain."

A' Mhaighdean, A' Mhaighdeann
"The maiden."

A' Mharconich, A' Mharcanaich
"The horse mountain."

Am Màm, Am Màm
"The gap" in Glenorchy.

Am Màm Mór, Am Màm Mór
"The large gap" in the Mamore Forest.

An Caisteal, An Caisteal
"The castle."

An Cruachan, An Cruachan
"The conical hill."

An Dun, An Dùn.
"The (hill)fort."

An Gearanach, An Gearanach
"The complainer."

Angel's Peak, Sgòr an Lochain Uaine
In Gaelic this is "the peak of the green lochan", and it is also given as *Sgor an Lochain Uaine* on maps.

An Riabhachan, An Riabhachan
"The brindled one."

An Ruadh-mheallan, An Ruadh Mheallan
"The small red-brown lumpy hill."

An Sgarsoch, An Sgairseach
"The knotty or fissured hill."

An Sgorr, An Sgòr
"The pinnacle."

An Sidhean, An Sìthean
"The fairy mound."

An Socach, An Socach
"The sow."

An Stac, An Stac
"The stack."

An Stuc, An Stùc
"The exposed rocky steep hill."

An Tudair, An Tughadair
"The thatcher."

Aodann Chleireig, Aodann Chlèireig
The second element in this name is unclear but *aodann* refers to a hill-face.

Aonach air Chrith, Aonach air Chrith
"Shaking steep hill."

Aonach Beag, An t-Aonach Beag
"The small steep hill."

Aonach Buidhe, An t-Aonach Buidhe
"The yellow steep hill."

Aonach Eagach, An t-Aonach Eagach
"The notched steep hill."

Aonach Meadhoin, An t-Aonach Meadhain
"The middle steep hill."

Aonach Mor, An t-Aonach Mór
"The great steep hill."

Aonach Shasuinn, Aonach Shasainn
"The steep hill of the English."

Argyll Hills, Am Monadh Leacanach
"The slabbed hills" north of Inveraray.

Arkle, Airceil *or* Arcail
The first part of this Norse mountain name is unclear.

Askerven, Àisgeirbheinn
This may be "ash field mountain", from Norse/Gaelic.

Askival, Aisgeabhal *or* Asgabhal
"Ash wood hill", from Norse.

Auchnafree Hill
Achadh na Frìthe is "field of the deer forest".

B

Bac an Eich, Bac an Eich
"Hollow of the horse."

Badandun Hill
Bad an Dùin is "place of the hill (fort)".

Baosbheinn, Badhais-bheinn *or* Baoghais-bheinn
This may be "drenched mountain".

Beinn a' Bha'ach Ard, Beinn a' Bhàthaich Àrd
"High mountain of the byre."

Beinn a' Bhuird, Beinn a' Bhùird
"Table mountain."

Beinn a' Bhuiridh, Beinn a' Bhùiridh
"Mountain of bellowing."

Beinn a' Chaisgein Beag, Beinn a' Chaisgein Bheag
"Small mountain of the impediment."

Beinn a' Chaisgein Mor, Beinn a' Chaisgein Mhór
"Large mountain of the impediment."

Beinn a' Chaisteal, Beinn a' Chaisteil
"Castle mountain."

Beinn a' Chaolais, Beinn a' Chaolais
"Mountain of the narrows."

Beinn a' Chaorainn, Beinn a' Chaorthainn
"Rowan mountain."

Beinn a' Chapuill, Beinn a' Chapaill
"Mountain of the horse."

Beinn a' Chearcaill, Beinn a' Chearcaill
"Mountain of the circle."

Beinn a' Chlachain, Beinn a' Chlachain
"Mountain of the kirkton or churchyard."

Beinn a' Chlachair, Beinn a' Chlachair
"The stonemason's mountain."

Beinn a' Chlaidheimh, Beinn a' Chlaidheimh
"Mountain of the sword."

Beinn a' Chleibh, Beinn a' Chléibh
"Creel mountain."

Beinn a' Chochuill, Beinn a' Chochaill
"Husk mountain."

Beinn a' Choin, Beinn a' Choin
"Mountain of the dog."

Beinn a' Chreachain, Beinn a'
Chreachainn
"Mountain with a bare rocky surface."

Beinn a' Chroin, Beinn a' Chroin
This may be "mountain of the cloven
hoof".

Beinn a' Chrulaiste, Beinn a'
Chrùlaiste
"Mountain with a rocky hill."

Beinn a' Chuallaich, Beinn a'
Chuallaich
"Mountain of the cattle (herding)."

Beinn a' Chuirn, Beinn a' Chùirn
"Horn mountain."

Beinn a' Ghlo, Beinn a' Ghlò *or* na
Beinnichean Glotha
The meaning of the second part of
this name is unclear. The second
Gaelic name was used locally.

Beinn a' Mhanaich, Beinn a'
Mhanaich
"Mountain of the monk."

Beinn a' Mheadhoin, Beinn a'
Mheadhain,
"Mountain of the middle."

Beinn a' Mhuinidh *or* Beinn a'
Mhunaidh
"Mountain of the hill range."

Beinn Achaladair, Beinn Ach
Chaladair
"Mountain of Achallater."

Beinn Airigh Charr, Beinn Àirigh a'
Charr
"Mountain with the sheiling at the
rock ledge."

Beinn an Dothaidh, Beinn an
Dòthaidh
"Mountain of singeing or burning."

Beinn an Eoin, Beinn an Eòin
"Bird mountain."

Beinn an Lochain, Beinn an Lochain
"Mountain of the little loch."

Beinn an Oir, Beinn an Òir
"Gold mountain."

Beinn Bhalgairean, Beinn
Bhalgairean
"Mountain of foxes."

Beinn Bhan, A' Bheinn Bhàn
"The white, or fair, mountain."

Beinn Bharrain, Beinn a' Bharrain
"Mountain of the crest."

Beinn Bheag, A' Bheinn Bheag
"The small mountain."

Beinn Bheoil, Beinn a' Bheòil
"Mouth mountain."

Beinn Bhreac, A' Bheinn Bhreac
"The speckled mountain."

Beinn Bhreac-liath, A' Bheinn
Bhreac Liath
"The speckled grey-blue mountain."

Beinn Bhrotain, Beinn a' Bhrodain
"The mountain of the bog."

Beinn Bhuidhe, A' Bheinn Bhuidhe
"The yellow mountain."

Beinn Chabhair, Beinn a' Chabhair
This is said to mean "mountain of
the hawk".

Beinn Challum, Beinn Chaluim
"Calum's mountain."

Beinn Chaorach, Beinn Chaorach
"Sheep mountain."

Beinn Chuirn, Beinn a' Chùirn
"The mountain of the cairn."

Beinn Clachach, A' Bheinn
Chlachach
"The stony mountain."

Beinn Damh, Beinn Damh
"Mountain of stags."

Beinn Damhain, Beinn an Damhain
"Mountain of the spider or little
stag."

Beinn Dearg, A' Bheinn Dearg
"The red mountain."

Beinn Dearg Bheag, A' Bheinn
Dearg Bheag
"The small red mountain."

Beinn Dearg Mhor, A' Bheinn Dearg
Mhór
"The large red mountain."

Beinn Dearg Mor, A' Bheinn Dearg
Mhór
"The large red mountain."

Beinn Dhorain, Beinn Dobhrain
"Mountain of the river."

Beinn Direach, A' Bheinn Dìreach
"The straight mountain."

Beinn Donachain, Beinn Donnchain
"Duncan's mountain."

Beinn Dorain, Beinn Dobhrain
"Mountain of the river."

Beinn Dronaig, Beinn Dronnaig
"Mountain with a small ridge."

Beinn Dubh, A' Bheinn Dubh
"The black mountain."

Beinn Dubhchraig, Beinn Dubh
Chreig
"Mountain of the black rock."

Beinn Each, Beinn Each
"Mountain of horses."

Beinn Eibhinn, Beinn Éibhinn
This is either "pleasant mountain" or
"Éibhinn's mountain", a personal
name.

Beinn Eich, Beinn Eich
"Horse mountain."

Beinn Enaglair, Beinn Eunacleit
"Brow cliff mountain", from Gaelic/
Norse.

Beinn Eunaich, Beinn Eunaich
This may be "hunting, or fowling,
mountain".

Beinn Fhada, A' Bheinn Fhada
"The long mountain."

Beinn Fhionnlaidh, Beinn
Fhionnlaigh
"Finlay's mountain."

Beinn Gaire, Beinn Gàire
"Mountain of the loud noise."

Beinn Ghlas, A' Bheinn Ghlas
"The grey mountain."

Beinn Ghobhlach, A' Bheinn
Ghobhlach
"The forked mountain."

Beinn Heasgarnich, Beinn
Sheasgarnaich
This may be "mountain of the barren
place".

Beinn Iaruinn, Beinn Iarainn
"Iron mountain."

Beinn Ime, Beinn Ime
"Butter mountain."

Beinn Iutharn Bheag, Beinn Iuthairn
Bheag
"Small mountain of hell."

Beinn Iutharn Mhor, Beinn Iuthairn
Mhór
"Large mountain of hell."

Beinn Lair, Beinn Làir
"Mare mountain."

Beinn Leoid, Beinn Leòid
"Ljót's mountain", a Norse personal
name.

Beinn Liath Mhor, A' Bheinn Liath
Mhór
"The large grey-blue mountain."

Beinn Liath Mhor a'Ghiubhais Li,
Beinn Liath Mhór a' Ghiuthais
Léith
"The large grey-blue mountain of
the grey-blue pine tree."

Beinn Liath Mhor Fannich, Beinn
Liath Mhór Fainich
"The large grey-blue mountain of
Fannich."

Beinn Lochain, Beinn an Lochain
"Mountain of the small loch."

Beinn Luibhean, Beinn Luibhean
"Mountain of small plants."

Beinn Maol Chaluim, Beinn Mhaol
Chaluim
"Calum's bare mountain."

Beinn Mhanach, Beinn Mhanach
"Mountain of monks."

Beinn Mheadhoin, A' Beinn
Mheadhain
"The middle mountain."

Beinn Mheadhonach, A' Bheinn
Mheadhanach
"The middle mountain."

Beinn Mhic Chasgaig, Beinn
MhicCasgaig
"MacAskaig's mountain."

Beinn Mhic Mhonaidh, Beinn Mhic
Mhonaidh
"Mountain of the son of the moor."

Beinn MhicCedidh, Beinn
MhicCéidigh
"MacKeady's mountain."

Beinn Mholach, A' Bheinn Mholach
"The grizzled mountain."

Beinn Mhor, A' Bheinn Mhór
"The large mountain."

Beinn na Caillich, Beinn na Caillich
"Mountain of the old woman."

Beinn na Cille, Beinn na Cille
"Mountain of the church."

Beinn na Cloiche, Beinn na Cloiche
"Mountain of the stone."

Beinn na Doire Leithe, Beinn na
Doire Léithe
"Mountain of the grey-blue
oak-grove."

Beinn na Feusaige, Beinn na Feusaig
"Mountain of the beard."

Beinn na Gainimh, Beinn na Gainimh
"Mountain of the sand."

Beinn na Gucaig, Beinn na Gucaig
"Mountain of the acorn."

Beinn na h-Eaglaise, Beinn na
h-Eaglais
"Mountain of the church."

Beinn na h-Uamha, Beinn na
h-Uamha
"Mountain of the cave."

Beinn na Lap, Beinn nan Lap
"Mountain of the spots or dapples."

Beinn nam Fuaran, Beinn nam
Fuaran
"Mountain of the springs."

Beinn na Muice, Beinn na Muice
"Mountain of the pig."

Beinn nan Aighenan, Beinn nan
Aigheanan
"Mountain of the stags."

Beinn nan Caorach, Beinn nan
Caorach
"Mountain of the sheep."

Beinn nan Eun, Beinn nan Eun
"Mountain of the birds."

Beinn nan Imirean, Beinn nan
Iomairean
"Mountain of the riggs."

Beinn nan Lus, Beinn nan Lus
"Mountain of the plants or herbs."

Beinn nan Oighreag, Beinn nan
Oighreag
"Mountain of the cloudberries."

Beinn nan Ramh, Beinn nan Ràmh
"Mountain of the oars."

Beinn Narnain
This name is commonly said to
mean "mountain of the notches" but
the pronunciation suggests *Beinn
Fheàrnain* or *Beinn an Fheàrnain*,
which is "mountain of the alder(s)".

Beinn na Sroine, Beinn na Sròine
"Mountain of the nose."

Beinn Odhar, A' Bheinn Odhar
"The dun-coloured mountain."

Beinn Odhar Bheag, A' Bheinn
Odhar Bheag
"The small dun-coloured mountain."

Beinn Resipol, Beinn Réiseapoil
"Mountain of Resipol."

Beinn Ruadh, A' Bheinn Ruadh
"The red-brown mountain."

Beinn Sgaillinish, Beinn Sgàilinis
"Mountain of Sgaillinish."

Beinn Sgritheall, Beinn Sgritheall
"Scree mountain."

Beinn Sgulaird, Beinn Sgulaird
This name is unclear.

Beinn Shiantaidh, Beinn Shiantaidh
This may be "holy mountain".

Beinn Spionnaidh, Beinn
Spionnaidh
"Mountain of strength or might."

Beinn Suidhe, Beinn Suidhe
"Sitting mountain."

Beinn Talaidh, Beinn Tàlaidh
"Enticing mountain."

Beinn Tarsuinn, Beinn Tarsainn
"Cross mountain."

Beinn Teallach, Beinn Teallach
This appears to be "mountain of the
hearths".

Beinn Tharsuinn, A' Bheinn Tarsainn
"The cross mountain."

Beinn Trilleachan, Beinn Trìlleachan
"Mountain of grey plovers."

Beinn Tulaichean, Beinn Tulaichean
"Mountain of green hills."

Beinn Udlaidh, A' Bheinn Ùdlaidh
"The gloomy mountain."

Beinn Udlamain, Beinn Ùdlamain
"Mountain of the swivel."

Belig, Beilg
This name is unclear.

Ben A'an, Am Binnein
"The pinnacle."

Ben Aden, Beinn Aodainn
"Mountain of the hill face."

Ben Aigan, Beinn Éiginn
"Mountain of extremity."

Ben Alder, Beinn Eallair
"Mountain of the rocky river."

Ben Alligin, Beinn Àiliginn
"Alligin mountain."

Ben Armine, Beinn Àrmainn
"Mountain of the steward or commander."

Ben Arthur, Beinn Artair
This appears to be "Arthur's mountain" but the derivation may lie elsewhere, with an element linked to the name of Arrochar. This mountain is also known as "The Cobbler" and *An Greusaiche Crom*, "the hunched cobbler".

Ben Aslak, Beinn Aslag
This contains a Norse element, possibly a personal name.

Ben Attow, A' Bheinn Fhada
"The long mountain."

Ben Aven, Beinn Athainn
"Mountain of the bright river."

Ben Bhraggie, Beinn Bhragaidh
It is unclear what the second element here means, although *brag* can denote a sharp sound.

Ben Buie, A' Bheinn Bhuidhe
"The yellow mountain."

Ben Challum, Beinn Chaluim
"Calum's mountain."

Ben Chonzie, Beinn Chomhainn
This name may be related to that found in "Glencoe", in which case it may be a tribal name.

Ben Cleuch
"Cleuch" is a Lowland Scots noun denoting a ravine or gully.

Ben Cruachan, Cruachan *or* Cruachan Bheann
"Roughly conical hill" or "roughly conical hill of the mountains". It is said of this mountain, *Teirgidh Cruachan Bheann gun dad a dhol ri cheann*, "Ben Cruachan will wear away if there's nothing put on top of it".

Ben Damph, Beinn Damh
"Mountain of stags."

Ben Donich, Beinn Dòmhnaich
"Mountain of the Lord."

Ben Edra, Beinn Eadarra
The second part of this may be a river name.

Beneveian, Beinn a' Mheadhain
"Mountain in the middle."

Ben Ever, Beinn Eimhir
"Eimhir's mountain."

Ben Gulabin, Beinn Ghulbain
"Beak mountain."

Ben Hee, A' Bheinn Shìth *or* Beinn Shìth
"The magic mountain."

Ben Hope, Beinn Hòb
"The mountain of Hope", referring to the place called *Hòb* or **Hope** in Sutherland.

Ben Hutig, Beinn Hùitig *or* Beinn Phùitig
The second element may be of Norse origin.

Ben Ketland, Beinn Ceiteilein
This name may contain a Brythonic element for "wood".

Ben Klibreck, Beinn Cleithbrig
"Klibreck mountain." See **Klibreck**.

Ben Lawers, Beinn Labhair
"Lawers mountain." See **Lawers**.

Ben Ledi, Beinn Lididh
This name is unclear.

Ben Lomond, Beinn Laomainn
This name may have its origin in a Brythonic term for "beacon".

Ben Loyal, Beinn Laghail
This is "law mountain", from Norse.

Ben Lui, Beinn Laoigh
"Calf mountain."

Ben Macdui, Beinn Mac Duibh
"Mountain of Dubh's son."

Ben More, A' Bheinn Mhór
"The large mountain."

Ben More Assynt, Beinn Mhór Asainte
"Large mountain of Assynt."

Ben More Coigach, Beinn Mhór na Cóigich
"Large mountain of Coigach."

Ben More Mull, Beinn Mhór Mhuile *or* A' Bheinn Mhór Mhuileach
"The large Mull mountain."

Ben Nevis, Beinn Nibheis
This name appears to have been applied in the first instance to the river and has an Indo-European root meaning "wet". It was commonly believed to stem from *uabhas*, "terror", and the area has a forbidding reputation. However, Ben Nevis is rather dismissed in a saying, *Beinn Nibheis mhór a' glaodh-aich na laighe-siubhla 's cha tàinig aiste ach an luchag-fheòir*, "Great Ben Nevis was howling with its birth pains and all that came out of it was a field mouse".

Ben Oss, Beinn Òis
"Mountain at the river mouth", from Gaelic/Norse.

Ben Rinnes, Beinn Ruaidhneis
"Mountain at the red-brown haugh."

Ben Stack, Beinn Stac
"Stack mountain", from Gaelic/Norse.

Ben Starav, Beinn Starabh
This may contain a personal name but is unclear.

Ben Tee, Beinn an t-Sithidh
"Mountain of the blast."

Ben Tirran
This name is unclear.

Benula, Beinn Fhionnlaigh
"Finlay's mountain."

Ben Vair, Beinn a' Bheithir
"Serpent mountain."

Ben Vane, A' Bheinn Mheadhain
"The middle mountain."

Ben Venue, A' Bheinn Mheanbh
"The tiny mountain."

Ben Vorlich, Beinn Mhùrlaig
"Mountain at the inlet."

Ben Vrackie, Beinn a' Bhreacaidh
"Mountain of the speckled stream."

Ben Vuirich, Beinn a' Bhùraich *or* Beinn Bhùraich nam Madadh Móra
"Mountain of bellowing" or "mountain of the bellowing of the great wolves or hounds".

Ben Wyvis, Beinn Uais
This may stem from *uabhas*, "terror".

Benyellary, Beinn na hIolaire
"Eagle mountain."

Ben y Hone, Beinn a' Chòinnich
"Moss mountain."

Bidean a' Ghlas-Thuill, Bidean a' Ghlas Thuill
"Pinnacle of the grey hole."

Bidean an Eoin Deirg, Bidean an Eòin Deirg
"Pinnacle of the red bird."

Bidean nam Bian, Bidean nam Bian
"Pinnacle of the hides."

Bidein a' Chabair, Bidean a' Chabair
"Pinnacle of the antler."

Bidein a' Choire Sheasgaich, Bidean a' Choire Sheasgaich
"Pinnacle of the barren, or reedy, corrie."

Binnein an Fhidhleir, Binnein an Fhìdhleir
"Fiddler's pinnacle."

Binnein Beag, Am Binnein Beag
"The small pinnacle."

Binnein Mor, Am Binnein Mór
"The large pinnacle."

Binnein Shios, Am Binnein Shìos
"Easter pinnacle."

Binnein Shuas, Am Binnein Shuas
"Wester pinnacle."

Biod an Fhithich *or* Bioda an Fhithich
"Hill top of the raven."

Birnam Hill, Branac
The Gaelic name is of unclear origin.

Black Corries, Na Coireacha Dubha
Both names mean the same.

Black Mount, Am Monadh Dubh
"The black mount or range of hills."

Blath Bhalg, Blàth Bhalg
This may be "bag-shaped place of blossom". See **Blebo** in the Settlement section.

Blaven, Blàbheinn
"Blue mountain", from Norse/Gaelic.

Bleaton Hill, Monadh Phladain
"The hill of Bleaton or *Pladan*", which is unclear. Locally the name was pronounced *Mon Phladain*.

Boar of Badenoch, An Torc
"The boar." Nearby is the Sow of
Atholl.

Brack, The, Am Breac
"The speckled one."

Braeriach, Am Bràigh Riabhach
"The brindled upland."

Braes of Greenock, Bràigh Ghrianaig
"Upper part of Greenock."

Braid Hills
"Braid" here either means "broad" or
comes from *bràigh*, "upper part", as
found in "Breadalbane". These are
thought to be the hills recorded as
Monadh Éideann, "upland of Eidyn".

Braigh Coire Chruinn-bhalgain,
Bràigh Coire a' Chruinn Bhalgain
"Upper part of the corrie of the
round bag."

Braigh nan Uamhachan, Bràigh nan
Uamhachan
"Upland of the caves."

Breabag
If this name is Norse it is "broad
bank" and if Gaelic it is unclear, but
suggests a kick or blow.

Broad Cairn, Càrn Bràghaid
"Upland cairn."

Brown Cow Hill, A' Bhó Dhonn
"The brown cow."

Bruach na Frithe, Bruthach na Frìthe
"Brae of the deer forest."

Buachaille Etive Beag, Buachaille
Éite Beag
"The small shepherd of Etive."

Buachaille Etive Mor, Buachaille
Éite Mór
"The large shepherd of Etive."

Buck, The, Am Boc
"The buck."

Buidheanach Bheag, A'
Bhuidheanach Bheag
"The small yellow hill."

Bynack Beg, A' Bheithneag Bheag
"The small little mountain."

Bynack More, A' Bheithneag Mhór *or*
Beinn Bheithneag
"The large little mountain."

C

Cac Carn Beag, Cadha a' Chàirn
Beag
"Small pass at the cairn."

Cac Carn Mor, Cadha a' Chàirn
Mór
"Large pass at the cairn."

Caenlochan, Cadha an Lochain
"Path at the small loch."

Cairn Bannoch, An Càrn Beannach
"The pointed cairn or hill."

Cairn Dye, Càrn an Tàilleir
This appears to be "tailor's hill", but
the origin of the name may be older
and obscure.

Cairngorm, An Càrn Gorm
"The blue hill."

Cairngorms, Am Monadh Ruadh
"The red-brown mountain range",
which contrasts with *am Monadh
Liath*, "the grey-blue mountain
range", nearby.

Cairn Lochan, Càrn an Lochain
"Cairn or hill at the small
loch."

Cairn of Claise, Càrn na Claise
"Cairn or hill with a furrow."

Cairn of Gowal, Càrn a' Ghobhail
"The forked cairn or hill."

Cairn O'Mount, Càrn Mhon
"Cairn at the hill range."

Cairnsgarroch, An Càrn Sgarach
"The fissured cairn or hill."

Cairntoul, Càrn an t-Sabhail
"Hill or cairn of the barn."

Cairnwell, Càrn a' Bhalg *or* An Càrn
Bhailg
"Bag-shaped hill or cairn."

Caisteal Abhail, Caisteal Ghabhail
"Forked castle."

Cam Chreag, Cam Chreag
"Bent or distorted rock."

Campsie Fells
These hills in the Campsie area are
thought to be those referred to as
am Monadh Beannach, "the peaked
range of hills".

Canisp, Canasp
This name is unclear.

Carlownie Hill
This is thought to be "elm fort", from *Cathair Leamhnach*.

Carn a' Chaochain, Càrn a' Chaochain
"Hill or cairn of the small stream."

Carn a' Chlamhain, Càrn a' Chlamhain
"Hawk hill or cairn."

Carn a' Choin Deirg, Càrn a' Choin Deirg
"Hill or cairn of the red dog."

Carn a'Choire Bhoidheach, Càrn a' Choire Bhòidhich
"Hill or cairn at the beautiful corrie."

Carn a' Choire Ghairbh, Càrn a' Choire Ghairbh
"Hill or cairn at the rough corrie."

Carn a' Chuilinn, Càrn a' Chuilinn
"Holly hill or cairn."

Carn a' Gheoidh, Càrn a' Gheòidh
"Goose hill or cairn."

Carn a' Ghille Chearr, Càrn a' Ghille Cheàrr
This appears to be "hill or cairn of the wrong boy", but *ceàrr* can also mean left-handed.

Carn a' Ghlas-uillt, Càrn a' Ghlas Uillt
"Hill or cairn of the grey stream."

Carn a' Mhaim, Càrn a' Mhàim
"Hill or cairn at the pass."

Carnan Cruithneachd, Càrnan Cruithneachd
This seems in its current form to mean "small hill or cairn of wheat" but originally may have been *Càrn nan Cruithneach*, "hill or cairn of the Picts".

Carn an Fhreiceadain, Càrn an Fhreiceadain
"Hill or cairn of the guard."

Carn an Righ, Càrn an Rìgh
"King's hill or cairn."

Carn an Tionail, Càrn an Tionail
"Hill or cairn of the gathering."

Carn an t-Sagairt Beag, Càrn an t-Sagairt Beag
"Priest's small hill or cairn."

Carn an t-Sagairt Mor, Càrn an t-Sagairt Mór
"Priest's large hill or cairn."

Carn an Tuirc, Càrn an Tuirc
"Boar's hill or cairn."

Carn Aosda, Càrn Aonghais
"Angus's hill or cairn."

Carn Ballach, An Càrn Ballach
"The ragged hill or cairn."

Carn Ban, An Càrn Bàn
"The white hill or cairn."

Carn Ban Mor, An Càrn Bàn Mór
"The large white hill or cairn."

Carn Bhac, Càrn a' Bhac
"Hill or cairn at the hollow."

Carn Bhinnein, Càrn a' Bhinnein
"Hill or cairn of the pinnacle."

Carn Breac, An Càrn Breac
"The speckled hill or cairn."

Carn Bhren, Càrn Bhrein
"Hill or cairn of rottenness."

Carn Chuinneag, Càrn Chuinneag
"Hill or cairn of the milking pails."

Carn Dearg, An Càrn Dearg
"The red hill or cairn."

Carn Dearg Meadhonach, An Càrn Dearg Meadhanach
"The middle red hill or cairn."

Carn Dearg Mor, An Càrn Dearg Mór
"The large red hill or cairn."

Carn Ealar, Càrn an Fhìdhleir
"Fiddler's hill or cairn."

Carn Ealasaid, Càrn Ealasaid
"Elizabeth's hill or cairn."

Carn Eas, Càrn an Eas
"Hill or cairn at the waterfall."

Carn Easgann Bana, Càrn nan Easgann Bàna
"Hill or cairn of the white eels."

Carn Eighe, Càrn Eighe
This may be "icy hill or cairn".

Carn Etchachan, Càrn Éiteachain
This may be "hill or cairn of the little foul one" including an element found in the river name *Éite*, or Etive.

Carn Ghluasaid, Càrn a' Ghluasaid
"Hill or cairn of movement."

Carn Glas-choire, Carn a' Ghlas
Choire
"Hill or cairn of the grey-green
corrie."

Carn Gorm, An Càrn Gorm
"The blue hill or cairn."

Carn Liath, An Càrn Liath
"The grey-blue hill or cairn."

Carn Loch nan Amhaichean, Càrn
Loch nan Amhaichean
"Hill or cairn of the loch of the
necks."

Carn Mairg, Càrn Mairg
"Merk cairn."

Carn Mhic an Toisich, Càrn Mhic
an Tòisich
"Macintosh's hill or cairn."

Carn Mor, An Càrn Mór
"The large hill or cairn."

Carn Mor Dearg, An Càrn Mór Dearg
"The large red hill or cairn."

Carn na Baintighearna, Càrn na
Baintighearna
"The lady's hill or cairn."

Carn na Breabaig, Càrn na Breabaig
This appears to be "hill or cairn of
the little kick".

Carn na Caim, Càrn na Caim
"Hill or cairn of the bend."

Carn na Coinnich, Càrn na Còinnich
"Hill or cairn of the moss."

Carn na Coire Mheadhoin, Càrn na
Coire Meadhain
"Hill or cairn at the middle corrie."

Carn na Con Dhu, Càrn nan Con
Dubh
"Hill or cairn of the black dogs."

Carn na Criche, Càrn na Crìche
"Hill or cairn at the boundary."

Carn na Drochaide, Càrn na
Drochaide
"Hill or cairn at the bridge."

Carn na h-Easgainn, Càrn na
h-Easgainn
"Hill or cairn of the eel."

Carn nam Fiaclan, Càrn nam Fiaclan
"Toothed hill or cairn."

Carn na Nathrach, Càrn na Nathrach
"Hill or cairn of the snake."

Carn nan Gabhar, Càrn nan Gobhar
"Hill or cairn of the goats."

Carn nan Gobhar, Càrn nan Gobhar
"Hill or cairn of the goats."

Carn nan Tri-tighearnan, Càrn nan
Trì Tighearnan
"Hill or cairn of the three lords."

Carn na Saobhaidhe, Càrn na
Saobhaidhe
"Hill or cairn at the lair."

Carn Salachaidh, Càrn Shalachaidh
"Hill or cairn of Sallachy."

Carn Sgulain, Càrn Sgùlain
"Basket-shaped hill or cairn."

Ceann na Baintighearna, Ceann na
Baintighearna
"The lady's head."

Chno Dearg, A' Chnò Dhearg
This appears to be "the red nut" but
the name may have an earlier different form.

Cir Mhor, A' Chìr Mhór
"The large comb."

Ciste Dhubh, A' Chiste Dhubh
"The black chest."

Clisham, An Cliseam
The meaning of this name is unclear.

Cnap a' Chleirich, Cnap a' Chléirich
"The cleric's lumpy hill."

Cnap Chaochan Aitinn, Cnap a'
Chaochan Aitinn
"Lumpy hill of the juniper stream."

Cnap Coire na Spreidhe, Cnap Coire
na Spréidhe
"Lumpy hill at the cattle corrie."

Cnap Cruinn, An Cnap Cruinn
"The round lumpy hill."

Cnoc Coinnich, Cnoc Còinnich
"Hill of moss."

Cobbler, An Greusaiche Crom
The Gaelic name is "the hunched
cobbler" and this mountain is also
known as **Ben Arthur**.

Coinneach Mhor, A' Chòinneach
Mhór
"The large moss."

Conachraig, Conachreag
"Hound rock."

Conival, Conamheall *or* Conabhal

The spelling of the first Gaelic form looks as though the name means "hound hill". However, the name is Norse and contains *fjall*, "mountain", but the first part is unclear and may be related to that which appears in the village name **Connista**.

Cook's Cairn, Càrn MhicCùga
"MacCook's hill."

Corra-bheinn, Corra Bheinn
"Uneven mountain."

Corrag Bhuidhe, A' Chorrag Bhuidhe
"The yellow index finger."

Corryhabbie Hill
Although of Gaelic origin, the second element of this name is unclear.

Corwharn
This may be *Corr Chàrn*, "uneven hill or cairn", or *Coire a' Chàirn*, "corrie of the cairn or hill".

Cowie Hill, Mon Chollaigh
"The hill at the hazel place."

Craig a' Chaorainn, Creag a' Chaorthainn
"Rowan rock."

Craig an Loch, Creag an Locha
"Rock by the loch."

Craig Coire na Fiar Bhealaich, Creag Coire na Fiar Bhealaich
"Rock at the corrie by the crooked pass."

Craig Dubh, A' Chreag Dhubh
"The black rock."

Craig Leek, Creag Lic
"Slab rock."

Craignaw
"Rock of waters", from *Creag n-Abha*, or "rock of the water", from *Creag an Abha*.

Craig of Gowal, Creag a' Ghobhail
"The forked, or split rock."

Craigowl Hill, Creag a' Ghobhail
"The forked or split rock."

Cranstackie, Cranstacaidh
This is said to mean "rugged stack", but the first element of the name is unclear.

Creach Beinn, Creach Bheinn
"Hill of plunder."

Creach Bheinn, Creach Bheinn
"Hill of plunder."

Creag a' Mhadaidh, Creag a' Mhadaidh
"Rock of the wolf."

Creag a' Mhaim, Creag a' Mhàim
"Rock at the pass."

Creagan a' Chaise, Creagan a' Chaise
"Little rock of the steepness."

Creagan a' Choire Etchachan, Creagan Choire Éiteachain
This may be "little rock of the corrie of the foul one". See **Carn Etchachan**.

Creagan na Beinne, Creagan na Beinne
"Rocks of the mountain."

Creag Bhalg, Creag Bhalg
"Rock of the bag shapes."

Creag Dhubh, A' Chreag Dhubh
"The black rock."

Creag Dhubh Mhor, A' Chreag Dhubh Mhór
"The big black rock."

Creag Each, Creag Each
"Rock of horses."

Creag Gharbh, A' Chreag Gharbh
"The rough rock."

Creag Ghuanach, A' Chreag Ghuanach
"The unsteady rock."

Creag Leacach, A' Chreag Leacach
"The slabbed rock."

Creag Liath, A' Chreag Liath
"The grey-blue rock."

Creag MacRanaich, Creag MhicRànaich
"MacRanaich's rock", but this surname is unusual.

Creag Meagaidh
"The rock at the boggy place."

Creag Mhor, A' Chreag Mhór
"The large rock."

Creag nan Damh, Creag nan Damh
"Rock of the stags."

Creag nan Gabhar, Creag nan Gobhar
"Rock of the goats."

Creag Pitridh, Creag Pitridh
"Petrie's rock."

Creag Rainich, Creag Rainich
"Bracken rock."

Creag Ruadh, A' Chreag Ruadh
"The red-brown rock."

Creag Tharsuinn, Creag Tharsainn
"Cross or over rock."

Creag Uanach
See **Creag Ghuanach**.

Creag Uchdag, Creag Uchdag
"Rock of small slopes."

Creise, Clach Leathad
The Gaelic name is "stone slope"
while the more common name is
from Gaelic for "grease, or fat".

Croit Bheinn, Croit Bheinn
"Hillock mountain", or "hump-
backed mountain".

Cruach an t-Sidhein, Cruach an
t-Sìthein
"Conical hill of the faiy mound."

Cruach Ardrain, Cruach Àrdrain
"Conical hill of the Ardran", as in
Inverardran.

Cruach Coireadail, Cruach
Choireadail
"Conical hill of Coireadal."

Cruach Innse, Cruach Innse
"Conical hill of Inch."

Cruach nam Mult, Cruach nam Mult
"Conical hill of the wedders."

Cruinn a' Bheinn, Cruinne Bheinn
"Rounded mountain."

Cruach nan Capull, Cruach nan
Capall
"Conical hill of the horses."

Cuidhe Crom, An Cuidhe Crom
"The bent fold."

Cuillins, An Cuiltheann
There have been many attempts at
interpreting this name but none
have proved satisfactory.

Cuillins of Rum, An Cuiltheann
Rumach
See **Cuillins**.

Culardoch, Cùl Àrdaich
"Back of the high place", but *cùl* was
used poetically to refer to long flowing hair and perhaps that sense is
intended here.

Cul Beag, A' Chuthaill Bheag
This may be of Norse origin,
containing *kvi*, "enclosure", and *fjall*,
"mountain", then qualified by Gaelic
beag, "small".

Cùl Mhàm, Cùl Mhàm
"The back gap", in Morvern.

Cul Mor, A' Chuthaill Mhór
This may be of Norse origin,
containing *kvi*, "enclosure", and *fjall*,
"mountain", then qualified by Gaelic
mòr, "large".

D

Dagrum, An Dà Dhruim
"The two ridges."

Dechmont
This is said to be *Deagh Mhonadh*,
"good hill", but see **Dechmont** in
the Settlements section.

Derry Cairngorm, Càrn Gorm an
Doire
"The blue hill or cairn of the
oak-grove."

Devil's Point, Bod an Deamhain
"The devil's penis" in Gaelic.

Doune Hill
"Hill of the Doune", which itself
means a hill, or hill fort.

Driesh, Drìs
This is said to be "thorn", but the
long vowel in the Gaelic name goes
against this.

Druim Fada, An Druim Fada
"The long ridge."

Druim nan Cnamh, Druim nan
Cnàmh
"Ridge of the bones."

Druim na Sgriodain, Druim na
Sgrìodain
"Ridge of the scree."

Druim Shionnach, Druim Shionnach
"Ridge of foxes."

Druim Tarsuinn, Druim Tarsainn
"Cross ridge."

Drumalban, Druim Albann
"The ridge of Scotland."

Duchray Hill, Meall nan Leitir
The names in the two languages are

different, the Gaelic name being "lumpy hill of the broad slopes".

Dumbarton Rock, Ail Chluaidh
The Gaelic name is "rock of the Clyde" and this was the capital of the Brythonic people of Strathclyde.

Dun Caan, Dùn Càna
This is said to be "white hill".

Dun da Ghaoidhe, Dùn Dà Ghaoithe
"Hill of the two winds."

E

Eididh nan Clach Geala, Éididh nan Clach Geala
This appears to be "web of the white stones".

F

Fafernie, Féith Feàrnaidh
"Boggy channel at the alder place", or "boggy channel of the alder stream".

Faochagach, Am Faochagach
"The whelk-like one."

Faochaig, Faochaig
This name may be connected to *faochag*, "whelk".

Fara, Am Fàradh
"The ladder."

Farragon Hill, Cnoc Fheargain
"Feargan's hill."

Fashven, Faisbheinn
This may be "mountain of the stance".

Fiarach, Feurach
"Grassy place."

Fionn Bheinn, Fionn Bheinn
"White mountain."

Firmounth, Am Monadh Giuthais
"The pine hill."

Five Sisters of Kintail, Beanntan Chinn Tàile *or* Peathraichean Chinn Tàile
The first Gaelic name is simply "the Kintail mountains", while the second is "the sisters of Kintail" and may have been influenced by the English name.

Foinaven, Foinne Bheinn
"Wart mountain."

Fonab Hill, An Suidhe
In English the hill is named after Fonab nearby, but the Gaelic name is "the seat".

Fourman Hill, Fuar Mhon *or* Fuar Mhonadh
"Cold hill."

Fraochaidh, Fraochaidh
"Heather place."

Fraoch Bheinn, Fraoch Bheinn
"Heather mountain."

Fuar Tholl, Fuar Tholl
"Cold crevice."

G

Gairbeinn, Garbh Bheinn
"Rough mountain."

Gairich, Gàirich
"Howling, or roaring."

Garbhanach, An Garbhanach
"The rough little one."

Garbh Bheinn, Garbh Bheinn
"Rough mountain."

Garbh Chioch Mhor, Garbh Chìoch Mhór
"Great rough breast."

Garelet Hill, Geàrr Leathad
"Short slope."

Geal-charn, Geal Chàrn
"White hill or cairn."

Geal-charn Mor, Geal Chàrn Mór
"Large white hill or cairn."

Gearanach, An Gearanach
This may be "the moaning one".

Glamaig, Glàmaig
This is said to be "deep gorge".

Glas Bheinn, Glas Bheinn
"Grey-green mountain."

Glas Bheinn Mhor, Glas Bheinn Mhór
"Large grey-green mountain."

Glas-charn, Glas Chàrn
"Grey-green hill or cairn."

Glas Maol, Glas Mheall
"Grey-green lumpy hill."

Glas Tulaichean, Glas Thulaichean
"Grey-green low hills."

Glen Quoich Hills, Monadh Chuaich
In Gaelic this is the "Quoich range".

Gleouraich, Gleadhraich
The Gaelic name suggests "great noise".

Goat Fell, Gaoda Bheinn
This is said to be "windy mountain", but the first element may be Norse.

Grampians, Am Monadh
The English name comes from a misreading of Latin *Mons Graupius*, while the Gaelic name is "the mountain range". East of Drumochter the hills are called *Monadh Miongaig*, "the Minigaig range", and to the west they are *Monadh Dhruim Uachdair*, "the Drumochter range".

Great Knock, An Cnoc Mór
"The large hill."

Groban, An Gnoban
"Little hillock."

Gulvain, Gaor Bheinn
The meaning of this name is unclear.

H

Hartaval, Hartabhal
"Hart hill", from Norse.

Hill of Fare, Fàir Mhon
The first element in the Gaelic name suggests the horizon, or a wide view, while the second reflects the local pronunciation of the common element *monadh* used widely in the north-east in place of *beinn*.

I

Inaccessible Pinnacle, An Stac
The modern English name has largely replaced the Gaelic name meaning "stack", or "pillar".

K

Kelman Hill, Caol Mhon *or* Caol Mhonadh
"Slender hill."

Knockmore Hill, An Cnoc Mór
"The large hill."

Knock of Alves, Cnoc na h-Àbhais
"The hill of Alves."

L

Ladder Hills, Monadh an Fhàraidh
The English name is a translation from Gaelic.

Ladhar Bheinn, Ladhar Bheinn
"Hoof mountain."

Ladylea Hill
This may be "the grey-blue slope", from *An Leathad Liath*.

Largo Law
Old forms of the name such as "Knocklargauch" show this to be from *Cnoc Leargach*, "the hill of Largo".

Lamentation Hill, Creag a' Chòinneachain
The Gaelic name is "the rock of moss" and the English is a mistranslation, replacing *còinneach*, "moss", with *caoineadh*, "lamenting".

Leana Mhor, An Lèana Mhór
"The big meadow."

Leathad an Taobhain, Leathad an Taobhain
"Slope of the rib, or rafter."

Leum Uilleim, Leum Uilleim
"William's leap."

Liathach, An Liaghaich
This may stem from *liath*, "grey-blue".

Lochnagar, Beinn Chìochain
The English form is from the loch at the mountain and is said to be from *Loch na Gàire*, "loch of the loud noise". The Gaelic name is "mountain of the little breast".

Lomond Hills, Cuspairean Ualais
The English form may be related to the element found in "Ben Lomond", meaning "beacon". The Gaelic name looks as though it means "Wallace's objects", but *ualais* may be a metathesis of *uasal* and may ultimately be related to "Ochil".

Luinne Bheinn, Luinne Bheinn
This may be "angry or unpredictable mountain".

Lurg Mhor, An Lurg Mhór
"The large ridge gradually extending to a plain."

M

Mam na Gualainn, Màm na Gualainn
"Gap of the shoulder or ridge."

Mamore, Am Màm Mór
"The large gap", referring to a pass.

Mam Sodhail, Màm Sabhail
"Gap of the barn."

Mannoch Hill, Cnoc nam Manach
"The monks' hill."

Maoile Lunndaidh, Maoile Lunndaidh
"Bare hill of Lundy."

Maol Chean-dearg, Maol Cheann Dearg
"Blunt red head."

Maovally, Maobhalaidh
This name is unclear.

Marsco, Marsgo
This seems to be "sea wood", from Norse.

Mayar
This name and its origins are obscure.

Meall a' Bhuachaille, Meall a' Bhuachaille
"Lumpy hill of the herdsman."

Meall a' Bhuiridh, Meall a' Bhùiridh
"Lumpy hill of the bellowing."

Meall a' Chaorainn, Meall a' Chaorthainn
"Lumpy hill of the rowan."

Meall a' Choire Leith, Meall a' Choire Léith
"Lumpy hill of the grey-blue corrie."

Meall a' Chrasgaidh, Meall a' Chrasgaidh
"Lumpy hill of the crossing place."

Meall a' Chrathaich, Meall a' Chrathaich
This appears to be "lumpy hill of the shaking".

Meall a' Churain, Meall a' Churrain
"Lumpy hill of the carrot."

Meall a' Ghiubhais, Meall a' Ghiuthais
"Lumpy hill of the fir or pine."

Meall a' Mhuic, Mealla Mhuicey
"Lumpy hill of the pig river." See **Inverwick** (Perth).

Meall a' Phubuill, Meall a' Phubaill
"Lumpy hill of the pavilion, or tent."

Meall an Fheur Loch, Meall an Fheur Loch
"Lumpy hill of the grassy loch."

Meall an Fhudair, Meall an Fhùdair
"Lumpy hill of the powder."

Meall an t-Seallaidh, Meall an t-Seallaidh
"Lumpy hill of the view."

Meallan a' Chuail, Meallan a' Chuail
"Small lumpy hill of the bundle (of sticks)."

Meallan Liath Coire Mhic Dhughaill, Meallan Liath Coire MhicDhùghaill
"Grey-blue lumpy hill at MacDougall's corrie."

Meallan nan Uan, Meallan nan Uan
"Small lumpy hill of the lambs."

Meall Blair, Meall a' Bhlàir
"Lumpy hill of the plain."

Meall Buidhe, Am Meall Buidhe
"The yellow lumpy hill."

Meall Chuaich, Meall Chuaich
"Lumpy hill of the hollow."

Meall Corranaich, Meall Corranaich
It is unclear what the second element of this name means.

Meall Dearg, Am Meall Dearg
"The red lumpy hill."

Meall Doire Faid, Meall Doire Fàid
"Lumpy hill of the furrowed oak grove."

Meall Dubh, Am Meall Dubh
"The black lumpy hill."

Meall Dubhag, Meall Dubhaig
"The lumpy hill at the black stream."

Meall Fuarvonie, Meall Fuar Mhonaidh
"Lumpy hill of the cold range of hills."

Meall Garbh, Am Meall Garbh
"The rough lumpy hill."

Meall Ghaordie, Meall Ghaoirdidh
The second part of this name is
unclear.

Meall Glas, Am Meall Glas
"The grey-green lumpy hill."

Meall Glas-Choire, Meall Ghlas
Choire
"The lumpy hill at the grey-green
corrie."

Meall Gorm, Am Meall Gorm
"The blue lumpy hill."

Meall Greigh, Meall Greighe
"Lumpy hill of the herd, or flock."

Meall Horn, Meall Horn
"Lumpy hill of the horn", from
Gaelic/Norse. A more purely Norse
version of the name can be seen in
Hornabhal, or Horneval in Skye.

Meall Lighiche, Meall an Lighiche
"Lumpy hill of the doctor."

Meall Mor, Am Meall Mór
"The large lumpy hill."

Meall na Faochaig, Meall na Faochaig
"Lumpy hill of the whelk."

Meall na Fearna, Meall na Feàrna
"Lumpy hill of the alder."

Meall na h-Aisre, Meall na h-Aisre
"Lumpy hill of the path."

Meall na h-Eilde, Meall na h-Éilde
"Lumpy hill of the hind."

Meall na Leitreach, Meall na
Leitreach
"Lumpy hill of the broad slope."

Meall na Meoig, Meall na Meòig
"Lumpy hill of the whey."

Meall nam Maigheach, Meall nam
Maigheach
"Lumpy hill of the hares."

Meall nan Aighean, Meall nan
Aighean
"Lumpy hill of the stags."

Meall nan Caorach, Meall nan
Caorach
"Lumpy hill of the sheep."

Meall nan Ceapraichean, Meall nan
Ceapraichean
"Lumpy hill of the stumpy hillocks."

Meall nan Damh, Meall nan Damh
"Lumpy hill of the stags."

Meallan nan Eagan, Meall nan
Eagan
"Lumpy hill of the notches."

Meall nan Eun, Meall nan Eun
"Lumpy hill of the birds."

Meall nan Gabhar, Meall nan
Gobhar
"Lumpy hill of the goats."

Meall nan Subh, Meall nan Subh
"Lumpy hill of the berries."

Meall Odhar, Am Meall Odhar
"The dun-coloured lumpy
hill."

Meall Onfhaidh, Meall Onfhaidh
"Blustery lumpy hill."

Meall Reamhar, Am Meall Reamhar
"The fat lumpy hill."

Meall nan Tarmachan, Meall nan
Tarmachan
"Lumpy hill of the ptarmigans."

Meall na Teanga, Meall na Teanga
"Lumpy hill of the tongue."

Meall Tairbh, Meall Tairbh
"Lumpy hill of the bull."

Meall Tairneachan, Meall
Tàirneachain
This name may be connected with
thunder.

Meaul, Am Meall
"The lumpy hill."

Meikle Pap, A' Chìoch Mhór
"The large breast."

Meith Bheinn, Mèith Bheinn
"Fat mountain."

Merrick
This may stem from *meur* (finger),
but is unclear.

Millfore
This is probably "cold lumpy hill",
from *Am Meall Fuar.*

Monadh Fergie, Monadh Fheargaidh
"Hill of the angry river."

Monadh Mor, Am Monadh Mór
"The big hill."

Mona Gowan
"Stirk hill", from *Mon(adh) a'
Ghamhainn.*

Monamenach, Am Monadh
Meadhanach
"The middle hill."

Monega, Mon Agha
The second part of this name is
unclear.

Mormond Hill, Mór Mhon *or* Mór
Mhonadh
"Large hill."

Morrone, Mór Bheinn
"Large mountain."

Moruisg, Mórusg
This name is unclear.

Morven, Mór Bheinn
"Large mountain."

Mount Battock
This may be "hill of the small tufts
of heather", from *Mon Badag.*

Mount Blair
"Hill of the plain", from *Mon(adh) a'
Bhlàir.*

Mount Eagle, Cnoc na h-Iolaire
"Hill of the eagle."

Mounth, Am Monadh
"The mountain range." This is an
alternative name for the Grampians.

Mount Keen, Mon Caoin
"Gentle hill."

Mullach an Rathain, Mullach an
Ràthain
"Summit of the small circular fort."

Mullach Clach a' Bhlair, Mullach
Clach a' Bhlàir
"Summit of the stone of the field or
battle."

Mullach Coire Mhic Fhearchair,
Mullach Coire MhicFhearchair
"Summit of Farquharson's
corrie."

Mullach Coire nan Geur-oirean,
Mullach Coire nan Geur Oirean
"Summit of the corrie of the sharp
edges."

Mullach Fraoch-choire, Mullach
Fraoch Choire
"Summit of heather corrie."

Mullach na Dheiragain, Mullach
nan Dearganan
"Summit of the kestrels."

Mullach nan Coirean, Mullach nan
Coirean
"Summit of the corries."

Mullwharchar, Maol Fhearchair
"Farquhar's blunt hill."

N

Na Gruagaichean, Na Gruagaichean
"The maidens."

O

Ochil Hills, Sliabh Ochaill *or* Na
Foicheallan
"Ochil" and *Ochaill* are from
Brythonic *uchel,* "high", which is
related to *uasal,* "noble". *Sliabh* is not
commonly used to refer to a hill in
Scotland although this is its
common meaning in Ireland. The
second name shows a not uncommon feature of Gaelic, where an
initial "f" is added to an existing
word.

Old Man of Storr, Bodach an Stòrr
The English form is a translation
from Gaelic, which itself is a euphe-
mism for *Bod an Stòrr,* "the penis of
Storr".

Ord Hill, An t-Òrd
"The rounded hill."

Oreval, Oireabhal
This may be "Orri's hill", from
Norse.

Ormond Hill, Cnoc Mhoire
The English form may contain
monadh, or its pre-Gaelic equivalent
for "hill". The Gaelic name is "St
Mary's hill".

P

Pap of Glencoe, Sgùrr na Cìche
In Gaelic this is "peak of the breast".

Paps of Jura, Beanntan Dhiùra
These breast-shaped hills are called
"the Jura mountains" in Gaelic.

Parallel Roads, Casan a' Ghlinne,
Casan Ghlinne Ruaidh *or* Na Casan
This natural feature is referred to as
"path of the glen", "path of Glen

Roy", or "the paths" in Gaelic. The generic term here is *casan*, an obsolete singular noun meaning "path", which was understood by Gaelic speakers as a plural.

Parlan Hill, Beinn Phàrlain
"Parlan's mountain." *Pàrlan* is often rendered as "Bartholomew" in English and is the name of the progenitor of the MacFarlane clan, *Clann MhicPhàrlain.* This hill is in the traditional lands of the MacFarlane clan near Loch Lomond.

Plock of Kyle, Ploc a' Chaoil
"The pimple of Kyle."

Pressendye
Although of Gaelic origin, this name is unclear but may derive from *Preas an Taighe,* "the bush of the house". There may be other more plausible derivations.

Pulpit Hill (Oban), Crannag a' Mhinisteir
The Gaelic name is "the minister's pulpit".

Pulpit Rock (Tarbet Loch Lomond), Clach nan Tarbh
The Gaelic name is "the stone of the bulls".

Q

Quinag, A' Chuinneag
"The milk pail."

Quirang, A' Chuith-raing
This name is unclear. This range is known as *A' Bheinne Mhóir,* "the big mountain", in Wester Ross Gaelic.

R

Ravens Craig (Cumbrae), Creag nam Fitheach
The names mean the same in both languages.

Roineaval, Ròineabhal
"Rough hill", from Norse.

Roshven, Roisbheinn
"Horse mountain", from Norse/ Gaelic.

Ruadh-stac Beag, Ruadh Stac Beag
"Small red-brown stack."

Ruadh-stac Mor, Ruadh Stac Mór
"Large red-brown stack."

S

Sabhal Beag, Sàbhal Beag
"Small saw mountain."

Saddle, An Dìollaid
The English name is a translation from Gaelic.

Sail Chaorainn, Sàil a' Chaorthainn
"The rowan heel."

Saileag, An t-Sàileag
"The small heel."

Sail Gharbh, An t-Sàil Gharbh
"The rough heel."

Sail Gorm, An t-Sàil Ghorm
"The blue heel."

Sail Liath, An t-Sàil Liath
"The grey-blue heel."

Sail Mhor, An t-Sàil Mhór
"The large heel."

Salisbury Crags, Creag nam Marbh
The Gaelic name of these crags at Arthur's Seat in Edinburgh is "the craig of the dead".

Saval, Sàbhal
"Saw mountain", from Norse.

Scaraben, Sgaire Bheinn
"Notched mountain", from Norse/ Gaelic.

Schiehallion, Sìth Chailleann
"Fairy hill of the Caledonians."

Scour Ouran, Sgùrr Odhrain
"Odhran's peak."

Seana Bhraigh, Seana Bhràigh
"Old upland."

Sgairneach Mhor, An Sgàirneach Mhór
"The large hill of loose stones."

Sgiath a' Chaise, Sgiath a' Chaise
"Wing of steepness."

Sgiath Chuil, Sgiath a' Chùil
"Wing of the back."

Sgoran Dubh Mor, An Sgòran Dubh Mór
"The large black pinnacle."

Sgor an Lochain Uaine, Sgòr an Lochain Uaine

"The pinnacle at the green lochan", also known as **Angel's Peak**.

Sgor Gaibhre, Sgòr Goibhre
"Goat pinnacle."

Sgor Gaoith, Sgòr Gaoithe
"Windy pinnacle."

Sgor Iutharn, Sgòr Iuthairn
"Pinnacle of hell."

Sgor Mor, An Sgòr Mór
"The great pinnacle."

Sgor na h-Ulaidh, Sgòr na h-Ulaidh
"Pinnacle of the treasure."

Sgorr a' Choise, Sgòr a' Choise
This may be "pinnacle of the cavern", or "steep pinnacle".

Sgorr Bhan, An Sgòr Bàn
"The white pinnacle."

Sgorr Craobh a' Chaorainn, Sgòr Craobh a' Chaorthainn
"Pinnacle of the rowan tree."

Sgorr Dhearg, An Sgòr Dearg
"The red pinnacle."

Sgorr Dhonuill, Sgòr Dhòmhnaill
"Donald's pinnacle."

Sgorr Mhic Eacharna, Sgòr MhicEacharna
"MacEachern's pinnacle."

Sgorr na Diollaid, Sgòr na Dìollaid
"The saddle pinnacle."

Sgorr nam Fiannaidh, Sgòr nam Fiannaidh
"Pinnacle of the Fianna warriors."

Sgorr nan Lochan Uaine, Sgòr nan Lochan Uaine
"Pinnacle of the small green lochs."

Sgor Ruadh, An Sgòr Ruadh
"The red-brown pinnacle."

Sguman Coinntich, Sgùman Còinntich
"Mound, or stack of moss."

Sgurr a' Bhac Chaolais, Sgùrr a' Bhac Chaolais
"Peak of the hollow at the narrows."

Sgurr a' Bhealaich Dheirg, Sgùrr a' Bhealaich Dheirg
"Peak of the red pass."

Sgurr a' Chaorachain, Sgùrr a' Chaorachain
This may be "peak of the rowan-berry place".

Sgurr a' Chaorainn, Sgùrr a' Chaorthainn
"Peak of the rowan."

Sgurr a' Choire-bheithe, Sgùrr a' Choire Bheithe
"Peak of the birch corrie."

Sgurr a' Choire Ghlais, Sgùrr a' Choire Ghlais
"Peak of the grey corrie."

Sgurr a' Dubh Doire, Sgùrr an Dubh Dhoire
"Peak of the black oak-grove."

Sgurr a' Fionn Choire, Sgùrr an Fhionn Choire
"Peak of the white corrie."

Sgurr a' Gharaidh, Sgùrr a' Ghàraidh
"Peak of the dyke."

Sgurr a' Ghreadaidh, Sgùrr a' Ghreadaidh
This may be "peak of the torment-ing, or thrashing".

Sgurr Alasdair, Sgùrr Alasdair
"Alasdair's peak." This name commemorates Sheriff Alexander Nicolson, the first man known to have reached the summit. Prior to this, the mountain was known as *An Sgùrr Biorach*, "the sharp peak".

Sgurr a' Mhadaidh, Sgùrr a' Mhadaidh
"Peak of the wolf, or fox."

Sgurr a' Mhaim, Sgùrr a' Mhàim
"Peak of the gap."

Sgurr a' Mhaoraich, Sgùrr a' Mhaoraich
"Peak of the shellfish."

Sgurr a' Mhuilinn, Sgùrr a' Mhuilinn
"Peak of the mill."

Sgurr an Airgid, Sgùrr an Airgid
"Peak of silver."

Sgurr an Doire Leathain, Sgùrr an Doire Leathainn
"Peak of the wide grove."

Sgurr an Fhidhleir, Sgùrr an Fhìdhleir
"Peak of the fiddler."

Sgurr an Fhuarain
See **Scour Ouran**.

Sgurr an Lochain, Sgùrr an Lochain
"Peak of the small loch."

Sgurr an Utha, Sgùrr an Ùtha
"Peak of the udder."

Sgurr Ban, An Sgùrr Bàn
"The fair-coloured peak."

Sgurr Breac, An Sgùrr Breac
"The speckled peak."

Sgurr Choinnich, Sgùrr Choinnich
"Kenneth's peak."

Sgurr Choinnich Mor, Sgùrr
Choinnich Mór
" Kenneth's big peak."

Sgurr Coire Choinnichean, Sgùrr
Coire Chòinnichean
"Peak of the corrie of mosses."

Sgurr Cos na Breachd-laoigh, Sgùrr
Còs nam Breac Laogh
"Peak at the den of the speckled
calves."

Sgurr Dearg, An Sgùrr Dearg
"The red peak."

Sgurr Dhomhnuill, Sgùrr
Dhòmhnaill
"Donald's peak."

Sgurr Dubh, An Sgùrr Dubh
"The black peak."

Sgurr Dubh Mor, An Sgùrr Dubh
Mór
"The large black peak."

Sgurr Eilde Mor, Sgùrr Eilde Mór
"Great peak of the hind."

Sgurr Fhuaran
See **Scour Ouran**.

Sgurr Fhuar-thuill, Sgùrr Fhuar
Thuill
"Peak of the cold hole."

Sgurr Fiona, Sgùrr Fìona
"Wine peak."

Sgurr Gaorsaic
This name is unclear.

Sgurr Ghiubhsachain, Sgùrr a'
Ghiuthsachain
"Peak at the small pine wood."

Sgurr Innse, Sgùrr Innse
"The peak of Inch."

Sgurr Mhic Bharraich, Sgùrr
MhicBharraich
"MacVarich's peak."

Sgurr Mhic Choinnich, Sgùrr
MhicChoinnich
"MacKenzie's peak."

Sgurr Mhor, An Sgùrr Mór
"The large peak."

Sgurr Mhurlagain, Sgùrr Mhùrlagain
or Sgùrr Mhùrbhlagain
"The peak of Murlaggan."

Sgurr Mor, An Sgùrr Mór
"The large peak."

Sgurr na Ba Glaise, Sgùrr na Bà
Glaise
"Peak of the grey-green cow."

Sgurr na Banachdich, Sgùrr na
Banachdaich
"The milkmaid's peak."

Sgurr na Carnach, Sgùrr na Càrnaich
"Peak of the rocky place."

Sgurr na Ciste Duibhe, Sgùrr na
Ciste Duibhe
"Peak of the black chest."

Sgurr na Coinnich, Sgùrr na
Còinnich
"Peak of the moss."

Sgurr na Fearstaig, Sgùrr na Feartaig
"Sea-pink peak."

Sgurr na Ciche, Sgùrr na Cìche
"Peak of the breast."

Sgurr na Lapaich, Sgùrr na Làpaich
"Peak of the bog."

Sgurr nan Ceannaichean, Sgùrr nan
Ceannaichean
"Peak of the merchants."

Sgurr nan Ceathreamhnan, Sgùrr
nan Ceathramhnan
"Peak of the quarters."

Sgurr nan Clach Geala, Sgùrr nan
Clach Geala
"Peak of the white stones."

Sgurr nan Cnamh, Sgùrr nan Cnàmh
"Peak of the bones."

Sgurr nan Coireachan, Sgùrr nan
Coireachan
"Peak of the corries."

Sgurr nan Conbhairean, Sgùrr nan
Conbhairean
"Peak at the confluences."

Sgurr nan Each, Sgùrr nan Each
"Peak of the horses."

Sgurr nan Eag, Sgùrr nan Eag
"Peak of the notches."

Sgurr nan Eugallt, Sgùrr nan Eugallt
This is said to be either "peak of the deathly streams", or "peak of the precipices".

Sgurr nan Fhir Duibhe, Sgùrr an Fhir Dhuibh
"The black(-haired) man's peak."

Sgurr nan Gillean, Sgùrr nan Gillean
"Peak of the lads."

Sgurr na Ruaidhe, Sgùrr na Ruaidhe
"Peak of red-brown-ness."

Sgurr na Sgine, Sgùrr na Sgìne
"Peak of the knife."

Sgurr Ruadh, An Sgùrr Ruadh
"The red-brown peak."

Sgurr Thuilm, Sgùrr Thuilm
"Peak of Holm."

Shalloch on Minnoch
This may be "middle willow place", from *Seileachan Meadhanach.*

Sheaval, Seubhal
"Sea hill."

Shee of Ardtalnaig, Sìth Àird Talanaig
"Fairy hill of Ardtalnaig."

Slat Bheinn, Slat Bheinn
"Rod mountain."

Slioch, Sleaghach
"Spear-like mountain."

Sow of Atholl, An Socach
"The sow." Nearby is the **Boar of Badenoch.**

Spidean a' Choire Leith, Spidean a' Choire Léith
"Pinnacle of the grey-blue corrie."

Spidean Coinich, Spidean Còinnich
"Mossy pinnacle."

Spidean Coire nan Clach, Spidean Coire nan Clach
"Pinnacle of the stony corrie."

Spidean Mealach, An Spidean Mialach
"The lousy pinnacle."

Sron a' Choire Chnapanich, Sròn a' Choire Chnapanaich
"Nose of the hillocky corrie."

Sron a' Choire Ghairbh, Sròn a' Choire Ghairbh
"Nose of the rough corrie."

Sron Garbh, An t-Sròn Gharbh
"The rough nose-shaped hill."

Sron nan Giubhas, Sròn nan Giuthas
"Nose-shaped hill of the pine trees."

Sron Riach, An t-Sròn Riabhach
"The brindled nose-shaped hill."

Stack Polly, Stac Pollaidh
"Stack at the pool river."

Stob, The, An Stob
"The stump."

Stob a' Bhruaich Leith, Stob a' Bhruthaich Léith
"Stump of the grey-blue slope."

Stob a' Choin, Stob a' Choin
"Stump of the dog."

Stob a' Choire Mheadhoin, Stob a' Choire Mheadhain
"Stump of the middle corrie."

Stob a' Choire Odhair, Stob a' Choire Odhair
"Stump of the dun-coloured corrie."

Stob an Aonaich Mhoir, Stob an Aonaich Mhóir
"The stump of Aonach Mór."

Stob an Cul Choire, Stob a' Chùl Choire
"Stump of the back corrie."

Stob Ban, An Stob Bàn
"The fair-coloured stump."

Stob Choire Claurigh, Stob Choire Clamhraidh
"Stump of the bellowing corrie."

Stob Coir' an Albannaich, Stob Coire an Albannaich
"Stump of the Scotsman's corrie."

Stob Coire a' Chairn, Stob Coire a' Chàirn
"Stump of the corrie of the cairn."

Stob Coire a' Chearcaill, Stob Coire a' Chearcaill
"Stump of the corrie of the circle."

Stob Coire an Laoigh, Stob Coire an Laoigh
"Stump of the corrie of the calf."

Stob Coire Creagach, Stob a' Choire Chreagaich
"Stump of the rocky corrie."

Stob Coire Dheirg, Stob a' Choire
Dheirg
"Stump at the red corrie."

Stob Coire Dubh, Stob a' Choire
Dhuibh
"Stump at the black corrie."

Stob Coire Easain, Stob Coire
Easain
"Stump of waterfall corrie."

Stob Coire Etchachan, Stob Coire
Éiteachain
"Stump at the corrie of the foul
one." See **Carn Etchachan**.

Stob Coire Leith, Stob a' Choire
Léith
"Stump at the grey-blue corrie."

Stob Corrie Lochan, Stob Coire an
Lochain
"Stump at the corrie by the small
loch."

Stob Coire na Gaibhre, Stob Coire
na Goibhre
"Stump at the goat's corrie."

Stob Coire nam Beith, Stob Coire
nam Beithe
"Stump at the corrie of the
birches."

Stob Coire Raineach, Stob Coire
Raineach
"Stump of the corrie of Rannoch."

Stob Coire Sgreamhach, Stob a'
Choire Sgreamhaich
"Stump of the dreadful corrie."

Stob Coire Sgriodain, Stob Coire
Sgrìodain
"Stump of the corrie of Sgridain", a
name referring to scree.

Stob Daimh, Stob Daimh
"Stag stump."

Stob Dearg, An Stob Dearg
"The red stump."

Stob Dubh, An Stob Dubh
"The black stump."

Stob Ghabhar, Stob Ghobhar
"Goats' stump."

Stobinian, Stob Binnein
"Pinnacle stump."

Stob na Broige, Stob na Bròige
"Stump of the shoe."

Stob na Cruaiche, Stob na Cruaiche
"Stump of the conical hill."

Stob Poite Coire Ardair, Stob Poite
Coire Àrdair
"Stump of the pot of corrie of the
high river."

Storr, The, An Stòrr
"The great one", from Norse.

Streap, An Streap
"The climbing."

Stuc a' Chroin, Stùc a' Chròthain
"Stump of the small sheep fold."

Stuc Beag, An Stùc Beag
"The small hill."

Stuchd an Lochain, Stùc an Lochain
"Hill by the small loch."

Stuc Mor, An Stùc Mór
"The large hill."

Suilven, Sula Bheinn
"Pillar mountain", from Norse/
Gaelic.

T

Teilesval, Teileasabhal
"Cave hill", from Norse.

Tigh Mor na Seilge, Taigh Mór na
Seilge
"The large hunting house."

Tinto
This name may be Gaelic, or
Brythonic and related to Gaelic
teine, or Brythonic *tân*, "fire". A
possible source is Gaelic *teinteach*,
"fiery, hot, fierce".

Tirga Mor, Tiorga Mór
"Great Tiorga." It is unclear what
the derivation of *Tiorga* is.

Toll Creagach, An Toll Creagach
"The rocky hole."

Tolmount, An Tulmon
"Naked hill", or "brow hill."

Tom a'Choinich, Tom a' Chòinnich
"Mossy knoll."

Toman Coinich, Toman Còinnich
"Mossy hillock."

Tom Buidhe, An Tom Buidhe
"The yellow knoll."

Tom Dubh, An Tom Dubh
"The black knoll."

Tom Meadhoin, Tom Meadhain
  "Middle knoll."
Tom na Gruagaich, Tom na Gruagaich
  "Knock of the maiden."
Trallaval, Trallabhal *or* Trollabhal
  "Troll hill", from Norse.
Traprain Law, Dùn Peilleir
  The English form has English *hláw*,
  "hill", attached to a settlement name
  of Brythonic origin. The Gaelic
  form is from Brythonic "fort of the
  spear shafts".
Trossachs, Na Tròisichean *or* Na
  Tròsaichean
  "The crossing place hills."

Trostan Hill, Cnoc Trostain
  "St Drostan's hill", the name of a
  Pictish saint.
Tullich Hill, An Tulach
  "The green hill."

U
Uamh Bheag, An Uamh Bheag
  "The small cave."
Uisgnaval Mor, Uisgneabhal Mór
  This may be "ox hill", from Norse.

W
White Mounth, Am Monadh Geal
  "The white hill, or range of hills."

Maps

The maps on the following pages show the distribution of tribes, language groups and placename elements.

Map 1: Tribes known to the Romans

Map 1 shows the approximate locations of
the tribes known to the Romans.

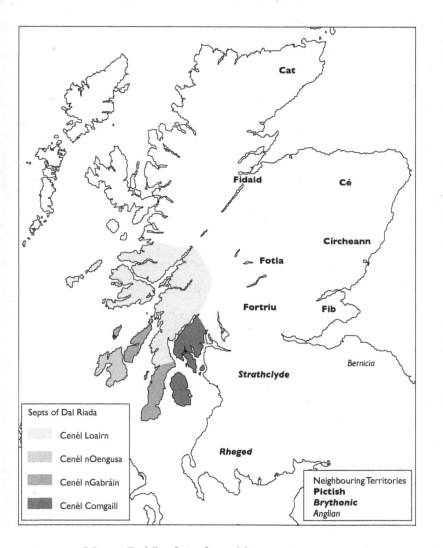

Map 2: Dal Riada and neighbouring territories

Map 2 shows the location of the different linguistic groupings in relation to the Scots of Dal Riada before the Scots began to expand into Pictish territory. Dal Riada itself was divided into the groups shown on the map on the basis of dynastic succession.

Map 3: Distribution of Brythonic *aber*

Map 3 shows the area in which Pictish/Brythonic *aber*,
"river mouth", is widely found as a placename element in
names such as Aberlady and Obar Dheathain, together with
isolated instances in Applecross and Dumfriesshire.

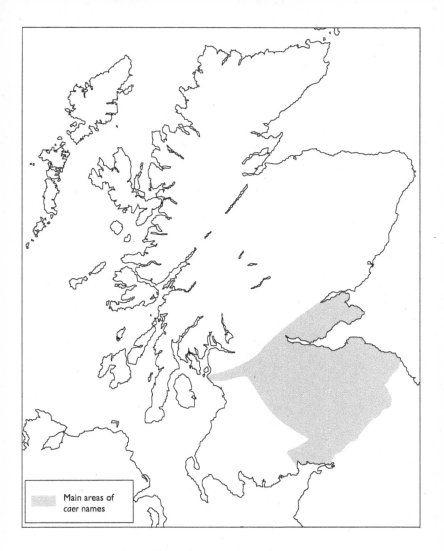

Map 4: Distribution of Brythonic *caer*

Map 4 shows the area over which Brythonic *caer*,
"fort", is commonly found as a placename element
in such names as Caerlaverock and Carfrae.

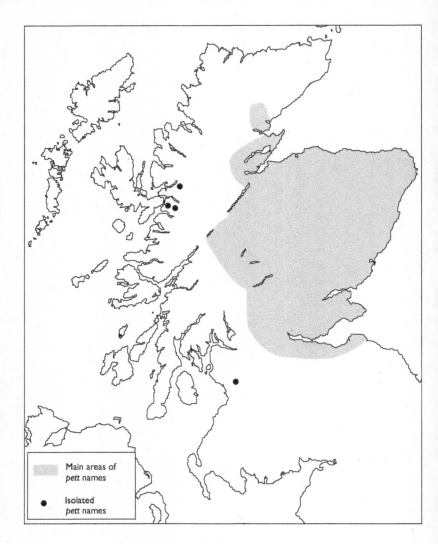

Map 5: Distribution of Pictish *pett*

Map 5 shows the distribution area of Pictish *pett*, together
with isolated examples. This generally becomes "Pit-" as in
Pitlochry and Pittenweem, but remains as "Pet-" in Petty
and is disguised as *Baile* in names in Gaelic such as Baile
Chloichrigh, where the English form retains the original *pett*.

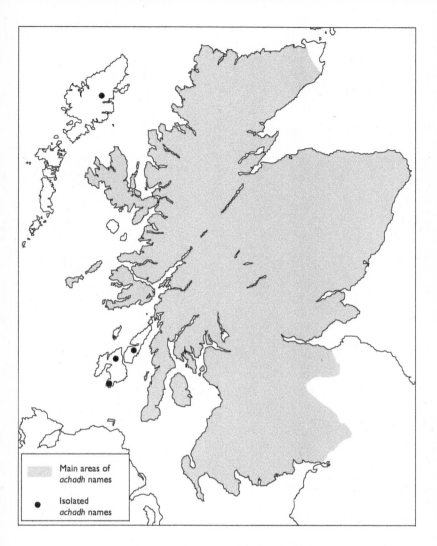

Map 6: Distribution of Gaelic *achadh*

Map 6 illustrates the area in which Gaelic *achadh*,
"field", is commonly found as an element in placenames
such as Achnasheen and Auchenrivock.

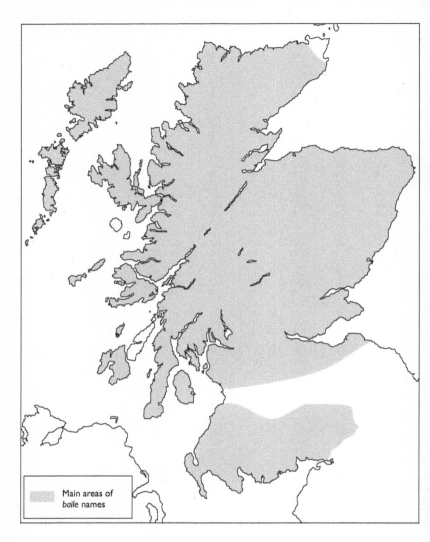

Main areas of
baile names

Map 7: Distribution of Gaelic *baile*

Map 7 shows where the Scots were long enough settled to have
begun farms and named them. This map shows that these names
are not as widely distributed as the *achadh* field names on Map 6.

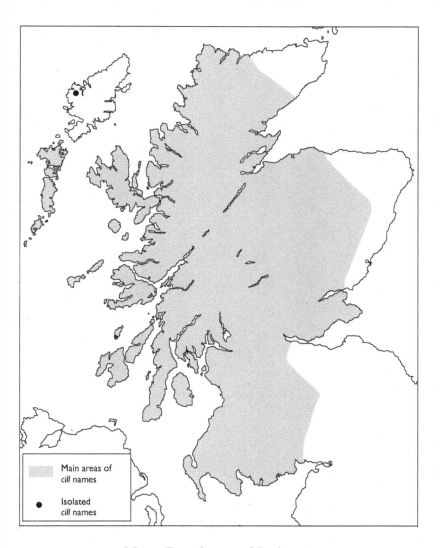

Map 8: Distribution of Gaelic *cill*

Map 8 shows the area over which Gaelic *cill*, "cell, church",
is found as an element in placenames such as Kilmarnock
and Kilbrare. While most *cill* names are followed by the
name of a holy person or saint, several are descriptive,
such as *Cill Duinn* or Kildun, "brown church".

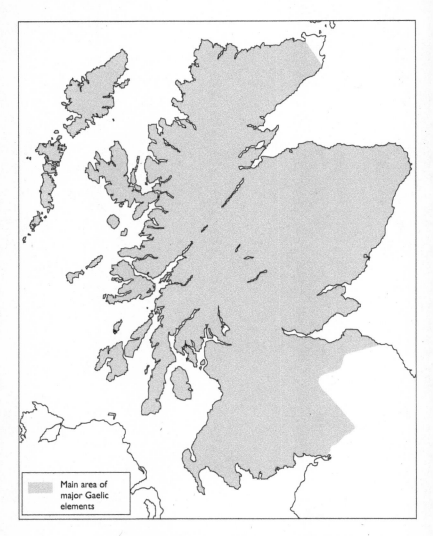

Main area of
major Gaelic
elements

Map 9: Combined distribution of Gaelic *achadh, baile* and *cill*

The combined distribution of the Gaelic elements, *achadh,*
baile and *cill*, as shown on Map 9, gives an indication of the
maximum extent of the Gaelic-speaking areas of the country.
Although placenames in the unshaded south-eastern area contain
personal names of a Gaelic origin, it is probable that Gaelic
speakers formed only the upper strata of society, the majority
and lower ranks of which would have spoken English.

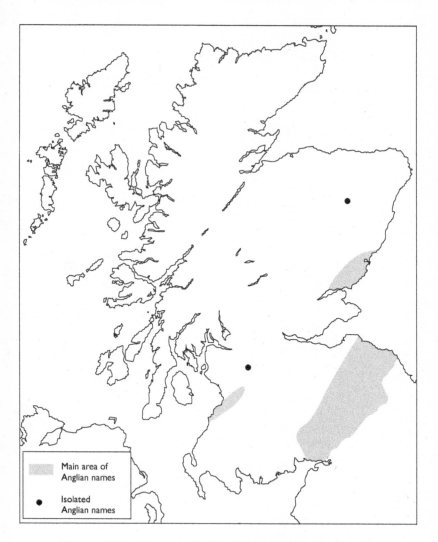

Map 10: Distribution of earliest English (Anglian) names

Map 10 shows the areas containing the oldest Anglian names – those including elements such as *wíc* (village), *hám* (farm), *bótl* (house), *tún* (farm) and *-ing-* (people), which indicate human habitation.

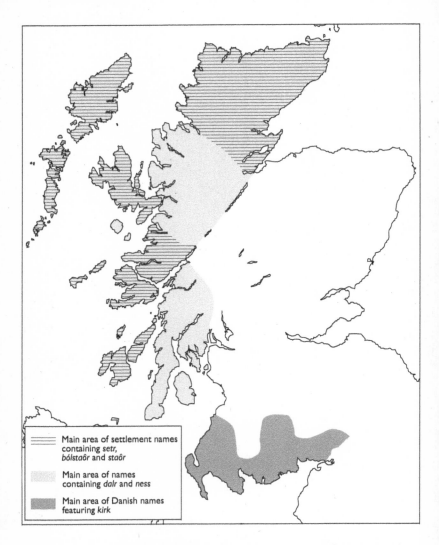

Legend:

Main area of settlement names containing *setr*, *bólstaðr* and *staðr*

Main area of names containing *dalr* and *ness*

Main area of Danish names featuring *kirk*

Map 11: Distribution of selected Norse names (including Danish)

Map 11 shows the extent of Norse and Danish penetration of Scotland, although only the area indicated by horizontal lines features Norse settlement elements.

Map 12: Districts of Scotland (in English)

Map 13: Districts of Scotland (in Gaelic)

Bibliography

Alexander, W.M. (1952) *Place-Names of Aberdeenshire*. Aberdeen: Third Spalding Club

An t-Suirbhéireacht Ordanáis (1989) *Gasaitéar na hÉireann*. Dublin: Rialtas na h-Éireann

Atkinson, T. (1997) *South West Scotland*. Edinburgh: Luath Press

Black, G.F. (1993) *Surnames of Scotland*. Edinburgh: Birlinn

Brownlie, N.M. (1995) *Bailtean is Ath-Ghairmean a Tiriodh*. Glendaruel: Argyll Publishing

Cox, R.A.V. (2002) *Place-names of Carloway, Isle of Lewis*. Dublin: Dublin Institute for Advanced Studies

Diack, F. (1944) *The Inscriptions of Pictland*. Aberdeen: Third Spalding Club

Dwelly, E. (1973) *Illustrated Gaelic – English Dictionary*. Glasgow: Gairm

Ellice, E.C. (1999) *Place Names of Glengarry and Glenquoich*. Exeter: Ashley House Printing

Ferguson, J. (1985) *The Place-names of Berneray*. Inverness: Gaelic Society of Inverness

Ferguson, K. & Perrons, M. (1990) *Place-names of Islay*. Islay: Islay Museums Trust

Flanagan, D. & Flanagan, L. (1994) *Irish Place Names*. Dublin: Gill and MacMillan

Forbes, A.R. (1923) *Place-names of Skye*. Paisley: A. Gardner

Fraser, I. (1988) *The Place-names of Argyll*. Inverness: Gaelic Society of Inverness

Fraser, I. (undated) *The Settlement Names of Gairloch Parish*. Gairloch: Ross and Cromarty Heritage Society

Fraser, I. (1999) *The Place-names of Arran*. Glasgow: Arran Society of Glasgow

Gillies, W. (1989) *Gaelic and Scotland/Alba agus a' Ghàidhlig*. Edinburgh: Edinburgh University Press

Grannd, S. (2013). *Gàidhlig Dhùthaich MhicAoidh*. Melness: Taigh na Gàidhlig

Holmer, N. (1942) *The Irish Language in Rathlin Island, Co. Antrim*. Dublin: Royal Irish Academy

Holmer, N. (1957) *The Gaelic of Arran*. Dublin: Dublin Institute for Advanced Studies

Holmer, N. (1962) *The Gaelic of Kintyre*. Dublin: Dublin Institute for Advanced Studies

Johnston, J.B. (1987) *Place-Names of Stirling District*. Stirling: Stirling District Libraries

Kerr, J. (1981) *Old Roads to Strathardle*. Kettering: John Kerr

King, J. (2019) *Scottish Gaelic Place-names. The Collected Works of Charles M Robertson 1864–1927*. Sleat: Clò Ainmean-Àite na h-Alba

King, J. (undated) *A (re-)examination of the work of F.C. Diack*. Unpublished presentation.

King, J. (undated) *Gaelic Place-names of North-East Scotland*. Unpublished presentation.

King, J. & Cotter, M. (undated) *Gaelic in the Landscape. Place-names in Islay and Jura/A' Ghàidhlig air Aghaidh na Tìre. Ainmean-àite ann an Ìle agus Diùra*. Perth: Scottish Natural Heritage

McArthur, C. (undated) *The Place-names of Jura*. Jura: privately published

MacBain, A. (1922) *Place Names, Highlands and Islands*. Stirling: Eneas MacKay

McCaffray, C. (1992) *Green's Guide to Sheriff Court Districts*. Edinburgh: W. Green

MacDhòmhnaill, M.M. (1997) *Ainmean Àite Sgìr' a' Bhac, Eilean Leòdhais*. Back: M.M. MacDhòmhnaill

MacDonald, A. (1941) *The Place-names of West Lothian*. Edinburgh: Oliver and Boyd

MacDonald, J. (undated) *The Place Names of Skye*. Duntulm: J. MacDonald

MacDonald, M. (1985) *Fort William and Nether Lochaber*. Oban: West Highland Publications

MacIlleathain, R. (undated) *Gaelic and Norse in the Landscape: Place names in Caithness and Sutherland/A' Ghàidhlig is Lochlannais air Aghaidh na Tìre: Ainmean-àite ann an Gallaibh, Cataibh is Dùthaich MhicAoidh*. Ullapool: Scottish Natural Heritage

MacIlleathain, R. (2007) *Gaelic in the Landscape: Place names in the North West Highlands/A' Ghàidhlig air Aghaidh na Tìre: Ainmean-àite ann an Iar-thuath na Gàidhealtachd*. Perth: Scottish National Heritage

MacKillop, D. (undated) *Sea Names of Berneray*. Inverness: Gaelic Society of Inverness

MacKinnon, L. (1973) *Place-names of Lochaber*. Fort William: Saltire Society

MacLean, R. (2004) *The Gaelic Place Names and Heritage of Inverness*. Inverness: Culcabock Publishing

MacLennan, J. (2001) *Place-names of Scarp*. Privately published.

MacLeod, F. (1989) *Togail Tìr*. Stornoway: Acair

MacNeill, P. & Nicholson, R. (1975) *Historical Atlas of Scotland c. 400–c. 1600*. St Andrews: Conference of Scottish Mediaevalists

McNeir, C.L. (ed.) (2001) *Faclair na Pàrlamaid, Dictionary of Terms*. Edinburgh: Scottish Parliament

McNiven, P.E. (2011) *Gaelic place-names and the social history of Gaelic speakers in Menteith*. PhD Thesis. Glasgow: University of Glasgow

Márkus, G. (2012) *The Place-names of Bute*. Donington: Shaun Tyas

Maxwell, H. (1894) *Scottish Land-names*. Edinburgh: William Blackwood and Sons

Maxwell, H. (1930) *The Place-names of Galloway*. Glasgow: Jackson, Wylie and Co.

Morgan, P. (1999) *Ainmean Àite Rùim, The Place-Names of Rùm*. Rum: Dualchas Nàdair na h-Alba

Newton, M. (2010) *Bho Chluaidh gu Calasraid/From the Clyde to Callander*. Glasgow: The Grimsay Press

NicIain, C.M. (1999) *Ainmean-Àiteachan Sgìre Sholais*. An Ceathramh Meadhanach: C.M. NicIain

Nicolaisen, W.F.H. (1986) *Scottish Place-names*. London: Batsford

Oftedal, M. (1954) "The Village Names of Lewis". Norsk Tidskift for Sprogvidenskap

Oileanaich Colaiste Inbhir Nis (2004) *Roghainn an Raoin Rèidh*. Inverness: Inverness College

Ó Murchú, M. (1989) *East Perthshire Gaelic*. Dublin: Dublin Institute for Advanced Studies

Redford, M. (1988) "Commemorations of Saints of the Celtic Church in Scotland". Unpublished MLitt Thesis. Edinburgh: University of Edinburgh

Room, A. (1988) *Dictionary of Irish Place-names*. Belfast: Appletree Press

Scottish Qualifications Authority (2009) *Gaelic Orthographic Conventions*. Glasgow: SQA

Skene, W.F. (1887) *Celtic Scotland*. Edinburgh: David Douglas

Taylor, S. (1998) *The Uses of Place-names*. Edinburgh: Scottish Cultural Press

— with Márkus, G. (2006–8) *The Place-names of Fife, Volumes 1–3*. Donington: Shaun Tyas

Watson, A. & Allan, E. (1984) *Place-names of Upper Deeside*. Aberdeen: Aberdeen University Press

Watson, A & Clement, D. (1983) *Aberdeenshire Gaelic*. Inverness: Gaelic Society of Inverness

Watson, S. (ed.) (2007) *Saoghal Bana-mharaiche*. Ceann Drochaid: Clann Tuirc

Watson, W.J. (2002) *Scottish Place-name Papers*. London: Steve Savage

— (1993) *The History of the Celtic Place-names of Scotland*. Dublin: Irish Academic Press

— (1976) *The Place-names of Ross and Cromarty*. Dingwall: Ross and Cromarty Heritage Society

Wentworth, R. (2006) *Gaelic Words and Phrases from Wester Ross*. Daviot: Clàr

Journals

In addition to the above, the publications of the Scottish Gaelic Texts Society, of local Comainn Eachdraidh, the newsletter of the Scottish Place-Name Society and the periodicals below contain much valuable information and sources on placenames.

Celtic Review
Celtic Studies
Cothrom

Gairm
Gath
Journal of Scottish Name Studies
Norsk Tidskrift for Sprogvidenskap
Revue Celtique
Scottish Gaelic Studies
Scottish History Society
Scottish Studies
Tocher
Transactions of the Gaelic Society of Inverness

Websites

The following websites are a valuable source of information.

Ainmean Àite na h-Alba – www.gaelicnames.org
Digital Archive of Scottish Gaelic – www.dasg.ac.uk
Sabhal Mòr Ostaig – www.smo.uhi.ac.uk
Scottish Place-Name Society – www.spns.org.uk
Tobar an Dualchas/Kist o Riches – www.tobarandualchais.co.uk